New
Mathematics
Counts

2nd Edition

Secondary
Normal (Academic)

2

Tay Choon Hong
Mark Riddington • Martin Grier

APPROVED BY MINISTRY OF EDUCATION
SINGAPORE
for use from 2008–2012

mc **Marshall Cavendish**
Education

© 2008 Marshall Cavendish International (Singapore) Private Limited

Published by Marshall Cavendish Education
A member of Times Publishing Limited
Times Centre, 1 New Industrial Road, Singapore 536196
Customer Service Hotline: (65) 6411 0820
E-mail: tmesales@sg.marshallcavendish.com
Website: www.marshallcavendish.com/education/sg

Adapted from **Blackwell Maths**
Published by Basil Blackwell Ltd

Mathematics Counts for Secondary 2
Normal (Academic) first published 1989

New Mathematics Counts for Secondary 2
Normal (Academic)
First published 2000
Second edition 2008

The websites cited in the book were reviewed and deemed suitable at the time of printing.

ISBN 978-981-01-0993-6

Editors: Cheryl Lee, Lee Ling Li, Nor Azean Abdullah, Ryan Bong
Senior Editor: Varsha Primalani
Illustrated by: Anuar Abdul Rahim

Printed in Singapore by Times Graphics Pte Ltd

Acknowledgements

7/25/08 finished G8/G9
Derek @ Taiwan (5th & 6th summer)

The publishers would like to thank the following:

- *The University of Cambridge Local Examinations Syndicate and the Singapore Examinations and Assessment Board (SEAB)* for permission to reproduce some of the questions from the Singapore-Cambridge GCE 'N' Level and GCE 'O' Level examinations. The answers in this publication are given by the publishers. UCLES and SEAB bear no responsibility for these answers. Any queries or comments on the answers should be forwarded to the publishers directly.

- *The Geometer's Sketchpad®, Key Curriculum Press*, 1150 65th Street, Emeryville, CA 94608. 1-800-995-MATH, www.keypress.com/sketchpad.

About the authors

Tay Choon Hong has accumulated more than 20 years of experience in teaching Mathematics at the secondary level. He is currently the Head of the Mathematics Department in his school. He graduated with a B.Sc.(Hons) degree in Mathematics from the University of Malaya. His professional qualifications include a Masters' degree in Education from the National University of Singapore.

Mark Riddington and **Martin Grier** are both B.Sc. degree holders and highly experienced Mathematics teachers in British secondary schools.

Preface

New Mathematics Counts (2nd Edition) is a revised version of the highly recommended **New Mathematics Counts**. This edition meets the requirements of the latest syllabuses for the GCE 'N' Level (Syllabus A) and 'O' Level examinations set by the Ministry of Education, Singapore.

Consisting of five textbooks designed specially for students following the Normal (Academic) Course, the material has been developed to help students excel in the GCE 'N' Level Mathematics examination and to prepare these students to proceed to sit for the GCE 'O' Level Mathematics examination thereafter. The material is arranged in a sound pedagogical sequence in which abstract reasoning is supported by concrete examples. Care is given to introducing concepts one at a time to allow students to grasp them with ease. Understanding of concepts is further enhanced by the judicious use of worked examples and graded exercises.

Chapter Opener
Each chapter starts out with an interesting story or example related to the topic covered to stimulate students' interest.

Use of diagrams
Diagrams are used intelligently to help students visualise mathematical concepts and ideas more clearly.

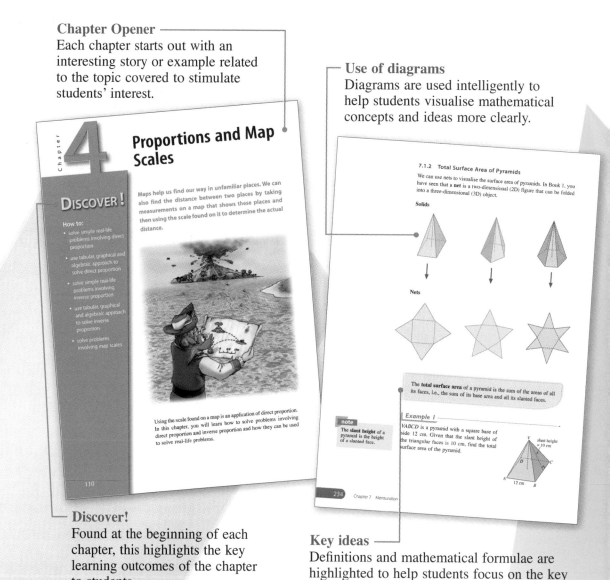

Discover!
Found at the beginning of each chapter, this highlights the key learning outcomes of the chapter to students.

Key ideas
Definitions and mathematical formulae are highlighted to help students focus on the key concepts covered.

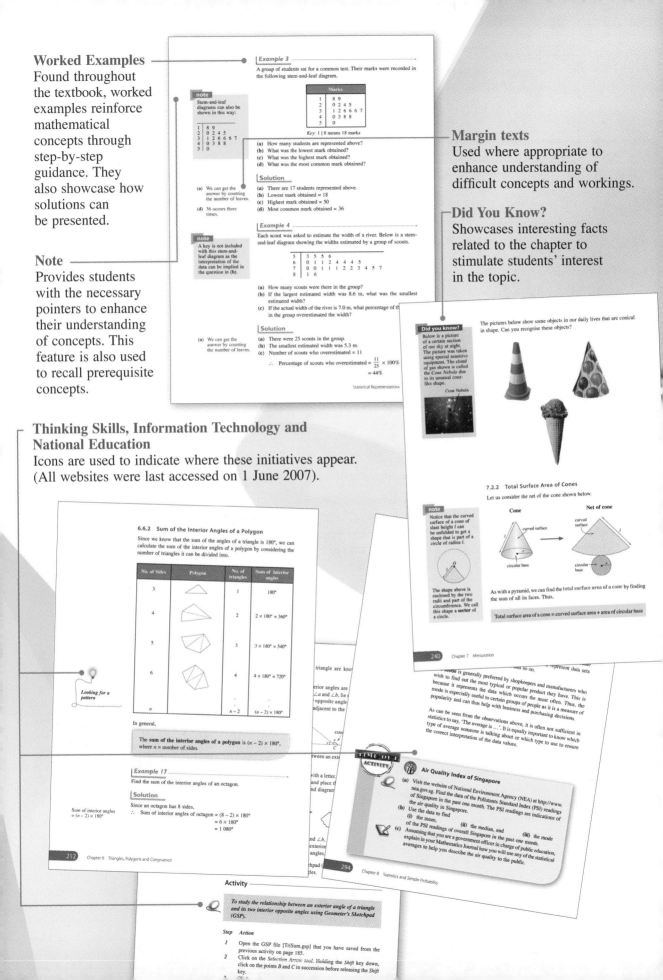

Worked Examples
Found throughout the textbook, worked examples reinforce mathematical concepts through step-by-step guidance. They also showcase how solutions can be presented.

Note
Provides students with the necessary pointers to enhance their understanding of concepts. This feature is also used to recall prerequisite concepts.

Thinking Skills, Information Technology and National Education
Icons are used to indicate where these initiatives appear. (All websites were last accessed on 1 June 2007).

Margin texts
Used where appropriate to enhance understanding of difficult concepts and workings.

Did You Know?
Showcases interesting facts related to the chapter to stimulate students' interest in the topic.

Example 3

A group of students sat for a common test. Their marks were recorded in the following stem-and-leaf diagram.

Marks

1	8 9
2	0 2 4 5
3	1 2 6 6 6 7
4	0 3 8 8
5	0

Key: 1 | 8 means 18 marks

(a) How many students are represented above?
(b) What was the lowest mark obtained?
(c) What was the highest mark obtained?
(d) What was the most common mark obtained?

note
Stem-and-leaf diagrams can also be shown in this way:

1	8 9
2	0 2 4 5
3	1 2 6 6 6 7
4	0 3 8 8
5	0

Solution

(a) There are 17 students represented above.
(b) Lowest mark obtained = 18
(c) Highest mark obtained = 50
(d) Most common mark obtained = 36

(a) We can get the answer by counting the number of leaves.
(d) 36 occurs three times.

Example 4

Each scout was asked to estimate the width of a river. Below is a stem-and-leaf diagram showing the widths estimated by a group of scouts.

5	3 5 5 6
6	0 1 1 2 4 4 4 5
7	0 0 1 1 1 2 2 3 4 5 7
8	1 6

note
A key is not included with this stem-and-leaf diagram as the interpretation of the data can be implied from the question in (b).

(a) How many scouts were there in the group?
(b) If the largest estimated width was 8.6 m, what was the smallest estimated width?
(c) If the actual width of the river is 7.0 m, what percentage of the scouts in the group overestimated the width?

Solution

(a) There were 25 scouts in the group.
(b) The smallest estimated width was 5.3 m.
(c) Number of scouts who overestimated = 11

∴ Percentage of scouts who overestimated = $\frac{11}{25} \times 100\%$
= 44%

(a) We can get the answer by counting the number of leaves.

Statistical Representations

Did you know?
Below is a picture of a certain section of our sky at night. The picture was taken using special sensitive equipment. The cloud of gas shown is called the *Cone Nebula* due to its unusual cone-like shape.

Cone Nebula

The pictures below show some objects in our daily lives that are conical in shape. Can you recognise these objects?

7.2.2 Total Surface Area of Cones

Let us consider the net of the cone shown below.

note
Notice that the curved surface of a cone of slant height *l* can be unfolded to get a shape that is part of a circle of radius *l*.

The shape above is enclosed by the two radii and part of the circumference. We call this shape a **sector** of a circle.

Cone   **Net of cone**

As with a pyramid, we can find the total surface area of a cone by finding the sum of all its faces. Thus,

Total surface area of a cone = curved surface area + area of circular base

240   Chapter 7 Mensuration

6.6.2 Sum of the Interior Angles of a Polygon

Since we know that the sum of the angles of a triangle is 180°, we can calculate the sum of the interior angles of a polygon by considering the number of triangles it can be divided into.

No. of Sides	Polygon	No. of triangles	Sum of interior angles
3		1	180°
4		2	2 × 180° = 360°
5		3	3 × 180° = 540°
6		4	4 × 180° = 720°
⋮		⋮	⋮
n		n − 2	(n − 2) × 180°

Looking for a pattern

In general,

The **sum of the interior angles of a polygon** is $(n - 2) \times 180°$, where n = number of sides.

Example 17

Find the sum of the interior angles of an octagon.

Solution

Since an octagon has 8 sides,
∴ Sum of interior angles of octagon = (8 − 2) × 180°
= 6 × 180°
= 1 080°

Sum of interior angles = $(n - 2) \times 180°$

212   Chapter 6 Triangles, Polygons and Congruence

---

mode is generally preferred by shopkeepers and manufacturers who wish to find out the most typical or popular product they have. This is because it represents the data which occurs the most often. This is especially useful to certain groups of people as it is a measure of popularity and can thus help with business and purchasing decisions.

As can be seen from the observations above, it is often not sufficient in statistics to say, 'The average is …'. It is equally important to know which type of average someone is talking about or which type to use to ensure the correct interpretation of the data values.

TIME-OUT ACTIVITY

Air Quality Index of Singapore

(a) Visit the website of National Environment Agency (NEA) at http://www.nea.gov.sg. Find the data of the Pollutants Standard Index (PSI) readings of Singapore in the past one month. The PSI readings are indications of the air quality in Singapore.
(b) Use the data to find
(i) the mean,   (ii) the median, and   (iii) the mode of the PSI readings of overall Singapore in the past one month.
(c) Assuming that you are a government officer in charge of public education, explain in your Mathematics Journal how you will use any of the statistical averages to help you describe the air quality to the public.

294   Chapter 8 Statistics and Simple Probability

Activity

To study the relationship between an exterior angle of a triangle and its two interior opposite angles using Geometer's Sketchpad (GSP).

Step   *Action*

1   Open the GSP file [TriSum.gsp] that you have saved from the previous activity on page 185.
2   Click on the *Selection Arrow tool*. Holding the *Shift* key down, click on the points B and C in succession before releasing the *Shift* key.

Exercise

Comprises carefully graded questions to ensure understanding and mastery of the topic. Challenging questions (marked with a ★) and past-year examination questions are also incorporated to develop higher-order thinking skills and build exam confidence.

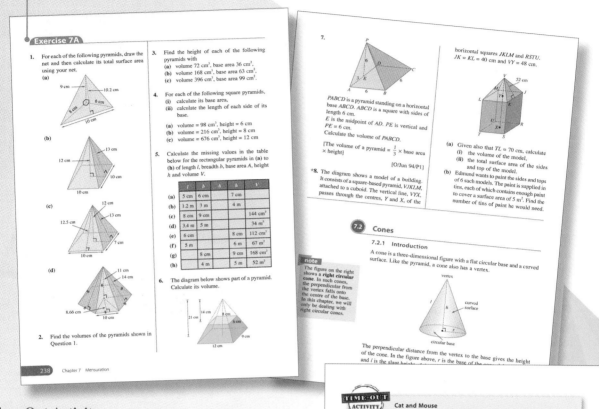

Time-Out Activity

Contains activities that engage students and make the learning process more enjoyable. Some of the activities found here incorporate the use of Information Technology, Thinking Skills, National Education messages or Journal Writing tasks.

Journal Writing Task

Comprises questions that encourage students to reflect, discuss or explain application of concepts. Students are also encouraged to write their explanations or thought processes in a journal, helping them to clarify their understanding.

Summary

Located at the end of every chapter, this serves as a recap and revision of the main concepts covered in the chapter.

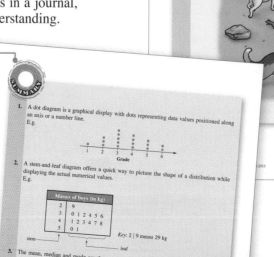

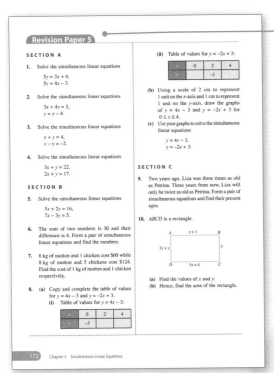

Revision Paper

Provided at the end of each chapter for consolidated practice, these questions are grouped into three different sections in increasing order of difficulty.

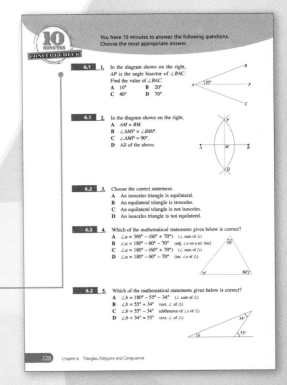

10 Minutes Concept Check

This section helps students diagnose their understanding of each section within a chapter. Each question has been labelled with the corresponding section number to allow students to identify their areas of weakness.

Review Paper

Serves as an overall revision to help students prepare for examinations.

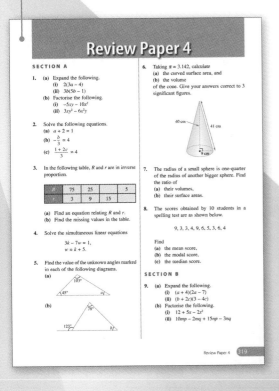

Enrichment Maths

Containing multi-faceted activities that allow students to investigate mathematical ideas or explore practical applications, this section provides excellent opportunities for class discussions as well as to cultivate higher-order thinking skills.

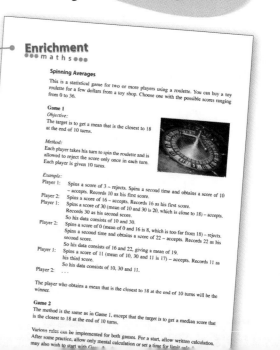

Contents

The chapters in the New Mathematics Counts (2nd Edition) series are colour-coded according to the three strands in the Secondary Mathematics syllabus as shown below:

■ Numbers and Algebra   ■ Geometry and Measurement   ■ Statistics and Probability

Mathematical Notation

1. Set Notation

$\in$	is an element of
$\notin$	is not an element of
$\{x_1, x_2, \ldots\}$	the set with elements $x_1, x_2, \ldots$
$\{x : \ldots\}$	the set of all x such that ...
$n(A)$	the number of elements in set A
$\varnothing$	the empty set
$\mathscr{E}$	the universal set
A'	the complement of the set A
$\mathbb{N}$	the set of positive integers, $\{1, 2, 3, \ldots\}$
$\mathbb{Z}$	the set of integers, $\{0, \pm1, \pm2, \pm3, \ldots\}$
$\mathbb{Z}^+$	the set of positive integers, $\{1, 2, 3, \ldots\}$
$\mathbb{R}$	the set of real numbers
$\subseteq$	is a subset of
$\subset$	is a proper subset of
$\nsubseteq$	is not a subset of
$\not\subset$	is not a proper subset of
$\cup$	union
$\cap$	intersection
$[a, b]$	the closed interval $\{x \in \mathbb{R}: a \le x \le b\}$
$[a, b)$	the interval $\{x \in \mathbb{R}: a \le x < b\}$
$(a, b]$	the interval $\{x \in \mathbb{R}: a < x \le b\}$
(a, b)	the open interval $\{x \in \mathbb{R}: a < x < b\}$

2. Miscellaneous Symbols

$=$	is equal to
$\ne$	is not equal to
$\equiv$	is identical to or is congruent to
$\approx$	is approximately equal to
$\propto$	is proportional to
$<$	is less than
$\le$	is less than or equal to
$\nless$	is not less than
$>$	is greater than
$\ge$	is greater than or equal to
$\ngtr$	is not greater than
∞	infinity

3. Operations

$a + b$	a plus b
$a - b$	a minus b
$a \times b, ab, a.b$	a multiplied by b
$a \div b, \frac{a}{b}, a/b$	a divided by b
$a : b$	the ratio of a to b
$\sqrt{a}$	the positive square root of the real number a
$|a|$	the modulus of the real number a

4. SI Units (Système International d'Unités)

The international system of units uses seven base units. All other units are derived from these base units by multiplying or dividing one unit by another.

Physical quantity	Name of SI base unit	Symbol for unit
length	metre	m
mass	kilogram	kg
time	second	s
electric current	ampere	A
thermodynamic temperature	kelvin	K
luminous intensity	candela	cd
amount of substance	mole	mol

The last three items are used mainly in more advanced scientific work. For ordinary purposes, temperature is measured on the Celsius (Centigrade) scale. The temperature intervals of the Kelvin and the Celsius scales are similar.

The multiples and sub-multiples of the base units are obtained by adding the approved prefix to the unit being used. Normally, we add a prefix to a unit so that the numeric part of the quantity is kept between 0.1 and 1 000 (i.e., not too small or too large a number). An exception is the 'kilogram', which is a base unit by itself.

Multiplication factor	Prefix	Symbol
10^{-12}	pico	p
10^{-9}	nano	n
10^{-6}	micro	μ
10^{-3}	milli	m
10^{-2}	centi	c
10^{3}	kilo	k
10^{6}	mega	M
10^{9}	giga	G
10^{12}	tera	T

Under the SI system, the presentation of numerical values is as follows:

1,000 is written as 1 000
12,005 is written as 12 005
1,000,500 is written as 1 000 500
0.00394 is written as 0.003 94

Some Conversion Tables

Length

10 millimetres (mm) = 1 centimetre (cm)
100 centimetres   = 1 metre (m)
1 000 metres   = 1 kilometre (km)

Mass

1 000 milligrams (mg) = 1 gram (g)
1 000 grams   = 1 kilogram (kg)
1 000 kilograms   = 1 tonne (t)

Area

10 000 m²   = 1 hectare (ha)
100 hectares = 1 km²

Volume and Capacity

1 000 cm³ = 1 litre (l)

Time

1 minute (min) = 60 seconds (s)
1 hour (h)   = 60 minutes
1 day   = 24 hours
1 week   = 7 days
1 year   = 365 days
1 leap year   = 366 days

Algebraic Expansions and Factorisations

Algebra is used extensively in many practical fields such as finance, business and meteorology.

In meteorology, which is the study of the weather system, algebra can be used to help predict the weather for the next day by describing the complicated weather system through simple algebraic expressions.

In this chapter, you will learn how to expand, simplify and factorise algebraic expressions.

1.1.1   Expansion of $a(b + c)$

We have learned in Book 1 that we can use the **distributive law** of multiplication over addition and subtraction to remove the brackets in simple linear algebraic expressions. This method is known as **expansion**.

For example:

$$2(3a + 4) = 2 \times 3a + 2 \times 4$$
$$= 6a + 8$$

Alternatively, we can also present the working as:

$$2(3a + 4) = (2)(3a) + (2)(4)$$
$$= 6a + 8$$

Similarly, we can apply the distributive law to remove the brackets in the expansion of the product of two linear algebraic expressions.

For example:

$$2a(3a + 4) = 2a \times 3a + 2a \times 4$$
$$= 6a^2 + 8a$$

In general,

> To **expand an expression of the form $a(b + c)$**, the term outside the brackets must be multiplied by each term within the brackets.
>
> $$a(b + c) = ab + ac$$

note

The rules for algebraic multiplication are similar to those for arithmetic multiplication.

Arithmetic multiplication:
$(+2) \times (+3) = 6$
$(-2) \times (-3) = 6$
$(+2) \times (-3) = -6$
$(-2) \times (+3) = -6$

Algebraic multiplication:
$(+a) \times (+b) = ab$
$(-a) \times (-b) = ab$
$(+a) \times (-b) = -ab$
$(-a) \times (+b) = -ab$

Spatial visualisation

Generally, the expansion of an expression of the form $a(b + c)$ can be visualised using the concept of area in geometry as shown below.

$$\Rightarrow \quad a(b + c) = ab + ac$$

Example 1

Expand the following.

(a) $2(x + 1)$

(b) $4(3x - 5)$

(c) $-2(a + 5)$

(d) $-3(2b - 7)$

Solution

(a) $2 \times x + 2 \times 1$ can also be written as $(2 \times x) + (2 \times 1)$ or $2(x) + 2(1)$.

note

If the number outside the brackets is negative, the sign of each term in the brackets is changed when the brackets are removed.

(a) $2(x + 1) = 2 \times x + 2 \times 1$
$= 2x + 2$

(b) $4(3x - 5) = 4 \times 3x + 4 \times (-5)$
$= 12x - 20$

(c) $-2(a + 5) = -2 \times a - 2 \times 5$
$= -2a - 10$

(d) $-3(2b - 7) = -3 \times 2b - 3 \times (-7)$
$= -6b + 21$

Example 2

Expand and simplify the following.

(a) $4(2a - 3) + 3(a + 2)$

(b) $5(b + 2) + 2(b - 1)$

(c) $4(c - 4) - 2(c + 1)$

(d) $2(d + 3) - 3(1 - d)$

Solution

(a) $4(2a - 3) + 3(a + 2) = 8a - 12 + 3a + 6$
$= 8a + 3a - 12 + 6$
$= 11a - 6$

(b) $5(b + 2) + 2(b - 1) = 5b + 10 + 2b - 2$
$= 5b + 2b + 10 - 2$
$= 7b + 8$

(c) $4(c - 4) - 2(c + 1) = 4c - 16 - 2c - 2$
$= 4c - 2c - 16 - 2$
$= 2c - 18$

(d) $2(d + 3) - 3(1 - d) = 2d + 6 - 3 + 3d$
$= 2d + 3d + 6 - 3$
$= 5d + 3$

Example 3

Expand the following.

(a) $a(a + 3)$ (b) $b(2b - 3)$

(c) $(2c + 1)c$ (d) $-d(2d + e)$

Solution

(a) $a(a + 3) = a \times a + a \times 3$
$$= a^2 + 3a$$

(b) $b(2b - 3) = b \times 2b + b \times (-3)$
$$= 2b^2 - 3b$$

(c) $(2c + 1)c = 2c \times c + 1 \times c$
$$= 2c^2 + c$$

(d) $-d(2d + e) = -d \times 2d - d \times e$
$$= -2d^2 - de$$

Example 4

Expand and simplify the following.

(a) $m(2m - 3) + 4(m - 5)$ (b) $3(n + 2) - 2n(n + 2)$

(c) $x(x + 1) + 2x(3x + 2)$ (d) $2y(y - 1) - 3y(5 - y)$

Solution

(a) $m(2m - 3) + 4(m - 5) = 2m^2 - 3m + 4m - 20$
$$= 2m^2 + m - 20$$

(b) $3(n + 2) - 2n(n + 2) = 3n + 6 - 2n^2 - 4n$
$$= 6 - n - 2n^2$$

(c) $x(x + 1) + 2x(3x + 2) = x^2 + x + 6x^2 + 4x$
$$= 7x^2 + 5x$$

(d) $2y(y - 1) - 3y(5 - y) = 2y^2 - 2y - 15y + 3y^2$
$$= 5y^2 - 17y$$

Example 5

Expand and simplify the following.

(a) $3(p - 3q) + 2(3p + q)$ (b) $-2(p - q) - 3(5p - q)$

(c) $4x(3x + 2y) + 2x(x + y)$ (d) $5y(y - 2x) - 2x(3x - y)$

Solution

(a) $3(p - 3q) + 2(3p + q) = 3p - 9q + 6p + 2q$
$$= 9p - 7q$$

(b) $-2(p - q) - 3(5p - q) = -2p + 2q - 15p + 3q$
$$= -17p + 5q$$

(c) $4x(3x + 2y) + 2x(x + y) = 12x^2 + 8xy + 2x^2 + 2xy$
$$= 14x^2 + 10xy$$

$xy = x \times y = y \times x = yx$
$\therefore\ 10yx = 10xy$

(d) $5y(y - 2x) - 2x(3x - y) = 5y^2 - 10yx - 6x^2 + 2xy$
$$= 5y^2 - 8xy - 6x^2$$

Exercise 1A

1. Expand the following.
   (a) $7(4f + 3)$
   (b) $6(7g - 5)$
   (c) $5(5 - z)$
   (d) $-5(x + 3)$
   (e) $-4(n - 7)$
   (f) $-5(3w + 8)$
   (g) $-7(5r - 3)$
   (h) $-8(2 - m)$

2. Expand and simplify the following.
   (a) $5(x + 4) + 2(x + 7)$
   (b) $5(y - 5) + 8(y - 1)$
   (c) $3(a + 2) - 2(a + 1)$
   (d) $6(n + 5) - 3(2n - 5)$
   (e) $4(5y - 6) - 5(3y - 1)$
   (f) $5(2 - a) + 8(a + 4)$

3. Expand the following.
   (a) $f(3f + 4)$
   (b) $3h(4h - 5)$
   (c) $-z(z + 3)$
   (d) $-y(y - 1)$
   (e) $-k(3k + 5)$
   (f) $-2x(2x - 3)$
   (g) $(4n + 3)n$
   (h) $(2p - 3)p$

4. Expand the following.
   (a) $a(a + b)$
   (b) $c(c - d)$
   (c) $-g(h - g)$
   (d) $-3m(m + n)$
   (e) $4p(2p + q)$
   (f) $-5r(3r - 2s)$

5. Expand and simplify the following.
   (a) $x(x + 1) + 2(x + 2)$
   (b) $2(y - 2) + y(y + 1)$
   (c) $2(3a + 1) - a(5a + 3)$
   (d) $4n(n + 2) - 3(3 - n)$
   (e) $3(x - 2) + 2x(x - 3)$
   (f) $5(y - 5) - 2y(5 - y)$

6. Expand and simplify the following.
   (a) $2b(b + 5) + b(2 - b)$
   (b) $k(2k + 5) - k(k + 1)$
   (c) $m(4 - m) - 3m(2m + 1)$
   (d) $7n(6n + 5) - n(2 - 3n)$
   (e) $5x(3x - 5) + 2x(3x - 5)$
   (f) $6y(2y - 3) - 5y(3 - 2y)$

7. Expand and simplify the following.
   (a) $2(3b + 5a) + 5(b - 3a)$
   (b) $3(5h - 8g) + 8(h + 5g)$
   (c) $5u(3u + 2v) - u(u - v)$
   (d) $3w(5w - 2x) + x(x - 4w)$
   (e) $-2n(3n + m) + 3m(2m - n)$
   (f) $2x(5y - 3x) - y(8y - x)$

1.1.2 Expansion of $(a + b)(c + d)$

Activity

Spatial visualisation

> **To expand $(a + b)(c + d)$ using the concept of area in geometry.**

The length of the sides of some rectangles are as shown in the diagram on the right.

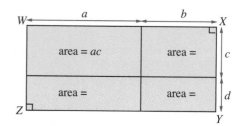

(a) Copy the diagram above and fill in the areas of the rectangles.

(b) Add all the areas to obtain an expression for the area of rectangle *WXYZ*.

(c) Write down the lengths of *WX* and *XY*. Hence, write down another expression for the area of rectangle *WXYZ*.

(d) What can you conclude from the results of **(b)** and **(c)**?

Let us now proceed to use the algebraic method to expand $(a + b)(c + d)$ and then compare the result with the method in the activity above. Let $(c + d) = k$.

$$\therefore \quad (a + b)(c + d) = (a + b)k$$
$$= ak + bk$$

Replace k by $(c + d)$.

$$= a(c + d) + b(c + d)$$
$$= ac + ad + bc + bd$$

Expanding directly, we get:

$$(a + b)(c + d) = ac + ad + bc + bd$$

Compare your expansion with the conclusion obtained in the activity above. Are they the same?

> To **expand an expression of the form $(a + b)(c + d)$**, each term in one pair of brackets must be multiplied by each term in the other pair of brackets.
>
> $$(a + b)(c + d) = ac + ad + bc + bd$$

Example 6

Expand the following.

(a) $(p + 2)(p + 5)$ **(b)** $(q + 3)(q - 5)$

(c) $(r - 2)(r + 3)$ **(d)** $(s - 4)(s - 6)$

Solution

We can also expand the algebraic expressions in **(a)** and **(b)** directly as shown in **(c)** and **(d)**.

(a) $(p + 2)(p + 5) = p(p + 5) + 2(p + 5)$
$$= p^2 + 5p + 2p + 10$$
$$= p^2 + 7p + 10$$

(b) $(q + 3)(q - 5) = q(q - 5) + 3(q - 5)$
$$= q^2 - 5q + 3q - 15$$
$$= q^2 - 2q - 15$$

$(-2) \times (+3) = -6$

(c) $(r - 2)(r + 3) = r^2 + 3r - 2r - 6$
$$= r^2 + r - 6$$

$(-4) \times (-6) = +24$

(d) $(s - 4)(s - 6) = s^2 - 6s - 4s + 24$
$$= s^2 - 10s + 24$$

Example 7

Expand the following.

(a) $(2a + 3)(a + 4)$ **(b)** $(3b + 2)(4b - 3)$

(c) $(2c - 3)(5 + 4c)$ **(d)** $(2 - d)(4 - 3d)$

Solution

Expanding directly, we get:

$(2a + 3)(a + 4)$

$= 2a(a) + 2a(4) +$
$\quad 3(a) + 3(4)$
$= 2a^2 + 8a + 3a + 12$
$= 2a^2 + 11a + 12$

(a) $(2a + 3)(a + 4) = 2a(a + 4) + 3(a + 4)$
$$= 2a^2 + 8a + 3a + 12$$
$$= 2a^2 + 11a + 12$$

(b) $(3b + 2)(4b - 3) = 3b(4b - 3) + 2(4b - 3)$
$$= 12b^2 - 9b + 8b - 6$$
$$= 12b^2 - b - 6$$

(c) $(2c - 3)(5 + 4c) = 10c + 8c^2 - 15 - 12c$
$$= 8c^2 - 2c - 15$$

(d) $(2 - d)(4 - 3d) = 8 - 6d - 4d + 3d^2$
$$= 8 - 10d + 3d^2$$

Example 8

Expand the following.

(a) $(x + y)(z + 5)$ **(b)** $(2k - l)(m + 2)$

Solution

(a) $(x + y)(z + 5) = xz + 5x + yz + 5y$

(b) $(2k - l)(m + 2) = 2km + 4k - lm - 2l$

Exercise 1B

1. Expand the following.
   - **(a)** $(a + 2)(a + 3)$
   - **(b)** $(2 + c)(9 + c)$
   - **(c)** $(e + 3)(e - 5)$
   - **(d)** $(2 + n)(3 - n)$
   - **(e)** $(k - 5)(k + 11)$
   - **(f)** $(3 - r)(6 + r)$
   - **(g)** $(g - 8)(g - 4)$
   - **(h)** $(5 - z)(3 - z)$
   - **(i)** $(q + 2)(q + 2)$
   - **(j)** $(m + 3)(m - 3)$
   - **(k)** $(w - 5)(w + 5)$
   - **(l)** $(s - 2)(s - 2)$

2. Expand the following.
   - **(a)** $(2c + 3)(3c + 5)$
   - **(b)** $(7 + 4t)(t + 2)$
   - **(c)** $(2 + 3x)(9 + 5x)$
   - **(d)** $(4a + 3)(3a - 4)$

   - **(e)** $(2d + 7)(2 - d)$
   - **(f)** $(3 + 5r)(2 - 3r)$
   - **(g)** $(3a - 2)(2a + 1)$
   - **(h)** $(5h - 2)(3 + h)$
   - **(i)** $(5 - 2t)(3 + t)$
   - **(j)** $(p - 2)(4p - 5)$
   - **(k)** $(4b - 1)(2 - 3b)$
   - **(l)** $(2 - 3p)(5 - 3p)$

3. Expand the following.
   - **(a)** $(a + b)(c + 2)$
   - **(b)** $(m + n)(n + 3)$
   - **(c)** $(p - q)(r - 4)$
   - **(d)** $(x + 2y)(y + 2)$
   - **(e)** $(l + m)(m - n)$
   - **(f)** $(a - b)(c + d)$
   - **(g)** $(y - 2x)(x - z)$
   - **(h)** $(p + q)(3p - 2q)$
   - **(i)** $(2y + z)(z + x)$
   - **(j)** $(3x - 2y)(x + z)$

1.1.3 Expansion of $(a + b)^2$ and $(a - b)^2$

Let us consider the following special case where $c = a$ and $d = b$ in the algebraic expressions of the form $(a + b)(c + d)$.

If $c = a$ and $d = b$,

$$(a + b)(c + d) = (a + b)(a + b)$$
$$= (a + b)^2$$

We have learned how to expand algebraic expressions of the form $(a + b)(c + d)$. Using the same method for $(a + b)^2$, we get:

$$(a + b)^2 = (a + b)(a + b)$$
$$= a(a + b) + b(a + b)$$
$$= a^2 + ab + ba + b^2$$
$$= a^2 + 2ab + b^2$$

We can also visualise the expansion on the previous page using the concept of area in geometry:

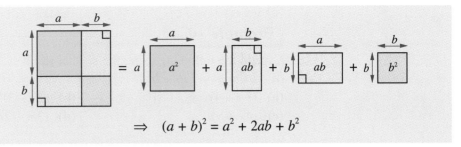

$$\Rightarrow \quad (a+b)^2 = a^2 + 2ab + b^2$$

Similarly using the algebraic method,

$$(a-b)^2 = (a-b)(a-b)$$
$$= a(a-b) - b(a-b)$$
$$= a^2 - ab - ba + b^2$$
$$= a^2 - 2ab + b^2$$

Here again, we can visualise the expansion above using the concept of area in geometry:

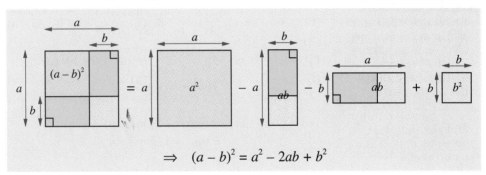

$$\Rightarrow \quad (a-b)^2 = a^2 - 2ab + b^2$$

Since we subtracted b^2 twice, we need to add it back once.

Example 9

Expand the following.

(a) $(x+4)^2$ **(b)** $(x-3)^2$

Solution

(a)

	x	4
x	x^2	$4x$
4	$4x$	16

(a) $(x+4)^2 = (x+4)(x+4)$
$$= x(x+4) + 4(x+4)$$
$$= x^2 + 4x + 4x + 16$$
$$= x^2 + 8x + 16$$

(b) $(x-3)^2 = (x-3)(x-3)$
$$= x(x-3) - 3(x-3)$$
$$= x^2 - 3x - 3x + 9$$
$$= x^2 - 6x + 9$$

In general,

$$(a+b)^2 = a^2 + 2ab + b^2$$
$$(a-b)^2 = a^2 - 2ab + b^2$$

In the next example, we shall make use of the special results of $(a + b)^2$ and $(a - b)^2$ that we have just found.

Example 10

Expand the following using the special result $(a + b)^2 = a^2 + 2ab + b^2$ or $(a - b)^2 = a^2 - 2ab + b^2$.

(a) $(3u + 4)^2$ **(b)** $(2v - 3)^2$

(c) $(4x + y)^2$ **(d)** $(3m - 2n)^2$

Solution

(a)
$$(a + b)^2 = a^2 + 2ab + b^2$$
$$(3u + 4)^2 = (3u)^2 + 2(3u)(4) + 4^2 \quad \longleftarrow \text{Replace } a \text{ with } 3u$$
$$= 9u^2 + 24u + 16 \qquad\qquad \text{and } b \text{ with } 4$$

(b)
$$(a - b)^2 = a^2 - 2ab + b^2$$
$$(2v - 3)^2 = (2v)^2 - 2(2v)(3) + 3^2 \quad \longleftarrow \text{Replace } a \text{ with } 2v$$
$$= 4v^2 - 12v + 9 \qquad\qquad \text{and } b \text{ with } 3$$

(c) $(4x + y)^2 = (4x)^2 + 2(4x)(y) + y^2$
$$= 16x^2 + 8xy + y^2$$

(d) $(3m - 2n)^2 = (3m)^2 - 2(3m)(2n) + (2n)^2$
$$= 9m^2 - 12mn + 4n^2$$

Exercise 1C

1. Expand the following using the special result $(a + b)^2 = a^2 + 2ab + b^2$ or $(a - b)^2 = a^2 - 2ab + b^2$.
   (a) $(x + 8)^2$ (b) $(x + 10)^2$
   (c) $(x - 7)^2$ (d) $(x - 4)^2$
   (e) $(p + q)^2$ (f) $(s + t)^2$
   (g) $(p - q)^2$ (h) $(s - t)^2$

2. Expand the following using the special result $(a + b)^2 = a^2 + 2ab + b^2$ or $(a - b)^2 = a^2 - 2ab + b^2$.
   (a) $(2x + 1)^2$ (b) $(3a + 1)^2$

   (c) $(3m + 2)^2$ (d) $(2a + 3)^2$
   (e) $(5a - 2)^2$ (f) $(4a - 3)^2$
   (g) $(7y - 4)^2$ (h) $(8n - 5)^2$

3. Expand the following using the special result $(a + b)^2 = a^2 + 2ab + b^2$ or $(a - b)^2 = a^2 - 2ab + b^2$.
   (a) $(2a + b)^2$ (b) $(3h + k)^2$
   (c) $(4m + 3n)^2$ (d) $(5p + 2q)^2$
   (e) $(2r - s)^2$ (f) $(3u - v)^2$
   (g) $(4v - 3w)^2$ (h) $(5x - 2y)^2$

1.1.4 Expansion of $(a + b)(a - b)$

Let us consider the special case of $(a + b)(a - b)$. Applying what we have learned earlier in this chapter, we have:

$$(a + b)(a - b) = a(a - b) + b(a - b)$$
$$= a^2 - ab + ba - b^2$$
$$= a^2 - b^2$$

Example 11

Expand the following.

(a) $(x + 4)(x - 4)$ **(b)** $(x - 3)(x + 3)$

Solution

(a) Note that $x^2 = x \times x$ and $16 = 4^2$. Therefore, the expansion of $(x + 4)(x - 4)$ results in the difference of two squares, x^2 and 16.

(b) The expansion results in the difference of two squares, x^2 and 9.

(a) $(x + 4)(x - 4) = x(x - 4) + 4(x - 4)$
$$= x^2 - 4x + 4x - 16$$
$$= x^2 - 16$$

(b) $(x - 3)(x + 3) = x(x + 3) - 3(x + 3)$
$$= x^2 + 3x - 3x - 9$$
$$= x^2 - 9$$

In general,

$$(a + b)(a - b) = a^2 - b^2$$

In the next example, we shall make use of the special result of $(a + b)(a - b)$ that we have just found.

Example 12

Expand the following using the special result $(a + b)(a - b) = a^2 - b^2$.

(a) $(h + 6)(h - 6)$ **(b)** $(2k - 3)(2k + 3)$

(c) $(3m + 2n)(3m - 2n)$

Solution

$$(a + b)(a - b) = a^2 - b^2$$
$$\uparrow \uparrow \uparrow \uparrow \quad \updownarrow \quad \uparrow$$
$$(h + 6)(h - 6) = h^2 - 6^2$$

(a) $(h + 6)(h - 6) = h^2 - 6^2$
$$= h^2 - 36$$

(b) $(2k - 3)(2k + 3) = (2k)^2 - 3^2$
$$= 4k^2 - 9$$

It is $(3m)^2$ and **not** $3m^2$.

(c) $(3m + 2n)(3m - 2n) = (3m)^2 - (2n)^2$
$$= 9m^2 - 4n^2$$

1. Expand the following using the special result $(a + b)(a - b) = a^2 - b^2$.
   (a) $(x + 1)(x - 1)$
   (b) $(m - 10)(m + 10)$
   (c) $(8 + u)(8 - u)$
   (d) $(9 - n)(9 + n)$
   (e) $(h + k)(h - k)$
   (f) $(r - s)(r + s)$

   (c) $(1 - 3x)(1 + 3x)$
   (d) $(1 + 5y)(1 - 5y)$
   (e) $(3a + 4)(3a - 4)$
   (f) $(5b - 3)(5b + 3)$
   (g) $(3 - 2k)(3 + 2k)$
   (h) $(2 + 5h)(2 - 5h)$

2. Expand the following using the special result $(a + b)(a - b) = a^2 - b^2$.
   (a) $(2p + 1)(2p - 1)$
   (b) $(4q - 1)(4q + 1)$

3. Expand the following using the special result $(a + b)(a - b) = a^2 - b^2$.
   (a) $(2x + y)(2x - y)$
   (b) $(x + 3y)(x - 3y)$
   (c) $(4a - 3b)(4a + 3b)$
   (d) $(2a - 5b)(2a + 5b)$

TIME-OUT ACTIVITY

Spot the Mistakes I

Study the expansions done by three students, Ali, Benny and Chandra as shown below.

Ali's expansion: $(2a + 3)^2 = 4a^2 + 9$
Benny's expansion: $(3a - 2)^2 = 9a^2 - 4$
Chandra's expansion: $(4a + 1)(4a - 1) = 16a^2 - 4a + 4a - 1$
$= 16a^2 - 8a - 1$

(a) By substituting numerical values, show that the above solutions are wrong.
(b) Discuss with your classmates and explain in your Mathematics Journal the mistakes in each of the above solutions.
(c) Finally, present the correct solutions in your Mathematics Journal.

Factorisation of Algebraic Expressions

1.2.1 Factorisation by Taking Out the Common Factor

In Section 1.1, you have learned about expansion by the distributive law. For example, $a(b + c) = ab + ac$. The reverse process, $ab + ac = a(b + c)$ is called **factorisation**. In this case, factorisation is done by '**taking out the common factor**'. Consider the expression $3x + 6$. The factors of $3x$ are 3 and x, and the factors of 6 are 3 and 2. Therefore, 3 is the common factor of $3x$ and 6.

$$\therefore \quad 3x + 6 = 3 \times x + 3 \times 2$$
$$\text{Since} \quad 3(x + 2) = 3 \times x + 3 \times 2 \quad \text{(Distributive law)}$$
$$\therefore \quad 3x + 6 = 3(x + 2)$$

From the above example, we see that the common factor has been taken out and placed in front of the brackets to get the factorised form. The expression inside the brackets is obtained by dividing each term by the common factor. The factorised form of an expression is considered to be the simplest form of that expression.

In general,

$$\overset{\text{factorisation}}{\underset{\text{expansion}}{\xrightleftharpoons{\hspace{2cm}}}}$$
$$ab + ac = a(b + c)$$

| **Example 13**

note

You can use expansion to check your factorised form.

Factorise the following.

(a) $2x + 6$ (b) $-3m - 12$

(c) $5x + 5y$ (d) $4b - 8c$

(e) $x^2 - x$ (f) $9x^2 + 24xy$

(g) $x(x + 2) + 3(x + 2)$ (h) $k(2k - 3) + (2k - 3)$

| **Solution**

The common factor of $2x$ and 6 is 2.

(a) $2x + 6 = 2 \times x + 2 \times 3$
$$= 2(x + 3)$$

The common factor of $-3m$ and -12 is -3.

(b) $-3m - 12 = (-3 \times m) + (-3 \times 4)$
$$= -3(m + 4)$$

The common factor of $5x$ and $5y$ is 5.

(c) $5x + 5y = 5 \times x + 5 \times y$
$$= 5(x + y)$$

To factorise completely, we take out the highest common factor (H.C.F.) of $4b$ and $-8c$ which is 4.

(d) $4b - 8c = 4 \times b - 4 \times 2c$
$$= 4(b - 2c)$$

The common factor of x^2 and x is x.

(e) $x^2 - x = x \times x - x \times 1$
$ = x(x - 1)$

The common factor of $9x^2$ and $24xy$ is $3x$.

(f) $9x^2 + 24xy = 3x \times 3x + 3x \times 8y$
$ = 3x(3x + 8y)$

The common factor $x(x + 2)$ and $3(x + 2)$ is $(x + 2)$.

(g) $x(x + 2) + 3(x + 2) = (x + 2)(x + 3)$ ← $(x + 2)$ is taken out, leaving x and $+3$ behind

(h) $(2k - 3)$ is common to $k(2k - 3)$ and $(2k - 3)$.

$(2k - 3)$ can be written as $1(2k - 3)$.

$\therefore \quad k(2k - 3) + (2k - 3) = k(2k - 3) + 1(2k - 3)$
$ = (2k - 3)(k + 1)$

Exercise 1E

1. Factorise the following.
(a) $3x + 12$ **(b)** $7x + 49$
(c) $56 + 7x$ **(d)** $98 + 49x$
(e) $4x - 16$ **(f)** $8x - 48$
(g) $16 - 8x$ **(h)** $12 - 48x$

2. Factorise the following.
(a) $6x + 21y$ **(b)** $4m + 6n$
(c) $8m + 12n$ **(d)** $10y + 25z$
(e) $18p - 27q$ **(f)** $15a - 12b$
(g) $14c - 49d$ **(h)** $16b - 40c$

3. Factorise the following.
(a) $x^2 + 4x$ **(b)** $y^2 - 4y$
(c) $3p + 4p^2$ **(d)** $5y^2 - 15y$
(e) $4a - 12a^2$ **(f)** $16s - 10s^2$
(g) $15y + 10y^2$ **(h)** $8a + 12a^2$

4. Factorise the following.
(a) $-48 - 8p$ **(b)** $-24 - 12m$
(c) $-15p - 10q$ **(d)** $-8y - 20z$
(e) $-4y - y^2$ **(f)** $-3p^2 - p$

5. Factorise the following.
(a) $a + ab$
(b) $c^2 - cd$
(c) $3e^2 + 6ef$
(d) $4g^2 - 6gh$
(e) $mn + mn^2$
(f) $p^2q - pq^2$

6. Factorise the following.
(a) $x(x + 1) + 2(x + 1)$
(b) $m(m + 1) + 4(m + 1)$
(c) $t(t - 2) + 2(t - 2)$
(d) $y(y - 5) + 5(y - 5)$
(e) $b(4b - 3) - 3(4b - 3)$
(f) $x(1 - 3x) + 2(1 - 3x)$
(g) $y(y + 1) + (y + 1)$
(h) $q(q - 4) - 4(q - 4)$

1.2.2 Factorisation by Grouping

Consider the expression $ac + ad + bc + bd$. You will notice that there is no common factor for all four terms, but we can factorise this expression by **grouping the terms** which have a common factor. Thus, we get:

$(c + d)$ is common to both terms in the expression $a(c + d) + b(c + d)$. Thus, we take it out as the common factor, leaving $a + b$ in the brackets.

$$ac + ad + bc + bd = a(c + d) + b(c + d)$$
$$= (c + d)(a + b)$$

terms with common factor a terms with common factor b

Notice the above factorisation is the reverse process of the expansion:

$$(a + b)(c + d) = a(c + d) + b(c + d)$$
$$= ac + ad + bc + bd$$

Refer to Section 1.1.2

In general,

$$\xrightarrow{\text{factorisation}}$$
$$ac + ad + bc + bd = (a + b)(c + d)$$
$$\xleftarrow{\text{expansion}}$$

Example 14

Factorise the following.
(a) $ac + ad + 2c + 2d$ **(b)** $3uv - 6uw + xv - 2xw$
(c) $mp + 3mq - 2np - 6nq$ **(d)** $hx + ky - hy - kx$

Solution

(a) $ac + ad + 2c + 2d = a(c + d) + 2(c + d)$
$$= (c + d)(a + 2)$$

note

We need to make the expressions in both brackets the same before taking it out as a common factor. For example, $(-p - 3q)$ can be expressed as $-(p + 3q)$.

(b) $3uv - 6uw + xv - 2xw = 3u(v - 2w) + x(v - 2w)$
$$= (v - 2w)(3u + x)$$

(c) $mp + 3mq - 2np - 6nq = m(p + 3q) + 2n(-p - 3q)$
$$= m(p + 3q) - 2n(p + 3q)$$
$$= (p + 3q)(m - 2n)$$

Arrange terms with common factors together.

(d) $hx + ky - hy - kx$
$\quad = hx - hy + ky - kx$
$\quad = h(x - y) + k(y - x)$
$\quad = h(x - y) - k(x - y)$
$\quad = (x - y)(h - k)$

Alternative method:
$hx + ky - hy - kx$
$= hx - hy - kx + ky$
$= h(x - y) - k(x - y)$
$= (x - y)(h - k)$

1. Factorise the following.
   (a) $a(z + 1) + 2(z + 1)$
   (b) $c(x - 3) + 3(x - 3)$
   (c) $e(v + 5) - 6(v + 5)$
   (d) $g(t - 6) - 7(t - 6)$
   (e) $m(2r + 1) + (2r + 1)$
   (f) $2a(z - 1) + 3(z - 1)$
   (g) $b(x + y) - c(x + y)$
   (h) $2f(t - 3u) - g(t - 3u)$

2. Factorise the following.
   (a) $mp + mq + np + nq$
   (b) $2ay + 2az + by + bz$
   (c) $fu - ft + gu - gt$
   (d) $4hs - 2hr + 2ks - kr$
   (e) $mp + mq - p - q$

   (f) $2ny + 2nz - y - z$
   (g) $ab + a - b - 1$
   (h) $3cd + c - 3d - 1$
   (i) $hk - 6 - 3h + 2k$
   (j) $4rs - 3 - 2r + 6s$
   (k) $6ap - 2bq - 3aq + 4bp$
   (l) $15my + 8nz - 6ny - 20mz$

3. Factorise the following.
   (a) $3uv + 12u + v + 4$ [N/86/P2]
   (b) $2mx - 6my + nx - 3ny$ [N/90/P2]
   (c) $ap + 2p + 3aq + 6q$ [N/93/P2]
   (d) $10ap + 5aq + 2bp + bq$ [N/94/P2]
   (e) $6a - 2b + 3ax - bx$ [N/96/P2]
   (f) $ac + 3bc - 2ad - 6bd$ [N/99/P2]

1.2.3 Factorisation by Using the Cross Method

An expression of the form $ax^2 + bx + c$ (where a, b and c are constants and $a \neq 0$) is called a **quadratic expression**. One method of factorising a quadratic expression is to use the reverse of the distributive law. For example:

$$x^2 + 7x + 12 = x^2 + 4x + 3x + 12$$
$$= x(x + 4) + 3(x + 4)$$
$$= (x + 4)(x + 3)$$

We can use the concept of area in geometry to visualise the factorisation shown on the right:

You will notice that $7x$ has been 'broken up' into $4x + 3x$. We have to make sure that in the final answer, the product of the two numbers within the brackets is the **constant term** of the quadratic expression. In the example above, we can see that $4 \times 3 = 12$. To do this systematically, we shall look at a method called the **cross method**.

Consider the expression $2x^2 + 7x + 3$. Let us see how we can use the cross method to factorise this expression.

Step 1 Determine the possible factors of the x^2 term and the constant term.

$$2x^2 + 7x + 3$$

$$x \times 2x \qquad (+1) \times (+3)$$

Step 2 Write the factors vertically as shown.

$$
\begin{array}{ll}
x & +1 \\
2x & +3
\end{array}
$$

Step 3 Multiply the factors as shown below and write the product in the last column.

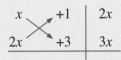

$$
\begin{array}{ll|l}
x & +1 & 2x \\
2x & +3 & 3x
\end{array}
$$

Step 4 Add the terms in the last column. Reject the work if the sum is not equal to the term in x in the given expression.

$$
\begin{array}{ll|l}
x & +1 & 2x \\
2x & +3 & 3x
\end{array} \Big\} \text{Add}
$$

$$5x \neq 7x \quad \text{(Rejected)}$$

Step 5 Exchange places of +1 and +3. Multiply the factors and add the terms in the last column again.

$$
\begin{array}{ll|l}
x & +3 & 6x \\
2x & +1 & x
\end{array}
$$

$$7x \quad \text{(Accepted)}$$

Step 6 As step **5** is accepted, the factors of the quadratic expression are those circled.

$$
\begin{array}{ll|l}
\boxed{x} & \boxed{+3} & 6x \\
\boxed{2x} & \boxed{+1} & x \\
\hline
 & & 7x
\end{array}
$$

$$\therefore \quad 2x^2 + 7x + 3 = (x + 3)(2x + 1)$$

note

Check your answer by expanding the factorised form.

$$(x + 3)(2x + 1)$$

$$= 2x^2 + 7x + 3$$

The steps above have been deliberately written in a lengthy way for you to follow. With sufficient practice, most of the steps can be mentally visualised as shown in the following examples.

Example 15

Factorise $a^2 + 11a + 30$.

Solution

$$a^2 + 11a + 30$$

$a \times a \qquad 1 \times 30$ or 2×15 or 5×6 or 3×10

note

Remember to check your answer by expanding the factorised form. You should obtain the original expression.

1st **Trial**			2nd **Trial**			3rd **Trial**		
a	1	a	a	2	$2a$	a	5	$5a$
a	30	$30a$	a	15	$15a$	a	6	$6a$
		$31a \neq 11a$			$17a \neq 11a$			$11a$
		(Rejected)			(Rejected)			(Accepted)

$\therefore \quad a^2 + 11a + 30 = (a + 5)(a + 6)$

Example 16

Factorise $y^2 - 8y + 12$.

Solution

$$y^2 - 8y + 12$$

$y \times y \qquad 2 \times 6$ or $(-2) \times (-6)$, 3×4 or $(-3) \times (-4)$, etc.

In the above expression, the term $-8y$ indicates that the factors of the positive constant term 12 should be both negative. Therefore, we should express 12 as $(-3) \times (-4)$ or $(-2) \times (-6)$ rather than 3×4 or 2×6.

note

If we choose to express 12 as 2×6 instead, our working will be as shown:

y	2	$2y$
y	6	$6y$
		$8y \neq -8y$
		(Rejected)

Since we get a positive coefficient of y instead of a negative coefficient, we reject the positive factors of 12.

1st **Trial**			2nd **Trial**		
y	3	$3y$	y	-2	$-2y$
y	-4	$-4y$	y	-6	$-6y$
		$-7y \neq -8y$			$-8y$
		(Rejected)			(Accepted)

$\therefore \quad y^2 - 8y + 12 = (y - 2)(y - 6)$

Example 17

Factorise $2m^2 + m - 3$.

Solution

$$2m^2 + m - 3$$

$m \times 2m$ $1 \times (-3)$ or $(-1) \times 3$

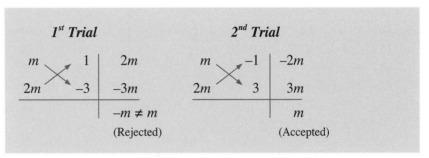

	1st Trial			**2nd Trial**	
m	1	$2m$	m	-1	$-2m$
$2m$	-3	$-3m$	$2m$	3	$3m$
		$-m \neq m$			m
		(Rejected)			(Accepted)

$\therefore \quad 2m^2 + m - 3 = (m - 1)(2m + 3)$

In the next example, we shall not show the rejected trials.

Example 18

Factorise the following.

(a) $x^2 + 7x + 10$ **(b)** $2y^2 + 8y + 6$

(c) $3 - m - 2m^2$ **(d)** $2p^2 + 3pr + r^2$

Solution

(a) $x^2 + 7x + 10 = (x + 2)(x + 5)$

x	2	$2x$
x	5	$5x$
		$7x$

Notice that all the three terms $2y^2$, $8y$ and 6 have the common factor 2. Always take out the common factor first.

(b) $2y^2 + 8y + 6 = 2(y^2 + 4y + 3)$
$\qquad\qquad\qquad\quad = 2(y + 1)(y + 3)$

y	1	y
y	3	$3y$
		$4y$

Alternatively, we can also rearrange the algebraic expression first:
$3 - m - 2m^2$
$= -(2m^2 + m - 3)$

(c) $3 - m - 2m^2 = (1 - m)(3 + 2m)$

1×3 $-m \times 2m$

1	$-m$	$-3m$
3	$2m$	$2m$
		$-m$

(d) $2p^2 + 3pr + r^2 = (p + r)(2p + r)$

$p \times 2p$ $r \times r$

p	r	$2pr$
$2p$	r	pr
		$3pr$

1. Factorise the following.
   (a) $z^2 + 3z + 2$ (b) $y^2 + 4y + 3$
   (c) $x^2 + 7x + 6$ (d) $w^2 + 6w + 5$
   (e) $v^2 + 12v + 36$ (f) $u^2 + 18u + 81$
   (g) $s^2 + 10s + 21$ (h) $r^2 + 11r + 18$
   (i) $p^2 - 12p + 36$ (j) $n^2 - 8n + 16$
   (k) $m^2 - 7m + 12$ (l) $k^2 - 11k + 30$
   (m) $h^2 + h - 12$ (n) $g^2 + 5g - 6$
   (o) $f^2 + 4f - 12$ (p) $e^2 + e - 6$
   (q) $d^2 - 5d - 24$ (r) $c^2 - 4c - 12$
   (s) $b^2 - 10b - 24$ (t) $a^2 - a - 12$

2. Factorise the following.
   (a) $2a^2 + 5a + 2$ (b) $3b^2 + 10b + 3$
   (c) $12c^2 + 17c + 6$ (d) $6d^2 + 13d + 6$
   (e) $12e^2 + e - 6$ (f) $6f^2 + 5f - 6$
   (g) $3g^2 - 4g + 1$ (h) $4h^2 - 17h + 4$
   (i) $5z^2 - 8z - 4$ (j) $6y^2 - y - 2$

(k) $2k^2 + 18k + 40$ (l) $2x^2 + 14x + 20$
(m) $3m^2 + 9m - 30$ (n) $3n^2 + 6n - 9$
(o) $2w^2 - 14w + 24$ (p) $2p^2 - 16p + 24$
(q) $3v^2 - 3v - 6$ (r) $5r^2 - 10r - 15$

3. Factorise the following.
   (a) $w^2 - 13w + 36$ [N/85/P2]
   (b) $y^2 + 10y + 25$ [N/91/P2]
   (c) $y^2 + 5y + 6$ [N/92/P2]
   (d) $x^2 - 3x - 10$ [N/93/P2]
   (e) $y^2 - 10y + 25$ [N/95/P2]
   (f) $x^2 - 4x - 5$ [N/98/P2]

★4. Factorise the following.
   (a) $u^2 + 9us + 20s^2$
   (b) $48d^2 + 2dy - y^2$
   (c) $5m^2 - 30mn + 40n^2$
   (d) $5s^2 - 15st - 20t^2$

1.2.4 Factorisation by Using the Special Results of $a^2 + 2ab + b^2$ and $a^2 - 2ab + b^2$

From section 1.1.3, we have seen that:

$$(a + b)^2 = a^2 + 2ab + b^2$$
$$(a - b)^2 = a^2 - 2ab + b^2$$

The reverse processes are shown below.

$$a^2 + 2ab + b^2 = (a + b)^2$$
$$a^2 - 2ab + b^2 = (a - b)^2$$

note

$a^2 + 2ab + b^2$

$= (a + b)^2$

$a^2 - 2ab + b^2$

$= (a - b)^2$

By using the special results obtained above, expressions of the forms $a^2 + 2ab + b^2$ and $a^2 - 2ab + b^2$ can be factorised directly. The above expressions can also be factorised by using the cross method. However, in this section, we will focus on factorising such expressions using the special results.

| *Example 19*

Factorise the following.
(a) $a^2 + 2a + 1$ (b) $a^2 - 6a + 9$

Solution

note

Check that the algebraic expression is in the form of $a^2 + 2ab + b^2$ or $a^2 - 2ab + b^2$ before applying the special results.

(a) $a^2 + 2a + 1 = a^2 + 2(a)(1) + 1^2$ ← Mentally visualise as
$$= (a + 1)^2$$

$$a^2 + 2ab + b^2 = (a + b)^2$$
$$a^2 + 2(a)(1) + 1^2 = (a + 1)^2$$

Alternative method:
$$a^2 + 2a + 1 = (a + 1)(a + 1)$$
$$= (a + 1)^2$$

$$
\begin{array}{c|c}
a \quad 1 & a \\
a \quad 1 & a \\
\hline
& 2a
\end{array}
$$

(b) $a^2 - 6a + 9 = a^2 - 2(a)(3) + 3^2$ ← Mentally visualise as
$$= (a - 3)^2$$

$$a^2 - 2ab + b^2 = (a - b)^2$$
$$a^2 - 2(a)(3) + 3^2 = (a - 3)^2$$

Alternative method:
$$a^2 - 6a + 9 = (a - 3)(a - 3)$$
$$= (a - 3)^2$$

$$
\begin{array}{c|c}
a \quad -3 & -3a \\
a \quad -3 & -3a \\
\hline
& -6a
\end{array}
$$

Example 20

Factorise the following.

(a) $4a^2 + 4a + 1$ **(b)** $18x^2 - 24x + 8$

Solution

(a) $4a^2 + 4a + 1 = (2a)^2 + 2(2a)(1) + 1^2$
$$= (2a + 1)^2$$

Mentally visualise as

$$a^2 + 2ab + b^2 = (a + b)^2$$
$$(2a)^2 + 2(2a)(1) + 1^2 = (2a + 1)^2$$

Alternative method:
$$4a^2 + 4a + 1 = (2a + 1)(2a + 1)$$
$$= (2a + 1)^2$$

$$
\begin{array}{c|c}
2a \quad 1 & 2a \\
2a \quad 1 & 2a \\
\hline
& 4a
\end{array}
$$

Take out the H.C.F. of all terms first, if there is any.

(b) $18x^2 - 24x + 8 = 2(9x^2 - 12x + 4)$
$$= 2[(3x)^2 - 2(3x)(2) + 2]^2$$
$$= 2(3x - 2)^2$$

Mentally visualise as

$$a^2 - 2ab + b^2 = (a - b)^2$$
$$(3x)^2 - 2(3x)(2) + 2^2 = (3x - 2)^2$$

Alternative method:
$$18x^2 - 24x + 8 = 2(9x^2 - 12x + 4)$$
$$= 2[(3x - 2)(3x - 2)]$$
$$= 2(3x - 2)^2$$

$$
\begin{array}{c|c}
3x \quad -2 & -6x \\
3x \quad -2 & -6x \\
\hline
& -12x
\end{array}
$$

Example 21

Factorise the following using the special result $a^2 + 2ab + b^2 = (a + b)^2$ or $a^2 - 2ab + b^2 = (a - b)^2$.

(a) $x^2 + 6xy + 9y^2$ **(b)** $4x^2 - 4xy + y^2$

Solution

(a) $x^2 + 6xy + 9y^2 = x^2 + 2(x)(3y) + (3y)^2$
$$= (x + 3y)^2$$

(b) $4x^2 - 4xy + y^2 = (2x)^2 - 2(2x)(y) + y^2$
$$= (2x - y)^2$$

Exercise 1H

1. Factorise the following using the special result $a^2 + 2ab + b^2 = (a + b)^2$ or $a^2 - 2ab + b^2 = (a - b)^2$.

(a) $a^2 + 4a + 4$

(b) $m^2 + 10m + 25$

(c) $b^2 - 2b + 1$

(d) $w^2 - 8w + 16$

2. Factorise the following using the special result $a^2 + 2ab + b^2 = (a + b)^2$ or $a^2 - 2ab + b^2 = (a - b)^2$.

(a) $4c^2 + 12c + 9$

(b) $25x^2 + 40x + 16$

(c) $4d^2 - 4d + 1$

(d) $64x^2 - 112x + 49$

3. Factorise the following using the special result $a^2 + 2ab + b^2 = (a + b)^2$ or $a^2 - 2ab + b^2 = (a - b)^2$.

(a) $2h^2 + 4h + 2$

(b) $75x^2 + 90x + 27$

(c) $3b^2 - 30b + 75$

(d) $72x^2 - 96x + 32$

4. Factorise the following using the special result $a^2 + 2ab + b^2 = (a + b)^2$ or $a^2 - 2ab + b^2 = (a - b)^2$.

(a) $m^2 + 2mn + n^2$

(b) $9x^2 + 30xy + 25y^2$

(c) $p^2 - 4pq + 4q^2$

(d) $25h^2 - 30hk + 9k^2$

1.2.5   Factorisation by Using the Special Result of $a^2 - b^2$

It has been shown using the distributive law in Section 1.1.4 that $(a + b)(a - b) = a^2 - b^2$. The reverse process $a^2 - b^2 = (a + b)(a - b)$ can be used to factorise expressions which are the difference of two squares. By identifying that an algebraic expression is in the form of $a^2 - b^2$, the above special result can be used for direct factorisation.

Example 22

Using the special result $a^2 - b^2 = (a + b)(a - b)$, factorise the following.

(a) $x^2 - 4$ **(b)** $64 - a^2$

(c) $4m^2 - 25$ **(d)** $2y^2 - 18$

Check that the algebraic expression is in the form of $a^2 - b^2$ before applying the special result.

(d) Always take out any common factor first.

Solution

(a) $x^2 - 4 = x^2 - 2^2$
$= (x + 2)(x - 2)$

(b) $64 - a^2 = 8^2 - a^2$
$= (8 + a)(8 - a)$

(c) $4m^2 - 25 = (2m)^2 - 5^2$
$= (2m + 5)(2m - 5)$

(d) $2y^2 - 18 = 2(y^2 - 9)$
$= 2(y^2 - 3^2)$
$= 2(y + 3)(y - 3)$

Example 23

Factorise the following using the special result $a^2 - b^2 = (a + b)(a - b)$.
(a) $m^2 - 9n^2$
(b) $4a^2 - 9b^2$
(c) $(c + 2)^2 - 9$
(d) $16 - (y - 3)^2$

Solution

(a) $m^2 - 9n^2 = m^2 - (3n)^2$
$= (m + 3n)(m - 3n)$

(b) $4a^2 - 9b^2 = (2a)^2 - (3b)^2$
$= (2a + 3b)(2a - 3b)$

(c) $(c + 2)^2 - 9 = (c + 2)^2 - 3^2$
$= [(c + 2) + 3][(c + 2) - 3]$
$= (c + 5)(c - 1)$

(d) $16 - (y - 3)^2 = 4^2 - (y - 3)^2$
$= [4 + (y - 3)][4 - (y - 3)]$
$= (4 + y - 3)(4 - y + 3)$
$= (y + 1)(7 - y)$

Example 24

Evaluate the following using the special result $a^2 - b^2 = (a + b)(a - b)$.
(a) $73^2 - 27^2$
(b) $\sqrt{6.8^2 - 3.2^2}$

Solution

(a) $73^2 - 27^2 = (73 + 27)(73 - 27)$
$= (100)(46)$
$= 4\ 600$

(b) $\sqrt{6.8^2 - 3.2^2} = \sqrt{(6.8 + 3.2)(6.8 - 3.2)}$
$= \sqrt{(10)(3.6)}$
$= \sqrt{36}$
$= 6$

1. Factorise the following using the special result $a^2 - b^2 = (a + b)(a - b)$.
   (a) $a^2 - 49$ (b) $b^2 - 25$
   (c) $144 - d^2$ (d) $100 - g^2$
   (e) $25m^2 - 1$ (f) $4z^2 - 81$
   (g) $1 - 64n^2$ (h) $121 - 25x^2$
   (i) $5w^2 - 500$ (j) $2p^2 - 32$
   (k) $108 - 3v^2$ (l) $64 - 4r^2$

2. Factorise the following using the special result $a^2 - b^2 = (a + b)(a - b)$.
   (a) $a^2 - z^2$ (b) $c^2 - 4x^2$
   (c) $16e^2 - v^2$ (d) $25f^2 - u^2$
   (e) $16g^2 - 25t^2$ (f) $49h^2 - 64s^2$
   (g) $(r + 1)^2 - 4$ (h) $(p + 1)^2 - 16$
   (i) $(k - 2)^2 - 100$ (j) $(a - 4)^2 - 25$
   (k) $144 - (m + 3)^2$ (l) $169 - (n - 4)^2$

3. Evaluate the following using the special result $a^2 - b^2 = (a + b)(a - b)$.
   (a) $88^2 - 12^2$ (b) $77^2 - 23^2$
   (c) $6.54^2 - 3.46^2$ (d) $5.43^2 - 4.57^2$
   (e) $\left(\dfrac{3}{4}\right)^2 - \left(\dfrac{1}{4}\right)^2$ (f) $\left(\dfrac{5}{8}\right)^2 - \left(\dfrac{3}{8}\right)^2$
   (g) $\dfrac{69^2 - 44^2}{4^2 + 3^2}$ (h) $\dfrac{78^2 - 22^2}{8^2 + 6^2}$
   (i) $\sqrt{8.2^2 - 1.8^2}$ (j) $\sqrt{1.105^2 - 0.105^2}$

4. Factorise the following.
   (a) $v^2 - 25$ [N/85/P2]
   (b) $9m^2 - 1$ [N/87/P2]
   (c) $x^2 - 9$ [N/92/P2]
   (d) $3c^2 - 12d^2$ [N/95/P2]

Spot the Mistakes II

Frankie and Hadi are each given an algebraic expression to factorise. Their workings are shown below.

Frankie's factorisation: $a^2 - 1 = (a - 1)^2$

Hadi's factorisation: $4a^2 + 24a + 36 = (2a + 6)^2$

$$
\begin{array}{c|c}
2a \quad\quad 6 & 12a \\
2a \quad\quad 6 & 12a \\
\hline
& 24a
\end{array}
$$

Discuss with your classmates and explain in your Mathematics Journal, how you would
(i) show that Frankie's factorisation is incorrect,
(ii) show that Hadi's factorisation is not complete,
(iii) show Hadi a better way to factorise the expression $4a^2 + 24a + 36$ completely.

1. Expansion of algebraic expression using the distributive law:

    (a) $a(b + c) = ab + ac$

    (b) $(a + b)(c + d) = a(c + d) + b(c + d)$
    $$= ac + ad + bc + bd$$

2. Factorisation is the reverse process of expansion. The methods of factorisation include:

    (a) $ab + ac = a(b + c)$ ← Taking out the common factor

    (b) $ac + ad + bc + bd = a(c + d) + b(c + d)$ ← Grouping method
    $$= (c + d)(a + b)$$

    (c) E.g. $2x^2 + 7x + 3 = (x + 3)(2x + 1)$ ← Cross method

    $$
    \begin{array}{cc|c}
    x & 3 & 6x \\
    2x & 1 & x \\
    \hline
     & & 7x
    \end{array}
    $$

    Always take out the common factor first in factorisation:

    E.g. $2y^2 + 8y + 6 = 2(y^2 + 4y + 3)$
    $$= 2(y + 1)(y + 3)$$

3. Expansion and factorisation by using special results:

    (a) $\underset{\text{factorisation}}{\overset{\text{expansion}}{(a + b)^2 = a^2 + 2ab + b^2}}$

    (b) $\underset{\text{factorisation}}{\overset{\text{expansion}}{(a - b)^2 = a^2 - 2ab + b^2}}$

    (c) $\underset{\text{factorisation}}{\overset{\text{expansion}}{(a + b)(a - b) = a^2 - b^2}}$

Enrichment
●●● m a t h s ●●●

Mental Squares

Kok Hua's friend showed him a method to work out the squares of some types of numbers. The method is shown below.

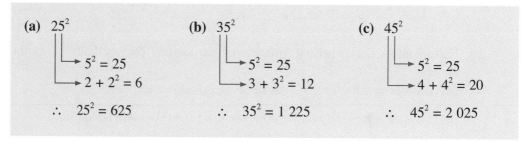

(a) 25^2

$5^2 = 25$
$2 + 2^2 = 6$

$\therefore 25^2 = 625$

(b) 35^2

$5^2 = 25$
$3 + 3^2 = 12$

$\therefore 35^2 = 1\ 225$

(c) 45^2

$5^2 = 25$
$4 + 4^2 = 20$

$\therefore 45^2 = 2\ 025$

Using the above method, evaluate
(i) 55^2, **(ii)** 65^2, **(iii)** 15^2.

Kok Hua noticed that all the numbers squared earlier had 5 as the unit digit. He decided to try the same method on numbers where the unit digits are other numbers.

(a) 24^2

$4^2 = 16$
$2 + 2^2 = 6$

$24^2 = 576 \neq 616$

(b) 16^2

$6^2 = 36$
$1 + 1^2 = 2$

$16^2 = 256 \neq 236$

 Kok Hua pondered why the above method only worked on numbers which had 5 as the unit digit. Finally, using algebra, he was able to understand why the method worked only on numbers which had 5 as the unit digit. Can you see why?
(*Hint:* You can use one of the three special results that you have learned in algebraic expansion.)

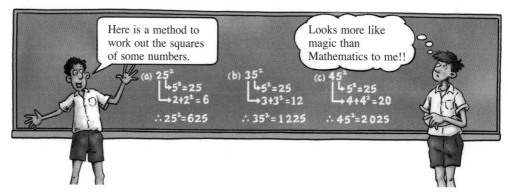

You have 10 minutes to answer the following questions.
Choose the most appropriate answer.

1.1 **1.** $-(a + 2) =$
- **A** $-a + 2$
- **B** $-a - 2$
- **C** $a - 2$
- **D** $a + 2$

1.1 **2.** $2(b - 3) - (b + 4) =$
- **A** $b - 10$
- **B** $b - 2$
- **C** $b - 7$
- **D** $3b - 10$

1.1 **3.** $(h + 4)(h - 3) =$
- **A** $h^2 - h - 12$
- **B** $h^2 - h + 12$
- **C** $h^2 + h + 12$
- **D** $h^2 + h - 12$

1.1 **4.** $(2u + 3)^2 =$
- **A** $2u^2 + 6u + 6$
- **B** $2u^2 + 6u + 9$
- **C** $4u^2 + 9$
- **D** $4u^2 + 12u + 9$

1.1 **5.** $(m + 5)(n - 3) =$
- **A** $mn - 15$
- **B** $mn + 5n - 3m + 15$
- **C** $m + 5n - 3$
- **D** $mn - 3m + 5n - 15$

1.2 **6.** $-6x - 9y =$
- **A** $-3(2x - 3y)$
- **B** $-3(2x + 3y)$
- **C** $-2(3x + 2y)$
- **D** $3(2x - 3y)$

1.2 **7.** $ax + by - ay - bx =$
- **A** $(a - b)(x - y)$
- **B** $(a - b)(x + y)$
- **C** $(a + b)(x - y)$
- **D** $(a + b)(x + y)$

1.2 **8.** $6y^2 - 25y + 25 =$
- **A** $(2y - 5)^2$
- **B** $(2y - 5)(3y - 5)$
- **C** $(3y + 5)^2$
- **D** $(2y + 5)(3y + 5)$

1.2 **9.** $x^2 - 18x + 81 =$
- **A** $(x - 9)^2$
- **B** $(x - 9)(x + 9)$
- **C** $(x + 9)^2$
- **D** $(x - 3)(x - 27)$

1.2 **10.** $w^2 - 9 =$
- **A** $(w - 9)^2$
- **B** $(w - 3)^2$
- **C** $(w - 3)(w + 3)$
- **D** $(w - 1)(w + 9)$

SECTION A

1. Expand the following.
   (a) $3(2 + a)$
   (b) $-6(5y - 4)$
   (c) $3(2a - b)$
   (d) $-5x(x + y)$

2. Factorise the following.
   (a) $20c + 15$
   (b) $6 - 12d$
   (c) $-8x - 12$
   (d) $-6y + 21$

3. Expand the following.
   (a) $4a(a + 3) + 2(a + 5)$
   (b) $7b(2b + 1) - b(b - 3)$
   (c) $2c(3c - d) - c(4c + 3d)$
   (d) $4e(2e - 3f) + 5f(3e - 2f)$

4. Factorise the following.
   (a) $6x - 9y$
   (b) $a^2b + ab^2$
   (c) $3x^2 - 6x$
   (d) $-10ky^2 - 4ky$

SECTION B

5. Expand the following.
   (a) $(m + 2)(3m + 4)$
   (b) $(3n - 5)(2n + 5)$
   (c) $(p - 3)(5p - 7)$

6. Factorise the following.
   (a) $h^2 + 3h + 2$
   (b) $k^2 + 5k - 6$
   (c) $r^2 - r - 6$

7. Expand the following.
   (a) $(6a + 5)^2$
   (b) $(4 - x)(4 + x)$
   (c) $(4x - 3y)^2$

8. Factorise the following.
   (a) $4e^2 - 36f^2$
   (b) $4x^2 - 4xy + y^2$
   (c) $2y^2 + 4xy + 2x^2$

SECTION C

9. (a) Factorise $a^2 - b^2$.
   (b) Hence, evaluate
   (i) $4.99^2 - 1.01^2$, and
   (ii) $\sqrt{26^2 - 24^2}$
   without using a calculator.

10. (a) Factorise the following.
    (i) $5a - ab + 10 - 2b$
    (ii) $5xy + x - 5y - 1$
    (iii) $35ac - 6bd + 10bc - 21ad$
    ★(b) Given that $x^2 + y^2 = 25$ and $xy = 12$, find the value of
    (i) $(x + y)^2$,
    (ii) $(x - y)^2$,
    (iii) $x^2 - y^2$.

Algebraic Fractions, Equations and Inequalities

You may see traffic signs such as the one shown below when you travel on certain roads. Do you know what signs like these represent?

Such signs indicate the speed limit that vehicles travelling on that particular stretch of road must adhere to. For instance, a traffic sign showing a speed limit of 80 km/h would imply that vehicles travelling on that stretch of road can only travel up to a speed of 80 km/h but not more. If we use x to denote the speed of any vehicle on this road, we can write the statement mathematically as $x \leq 80$. Such a mathematical statement is known as an inequality. What are the possible values that x can take?

In this chapter, you will be learning more about simple inequalities together with algebraic fractions and equations. You will see how problems that we encounter in our daily lives can be translated into equations and inequalities and solved algebraically.

In arithmetic, you have seen numerical fractions such as $\frac{1}{2}$, $\frac{3}{4}$ and $\frac{5}{10}$. Similarly, in algebra, we have **algebraic fractions** which are also written in the form $\frac{A}{B}$, where A is the numerator and B ($B \neq 0$) is the denominator.

In algebraic fractions, either **both A and B are algebraic expressions** or **at least one of them is an algebraic expression**. Some examples of algebraic fractions are given below.

E.g.

$\frac{5a \;\leftarrow \text{expression}}{2 \;\leftarrow \text{number}}$
$\qquad$
$\frac{1 \;\leftarrow \text{number}}{b^2 \;\leftarrow \text{expression}}$
$\qquad$
$\frac{a - b \;\leftarrow \text{expression}}{a + b \;\leftarrow \text{expression}}$

> **Algebraic fractions** are fractions that contain an algebraic expression in the numerator or denominator, or both.

2.1.1 Simplification of Algebraic Fractions

We simplify algebraic fractions in the same way we simplify numerical fractions, i.e., by 'cancelling' (dividing) factors common to both the numerator and the denominator.

Numerical fraction	Algebraic fraction
E.g. $\dfrac{8}{12} = \dfrac{{}^1\!\!\!4 \times 2}{{}_1\!\!\!4 \times 3} = \dfrac{2}{3}$	E.g. $\dfrac{15m}{10} = \dfrac{{}^1\!\!\!5 \times 3 \times m}{{}_1\!\!\!5 \times 2} = \dfrac{3m}{2}$

> Algebraic fractions can be **simplified** by 'cancelling' the factors which are common to both the numerator and denominator.

Example 1

Simplify the following.

(a) $\dfrac{8a}{6}$
$\qquad\qquad$
(b) $\dfrac{4b^3}{b}$

(c) $\dfrac{21cd}{7d}$
$\qquad\qquad$
(d) $\dfrac{6e}{9e^2f}$

Solution

b^3 means $b \times b \times b$.
b^2 means $b \times b$.

(a) $\dfrac{8a}{6} = \dfrac{4 \times {}^1\!\cancel{2} \times a}{3 \times \cancel{2}_1}$

$= \dfrac{4a}{3}$

(b) $\dfrac{4b^3}{b} = \dfrac{4 \times {}^1\!\cancel{b} \times b \times b}{\cancel{b}_1}$

$= 4b^2$

(c) $\dfrac{21cd}{7d} = \dfrac{3 \times {}^1\!\cancel{7} \times c \times \cancel{d}{}^1}{{}_1\cancel{7} \times \cancel{d}_1}$

$= 3c$

(d) $\dfrac{6e}{9e^2f} = \dfrac{2 \times {}^1\!\cancel{3} \times \cancel{e}{}^1}{3 \times \cancel{3}_1 \times \cancel{e}_1 \times e \times f}$

$= \dfrac{2}{3ef}$

| **Example 2** |

Simplify the following.

(a) $\dfrac{(a-b)^2}{3(a-b)}$

(b) $\dfrac{(x+2)(x-3)}{(x-3)(x+4)}$

Solution

(a) $\dfrac{(a-b)^2}{3(a-b)}$

$= \dfrac{(a-b)(\cancel{a-b})^1}{3\,(\cancel{a-b})_1}$

$= \dfrac{a-b}{3}$

(b) $\dfrac{(x+2)(x-3)}{(x-3)(x+4)}$

$= \dfrac{(x+2)(\cancel{x-3})^1}{{}_1(\cancel{x-3})(x+4)}$

$= \dfrac{x+2}{x+4}$

Exercise 2A

1. Simplify the following.

(a) $\dfrac{8y}{12}$ **(b)** $\dfrac{27x}{36}$ **(c)** $\dfrac{72p}{64}$

(d) $\dfrac{w^3}{w}$ **(e)** $\dfrac{6e^3}{2e^2}$ **(f)** $\dfrac{8x^3}{6x}$

(g) $\dfrac{z}{z^2}$ **(h)** $\dfrac{18d}{9d^2}$ **(i)** $\dfrac{18f^2}{27f^4}$

2. Simplify the following.

(a) $\dfrac{4b}{8ab}$ **(b)** $\dfrac{12bc}{6c}$ **(c)** $\dfrac{14cd}{21d}$

(d) $\dfrac{9d^2e}{24e}$ **(e)** $\dfrac{6f}{27e^2f}$ **(f)** $\dfrac{gv^2}{2g^2v}$

(g) $\dfrac{3h^3w}{4hw}$ **(h)** $\dfrac{5kx^2}{10k^3x}$ **(i)** $\dfrac{39x^2y}{26xy^2}$

3. Simplify the following.

(a) $\dfrac{a(a+b)}{b(a+b)}$ **(b)** $\dfrac{(a-b)c}{(a+b)c}$

(c) $\dfrac{x^2}{x(x+y)}$ **(d)** $\dfrac{3(x+y)}{5(x+y)^2}$

(e) $\dfrac{pqr}{p(q+r)}$ **(f)** $\dfrac{f(a-t)}{f^3}$

(g) $\dfrac{t(a+f)^2}{a+f}$ **(h)** $\dfrac{(k+1)(k-1)}{(k-1)^2}$

2.1.2 Multiplication and Division of Simple Algebraic Fractions

We multiply algebraic fractions in the same way we multiply numerical fractions, i.e., by crossing out the common factors where possible followed by multiplying the numerators and multiplying the denominators.

Numerical fraction	Algebraic fraction
E.g. $$\frac{\overset{1}{\cancel{7}}}{\underset{3}{\cancel{15}}} \times \frac{\overset{8}{\cancel{40}}}{\underset{7}{\cancel{49}}} = \frac{1 \times 8}{3 \times 7}$$ $$= \frac{8}{21}$$	E.g. $$\frac{\overset{1}{\cancel{4}}xy}{\underset{2}{\cancel{z}}} \times \frac{3\overset{1}{\cancel{z}}}{\underset{2}{\cancel{8}}\cancel{x}_1} = \frac{y \times 3}{1 \times 2}$$ $$= \frac{3y}{2}$$

When **multiplying algebraic fractions**,

1. Cross out the common factors where possible.
2. Multiply the numerators; multiply the denominators.

note

Try using your calculator to verify if the results obtained in the multiplication and division of the numerical fractions shown are correct.

Visit the following websites for activities that will help you revise the multiplication and division of fraction: http://www.math. com/school/subject1/ practice/s1u4L4/ s1u4L4Pract.html and http://www.math. com/school/subject1/ practice/s1u4L5/ s1u4L5Pract.html

Similarly, we divide algebraic fractions in the same way we divide numerical fractions, i.e., by changing '÷' to '×', inverting the divisor and then proceeding with multiplication.

Numerical fraction	Algebraic fraction
E.g. $$\frac{5}{12} \div \frac{35}{39} = \frac{\overset{1}{\cancel{5}}}{\underset{4}{\cancel{12}}} \times \frac{\overset{13}{\cancel{39}}}{\underset{7}{\cancel{35}}}$$ $$= \frac{1 \times 13}{4 \times 7}$$ $$= \frac{13}{28}$$	E.g. $$\frac{5m}{6} \div \frac{2mn}{12} = \frac{5\overset{1}{\cancel{m}}}{\underset{1}{\cancel{6}}} \times \frac{\overset{2}{\cancel{12}}\overset{1}{}}{\underset{1}{\cancel{2}}\cancel{m}n}$$ $$= \frac{5 \times 1}{1 \times n}$$ $$= \frac{5}{n}$$

When **dividing algebraic fractions**,

1. Change the '÷' sign to '×'.
2. Invert the second fraction.
3. Proceed with multiplication.

Example 3

Simplify the following.

(a) $\dfrac{5a}{12} \times \dfrac{4}{a}$

(b) $\dfrac{8pq}{9r} \times \dfrac{3r}{4p}$

(c) $\left(\dfrac{4x}{15z}\right)\left(\dfrac{3z^2}{8}\right)$

(d) $\left(\dfrac{2s}{3t^2}\right)\left(\dfrac{9st}{16}\right)$

Solution

(a) $\dfrac{5a^1}{12_3} \times \dfrac{1\,4}{1\,a} = \dfrac{5}{3}$

$= 1\dfrac{2}{3}$

(b) $\dfrac{2\,8p^1q}{3\,9r_1} \times \dfrac{1\,3r^1}{1\,4p_1} = \dfrac{2q}{3}$

(c) $\left(\dfrac{4x}{15z}\right)\left(\dfrac{3z^2}{8}\right)$

$= \dfrac{4x}{15z} \times \dfrac{3z^2}{8}$

$= \dfrac{1\,4x}{5\,15z_1} \times \dfrac{1\,3 \times z \times z^1}{8_2}$

$= \dfrac{x \times z}{5 \times 2}$

$= \dfrac{xz}{10}$

(d) $\left(\dfrac{2s}{3t^2}\right)\left(\dfrac{9st}{16}\right)$

$= \dfrac{2s}{3t^2} \times \dfrac{9st}{16}$

$= \dfrac{1\,2s}{1\,3 \times t \times t_1} \times \dfrac{3\,9st^1}{16_8}$

$= \dfrac{s \times 3 \times s}{t \times 8}$

$= \dfrac{3s^2}{8t}$

Example 4

Simplify the following.

(a) $\dfrac{6h}{7} \div \dfrac{2k}{14}$

(b) $\dfrac{4ac}{7} \div \dfrac{16c}{5a}$

(c) $\dfrac{\left(\dfrac{3m}{5}\right)}{\left(\dfrac{3}{4n}\right)}$

(d) $\dfrac{\left(\dfrac{8a}{9b}\right)}{\left(\dfrac{16}{ab}\right)}$

Solution

(a) $\dfrac{6h}{7} \div \dfrac{2k}{14} = \dfrac{6h}{1\,7} \times \dfrac{14^{\,2^1}}{1\,2k}$

$= \dfrac{6h}{k}$

(b) $\dfrac{4ac}{7} \div \dfrac{16c}{5a}$

$= \dfrac{1\,4ac^1}{7} \times \dfrac{5a}{4\,16c_1}$

$= \dfrac{a \times 5a}{7 \times 4} = \dfrac{5a^2}{28}$

(c) $\dfrac{\left(\dfrac{3m}{5}\right)}{\left(\dfrac{3}{4n}\right)} = \dfrac{3m}{5} \div \dfrac{3}{4n}$

$= \dfrac{{}^1\cancel{3}m}{5} \times \dfrac{4n}{\cancel{3}_1}$

$= \dfrac{4mn}{5}$

(d) $\dfrac{\left(\dfrac{8a}{9b}\right)}{\left(\dfrac{16}{ab}\right)} = \dfrac{8a}{9b} \div \dfrac{16}{ab}$

$= \dfrac{{}^1\cancel{8}a}{9\cancel{b}_1} \times \dfrac{a\cancel{b}^1}{\cancel{16}_2}$

$= \dfrac{a \times a}{9 \times 2} = \dfrac{a^2}{18}$

Example 5

Simplify the following.

(a) $\dfrac{(x-1)^2}{2x} \times \dfrac{x^2}{x-1}$

(b) $\dfrac{(2x-3)(2x+3)}{x} \div \dfrac{2x-3}{x^2}$

Solution

(a) $\dfrac{(x-1)^2}{2x} \times \dfrac{x^2}{x-1} = \dfrac{{}^1\cancel{(x-1)}(x-1)}{2x_1} \times \dfrac{x \times x^1}{\cancel{(x-1)}_1}$

$= \dfrac{x(x-1)}{2}$

(b) $\dfrac{(2x-3)(2x+3)}{x} \div \dfrac{2x-3}{x^2} = \dfrac{(2x-3)(2x+3)}{x} \times \dfrac{x^2}{2x-3}$

$= \dfrac{{}^1\cancel{(2x-3)}(2x+3)}{x_1} \times \dfrac{x \times x^1}{\cancel{(2x-3)}_1}$

$= x(2x+3)$

Exercise 2B

1. Simplify the following.

(a) $\dfrac{3h}{11} \times \dfrac{22}{h}$

(b) $\dfrac{3}{8s} \times \dfrac{5t}{6}$

(c) $\dfrac{7rs}{14t} \times \dfrac{3t}{r}$

(d) $\dfrac{3gh}{2k} \times \dfrac{5}{6hk}$

(e) $\dfrac{8}{7xy} \times \dfrac{21}{4x}$

(f) $\left(\dfrac{3ef}{10}\right)\left(\dfrac{15f}{9e}\right)$

(g) $\left(\dfrac{5m^2n}{22}\right)\left(\dfrac{11}{13mn^2}\right)$

(h) $\left(\dfrac{9w^2}{14uv}\right)\left(\dfrac{7u^2}{24w^2v}\right)$

2. Simplify the following.

(a) $\dfrac{4b}{5} \div \dfrac{c}{5}$

(b) $\dfrac{5mn}{6} \div \dfrac{2n}{12m}$

(c) $\dfrac{9a}{mn} \div \dfrac{3a}{4m}$

(d) $\dfrac{6t}{7y} \div \dfrac{9t}{8yz}$

(e) $\dfrac{\left(\dfrac{5de}{6}\right)}{\left(\dfrac{7d}{4}\right)}$

(f) $\dfrac{\left(\dfrac{3u}{4v^2}\right)}{\left(\dfrac{5}{2uv}\right)}$

(g) $\dfrac{\left(\dfrac{2ab}{c}\right)}{\left(\dfrac{6b}{4c}\right)}$

(h) $\dfrac{\left(\dfrac{8y}{9z}\right)}{\left(\dfrac{4y^2}{5xz}\right)}$

3. Simplify the following.

(a) $\dfrac{a-3b}{2a} \times \dfrac{4}{3(a-3b)}$

(b) $\dfrac{(h+3)(h-2)}{h+3} \times \dfrac{h}{2(h-2)}$

(c) $\dfrac{(3k-2)^2}{3k} \times \dfrac{9}{2(3k-2)}$

(d) $\dfrac{a(a-3b)}{2b} \div \dfrac{a-3b}{4a}$

(e) $\dfrac{(m-9)(m+5)}{m-5} \div \dfrac{m-9}{m}$

(f) $\dfrac{(r+2)^2}{4(r+2)} \div \dfrac{r+2}{3}$

★**(g)** $\dfrac{x^2+xy}{xy-y^2} \times \dfrac{x-y}{x+y}$

★**(h)** $\dfrac{w^2+3w+2}{w+3} \div \dfrac{w+2}{w^2+3w}$

 2.2 **Solving Simple Equations**

Consider the following mathematical statements:

$$7 + 5 = 12 \dots\dots\dots\dots\dots\dots\dots\dots (1)$$
$$5 - 3 = 2 \dots\dots\dots\dots\dots\dots\dots\dots (2)$$

In *(1)*, the two numbers, 7 and 5 on the left-hand side (LHS) of the equal sign add up to give the number 12 on the right-hand side (RHS). Similarly, in *(2)*, the difference between the two numbers, 5 and 3 on the LHS of the equal sign, gives us the number 2 on the RHS. We say that the mathematical statements *(1)* are *(2)* are **true** as the value on the LHS of the equal sign is equal to that on the RHS. We call such mathematical statements **equations**.

As unknowns can be used to take the place of numbers, equations can contain unknowns as well as numbers.

> **note**
> We use letters to represent unknowns.

E.g. $a + 5 = 12$
           $b - 3 = 2$

> An **equation** is a mathematical statement that has two quantities joined by an equal sign. The quantity on the LHS of the equal sign has the same value as the quantity on the RHS.

Think of an equation as a balance where the LHS is always balanced by its RHS.

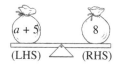

(LHS)　　(RHS)

You may wish to visit the following website where you can create your own equations and solve them using a virtual beam balance: http://nlvm.usu.edu/en/nav/frames_asid_201_g_4_t_2.html?open=instructions

Consider the equation $a + 5 = 8$. Let us try to 'guess' the value of a and determine its correct value by substituting each possible value into the LHS of the equation to see which one makes the equation true.

Taking $a = 1$, we have:

$$\text{LHS} = a + 5 = 1 + 5$$
$$= 6 \neq 8 \text{ (from RHS)}$$

$\therefore$　$a = 1$ is not the correct value that will make the equation true.

Let us now try another value, $a = 2$. We have:

$$\text{LHS} = a + 5 = 2 + 5$$
$$= 7 \neq 8 \text{ (from RHS)}$$

Again, $a = 2$ is not the correct value.

Trying another value, $a = 3$, we have:

$$\text{LHS} = a + 5 = 3 + 5$$
$$= 8 \text{ (from RHS)}$$

$\therefore$　$a = 3$ is the correct value that will make the equation true. We say that $a = 3$ **satisfies** the equation $a + 5 = 8$.

The value that satisfies an equation is called the **solution** or **root** of the equation. Finding the value of the unknown in an equation is called **solving the equation**.

2.2.1　Solving Equations Involving Addition or Subtraction

We can find the solution to the equation $a + 5 = 8$ in a more systematic way rather than through guessing. In trying to solve the equation, we are actually trying to find the value of a. As such, we will need to manipulate the equation so that 'a' appears on its own on the LHS.

$$a + 5 = 8$$
$$a = ?$$

To do so, we have to take away '+5' from the LHS of the equation.

The equation $a + 5 = 8$ can be represented on a balanced scale.

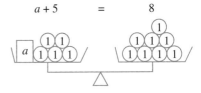

When we take away '+5' on the LHS, the scale becomes unbalanced.

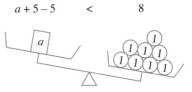

In order to balance it, we will need to take away 5 from the RHS as well.

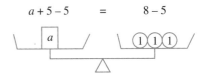

The steps can be summarised as follows:

To eliminate the '+5', we subtract 5 from both sides.

$$a + 5 = 8$$
$$a + 5 - 5 = 8 - 5 \quad \longleftarrow \quad \text{Subtract 5 from both sides.}$$
$$\therefore \quad a = 3$$

Similarly, to solve $b - 2 = 7$, we do the following:

To eliminate the '–2', we add 2 to both sides.

$$b - 2 = 7$$
$$b - 2 + 2 = 7 + 2 \quad \longleftarrow \quad \text{Add 2 to both sides.}$$
$$\therefore \quad b = 9$$

From the above examples, we can see that subtraction (–) is the inverse operation of addition (+) and vice versa.

Example 6

Solve the following equations.
(a) $a + 9 = 11$
(b) $b - 7 = -10$

Check your answer by substitution.
(a) LHS = $a + 9$
  = $2 + 9$
  = 11 = RHS
  ∴ $a = 2$ is the solution.

(b) LHS = $b - 7$
  = $-3 - 7$
  = -10 = RHS
  ∴ $b = -3$ is the solution.

Solution

(a) $\qquad a + 9 = 11$
$\qquad a + 9 - 9 = 11 - 9 \quad \longleftarrow \quad \text{Subtract 9 from both sides.}$
$\qquad \therefore \quad a = 2$

(b) $\qquad b - 7 = -10$
$\qquad b - 7 + 7 = -10 + 7 \quad \longleftarrow \quad \text{Add 7 to both sides.}$
$\qquad \therefore \quad b = -3$

2.2.2 Solving Equations Involving Multiplication or Division

Recall that the term $3a$ means $3 \times a$ or $a \times 3$. To solve an equation such as $3a = 12$, we need to manipulate it such that 'a' appears on its own on the LHS as shown below.

To eliminate the coefficient '3', we divide both sides by 3.

$$3a = 12$$

$$\frac{{}^{1}\cancel{3}a}{{}_{1}\cancel{3}} = \frac{\cancel{12}^{4}}{\cancel{3}_{1}} \quad \longleftarrow \text{ Divide both sides by 3.}$$

$$\therefore \quad a = 4$$

Similarly, to solve $\dfrac{a}{5} = 6$, we need to manipulate the equation such that 'a' appears on its own on the LHS as shown below.

$\dfrac{a}{5}$ means $a \div 5$.

To eliminate the denominator '5', we multiply both sides by 5.

$$\frac{a}{5} = 6$$

$$\frac{a}{{}_{1}\cancel{5}} \times \cancel{5}^{1} = 6 \times 5 \quad \longleftarrow \text{ Multiply both sides by 5.}$$

$$\therefore \quad a = 30$$

From the above examples, we can see that division ($\div$) is the inverse operation of multiplication ($\times$) and vice versa.

Example 7

Solve the following equations.

(a) $4c = 6$ **(b)** $\dfrac{d}{4} = -2\dfrac{1}{2}$

Solution

Check your answer by substitution.

(a) LHS $= 4c$

$= 4 \times \dfrac{3}{2}$

$= 6 = $ RHS

$\therefore \quad c = 1\dfrac{1}{2}$ is the solution.

(b) LHS $= \dfrac{d}{4}$

$= \dfrac{-10}{4}$

$= -\dfrac{5}{2}$

$= -2\dfrac{1}{2} = $ RHS

$\therefore \quad d = -10$ is the solution.

(a)

$$4c = 6$$

$$\frac{4c}{4} = \frac{6}{4} \quad \longleftarrow \text{ Divide both sides by 4.}$$

$$\therefore \quad c = \frac{3}{2} = 1\frac{1}{2}$$

(b)

$$\frac{d}{4} = -2\frac{1}{2}$$

$$\frac{d}{4} \times 4 = -2\frac{1}{2} \times 4 \quad \longleftarrow \text{ Multiply both sides by 4.}$$

$$\frac{d}{{}_{1}\cancel{4}} \times \frac{\cancel{4}^{1}}{1} = -\frac{5}{{}_{1}\cancel{2}} \times \frac{\cancel{4}^{2}}{1}$$

$$\therefore \quad d = -10$$

1. Solve the following equations.
   (a) $b + 3 = 9$ (b) $d + 8 = 5$
   (c) $f + 2 = -4$ (d) $h + 0.9 = 3.9$
   (e) $y + \dfrac{1}{8} = \dfrac{5}{8}$ (f) $w + \dfrac{1}{5} = -\dfrac{4}{5}$
   (g) $8 + n = 12$ (h) $8 + v = 2$

2. Solve the following equations.
   (a) $a - 2 = 3$ (b) $c - 4 = -1$
   (c) $e - 1 = -2$ (d) $g - 0.6 = 0.3$
   (e) $x - 0.7 = -0.3$ (f) $k - 0.3 = -0.7$
   (g) $m - \dfrac{1}{4} = \dfrac{1}{4}$ (h) $u - \dfrac{3}{7} = -\dfrac{2}{7}$

3. Solve the following equations.
   (a) $2a = 6$ (b) $2c = -10$
   (c) $-3b = 12$ (d) $-4g = -24$

   (e) $6x = 2$ (f) $10c = -2$
   (g) $-12m = 3$ (h) $-24u = -4$

4. Solve the following equations.
   (a) $\dfrac{b}{5} = 7$ (b) $\dfrac{d}{3} = -6$
   (c) $\dfrac{y}{5} = \dfrac{1}{8}$ (d) $\dfrac{w}{2} = 2\dfrac{1}{2}$
   (e) $-\dfrac{f}{7} = 4$ (f) $-\dfrac{h}{9} = -8$

5. Solve the following equations.
   (a) $d + 5 = 6$ (b) $f - 7 = 8$
   (c) $3b = 4$ (d) $\dfrac{h}{9} = 10$
   (e) $w + 13 = -14$ (f) $y - 11 = -12$
   (g) $16n = -4$ (h) $-\dfrac{v}{18} = \dfrac{1}{3}$

2.2.3 Solving Equations Involving More Than One Operation

Sometimes it is necessary for us to use more than one inverse operation in order to obtain the unknown by itself on the LHS of the equation.

Consider the expression $2 \times 4 + 5$. To evaluate this operation, we carry out multiplication first followed by addition.

$$\underbrace{2 \times 4} + 5$$
$$= \quad 8 \quad + 5$$
$$= \quad 13$$

Similarly, in the algebraic expression **2y + 5**, the unknown y is first multiplied by 2 followed by adding 5 to it.

Now, consider the equation **2y + 5 = 7**. In order to find the value of y, the expression $2y + 5$ must be 'broken down' in the reverse order to that which it was 'built up'.

'Building up': $y \xrightarrow{\times 2} 2y \xrightarrow{+5} 2y + 5$

'Breaking down': $y \xleftarrow{\div 2} 2y \xleftarrow{-5} 2y + 5$

Now, we shall proceed to solve the equation.

$$2y + 5 = 7$$
$$2y + 5 - 5 = 7 - 5 \longleftarrow \text{Subtract 5 from both sides.}$$

$$\therefore \quad 2y = 2$$
$$\frac{{}^1\cancel{2}y}{{}_1\cancel{2}} = \frac{\cancel{2}^1}{\cancel{2}_1} \longleftarrow \text{Divide both sides by 2.}$$
$$\therefore \quad y = 1$$

Example 8

Solve the following equations.

(a) $4x + 2 = 18$

(b) $4 - 3y = 19$

(c) $3m + \dfrac{1}{5} = \dfrac{7}{5}$

(d) $2p - 0.6 = 4.2$

Solution

Check your answer by substitution.

(a) LHS $= 4x + 2$
$= 4 \times 4 + 2$
$= 16 + 2$
$= 18$
$= $ RHS

(b) LHS $= 4 - 3y$
$= 4 - 3 \times (-5)$
$= 4 + 15$
$= 19$
$= $ RHS

Now, try checking the answers for parts (c) and (d) on your own.

(a)
$$4x + 2 = 18$$
$$4x + 2 - 2 = 18 - 2$$
$$4x = 16$$
$$\frac{4x}{4} = \frac{16}{4}$$
$$\therefore \quad x = 4$$

(b)
$$4 - 3y = 19$$
$$4 - 4 - 3y = 19 - 4$$
$$-3y = 15$$
$$\frac{-3y}{-3} = \frac{15}{-3}$$
$$\therefore \quad y = -5$$

(c)
$$3m + \frac{1}{5} = \frac{7}{5}$$
$$3m + \frac{1}{5} - \frac{1}{5} = \frac{7}{5} - \frac{1}{5}$$
$$3m = \frac{6}{5}$$
$$3m \div 3 = \frac{6}{5} \div 3$$
$$\frac{3m}{3} = \frac{{}^2\cancel{6}}{5} \times \frac{1}{\cancel{3}_1}$$
$$\therefore \quad m = \frac{2}{5}$$

(d)
$$2p - 0.6 = 4.2$$
$$2p - 0.6 + 0.6 = 4.2 + 0.6$$
$$2p = 4.8$$
$$\frac{2p}{2} = \frac{4.8}{2}$$
$$\therefore \quad p = 2.4$$

Example 9

Solve the following equations.

(a) $4(2x + 5) = 4$

(b) $2(3m - 4) = 5$

(c) $2(3 - a) = 7$

(d) $5(1 - 2v) = -25$

Solution

Check your answer by substitution.

(a) LHS $= 4(2x + 5)$
$= 4[2(-2) + 5]$
$= 4[-4 + 5]$
$= 4 \times 1$
$= 4 =$ RHS

Now, try checking the answers for parts (b), (c) and (d) on your own.

(a) $\quad 4(2x + 5) = 4$

$8x + 20 = 4$

$8x + 20 - 20 = 4 - 20$

$8x = -16$

$\dfrac{8x}{8} = \dfrac{-16}{8}$

$\therefore \quad x = -2$

(b) $\quad 2(3m - 4) = 5$

$6m - 8 = 5$

$6m - 8 + 8 = 5 + 8$

$6m = 13$

$\dfrac{6m}{6} = \dfrac{13}{6}$

$\therefore \quad m = 2\dfrac{1}{6}$

(c) $\quad 2(3 - a) = 7$

$6 - 2a = 7$

$6 - 6 - 2a = 7 - 6$

$-2a = 1$

$\dfrac{-2a}{-2} = \dfrac{1}{-2}$

$\therefore \quad a = -\dfrac{1}{2}$

(d) $\quad 5(1 - 2v) = -25$

$5 - 10v = -25$

$5 - 5 - 10v = -25 - 5$

$-10v = -30$

$\dfrac{-10v}{-10} = \dfrac{-30}{-10}$

$\therefore \quad v = 3$

Exercise 2D

1. Solve the following equations.
   (a) $7b + 4 = 25$
   (b) $3d + 9 = 6$
   (c) $7f - 5 = 9$
   (d) $5h + 6 = -4$
   (e) $6y - 2 = -5$
   (f) $7 + 3n = 9$
   (g) $8 - 2r = 11$
   (h) $-9 - 3v = -15$

2. Solve the following equations.
   (a) $2b + \dfrac{1}{8} = \dfrac{3}{8}$
   (b) $2d + \dfrac{3}{5} = \dfrac{1}{5}$
   (c) $8h - \dfrac{2}{3} = 1$
   (d) $3k - \dfrac{2}{5} = -1$
   (e) $3y + 0.5 = 1.7$
   (f) $8w + 2.8 = 0.4$
   (g) $2v - 2.6 = 2.4$
   (h) $4x - 3.6 = -0.4$

3. Solve the following equations.
   (a) $2(a + 4) = 16$
   (b) $3(c + 5) = 4$
   (c) $5(3y + 2) = -5$
   (d) $7(e - 3) = 14$
   (e) $8(2k - 1) = -12$
   (f) $4(3 + 2z) = 36$
   (g) $2(4 - m) = 5$
   (h) $6(2 - 3u) = 4$

Example 10

Solve the following equations.

(a) $2a = a + 5$

(b) $5b = 3b - 8$

(c) $3a + 5 = 2a + 4$

(d) $5b + 9 = 7b - 3$

Solution

The equations in this example have unknown like terms on both sides. We begin by subtracting the unknown term on the RHS from both sides of the equation. This will help to eliminate the unknown term that appears on the RHS.

Check your answer by substitution.

(a) LHS $= 2a$
$= 2 \times 5$
$= 10$
RHS $= a + 5$
$= 5 + 5$
$= 10$
Since LHS = RHS, $a = 5$ is the solution. Now, try checking the answer for parts **(b)**, **(c)** and **(d)** on your own.

(a)
$$2a = a + 5$$
$$2a - a = a - a + 5$$
$$\therefore \quad a = 5$$

(b)
$$5b = 3b - 8$$
$$5b - 3b = 3b - 3b - 8$$
$$2b = -8$$
$$\frac{2b}{2} = \frac{-8}{2}$$
$$\therefore \quad b = -4$$

(c)
$$3a + 5 = 2a + 4$$
$$3a - 2a + 5 = 2a - 2a + 4$$
$$a + 5 = 4$$
$$a + 5 - 5 = 4 - 5$$
$$\therefore \quad a = -1$$

(d)
$$5b + 9 = 7b - 3$$
$$5b - 7b + 9 = 7b - 7b - 3$$
$$-2b + 9 = -3$$
$$-2b + 9 - 9 = -3 - 9$$
$$-2b = -12$$
$$\frac{-2b}{-2} = \frac{-12}{-2}$$
$$\therefore \quad b = 6$$

Example 11

Solve the following equations.

(a) $3(a - 2) = 4(2a + 1)$

(b) $5(x + 4) - 2(x - 3) = 2$

Solution

'Remove' the brackets first by expansion.

(a)
$$3(a - 2) = 4(2a + 1)$$
$$3a - 6 = 8a + 4$$
$$3a - 8a - 6 = 8a - 8a + 4$$
$$-5a - 6 = 4$$
$$-5a - 6 + 6 = 4 + 6$$
$$-5a = 10$$
$$\frac{-5a}{-5} = \frac{10}{-5}$$
$$\therefore \quad a = -2$$

(b)
$$5(x + 4) - 2(x - 3) = 2$$
$$5x + 20 - 2x + 6 = 2$$
$$5x - 2x + 20 + 6 = 2$$
$$3x + 26 = 2$$
$$3x + 26 - 26 = 2 - 26$$
$$3x = -24$$
$$\frac{3x}{3} = \frac{-24}{3}$$
$$\therefore \quad x = -8$$

1. Solve the following equations.
   (a) $3a = a + 4$ (b) $5c = 4 + 3c$
   (c) $8d = -4d + 12$ (d) $6e = 4e - 8$
   (e) $2g = 3 - g$ (f) $4h = 5 - h$
   (g) $3x = 7 - 4x$ (h) $y = -4 - y$

2. Solve the following equations.
   (a) $7a + 5 = 3a + 9$ (b) $3c + 4 = 5c - 8$
   (c) $5 + 2g = 10 - 3g$ (d) $7k - 3 = 3k + 5$
   (e) $2u - 3 = 6 - u$ (f) $2q - 3 = 7 - 3q$
   (g) $9w - 3 = 16w + 11$
   (h) $2y - 4 = 5y - 1$

3. Solve the following equations.
   (a) $2(2a + 1) = 3(a + 4)$
   (b) $5(2 + 2c) = 6(3c - 2)$

   (c) $7(2 + d) = 3(4 - 2d)$
   (d) $5(3f - 4) = 2(6f + 5)$
   (e) $6(2g - 3) = 3(g - 2)$
   (f) $3(3h - 5) = 4(2 - h)$

4. Solve the following equations.
   (a) $6(x + 3) - 4(x + 5) = 0$
   (b) $7(2 + x) - 3(4 - 2x) = -11$
   (c) $6(x - 4) - 4(x - 3) = 4(2x - 7)$
   (d) $10x - (3x + 1) = 5(2x - 1) - (x - 8)$

5. Solve the following equations.
   (a) $3x + 7 = x + 16$ [N/96/P1]
   (b) $3p - 2 = p + 18$ [N/98/P1]
   (c) $3(x - 4) - 2(1 - x) = 0$ [N/86/P2]
   (d) $6(y - 4) + 2(y + 1) = 4$ [N/87/P2]

---

note

Recall that the number attached to an unknown is called its **coefficient**.
$\frac{1}{3}$ is the coefficient of x in the term $\frac{1}{3}x$.

$\frac{1}{3}x = \frac{1}{3} \times x$
$= \frac{x}{3}$

Notice that the equations that you have learned to solve so far are those with **integer coefficients** in their terms. We shall now proceed to solve equations that have terms with **fractional coefficients**.

Consider the equation $\frac{1}{3}x + 1 = 4$. Notice that $\frac{1}{3}x + 1$ is the same as $\frac{x}{3} + 1$. Therefore, we have:

'Building up': $x \xrightarrow{\div 3} \frac{x}{3} \xrightarrow{+1} \frac{x}{3} + 1$

'Breaking down': $x \xleftarrow{\times 3} \frac{x}{3} \xleftarrow{-1} \frac{x}{3} + 1$

$$\frac{1}{3}x + 1 = 4$$

$$\frac{x}{3} + 1 = 4$$

$$\frac{x}{3} + 1 - 1 = 4 - 1 \quad \longleftarrow \text{Subtract 1 from both sides.}$$

$$\frac{x}{3} = 3$$

$$\frac{x}{3} \times 3 = 3 \times 3 \quad \longleftarrow \text{Multiply both sides by 3.}$$

$$\therefore \quad x = 9$$

Example 12

Solve the following equations.

(a) $\dfrac{1}{4}x - 1 = 3$

(b) $\dfrac{x}{5} + 2 = 6$

Solution

(a)
$$\dfrac{1}{4}x - 1 = 3$$
$$\dfrac{x}{4} - 1 = 3$$
$$\dfrac{x}{4} - 1 + 1 = 3 + 1$$
$$\dfrac{x}{4} = 4$$
$$\dfrac{x}{4} \times 4 = 4 \times 4$$
$$\therefore \quad x = 16$$

(b)
$$\dfrac{x}{5} + 2 = 6$$
$$\dfrac{x}{5} + 2 - 2 = 6 - 2$$
$$\dfrac{x}{5} = 4$$
$$\dfrac{x}{5} \times 5 = 4 \times 5$$
$$\therefore \quad x = 20$$

Example 13

Solve the following equations.

(a) $\dfrac{2x}{3} = 4$

(b) $\dfrac{2x}{3} = \dfrac{1}{4}$

note

To solve an equation, we must manipulate the equation until the unknown appears alone on the LHS.

Solution

(a)
$$\dfrac{2x}{3} = 4$$
$$\dfrac{2x}{3} \times 3 = 4 \times 3$$
$$2x = 12$$
$$\dfrac{2x}{2} = \dfrac{12}{2}$$
$$\therefore \quad x = 6$$

(b)
$$\dfrac{2x}{3} = \dfrac{1}{4}$$
$$\dfrac{2x}{3} \times 3 = \dfrac{1}{4} \times 3$$
$$2x = \dfrac{3}{4}$$
$$\dfrac{2x}{2} = \dfrac{3}{4} \div 2$$
$$x = \dfrac{3}{4} \times \dfrac{1}{2}$$
$$\therefore \quad x = \dfrac{3}{8}$$

Example 14

Solve the following equations.

(a) $\dfrac{2x}{3} + 1 = 3$

(b) $\dfrac{3x}{4} - 1 = 5$

(c) $\dfrac{1}{3}x + \dfrac{1}{3} = 2$

(d) $2 - \dfrac{3x}{2} = 4$

Solution

(a)
$$\frac{2x}{3} + 1 = 3$$
$$\frac{2x}{3} + 1 - 1 = 3 - 1$$
$$\frac{2x}{3} = 2$$
$$\frac{2x}{3} \times 3 = 2 \times 3$$
$$2x = 6$$
$$\frac{2x}{2} = \frac{6}{2}$$
$$\therefore \quad x = 3$$

(b)
$$\frac{3x}{4} - 1 = 5$$
$$\frac{3x}{4} - 1 + 1 = 5 + 1$$
$$\frac{3x}{4} = 6$$
$$\frac{3x}{4} \times 4 = 6 \times 4$$
$$3x = 24$$
$$\frac{3x}{3} = \frac{24}{3}$$
$$\therefore \quad x = 8$$

(c) Recognise that $\frac{x}{3}$ and $\frac{1}{3}$ have the same denominator.

(c)
$$\frac{1}{3}x + \frac{1}{3} = 2$$
$$\frac{x}{3} + \frac{1}{3} = 2$$
$$\frac{x+1}{3} = 2$$
$$\frac{x+1}{3} \times 3 = 2 \times 3$$
$$x + 1 = 6$$
$$x + 1 - 1 = 6 - 1$$
$$\therefore \quad x = 5$$

(d)
$$2 - \frac{3x}{2} = 4$$
$$2 - 2 - \frac{3x}{2} = 4 - 2$$
$$-\frac{3x}{2} = 2$$
$$-\frac{3x}{2} \times 2 = 2 \times 2$$
$$-3x = 4$$
$$\frac{-3x}{-3} = \frac{4}{-3}$$
$$\therefore \quad x = -\frac{4}{3} = -1\frac{1}{3}$$

Exercise 2F

1. Solve the following equations.

(a) $\frac{a}{5} + 2 = 7$

(b) $\frac{b}{4} + 2 = -5$

(c) $\frac{c}{9} + 4 = -2$

(d) $\frac{d}{7} - 1 = 3$

(e) $5 - \frac{e}{7} = 2$

(f) $\frac{f}{2} - 4 = -3$

2. Solve the following equations.

(a) $\frac{4b}{5} = 8$

(b) $\frac{5d}{6} = -1$

(c) $\frac{q}{2} = \frac{3}{4}$

(d) $\frac{3g}{2} = -\frac{1}{4}$

(e) $\frac{4p}{3} = \frac{5}{6}$

(f) $\frac{2r}{3} = -\frac{3}{8}$

3. Solve the following equations.

(a) $1 + \frac{2a}{3} = 5$

(b) $\frac{2b}{5} + 2 = 6$

(c) $\frac{3c}{2} - 1 = 5$

(d) $\frac{3d}{7} - 1 = -4$

(e) $4 - \frac{5l}{2} = 8$

(f) $7 - \frac{7m}{9} = 7$

4. Solve the following equations.

(a) $\frac{1}{2}e + \frac{5}{2} = 4$

(b) $\frac{1}{6}h - \frac{2}{3} = -2$

(c) $\frac{5}{4} - \frac{k}{4} = 1$

(d) $\frac{2}{5}n + \frac{3}{5} = 3$

(e) $\frac{5p}{6} - \frac{3}{4} = 1$

(f) $\frac{3}{4} - \frac{r}{2} = 2$

Fun with Algebra

You may wish to work in pairs for the following activity.

Step	Operation
1	Think of a number
2	Add 2 to it
3	Multiply by 3
4	Subtract 5
5	Divide by 3
6	Subtract the number you started with from the number you obtained after step 5

(a) What is the answer?

(b) Start with a different number and check the final answer.

 (c) Making use of your knowledge of algebra, prove that the result is true for all numbers.

2.3   Solving Equations Involving Algebraic Fractions

note

In Book 1, you have learned how to add and subtract algebraic expressions with fractional coefficients. Do you realise that an **algebraic fraction that has a numerical denominator** can also be expressed as an **algebraic expression with a fractional coefficient**?

E.g. $\frac{x+1}{3}$ is the same as $\frac{1}{3}(x+1)$.

In Section 2.1, you have learned that algebraic fractions are fractions that contain an algebraic expression in the numerator or denominator, or both.

Before we can proceed to solve equations involving algebraic fractions, let us recall how to add or subtract two algebraic fractions that each have a numerical denominator.

Algebraic fractions must have the same denominator before they can be added or subtracted. For algebraic fractions with different denominators, we can rewrite them with the same denominator using the **L.C.M. (Lowest Common Multiple)** of the denominators.

E.g.

$$\frac{x+1}{3} + \frac{x}{2} = \frac{(x+1) \times 2}{3 \times 2} + \frac{x \times 3}{2 \times 3}$$ ⟵ Find the L.C.M. of the denominators.

$$= \frac{2(x+1)}{6} + \frac{3x}{6}$$ ⟵ Rewrite the algebraic fractions with same denominator using the L.C.M. found.

$$= \frac{2(x+1)+3x}{6}$$

$$= \frac{2x+2+3x}{6}$$ ⟵ Then, add or subtract the numerators as required.

$$= \frac{5x+2}{6}$$

Now, consider the equation:

$$\frac{x+1}{3} + \frac{x}{2} = 3$$

$$\frac{2(x+1)+3x}{6} = 3 \qquad \longleftarrow \text{From previous working}$$

$$\frac{5x+2}{6} = 3$$

$$\frac{(5x+2)}{6} \times 6 = 3 \times 6 \qquad \longleftarrow \text{Multiply both sides by 6.}$$

$$5x + 2 = 18$$

$$5x + 2 - 2 = 18 - 2 \qquad \longleftarrow \text{Subtract 2 from both sides.}$$

$$5x = 16$$

$$\therefore \quad x = \frac{16}{5} = 3\frac{1}{5}$$

Let us now consider another form of equations where the algebraic fractions lie on opposite sides of the equal sign.

E.g. $\quad \dfrac{x+1}{3} = \dfrac{x}{2}$

How do we solve such an equation?

We have: $\qquad \dfrac{x+1}{3} = \dfrac{x}{2}$

$$\frac{(x+1)}{3} \times 3 = \frac{x}{2} \times 3 \qquad \longleftarrow \text{Multiply both sides by 3.}$$

$$x + 1 = \frac{3x}{2}$$

$$(x+1) \times 2 = \frac{3x}{2} \times 2 \qquad \longleftarrow \text{Multiply both sides by 2.}$$

$$2(x+1) = 3x$$

$$2x + 2 = 3x$$

$$2 = 3x - 2x$$

$$2 = x$$

$$\therefore \quad x = 2$$

$\left.\vphantom{\begin{array}{c}a\\b\\c\\d\end{array}}\right\} (*)$

We need to eliminate 2 in the denominator of $\frac{3x}{2}$ on the RHS.

A more effective method, however, known as **cross-multiplication** where the steps marked (*) can be replaced by a shorter calculation (**), can be applied to solve such equations.

$$\frac{x+1}{3} \diagdown\hspace{-1em}\diagup \frac{x}{2} \left.\vphantom{\begin{array}{c}a\\b\end{array}}\right\} (**)$$

$$2(x + 1) = 3x$$
$$2x + 2 = 3x$$
$$2 = 3x - 2x$$
$$2 = x$$
$$\therefore \quad x = 2$$

note

(1) Do not confuse the cross-multiplication method with the cross method learned in Chapter 1.

(2) Cross-multiplication can only be carried out if there is a **single fraction on both sides of the equal sign.**

Example 15

Solve the equation $\dfrac{a-2}{3} - \dfrac{a-3}{4} = 1$.

Solution

L.C.M. of 3 and 4 is 12.

We can combine the terms on the LHS into a single fraction first before we multiply throughout by 12.

$$\frac{a-2}{3} - \frac{a-3}{4} = 1$$

$$\frac{4(a-2) - 3(a-3)}{12} \times 12 = 1 \times 12$$

$$4a - 8 - 3a + 9 = 12$$

$$a + 1 = 12$$

$$\therefore \quad a = 12 - 1$$

$$= 11$$

Example 16

Solve the equation $\dfrac{w-1}{2} + 3 = 4w$.

Solution

Multiply throughout by 2.

$$\frac{w-1}{2} + 3 = 4w$$

$$\frac{w-1+6}{2} = 4w$$

$$\frac{w-1+6}{2} \times 2 = 4w \times 2$$

$$w - 1 + 6 = 8w$$

$$-1 + 6 = 8w - w$$

$$5 = 7w$$

$$\frac{5}{7} = w$$

$$\therefore \quad w = \frac{5}{7}$$

Alternative method:

$$\frac{w-1}{2} + 3 = 4w$$ Combine the terms on the

$$\frac{w-1+6}{2} = 4w \longleftarrow$$ LHS into a single fraction.

$$\frac{w+5}{2} \diagtimes \frac{4w}{1} \longleftarrow$$ Cross-multiply

$$w + 5 = 8w$$

$$5 = 8w - w$$

$$5 = 7w$$

$$\frac{5}{7} = w$$

$$\therefore \quad w = \frac{5}{7}$$

Example 17

Solve the following equations.

(a) $\dfrac{5}{x} = \dfrac{2}{x-3}$

(b) $\dfrac{2}{3x+4} = \dfrac{1}{2x+3}$

Solution

note

Recognise that the denominator of each of the algebraic fractions is an algebraic expression.
We also apply cross-multiplication to solve such equations.

(a) $\dfrac{5}{x} \diagtimes \dfrac{2}{x-3}$

$$5(x-3) = 2x$$

$$5x - 15 = 2x$$

$$5x - 2x = 15$$

$$3x = 15$$

$$\therefore \quad x = 5$$

(b) $\dfrac{2}{3x+4} \diagtimes \dfrac{1}{2x+3}$

$$2(2x+3) = 1(3x+4)$$

$$4x + 6 = 3x + 4$$

$$4x - 3x = 4 - 6$$

$$\therefore \quad x = -2$$

1. Solve the following equations.

   (a) $\dfrac{a}{3} = \dfrac{4}{5}$ (b) $\dfrac{1}{2} = \dfrac{2v}{9}$

   (c) $\dfrac{2}{3} = \dfrac{3}{c}$ (d) $\dfrac{1}{2u} = \dfrac{3}{4}$

   (e) $\dfrac{3}{e} - 3 = 2$ (f) $3 - \dfrac{x}{2} = 7$

   (g) $\dfrac{5w}{3} - \dfrac{w}{3} = 4$ (h) $\dfrac{3z}{4} - \dfrac{z}{6} = 7$

2. Solve the following equations.

   (a) $\dfrac{2h+1}{5} = \dfrac{h}{3}$

   (b) $\dfrac{y-3}{4} = \dfrac{2y+4}{3}$

   (c) $\dfrac{7}{k} = \dfrac{5}{k-2}$

   (d) $\dfrac{6}{z+3} = \dfrac{5}{z-4}$

   (e) $\dfrac{m-2}{3} + 4 = 5m$

   (f) $5n + 4 = \dfrac{2n+1}{3}$

   (g) $\dfrac{r-1}{3} - 1 = 2r$

   (h) $5s - 8 = \dfrac{13s+2}{3}$

3. Solve the following equations.

   (a) $\dfrac{x-3}{4} - \dfrac{x-4}{5} = \dfrac{1}{2}$

   (b) $\dfrac{2x-3}{6} + \dfrac{3x-4}{8} = -1$

   (c) $\dfrac{x+1}{2} - \dfrac{3x-5}{8} = 1\dfrac{1}{2}$

   (d) $\dfrac{x-3}{2} - \dfrac{x+3}{4} = 5$

   (e) $\dfrac{y-5}{8} + \dfrac{9y+1}{4} = 4$

   (f) $\dfrac{4y+2}{3} - \dfrac{3y+3}{7} = 7$

   (g) $\dfrac{6y+1}{9} + 8y - 7 = 0$

   ★(h) $\dfrac{x}{3} - \dfrac{3(x-2)}{4} = \dfrac{1}{4} - \dfrac{x}{6}$

4. Solve the equation $\dfrac{1}{3}(x-2) + 2(x-1) = 9$.
   [N/97/P2]

5. Solve the following equations.

   (a) $\dfrac{3}{x} = 4$ [O/Jun 97/P1]

   (b) $\dfrac{x-1}{3} + \dfrac{x+5}{2} = 8$ [O/Jun 99/P1]

(2.4) **Application of Equations**

2.4.1 Problems Involving Simple Equations

Equations are very useful in helping us to solve practical problems. Each problem can first be translated into a mathematical equation. The equation is then solved algebraically. The result is translated back into the context of the problem, as shown in the following examples on the next page.

Example 18

What do I add to 5 to get 11?

Solution

Let the number to be added be a.

What do I add to 5 to give 11?

$$a \qquad + \quad 5 \quad = \quad 11$$

$\therefore$ the equation is: $a + 5 = 11$

Solving the equation: $a + 5 - 5 = 11 - 5$
$$a = 6$$

$\therefore$ the number to be added is 6.

Example 19

Five less than b is 9. What is the value of b?

Solution

Five less than b is 9

The equation is: $b - 5 \qquad = 9$

Solving the equation: $b - 5 + 5 = 9 + 5$
$$b = 14$$

$\therefore$ the value of b is 14.

We can check our answer by translating the result back into the context of the question. 5 less than 14 is 9. Therefore, the answer is correct.

Example 20

If I double a certain number and subtract 7, the result is 9. What is the number?

Solution

Let the number be m.

I double the number and subtract 7. The result is 9.

$$2 \quad \times \quad m \qquad\qquad - \quad 7 \qquad = \quad 9$$

$\therefore$ the equation is: $2m - 7 = 9$

Solving the equation: $2m - 7 + 7 = 9 + 7$
$$2m = 16$$
$$\frac{2m}{2} = \frac{16}{2}$$
$$m = 8$$

$\therefore$ the number is 8.

Example 21

A woman is four times as old as her daughter. If the difference in their ages is 21 years, find their ages.

note

Always let the unknown represent just the number (no units).

Daughter's age: $\boxed{x}$

Mother's age: $\boxed{x}\,\boxed{x}\,\boxed{x}\,\boxed{x}$

$\underbrace{}_{21}$

Solution

Let the age of the daughter be x years.
Then the mother is $4x$ years old.

Difference in age $= 21$ years
$$\therefore \quad 4x - x = 21$$
$$3x = 21$$
$$\frac{3x}{3} = \frac{21}{3}$$
$$\therefore \quad x = 7$$
and $\quad 4x = 4 \times 7$
$$= 28$$

$\therefore$ the daughter is 7 years old and the mother is 28 years old.

Example 22

The sum of two consecutive odd numbers is 40. What are the numbers?

note

Odd numbers:

$$\overset{+2}{\frown}\ \overset{+2}{\frown}\ \overset{+2}{\frown}\ \overset{+2}{\frown}$$
... 5   7   9   11   13 ...

$$\overset{+2}{\frown}$$
$\Rightarrow\ n\quad n + 2$

If however, we let the larger number be n instead, then the smaller number will be $n - 2$.

$$\overset{-2}{\frown}\ \overset{-2}{\frown}\ \overset{-2}{\frown}\ \overset{-2}{\frown}$$
... 5   7   9   11   13 ...

$$\overset{-2}{\frown}$$
$\Rightarrow\ n - 2\quad n$

Solution

Let the smaller odd number be n.
Then the larger odd number is $n + 2$.

$$\therefore \quad n + (n + 2) = 40$$
$$2n + 2 = 40$$
$$2n + 2 - 2 = 40 - 2$$
$$2n = 38$$
$$\frac{2n}{2} = \frac{38}{2}$$
$$\therefore \quad n = 19$$
and $\quad n + 2 = 19 + 2$
$$= 21$$

$\therefore$ the numbers are 19 and 21.

Example 23

The cost of 4 ballpoint pens and 6 pencils is $5.30. If the cost of a ballpoint pen is 20 cents more than the cost of a pencil, find the cost of one ballpoint pen.

Solution

Let the cost of each pencil be c cents.
The cost of each ballpoint pen is then $(c + 20)$ cents.

$$\text{Cost of 4 ballpoint pens} = 4 \times (c + 20) \text{ cents} = 4(c + 20) \text{ cents}$$
$$\text{Cost of 6 pencils} = 6c \text{ cents}$$
$$\text{Total cost} = \$5.30 = 530 \text{ cents}$$
$$\therefore \quad 4(c + 20) + 6c = 530$$
$$4c + 80 + 6c = 530$$
$$10c + 80 = 530$$
$$10c + 80 - 80 = 530 - 80$$
$$10c = 450$$
$$\frac{10c}{10} = \frac{450}{10}$$
$$\therefore \quad c = 45 \quad \text{and} \quad c + 20 = 45 + 20 = 65$$

$\therefore$ the cost of one ballpoint pen is 65 cents.

> **note**
>
> Make sure that the LHS and RHS are both expressed in the same units first before proceeding to solve the equation.

Exercise 2H

1. Letting the unknown number be n, write each of the following as an equation and then find the value of the number.
   (a) What do I add to 4 to get 7?
   (b) From what number do I subtract 23 to get 12?
   (c) Three times what number is 15?
   (d) What number must be multiplied by 8 to get 32?
   (e) What number must be divided by 3 to get −12?
   (f) A quarter of what number is 3?

2. For each of the following, write an equation and then solve it.
   (a) Three more than a is five.
   (b) Eleven more than c is six.
   (c) Two less than e is eight.
   (d) Seven less than f is one.

3. I think of a number n and add 5 to it. If the result is 12,
   (a) form an equation in n,
   (b) what is the number n?

4. I think of a number and subtract 5 from it. If the result is −2, what is the number?

5. I think of a number and double it. If the result is −12, what is the number?

6. If I subtract 6 from five times of a certain number, the result is 19. What is the number?

7. If I subtract 8 from twice a certain number, the result is 10. What is the number?

8. A boy is x years old. His father is five times as old as he is. If the difference in their ages is 32 years,
  (a) form an equation in x,
  (b) solve the equation to find the boy's age.

9. A goat is six times as heavy as its kid. If their total mass is 70 kg, find each of their masses in kg.

10. A mother is presently four times as old as her daughter. If the sum of their ages 6 years ago was 48, find their present ages.

11. A boy is 12 years old. His mother is four times as old as he is. In x years' time, the mother will be three times as old as the son. Form an equation in x and hence find x.

12. The sum of two consecutive even numbers is 42. Let n be the smaller number.
  (a) Express the bigger number in terms of n.
  (b) Form an equation in n.
  (c) Hence, find the two numbers.

13. The sum of three consecutive odd numbers is 99. What are the numbers?

14. The cost of 3 kg of mangosteens and 4 kg of durians is $29. The cost of 1 kg of mangosteens is $2 less than the cost of 1 kg of durian.
Let the cost of 1 kg of mangosteens be m.
  (a) State the cost of 1 kg of durian in terms of m.
  (b) Form an equation in m.
  (c) Hence, find the cost of 1 kg of durian.

15. The cost of 7 buns and 8 slices of cake is $10.60. If the cost of a slice of cake is 20 cents more than the cost of a bun, find the cost of a slice of cake.

16. For the given rectangle, find
  (a) the value of x,
  (b) the perimeter of the rectangle.

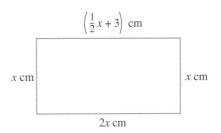

$\left(\frac{1}{2}x + 3\right)$ cm

x cm x cm

$2x$ cm

2.4.2 Problems Involving Simple Algebraic Fractions

Example 24

A car took 2 hours to travel a distance of x km. A truck took 3 hours to travel the same distance. If the speed of the car is 15 km/h more than the speed of the truck, calculate x.

Solution

$$\text{Speed} = \frac{\text{Distance}}{\text{Time}}$$

$\therefore$ Speed of car $= \dfrac{x}{2}$ km/h; Speed of truck $= \dfrac{x}{3}$ km/h

Speed of car $-$ Speed of truck $= 15$ km/h

$$\therefore \quad \frac{x}{2} - \frac{x}{3} = 15$$

$$\frac{3x - 2x}{6} = 15$$

$$\frac{x}{6} = 15$$

$$\therefore \quad x = 90$$

note

$$\frac{x}{2} > \frac{x}{3}$$

It is important to know the order of the terms when performing subtraction.

Example 25

If the numerator and denominator of $\dfrac{13}{17}$ are respectively decreased and increased by the same number, the result is $\dfrac{1}{2}$. Find the number.

Solution

Let the required number be x.

The new fraction is $\dfrac{13 - x}{17 + x}$ Numerator decreased by x / Denominator increased by x

Thus,
$$\frac{13 - x}{17 + x} = \frac{1}{2}$$
$$2(13 - x) = 1(17 + x)$$
$$26 - 2x = 17 + x$$
$$26 - 17 = x + 2x$$
$$9 = 3x$$
$$\frac{9}{3} = x$$
$$\therefore \quad x = 3$$

The required number is 3.

1. A van travels at a constant speed of x km/h over a distance of 45 km. If the van increases its speed by 4 km/h, it will be able to travel a distance of 48 km in the same amount of time. Calculate x.

2. A biker travels at a constant speed of x km/h over a distance of 6 km. If the biker reduces his speed by 2 km/h, he will only cover a distance of 5 km in the same amount of time. Calculate x.

3. A speeding boat travelled a distance of x km at a constant speed of 80 km/h. An ocean liner travelled the same distance at 60 km/h. If the difference in time taken was 2 hours, calculate x.

4. The LRT travels a distance of x km at a constant speed of 60 km/h. The MRT travels the same distance of x km at 80 km/h. If the difference in time taken is 1 minute, calculate x.

5. If the numerator and denominator of $\frac{5}{19}$ are increased and decreased respectively by x, the result is $\frac{3}{5}$.
   (a) Express the new fraction in terms of x.
   (b) Find x.

6. If a number x is subtracted from both the numerator and denominator of $\frac{13}{23}$, the resulting fraction is $\frac{1}{3}$. Calculate x.

7. The denominator of a fraction is 6 more than the numerator. Let the numerator be x.
   (a) Express the fraction in terms of x.
   (b) If both the numerator and denominator are increased by 4, the resulting fraction is $\frac{5}{7}$. Find x.

8. An aircraft flew a distance of x km from Amsterdam to Cairo at an average speed of 820 km/h and returned non-stop by the same route at an average speed of 656 km/h. Given that the aircraft took 1 hour more for the return trip, calculate x.

9. A coach took $3\frac{1}{2}$ hours to travel a distance of 240 km from Kuala Lumpur to Cameron Highlands. It travelled part of the journey at an average speed of 60 km/h and the rest of the journey at 75 km/h. Calculate the distance it travelled at 60 km/h.

★10. The distance from Amy's house to the nearest bus-stop is 240 m. On a particular day, Amy walks towards the bus-stop at an average speed of 30 metres per minute from the instant she leaves her house. After walking for a distance of x m, Amy sees her bus approaching. She then runs towards the bus-stop at an average speed of 150 metres per minute.
   (a) Find, in terms of x, an expression for
       (i) the distance that Amy runs in metres,
       (ii) the number of minutes that Amy walks,
       (iii) the number of minutes that Amy runs.
   (b) Given that the time taken by Amy to reach the bus-stop is 6 minutes, find the value of x.

11. To reach his office on time, Mr Chin usually drives to work at an average speed of 75 km/h. However, if Mr Chin increases his average driving speed by 5 km/h, he will reach his office 10 minutes earlier. If the distance Mr Chin needs to travel to reach his office is represented by x km, form an equation in x and solve for x.

12. The following diagram shows a rectangular tank and two taps A and B.

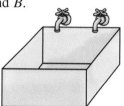

Tap A alone can fill the tank in 4 hours while tap B alone can fill the tank in 6 hours. Taps A and B together can fill the tank in t minutes. Form an equation in t and solve it to find the time, t, in minutes, taps A and B together would take to fill the tank.

The Diophantus Riddle

Diophantus (100 AD – 400 AD) was one of the greatest mathematicians of his time. He is often known as the 'father of algebra' although al-Khwarizmi is given the same title by some other mathematicians.

Diophantus is said to have lived some time between 100 and 400 AD. Although the exact dates of his birth and death are not known, the exact number of years he lived is known. This has been recorded in the form of an algebraic riddle by one of his admirers. This riddle, which is given below, divides Diophantus' life into 6 segments.

Diophantus' youth lasted $\frac{1}{6}$ of his life; he grew a beard after $\frac{1}{12}$ more; after $\frac{1}{7}$ more of his life, he married; five years later, he had a son; his son lived exactly $\frac{1}{2}$ as long as him; he died 4 years after his son.

Can you solve this riddle and find out the exact number of years that Diophantus lived? (*Hint:* Let the number of years Diophantus lived be x; form an equation in x and then solve it to find Diophantus' lifespan.)

2.5   Inequalities and Their Applications

2.5.1   Inequalities

In Book 1, we have seen how integers can be represented on a number line based on their order.

We have also learned how to write mathematical statements symbolically. For example, the statement '3 is greater than 2' can be written symbolically as '3 > 2'. We call such a mathematical statement an **inequality**. Another example of an inequality is '1 < 2'.

Just like equations, which involve the use of unknowns, inequalities too can contain an unknown.

Consider this: We have an unknown number that is greater than 3. A few out of the many possible values that the number can take are 3.001, $4\frac{1}{2}$ and even 1 000 000. As long as the number is greater than 3, it is a possible answer. Thus, if we were to list down all the possible values of the unknown number, our list will go on indefinitely.

note

A **variable** is a letter that can be used to represent an unknown quantity. A variable can take on any value that satisfies the inequality. Any other letter can be used in place of x.

However, we can use an inequality to represent the set of all possible values for the above. We write:

$$x > 3$$

where x is a variable that can assume any real value that is greater than 3. We call the set of all possible values that satisfy an inequality its **solution set**.

The inequality '$x > 3$' can be illustrated on the number line as follows:

note

An open dot (as indicated by the circle or empty dot) indicates that the value below the dot is **not included** in the solution set for the inequality.

Similarly, if we have an unknown number that can be greater than or equal to 3, we can represent the statement using an inequality. In this case, we write:

$$x \geq 3$$

The inequality '$x \geq 3$' can be illustrated on the number line as follows:

note

A closed dot (as indicated by the shaded circle) indicates that the value below the dot is **included** in the solution set for the inequality.

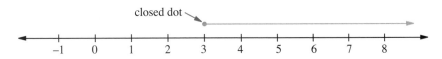

Consider the inequality $5 > 2$. We know that it is a true statement. What do you think will happen if we multiply or divide both sides of the inequality by the same positive number? Will we still have a true statement?

We have: $5 > 2$

Multiplying both sides by 2, we have: $5 \times 2 > 2 \times 2$

This gives us: $10 > 4$

$10 > 4$ is indeed a true statement.

Now, consider the following inequality: $\qquad 12 > 6$

Dividing both sides by 3, we have: $\qquad \dfrac{12}{3} > \dfrac{6}{3}$

This gives us: $\qquad 4 > 2$

$4 > 2$ is indeed a true statement.

> Multiplying or dividing both sides of an inequality by a positive number will still give us a true mathematical statement.

We can make use of the above property to solve inequalities such as the one shown below.

$$3m < 12$$
$$\dfrac{3m}{3} < \dfrac{12}{3} \qquad \longleftarrow \text{Divide both sides by 3.}$$
$$\therefore \quad m < 4$$

note

Recall:
For any unknown x and any number a,
- $x > a$ means that 'x is greater than a',
- $x < a$ means that 'x is less than a',
- $x \geq a$ means that 'x is greater than or equal to a',
- $x \leq a$ means that 'x is less than or equal to a'.

The solution set to the inequality $3m < 12$ is the set of all real values that are less than 4. This means that m can take all possible real values that are less than 4.

Example 26

Solve the following inequalities.

(a) $6w < 18$

(b) $5x \geq -10$

(c) $\dfrac{y}{2} > -3$

(d) $\dfrac{3z}{2} \leq 6$

Solution

(a) Divide both sides by 6.
(b) Divide both sides by 5.
(c) Multiply both sides by 2.
(d) Multiply both sides by $\dfrac{2}{3}$.

(a) $\qquad 6w < 18$
$$\dfrac{6w}{6} < \dfrac{18}{6}$$
$$\therefore \quad w < 3$$

(b) $\qquad 5x \geq -10$
$$\dfrac{5x}{5} \geq \dfrac{-10}{5}$$
$$\therefore \quad x \geq -2$$

(c) $\qquad \dfrac{y}{2} > -3$
$$\dfrac{y}{{}_1\cancel{2}} \times \cancel{2}^{1} > -3 \times 2$$
$$\therefore \quad y > -6$$

(d) $\qquad \dfrac{3z}{2} \leq 6$
$$\dfrac{{}^1\cancel{3}z}{{}_1\cancel{2}} \times \dfrac{\cancel{2}^{1}}{\cancel{3}_1} \leq \cancel{6}^{2} \times \dfrac{2}{\cancel{3}_1}$$
$$\therefore \quad z \leq 4$$

Example 27

Solve $3x \le 16$.

Hence, write down

(a) the greatest value of x if x is a positive integer,

(b) the greatest value of x if x is a perfect square,

(c) the least value of x if x is a prime number.

Solution

$$3x \le 16$$

$$\frac{3x}{3} \le \frac{16}{3}$$

$$\therefore \quad x \le 5\frac{1}{3}$$

(a) If x is a positive integer, greatest value of $x = 5$.

(b) If x is a perfect square, greatest value of $x = 4$.

(c) If x is a prime number, least value of $x = 2$.

2.5.2 Application of Inequalities

In Section 2.4, we have seen how equations can be used to represent word problems. However, not all word problems can be represented using equations. Consider the problem in Example 28 given below: Arul has $100. He wants to buy x number of durians at $8 each. What is the maximum number of durians that he can buy? This is a typical problem that can be solved using an **inequality**.

Example 28

Arul has $100. He can buy x number of durians at $8 each.

(a) Form an inequality in x.

(b) Solve the inequality.

(c) Hence, find the maximum number of durians that Arul can buy.

Solution

(a) Cost of 1 durian = $8

$\therefore$ Cost of 8 durians = $8 \times x$

$\qquad\qquad\qquad\quad = \$8x$

Maximum amount of money Arul can spend = $100

$\therefore$ the inequality for this problem is given by:

$$8x \le 100$$

(b) $\qquad 8x \leq 100$

$$\frac{8x}{8} \leq \frac{100}{8}$$

$$x \leq \frac{25}{2}$$

$$\therefore \quad x \leq 12\frac{1}{2}$$

(c) The greatest whole number that satisfies the inequality $x \leq 12\frac{1}{2}$ is 12.

$\therefore$ the maximum number of durians Arul can buy is 12.

Exercise 2J

1. For each of the following, replace each box with the correct inequality sign.

   (a) $5 \;\square\; 3$ **(b)** $-5 \;\square\; 3$

   (c) $5 \;\square\; -3$ **(d)** $-5 \;\square\; -3$

   (e) $2 \;\square\; 8$ **(f)** $-2 \;\square\; 8$

   (g) $2 \;\square\; -8$ **(h)** $-2 \;\square\; -8$

2. Copy and complete each of the following.

   (a) $\qquad 3a > 15$

   $$\frac{3a}{\square} > \frac{15}{\square}$$

   $$a > \square$$

   (b) $\qquad \dfrac{b}{3} < -2$

   $$\frac{b}{3} \times \square < -2 \times \square$$

   $$b < \square$$

   (c) $\qquad \dfrac{2c}{3} \geq -4$

   $$\frac{2c}{3} \times \square \geq -4 \times \square$$

   $$c \geq \square$$

3. Solve the following inequalities.

   (a) $2a \leq 6$ **(b)** $3b > -12$

   (c) $\dfrac{c}{5} < -1$ **(d)** $\dfrac{d}{8} \geq 2$

   (e) $\dfrac{3m}{2} > 9$ **(f)** $\dfrac{2n}{5} < -8$

4. Solve $5x > 45$.
   Hence, write down
   (a) the least value of x if x is an integer,
   (b) the least value of x if x is a perfect square,
   (c) the least value of x if x is a prime number.

5. Solve $6x < 50$.
   Hence, write down the
   (a) the greatest value of x if x is an integer,
   (b) the greatest value of x if x is a perfect square,
   (c) the greatest value of x if x if a prime number.

6. **(a)** Find the largest integer n such that $5n < 23$.
   (b) Find the smallest prime number p such that $6p > 58$.
   (c) Find the largest rational number r such that $4r \leq 49$.

7. Julia's average mark for four Mathematics tests is represented by x marks. To score a distinction, her total marks for the four tests must be at least 300.
   (a) Form an inequality in x.
   (b) Solve the inequality.
   (c) Hence, state the minimum average mark that Julia must score for the four tests if she is to obtain a distinction.

8. Given that the perimeter of a certain square of side x cm cannot be more than 60 cm,
   (a) form an inequality in x.
   (b) Solve the inequality.
   (c) Hence, find the largest possible area of the square.

9. Ben has 69 planks that are of standard size. He would need 5 such planks to make a bookshelf. Find the maximum number of bookshelves Ben can make.

10. Excel Secondary School wants to send its students for an educational trip and has found an organisation that is willing to sponsor up to an amount of $2 500 for the trip. Given that the cost of sending a student for the trip is $12, what is the maximum number of students the school can send for the trip if it relies only on the sponsorship?

SUMMARY

1. Algebraic fractions are fractions that contain an algebraic expression in the numerator or denominator, or both.

2. Algebraic fractions can be simplified by 'cancelling' the factors which are common to both the numerator and denominator.
   E.g. $\dfrac{8a}{6} = \dfrac{4 \times \overset{1}{\cancel{2}} \times a}{3 \times \underset{1}{\cancel{2}}} = \dfrac{4a}{3}$

3. We multiply and divide algebraic fractions in the same way as we multiply and divide arithmetic fractions.

4. An equation is a mathematical statement that has two quantities joined by an equal sign. The quantity on the LHS of the equal sign in the equation has the same value as the quantity on the RHS.
   E.g. $7 + 5 = 12$, $a + 5 = 12$

5. The value that satisfies an equation is called the solution or root of the equation. Finding the value of the unknown in an equation is called solving the equation.

6. Rules for solving equations:

    *   To eliminate a positive number from one side, **subtract** the number from both sides.

        E.g. $a + 5 = 8$
        $\Rightarrow a + 5 - 5 = 8 - 5$
        $\therefore \quad a = 3$

    *   To eliminate a negative number from one side, **add** the number to both sides.

        E.g. $b - 2 = 7$
        $\Rightarrow b - 2 + 2 = 7 + 2$
        $\therefore \quad b = 9$

    *   To eliminate a coefficient from one side, **divide** both sides by the coefficient.

        E.g. $3a = 12$
        $\Rightarrow \dfrac{3a}{3} = \dfrac{12}{3}$
        $\therefore \quad a = 4$

    *   To eliminate a denominator from one side, **multiply** both sides by the denominator.

        E.g. $\dfrac{a}{5} = 6$
        $\Rightarrow \dfrac{a}{5} \times 5 = 6 \times 5$
        $\therefore \quad a = 30$

7. To transform equations involving algebraic fractions into simple equations, we can use cross-multiplication.

    E.g. $\dfrac{x+1}{3} \diagdown\!\!\!\!\!\diagup \dfrac{x}{2}$
    $2(x + 1) = 3x$
    $2x + 2 = 3x$

8. An inequality is a mathematical statement built from expressions using the symbols '<', '>', '≤' and '≥'.

    E.g. $1 < 2$, $3 > 2$, $5x \geq -10$, $\dfrac{3z}{2} \leq 6$.

9. Multiplying or dividing both sides of an inequality by the same positive number will still give us a true mathematical statement.

    E.g. $5 > 2$ $\qquad\qquad\qquad$ $10 > 4$
    $\Rightarrow 5 \times 2 > 2 \times 2$ $\qquad$ $\Rightarrow \dfrac{10}{2} > \dfrac{4}{2}$
    $\therefore \quad 10 > 4$ $\qquad\qquad$ $\therefore \quad 5 > 2$

Enrichment
●●● m a t h s ●●●

Identifying Patterns

1. Study the following equilateral triangles formed by using matches.

Fig. 1   Fig. 2   Fig. 3

    (a) Draw the next two figures.

    (b) Copy and complete the table below.

Figure no.	1	2	3	4	5
No. of matches used	3	7			

    (c) Without making any further drawings, find the number of matches used in

        (i) Figure 10,   **(ii)** Figure 20.

    (d) If m matches are used in Figure n, find an equation connecting m and n.

    (e) Explain why there cannot be any figure that is made up of 100 matches.

2. Each figure in the sequence shown below is made up by arranging a certain number of beads.

Fig. 1   Fig. 2   Fig. 3

    (a) Draw the fourth figure of the sequence.

    (b) Copy and complete the table below.

Figure no.	1	2	3	4
No. of beads used	5	9		

    (c) Without making any further drawings, find the number of beads used in

        (i) Figure 10,   **(ii)** Figure 20.

    (d) If Figure n is made up of m beads, find an equation connecting m and n.

    (e) Which figure is made up of 189 beads?

You have 10 minutes to answer the following questions.
Choose the most appropriate answer.

2.1   **1.**   Simplify $\dfrac{a^2b}{c} \div \dfrac{ab^2}{c}$.

    A ab **B** $\dfrac{a}{b}$ **C** abc **D** $\dfrac{ab}{c^2}$

2.2   **2.**   I $3 + 4 = 7$ II $3 + a = 8$ III $3a$
    Which of the following is correct?
    A   Only I is an equation.   **B**   Only II is an equation.
    C   Both I and II are equations.   **D**   Both II and III are equations.

2.2   **3.**   If $-2f = 6$, then $f =$ _____.

    A   8   **B** $-\dfrac{1}{3}$ **C**   4   **D** -3

2.2   **4.**   Given $3x - 4 = -5$, find the value of x.

    A $\dfrac{1}{3}$ **B** $-\dfrac{1}{3}$ **C**   3   **D** -3

2.2   **5.**   Given $4(y - 3) = 2(y - 1)$, find the value of y.
    A   5   **B**   1   **C** -2 **D** -7

2.3   **6.**   Solve the equation $\dfrac{3h}{10} + \dfrac{3h}{5} = 4\dfrac{1}{2}$.

    A $h = 1$ **B** $h = 4$ **C** $h = 5$ **D** $h = 9$

2.3   **7.**   Solve the equation $\dfrac{2}{9z} = \dfrac{1}{9}$.

    A $z = \dfrac{1}{9}$ **B** $z = \dfrac{1}{2}$ **C** $z = 1$ **D** $z = 2$

2.4   **8.**   A father is three times as heavy as his son. Given that the difference
    between their masses is 50 kg, find the son's mass.
    A   20 kg   **B**   25 kg   **C**   50 kg   **D**   75 kg

2.5   **9.**   Solve $\dfrac{1}{2}x > 2$.

    A $x > 1$ **B** $x > -1$ **C** $x > 4$ **D** $x > -4$

2.5   **10.**   Alison wants to buy some bars of chocolate to distribute at her birth-
    day party. Given that she has $55 and each bar of chocolate costs $2,
    what is the maximum number of bars of chocolate that she can buy?
    A   20   **B**   25   **C**   27   **D**   28

SECTION A

1. Simplify the following.

   (a) $\dfrac{2c}{ba} \times \dfrac{3a}{4c}$

   (b) $\dfrac{3n}{4} \div \dfrac{6m}{7}$

2. Solve the following equations.
   (a) $2(a - 3) = 15$

   (b) $5(b - 4) = \dfrac{10}{3}$

3. Solve the following equations.
   (a) $2x - 3(4x - 5) = 6$
   (b) $7(y - 2) + 3(4y - 5) = 6$

4. Solve the following equations.

   (a) $\dfrac{4u}{9} + \dfrac{2u}{9} = 2$

   (b) $2 - \dfrac{w}{8} = \dfrac{1}{4}$

SECTION B

5. Solve the following equations.

   (a) $\dfrac{3}{2k} = 6$

   (b) $\dfrac{s}{3} - \dfrac{s}{5} = 2$

   (c) $\dfrac{4}{m} = \dfrac{2}{m - 2}$

6. Solve the following equations.

   (a) $\dfrac{1}{n + 2} = \dfrac{3}{5n + 8}$

   (b) $\dfrac{u - 1}{4} - 2 = \dfrac{u}{3}$

   (c) $\dfrac{x}{2} - (x - 2) = \dfrac{5}{2}$

7. Solve the following inequalities.
   (a) $5u > -20$

   (b) $\dfrac{v}{2} < -7$

   (c) $\dfrac{2w}{3} \geq 3\dfrac{1}{3}$

8. (a) A woman's age is four times her son's age. If her son is y years old and the sum of their ages is 50, form an equation in y and find their ages.

   (b) A man's mass is four times his daughter's mass of m kg. If the father is 51 kg heavier than the daughter, form an equation in terms of m. Hence, find the daughter's mass.

SECTION C

9. (a) As part of a fundraising programme, a charity concert was organised. For every ticket that is sold, $15 will be donated to charity. Find the minimum number of tickets that have to be sold to raise an amount of at least $50 000.

   (b) The sum of two consecutive odd numbers is 96. If the smaller number is x, form an equation in x and hence find the two numbers.

10. (a) Adding 6 to a number, n, and then multiplying it by 3 gives the same result as subtracting 2 from the number and then multiplying it by 7. Form an equation in terms of n and hence find the number.

    (b) The distance from Mr Tan's home to his office is x km. To reach his office on time, Mr Tan normally drives to work at an average speed of 75 km/h. On one rainy day however, he drove to his office at an average speed of 60 km/h. Given that he reached his office 5 minutes late, form an equation in x and solve for x.

Cartesian Coordinates and Linear Graphs

How did you manage to find your seat the last time you went to a cinema?

You would have probably done so by first locating the row you would be seated in, followed by counting the position of your seat down the row. The system for the ordering of seats in a cinema is an example of a coordinate system. It makes use of a set of letters and numbers for identifying the rows and columns of seats in the cinema.

In Mathematics, the system used for locating the position of any point on a plane is based on pairs of numbers known as ordered pairs. This system was invented by the French mathematician and philosopher, René Descartes (1596–1650). It is thus named the Cartesian coordinate system in his honour.

Besides the ordering of seats in a cinema, can you think of other examples in our daily lives where we make use of coordinate systems?

In Book 1, you have learned that a horizontal number line can be used to represent the set of all real numbers.

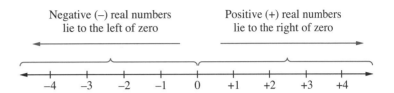

A vertical number line can also be constructed. Just as 'right' ($\rightarrow$) and 'left' ($\leftarrow$) are opposites of each other, so are 'up' ($\uparrow$) and 'down' ($\downarrow$). Hence, on a vertical number line, positive (+) numbers lie above zero while negative (–) numbers lie below zero.

Placing the vertical number line perpendicular to the horizontal number line such that the zeroes intersect gives rise to the diagram shown below on the left. The horizontal number line is called the **x-axis** while the vertical number line is called the **y-axis**. The point where the two axes meet is called the **origin** (denoted by the letter '**O**').

<table>
<tr>
<td>

note

Both the x-axis and y-axis extend indefinitely on either side of the origin. However, by convention, we mark arrows only for the positive directions, i.e., 'right' and 'up'.

</td>
<td>

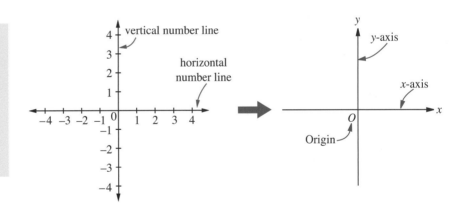

</td>
</tr>
</table>

note

A **plane** is an endless two-dimensional flat surface. The Cartesian plane can also be known as the **x–y plane** or the **rectangular coordinate plane**.

The plane on which the axes are drawn is known as the **Cartesian plane**. The system used for describing the position of any point on the Cartesian plane is known as the **Cartesian coordinate system**. In this system, the origin acts as the reference point for describing the position of all other points on the plane.

To state the position of any point on a plane, we need to state its horizontal and vertical distance (1, 2, 3, ...) and direction (+, –) from the origin, i.e., how far to the right or left of the origin and how far up or down from the origin the point lies.

Look at the point, P, in the diagram below. It can be seen that point P is 2 units to the right (+2) of the origin and 3 units up (+3) from the origin.

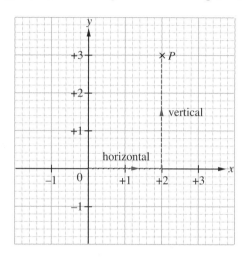

For the point P,
- '+2', the real number that represents its horizontal position from the origin is known as its **x-coordinate**.
- '+3', the real number that represents its vertical position from the origin is known as its **y-coordinate**.

To specify the position of a point on the Cartesian plane, we write its x and y coordinates in the form of an **ordered pair (x, y)**, with the x-coordinate followed by the y-coordinate.

note

An **ordered pair** (a, b) is one in which its terms a and b follow a specified order.

$$\therefore \quad (a, b) \neq (b, a)$$

E.g. $(2, 3) \neq (3, 2)$

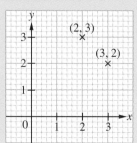

Thus, the **coordinates** of the above point P are (+2, +3) or more simply **(2, 3)**. On the Cartesian plane, we mark the point P as P(2, 3).

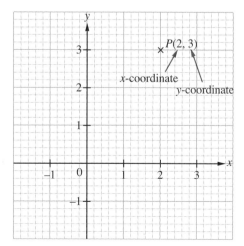

In general,

note

The coordinates of the origin, *O*, are (0, 0) since it is the point where the two axes meet (i.e., where the two zeroes coincide).

1. On a Cartesian plane, the **x-axis** is a **horizontal number line** while the **y-axis** is a **vertical number line**.
2. The *x*-axis and *y*-axis meet at a point called the **origin** (denoted by the letter '*O*').
3. The position of any point on the Cartesian plane can be expressed in terms of an **ordered pair of real numbers** (***x, y***) where *x* represents the *x*-coordinate and *y* represents the *y*-coordinate.

Now, let us learn how to **plot** a point on a Cartesian plane.

Consider the point $Q(-2, 3)$.

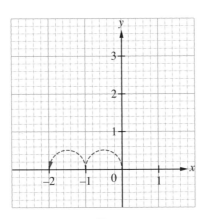

Since the *x*-coordinate is '–2', we first move 2 units to the left of the origin.

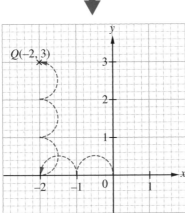

Since the *y*-coordinate is 3, we next move 3 units up to get the point *Q*.

Visit the following website for an interactive game that tests your knowledge of the Cartesian coordinate system: http://www.shodor.org/ interactivate/activities/ SimpleMazeGame

Example 1

State the coordinates of the points marked on the Cartesian plane below.

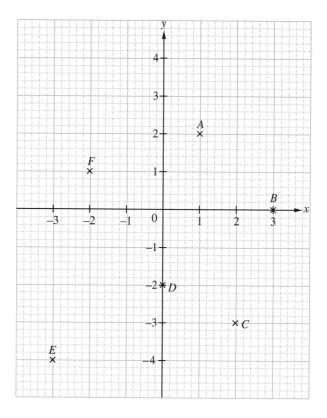

Solution

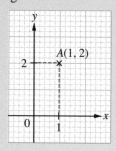
The point marked A is:

1 unit to the right of the origin, i.e., its x-coordinate is 1.

2 units above the origin, i.e., its y-coordinate is 2.

$\therefore$ the coordinates of A are $(1, 2)$.

The point marked B is:

3 units to the right of the origin, i.e., its x-coordinate is 3.

0 units above the origin (as it is on the x-axis), i.e., its y-coordinate is 0.

$\therefore$ the coordinates of B are $(3, 0)$.

Similarly,

the coordinates of C are $(2, -3)$,

the coordinates of D are $(0, -2)$,

the coordinates of E are $(-3, -4)$, and

the coordinates of F are $(-2, 1)$.

Example 2

Plot the following points on the same Cartesian plane:

$A(5, 3)$	$B(0, 2)$
$C(-3, 2)$	$D(-4, 0)$
$E(-2, -2)$	$F(3, -3)$

Solution

For $A(5, 3)$:   Starting at the origin, move **5 units to the right** and then **3 units up**.

For point B, we do not move to the left or right as the x-coordinate is 0.

For $B(0, 2)$:   Starting at the origin, move **2 units up**.

For $C(-3, 2)$:   Starting at the origin, move **3 units to the left** and then **2 units up**.

Doing similarly for the coordinates of D, E and F, we get the following points:

Since the x-coordinate of B is 0, the point is on the y-axis, i.e., it is neither to the left nor to the right of the origin.

Since the y-coordinate of D is 0, the point is on the x-axis, i.e., it is neither above nor below the origin.

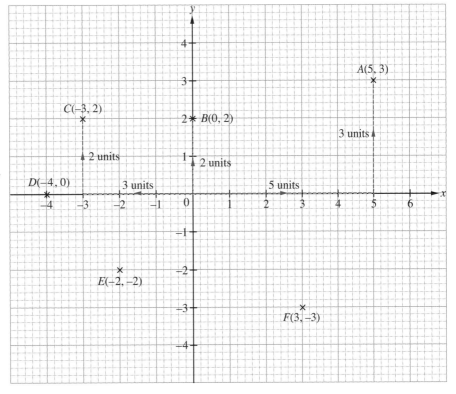

1. State the coordinates of the points *A* to *L* marked on the Cartesian plane below.

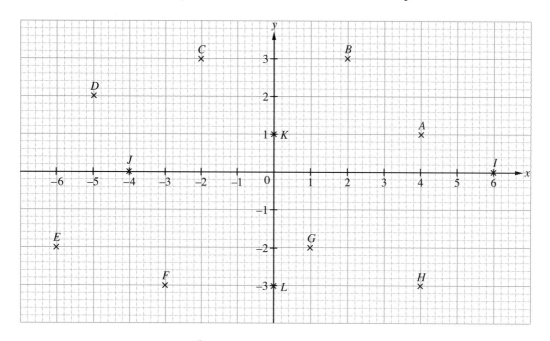

2. State the coordinates of the points *A* to *L* marked on the Cartesian plane below.

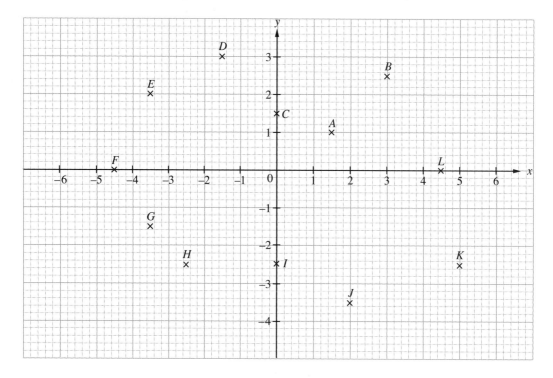

3. On a piece of graph paper, draw a set of Cartesian axes so that the x-axis and y-axis can each be marked off from –5 to 5. Then, mark the following points.
   (a) A(4, 5)
   (b) B(–3, 1)
   (c) C(–3, –2)
   (d) D(3, –2)
   (e) E(–2, 0)
   (f) F(0, –4)

4. Draw a set of x-y axes on a graph paper with both the x-axis and the y-axis extending from –5 to 5. Mark the following points.
   (a) $M\left(5, 3\frac{1}{2}\right)$
   (b) $N\left(4\frac{1}{2}, -2\right)$
   (c) $P\left(-1\frac{1}{2}, 3\right)$
   (d) $Q\left(-3, -4\frac{1}{2}\right)$
   (e) $R\left(0, 2\frac{1}{2}\right)$
   (f) $S\left(4\frac{1}{2}, 0\right)$
   (g) $T\left(1\frac{1}{2}, -4\frac{1}{2}\right)$
   (h) $U\left(-2\frac{1}{2}, 1\frac{1}{2}\right)$

5. (a) Mark the following two sets of points on the same Cartesian plane.
   Set A → (–2, 0), (0, 0), (1, 0), (3, 0)
   Set B → (0, –3), (0, –1), (0, 2), (0, 5)
   (b)  (i) Where do the points in Set A lie? What do they have in common?

(ii) Where do the points in Set B lie? What do they have in common?

6. (a) Draw a set of x-y axes on a graph paper and mark the following points.
   (i) A(0, 4)
   (ii) B(2, 1)
   (iii) C(5, 1)
   (iv) D(3, –2)
   (v) E(4, –5)
   (vi) F(0, –3)
   (vii) G(–4, –5)
   (viii) H(–3, –2)
   (ix) I(–5, 1)
   (x) J(–2, 1)
   (b) Join the points given in (a) by a series of straight lines, i.e., join A to B, B to C, C to D, etc. and finishing with J back to A. Describe the figure obtained.

7. (a) On a set of x-y axes, mark the following points.
   (i) A(–3, –6)
   (ii) B(–2, –4)
   (iii) C(–1, –2)
   (iv) D(0, 0)
   (v) E(1, 2)
   (vi) F(2, 4)
   (vii) G(3, 6)
   (viii) H(4, 8)
   (b) Join the points given in (a), i.e., join A to B to C to D, etc. finishing with G to H. Describe the pattern obtained.
   (c) What is the relationship between the x-coordinate and y-coordinate in each pair?

TIME-OUT ACTIVITY

Treasure Hunt

The map of Treasure Island (shown on the next page) is drawn on a set of axes labelled 0 to 12 (in km). A group of pirates landed at Camp Cove (3, 3) looking for the gold which the pirate Red Beard had buried in one of the locations marked on a grid map of the island. The pirates walked through the Marshes to Peak Hill (2, 6) where they camped overnight. The next morning they crossed Alligator River to arrive at Lone Palm (4, 9). However, they could not find the treasure there either.

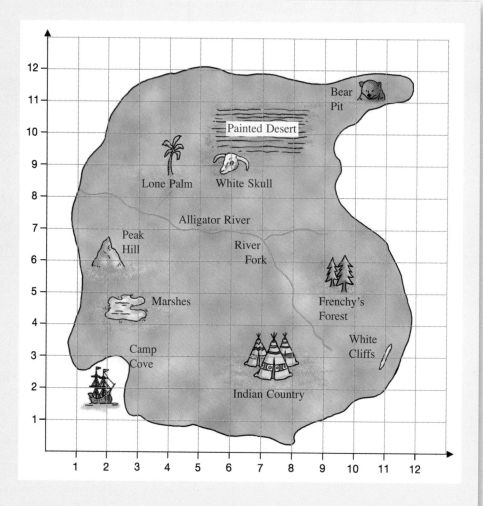

Caught in the Painted Desert (7, 10) overnight, they left for Alligator River (8, 7) the next morning. There, they were happy to find fresh, though dangerous, water.

Soon, they lost their way. They wandered for three days through Frenchy's Forest (9, 6) to (10, 5), then to White Cliffs (11, 3), Indian Country (7, 3) and beyond Indian Country (8, 4). Exhausted, they followed the river to a spot (7, 7) just past River Fork, where they camped until the next day. They had been away from their ship for over a week and were running short of supplies.

They decided to return to their ship by the way of White Skull (6, 9), across the river to Peak Hill (2, 6), the Marshes (3, 5) to (2, 4), and finally to Camp Cove (3, 3). Captain Bootleg was very angry when he found out that they had returned without the gold and decided to mark their journey on the grid map of the island. When he finished, he immediately realised where the gold was hidden.

Can you tell where the gold was hidden?

Linear Functions and Graphs

3.2.1 Linear Functions

The last question in Exercise 3A, which involved plotting points on the Cartesian plane, gave rise to a straight line. In this section, we will investigate relationships between points that join up to form straight lines.

Consider the points $(-2, -4)$, $(-1, -2)$, $(1, 2)$ and $(2, 4)$. Let us draw up a table and write the x and y coordinates of all the points in two rows.

x	-2	-1	1	2
y	-4	-2	2	4

Looking for a pattern

What is the relationship between the x-coordinate and y-coordinate in each of the points given above?

It can be observed that, in each of the given points, the value of the y-coordinate is twice the value of the x-coordinate.

E.g.
When $x = -2$, $y = 2(-2) = -4 \Rightarrow$ we have the point $(-2, -4)$
When $x = 1$, $y = 2(1) = 2 \Rightarrow$ we have the point $(1, 2)$

Now, check whether the x-coordinate and the y-coordinate in each of the other two points in the table above share the same relationship.

As each y-coordinate is twice its corresponding x-coordinate, we say that there exists a relation between the two variables. This relation is defined by $y = 2x$. Notice also that for the relation $y = 2x$, every value of x will give exactly one value of y.

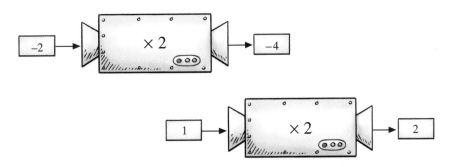

Mathematically, we can also call this type of relation a **function**.

> A variable y is said to be a **function** of another variable x if every value of x gives exactly one value of y.

Under the given function $y = 2x$, we can continue to form ordered pairs where the y-value is always twice the x-value. Thus, it would be impossible for us to write down all the ordered pairs that obey the function $y = 2x$.

However, we can represent all the ordered pairs that obey the function $y = 2x$ graphically as shown below.

Visit the following website for an interactive activity that puts your understanding of functions to the tests: http://www.shodor.org/interactivate/activities/FunctionMachine

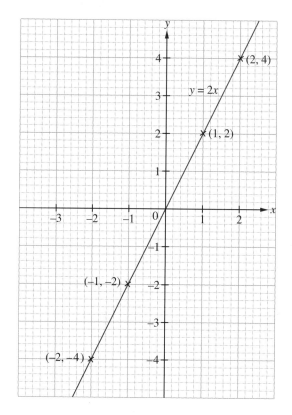

All the ordered pairs that obey the function $y = 2x$ can be represented as points that lie on the straight line. We call this straight line the graph of $y = 2x$.

note

An equation of a straight line graph is also known as a **linear equation**.

Straight line graphs are also known as **linear graphs**. Functions that give rise to linear graphs are known as **linear functions**. $y = 2x$ is an example of a linear function. $y = 2x$ is also known as the **equation of the straight line** graph above.

Note that every point lying on this straight line **satisfies** the equation $y = 2x$. For example, let us take the point $P(0.5, 1)$ on the line. Here, $x = 0.5$ and $y = 2(0.5) = 1$. Therefore, the coordinates of P satisfy the equation $y = 2x$.

Did you know?

The word 'linear' comes from the Latin word 'linearis' which means created by lines.

3.2.2 Graphs of Linear Equations

Consider the following:

> Draw the graph of $y = 3x$ for values of x from –3 to 3. Use a scale of 1 cm to 1 unit on the x-axis and 1 cm to 2 units on the y-axis.

To draw this graph, we first find the coordinates of a few points that satisfy the equation. Since the values of x lie between '–3' and '3', we tabulate the pairs of points whose x-coordinate lie between –3 and 3.

We thus set up a **table of values** using the given equation $y = 3x$ as shown:

x	–3	–2	–1	0	1	2	3
y							
(x, y)							

To complete the table, we substitute each value of x into $y = 3x$.

E.g.

When $x = -3$, $y = 3x$
$$= 3 \times (-3)$$
$$= -9 \qquad \Rightarrow \therefore \text{ we have the point } (-3, -9)$$

Similarly, when $x = -2$, $y = 3x$
$$= 3 \times (-2)$$
$$= -6 \qquad \Rightarrow \therefore \text{ we have the point } (-2, -6)$$

Continuing in this way for $x = -1, 0, 1, 2$ and 3, we would have the points $(-1, -3), (0, 0), (1, 3), (2, 6)$ and $(3, 9)$. The completed table of values for $y = 3x$ is as follows:

x	–3	–2	–1	0	1	2	3
y	–9	–6	–3	0	3	6	9
(x, y)	(–3, –9)	(–2, –6)	(–1, –3)	(0, 0)	(1, 3)	(2, 6)	(3, 9)

Next, we can proceed to draw our graph using the scale given in the question. The scale given is 1 cm to 1 unit on the x-axis and 1 cm to 2 units on the y-axis.

This means that, on graph paper, we can use 1 cm to represent 1 unit on the x-axis and 1 cm to represent 2 units on the y-axis. This representation of units is called the **scale** of the graph.

In short, we can write the scale as:

- For the x-axis, 1 cm : 1 unit
- For the y-axis, 1 cm : 2 units

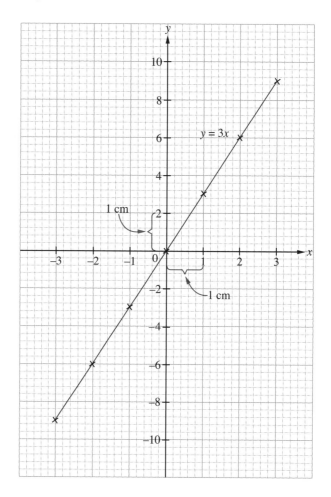

In cases where no scale is provided, we would need to come up with a suitable scale for each of the axes.

Some useful guidelines for deciding on a scale:

1. Look at the smallest and largest values of x and do a rough calculation to decide the scale that would give the largest possible graph. Do the same for the values of y.

2. Choose a suitably large scale for both axes. The vertical and horizontal distances between the first point and the last point should preferably cover 8 cm of space or more. Bigger graphs give more accurate results.

3. Use scales that are easy to read. Avoid awkward scales, for e.g., 1 cm to represent 3 units and 1 cm to represent 1.5 units.

Example 3

Draw the graph of $y = -2x$ for $-3 \leq x \leq 3$. Use 1 cm to represent 1 unit on both axes.

Solution

The table of values for $y = -2x$ is as follows:

When $x = -3$,
$$y = -2(-3)$$
$$= 6$$
$$\Rightarrow (-3, 6)$$

x	-3	-2	-1	0	1	2	3
y	6	4	2	0	-2	-4	-6
(x, y)	$(-3, 6)$	$(-2, 4)$	$(-1, 2)$	$(0, 0)$	$(1, -2)$	$(2, -4)$	$(3, -6)$

> **note**
>
> Always remember to label your completed graph with its equation.

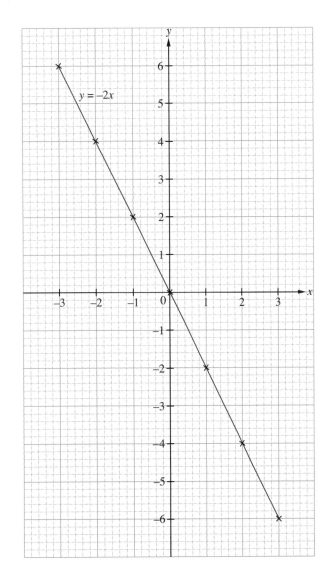

Example 4

Draw the graph of $y = x - 2$ for $-2 \leq x \leq 3$. Use a scale of 1 cm to 1 unit on both axes.

Solution

The table of values for $y = x - 2$ is as follows:

x	-2	-1	0	1	2	3
y	-4	-3	-2	-1	0	1
(x, y)	$(-2, -4)$	$(-1, -3)$	$(0, -2)$	$(1, -1)$	$(2, 0)$	$(3, 1)$

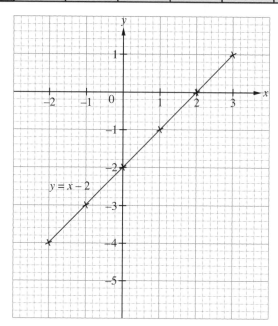

Exercise 3B

1. Deduce the relationship between the x-value and y-value in each of the following sets of ordered pairs. Hence, write down the function that defines the relationship in each case.

(a)

x	-2	-1	1	2
y	-2	-1	1	2

(b)

x	2	1	-1	-2
y	-2	-1	1	2

(c)

x	-2	-1	1	2
y	-8	-4	4	8

(d)

x	-2	-1	1	2
y	0	1	3	4

(e)

x	-2	-1	1	2
y	-3	-2	0	1

(f)

x	-2	-1	1	2
y	3	2	0	-1

2. Copy and complete each of the following tables for the equations given.

(a) $y = 5x$

x	−2	−1	0	1	2
y	−10			5	
(x, y)				(1, 5)	

(b) $y = -x$

x	−2	−1	0	1	2
y	2				
(x, y)					

(c) $y = -3x$

x	−2	−1	0	1	2
y	6				
(x, y)					

(d) $y = x + 5$

x	−3	−2	−1	0	1
y					
(x, y)					

(e) $y = x - 3$

x	−1	0	1	2	3
y					
(x, y)					

3. Using the completed tables of values in Question 2, plot the graphs of
   (a) $y = 5x$ for $-2 \le x \le 2$,
   (b) $y = -x$ for $-2 \le x \le 2$,
   (c) $y = -3x$ for $-2 \le x \le 2$,
   (d) $y = x + 5$ for $-3 \le x \le 1$,
   (e) $y = x - 3$ for $-1 \le x \le 3$.

4. The following is a table of values for the equation $y = 7x$. Copy and complete it.

x	−2	0	2
y			

Using a scale of 2 cm to represent 1 unit on the x-axis and a scale of 1 cm to represent 2 units on the y-axis, draw the graph of $y = 7x$ for values of x from −2 to 2.

5. Copy and complete the following table of values for the equation $y = x - 6$.

x	−1	0	1	2	3	4
y		−6		−4		−2

Using 1 cm to represent 1 unit on both axes, draw the graph of $y = x - 6$ for values of x from −1 to 4.

6. Draw the graph of each of the following equations.
   (a) $y = x$ for $-3 \le x \le 3$
   (b) $y = 6x$ for $-2 \le x \le 2$
   (c) $y = -4x$ for $-2 \le x \le 2$
   (d) $y = x + 7$ for $-3 \le x \le 1$
   (e) $y = x - 5$ for $-1 \le x \le 4$

Example 5

Draw the graph of $y = -x + 3$ for $-2 \leq x \leq 3$. Use a scale of 1 cm to 1 unit for both the axes.

Solution

The table of values for $y = -x + 3$ is as follows:

x	-2	-1	0	1	2	3	
$-x$	2	1	0	-1	-2	-3	$\left.\begin{matrix} \\ \\ \end{matrix}\right\}$ Add
$+3$	$+3$	$+3$	$+3$	$+3$	$+3$	$+3$	
y	5	4	3	2	1	0	
(x, y)	$(-2, 5)$	$(-1, 4)$	$(0, 3)$	$(1, 2)$	$(2, 1)$	$(3, 0)$	

note

At this point of time, you would have noticed that the coordinates of the points to be plotted, (x, y), can be read off from the rows of x- and y-values. As such, in the subsequent examples, the last row, (x, y), of the table will be omitted.

The table above helps us to work out the values of y neatly instead of a series of working of the type:

'when $x = -2$, $y = -(-2) + 3 = 5$'

which has to be done to find the corresponding y-value for each value of x.

Using the coordinates obtained in the table of values above, we have the following graph:

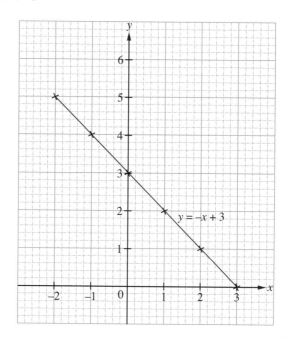

Example 6

Draw the graph of $y = 2x - 1$ for $-2 \leq x \leq 2$. Use a scale of 1 cm to 1 unit for both the axes.

Solution

The table of values for $y = 2x - 1$ is as follows:

x	-2	-1	0	1	2
$2x$	-4	-2	0	2	4
-1	-1	-1	-1	-1	-1
y	-5	-3	-1	1	3

} Add

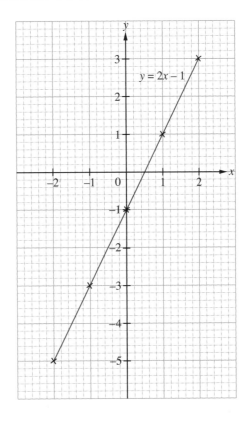

Example 7

Draw the graph of $y = 3(x - 1)$ for $-2 \leq x \leq 2$. Use 2 cm to represent 1 unit on the x-axis and 1 cm to represent 1 unit on the y-axis.
From the graph, find the corresponding value of
(a) y when $x = 0.8$,   **(b)** x when $y = -6.6$.

Solution

The table of values for $y = 3(x - 1)$ is as follows:

When $x = -2$,
$$y = 3(-2 - 1)$$
$$= 3(-3)$$
$$= -9$$
$$\Rightarrow (-2, -9)$$

x	-2	-1	0	1	2
$y = 3(x - 1)$	-9	-6	-3	0	3

On the x-axis, each division represents 0.1 units. On the y-axis, however, each division represents 0.2 units.

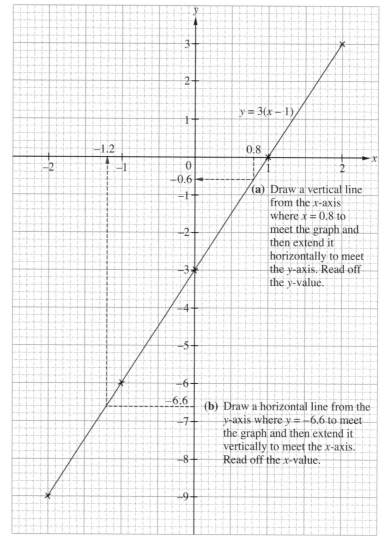

(a) Draw a vertical line from the x-axis where $x = 0.8$ to meet the graph and then extend it horizontally to meet the y-axis. Read off the y-value.

(b) Draw a horizontal line from the y-axis where $y = -6.6$ to meet the graph and then extend it vertically to meet the x-axis. Read off the x-value.

(a) $y = -0.6$ when $x = 0.8$ (b) $x = -1.2$ when $y = -6.6$

Example 8

Draw the graph of $x + y = 2$ for $-2 \le x \le 2$. Use 1 cm to represent 1 unit on both the axes.
From the graph, find the corresponding value of
(a) y when $x = 1.5$,   (b) x when $y = 3.6$.

Solution

The table of values for $x + y = 2$ is as follows:

x	–2	–1	0	1	2
y	4	3	2	1	0

When $x = -2$,
$-2 + y = 2$
$\therefore \quad y = 2 + 2$
$\qquad = 4$
$\Rightarrow (-2, 4)$

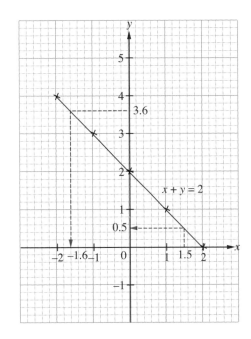

(a) $y = 0.5$ when $x = 1.5$ **(b)** $x = -1.6$ when $y = 3.6$

Example 9

Draw the graph of $4x + 2y = 6$ for $-2 \leq x \leq 2$. Use 2 cm to represent 1 unit on the x-axis and 1 cm to represent 1 unit on the y-axis.

Solution

When $x = -2$,
$4(-2) + 2y = 6$
$\quad -8 + 2y = 6$
$\qquad\quad 2y = 6 + 8$
$\qquad\qquad = 14$
$\therefore \quad y = 7$
$\Rightarrow (-2, 7)$

The table of values for $4x + 2y = 6$ is as follows:

x	–2	–1	0	1	2
y	7	5	3	1	–1

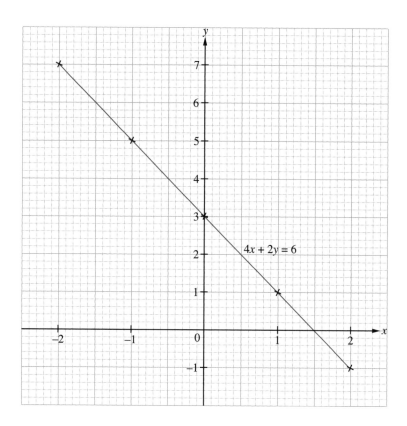

Alternative method:

We can first manipulate the equation such that y appears on its own on the left hand side.

$$4x + 2y = 6$$
$$2y = 6 - 4x$$
$$y = \frac{6 - 4x}{2}$$
$$y = 3 - 2x$$

Next, find the y values by directly substituting the x values in the equation $y = 3 - 2x$. Thus, we draw a table of values for $y = 3 - 2x$ instead. Plotting the x and y values from this table will give us the same graph as the one above.

Example 10

The amount, y, that a furniture company charges for delivery service is represented by the equation

$$y = 5d + 20$$

where d is the distance, in kilometres, travelled to make the delivery.
(a) Draw the graph of $y = 5d + 20$ for $0 \leq d \leq 20$.
(b) From the graph, find the basic fee charged by the furniture company.
(c) The charge for a certain delivery job is $100. Use the graph to find the distance travelled to make the delivery.

Solution

(a) The table of values for $y = 5d + 20$ is as follows:

d	0	5	10	15	20
$y = 5d + 20$	20	45	70	95	120

In this graph, each division on the x-axis represents 0.5 km and each division on the y-axis represents $2.

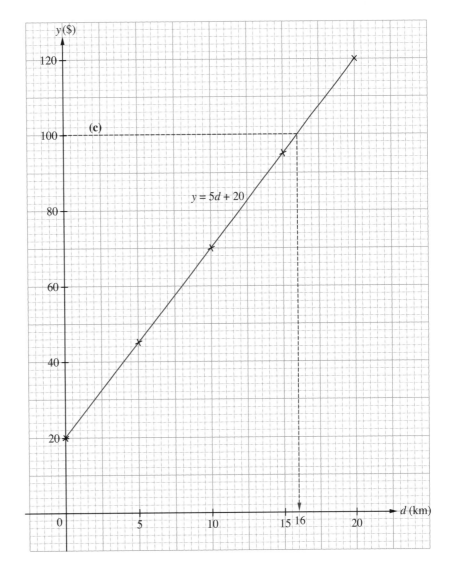

(b) The basic fee can be found by finding the amount charged when $d = 0$.

(b) From the graph, the basic fee is $20.

(c) The distance travelled to make the delivery was 16 km.

1. Copy and complete the following table of values for the equation $y = 4x + 5$.

x	−2	−1	0	1	2
y		1		9	

Using a scale of 2 cm to represent 1 unit on the x-axis and a scale of 1 cm to represent 2 units on the y-axis, draw the graph of $y = 4x + 5$ for $-2 \le x \le 2$.

2. For each of the following equations, form a table and draw the graph for $-2 \le x \le 2$.
   (a) $y = -x + 1$
   (b) $y = -x - 3$
   (c) $y = 3x - 2$
   (d) $y = 2x + 3$
   (e) $y = -2x - 5$
   (f) $y = -3x + 7$
   (g) $y = 3(x - 2)$
   (h) $y = 2(x + 3)$
   (i) $y = -4(x + 1)$
   (j) $y = -3(x - 1)$

3. For each of the following equations, form a table and draw the graph for $-2 \le x \le 2$.
   (a) $x + y = 1$
   (b) $x + y = -4$
   (c) $x - y = 3$
   (d) $x - y = -1$
   (e) $4x + 2y = 5$
   (f) $3x + 2y = 6$
   (g) $x - 2y = 4$
   (h) $2x + y - 1 = 0$

4. Calculate the values of a and b in the following table for the equation $6x + 2y = 8$.

x	−2	−1	0	1	2
y	10	a	4	b	−2

Using 2 cm to represent 1 unit on the x-axis and 1 cm to represent 1 unit on the y-axis, draw the graph of $6x + 2y = 8$ for $-2 \le x \le 2$.
From your graph, find
   (a) the values of y when $x = 1.8$ and -0.8.
   (b) the values of x when $y = 2.5$ and 8.5.

5. The amount $\$A$, that a postal company charges for sending a parcel is given by the equation

$$A = 3m + 20$$

where m is the mass of the parcel in kg.

   (a) Draw the graph of $A = 3m + 20$ for $0 \le m \le 10$. Use a scale of 2 cm to represent 2 kg on the horizontal axis and 2 cm to represent $\$10$ on the vertical axis.
   (b) Maria paid $\$35$ to the company for sending a parcel. From your graph, find the mass of the parcel that Maria sent.

6. The cost, $\$C$, that a factory takes to manufacture a certain type of toy is given by the equation

$$C = 4n + 280$$

where n is the number of toys produced.
   (a) Draw the graph of $C = 4n + 280$ for $0 \le n \le 100$. Use a scale of 2 cm to represent 20 toys on the horizontal axis and 1 cm to represent $\$20$ on the vertical axis. Start your vertical axis at $\$280$.
   (b) From the graph, it costs $\$280$ to manufacture 0 toys. Discuss with your classmates and write down an explanation to this in your Mathematics Journal.
   (c) Given that the manufacturing cost for this type of toy on a particular day was $\$500$, use your graph to find the number of toys produced on that day.

Drawing Graphs of Straight Lines

Bala drew the graph of the line $y = 3 - \frac{1}{2}x$ using two points as shown below.

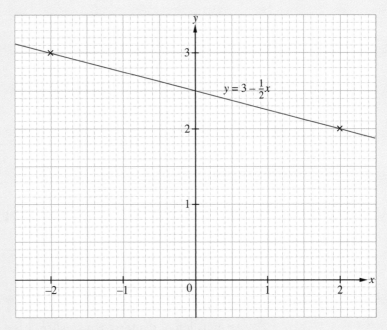

Discuss with your classmates and explain in your Mathematics Journal,
(a) the simplest method we can use to show that Bala's graph is wrong,
(b) how we can avoid the type of mistake Bala made whenever we want to draw a straight line graph.

3.2.3 Horizontal and Vertical Linear Relationships

Consider the following points:

(–3, 3)	(–3, 1)	(–2, 2)	(–2, 3)	(–1, 3)	(0, 3)
(1, 2)	(1, 3)	(2, 0)	(2, 3)	(3, 2)	(3, 4)

Which of the above points conform to the rule $y = 3$?

Notice that the rule $y = 3$ places no restriction on the value x may take. However, the value of y **must** be 3. Thus, the points above that conform to the rule $y = 3$ are:

$$(-3, 3), (-2, 3), (-1, 3), (0, 3), (1, 3), (2, 3)$$

By plotting and joining up the points which conform to the rule $y = 3$, we have:

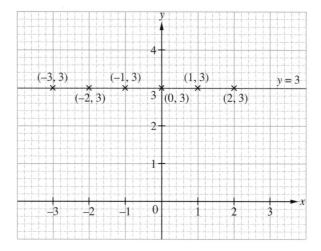

These points all lie on the same **horizontal** line. The equation of this horizontal line is $y = 3$.

In general,

> An equation of the form $y = k$, where k is a constant, is represented graphically by a **horizontal** line.

Now, consider the following points:

$(-3, -3)$	$(1, -3)$	$(1, -2)$	$(0, -2)$	$(1, -1)$	$(1, 0)$
$(0, 1)$	$(2, 1)$	$(1, 1)$	$(3, 1)$	$(1, 2)$	$(2, 3)$

Which of the above points conform to the rule $x = 1$?

Notice that the rule $x = 1$ places no restriction on the value y may take. However, the value of x **must** be 1. Thus, the points above that conform to the rule $x = 1$ are:

$$(1, -3), (1, -2), (1, -1), (1, 0), (1, 1), (1, 2)$$

By plotting and joining up the points which conform to the rule $x = 1$, we have:

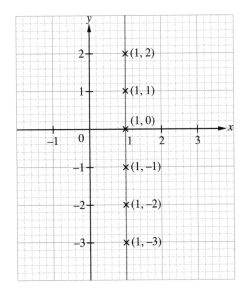

These points all lie on the same **vertical** line. This equation of this vertical line is $x = 1$.

In general,

An equation of the form $x = h$, where h is a constant, is represented graphically by a **vertical** line.

Exercise 3D

1. **(a)** Which of the points given below conform to the rule

   (i) $y = -2$,   **(ii)** $x = 3$?

(−1, −2)	(−2, −3)	(3, 3)
(3, −2)	(0, 3)	(3, −1)
(−2, −3)	(0, −2)	(3, 0)

   (b) Plot on separate graphs the points given in **(a)** which conform to rule **(i)** and rule **(ii)**.

2. **(a)** Which of the points given below conform to the rule

   (i) $y = 1$,   **(ii)** $x = -1$?

(3, −1)	(0, 1)	(1, −1)
(−1, 0)	(1, −2)	(2, 1)
(−1, 1)	(−1, −3)	(−3, 1)

   (b) Plot on separate graphs the points given in **(a)** which conform to rule **(i)** and rule **(ii)**.

3. Sketch the following lines on the same Cartesian plane for $-3 \leq x \leq 3$.

   (a) $y = 6$,   **(b)** $y = -3$

4. Sketch the following lines on the same Cartesian plane for $-3 \leq y \leq 3$.

   (a) $x = 2$ **(b)** $x = -5$

5. State the equation for each of the following straight lines.

(a)

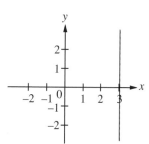

(b)

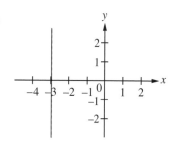

(c)

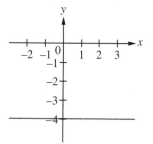

(d)

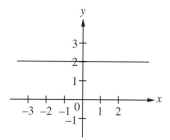

(e)

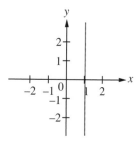

(f)

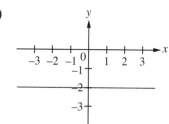

(g)

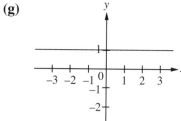

(h)

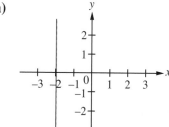

6. State the equation of
   (a) the x-axis,
   (b) the y-axis.

Gradients of Straight Line Graphs

The gradient or slope of a hill is a measure of how steep the hill is. The steeper the slope, the greater its gradient.

3.3.1 Positive and Negative Gradients

In Mathematics, the **gradient** of a line is defined as the ratio of the vertical change (increase or decrease) to the horizontal change.

$$\textbf{Gradient} = \frac{\text{vertical change}}{\text{horizontal change}}$$

Vertical change and horizontal change may be classified as positive change (increase) or negative change (decrease) according to the direction of change as shown in the table below.

Change	Direction of change	Sign
Vertical increase	↑	+
Vertical decrease	↓	−
Horizontal increase	→	+
Horizontal decrease	←	−

The gradient of the straight line *AC* shown below can be calculated as follows:

Gradient of $AC = \dfrac{\text{vertical change}}{\text{horizontal change}}$

$$= \frac{+2}{+3}$$

$$= \frac{2}{3}$$

Similarly, the gradient of the straight line *PR* shown below can be calculated as follows:

Gradient of $PR = \dfrac{\text{vertical change}}{\text{horizontal change}}$

$$= \frac{-2}{+3}$$

$$= -\frac{2}{3}$$

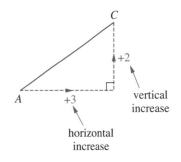

Example 11

Find the gradient of the line joining the points A and B.

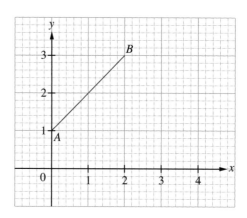

Solution

Vertical change $= +2$

Horizontal change $= +2$

Gradient of AB

$= \dfrac{\text{vertical increase}}{\text{horizontal increase}}$

$\therefore$ Gradient of AB

$= \dfrac{\text{vertical change}}{\text{horizontal change}}$

$= \dfrac{+2}{+2}$

$= 1$

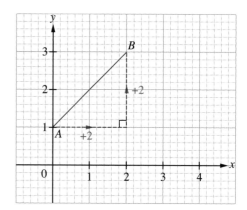

Example 12

For the diagram shown below, find the gradient of
(a) AB,   **(b)** PQ.

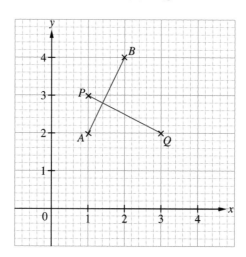

Solution

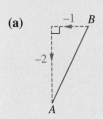
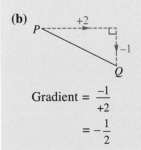
(a) Gradient of AB

$= \dfrac{\text{vertical change}}{\text{horizontal change}}$

$= \dfrac{+2}{+1}$

$= 2$

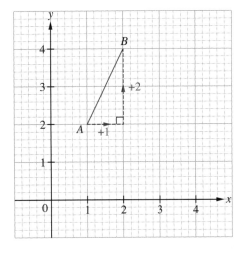

(b) Gradient of PQ

$= \dfrac{\text{vertical change}}{\text{horizontal change}}$

$= \dfrac{-1}{+2}$

$= -\dfrac{1}{2}$

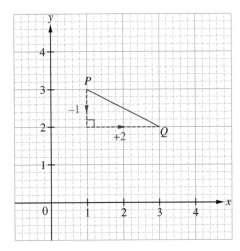

Example 13

(a) Using a scale of 2 cm to represent 1 unit on each axis, draw the graphs of

(i) $y = \dfrac{1}{2}x + 1$ for $-2 \le x \le 0$, and

(ii) $y = -x + 1$ for $0 \le x \le 2$.

(b) Hence, find the gradient of the lines

(i) $y = \dfrac{1}{2}x + 1$, and

(ii) $y = -x + 1$.

Solution

(a) (i) Table of values for $y = \dfrac{1}{2}x + 1$:

x	-2	-1	0
y	0	$\dfrac{1}{2}$	1

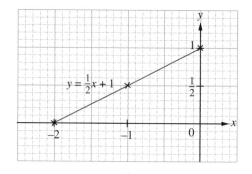

(ii) Table of values for $y = -x + 1$:

x	0	1	2
y	1	0	-1

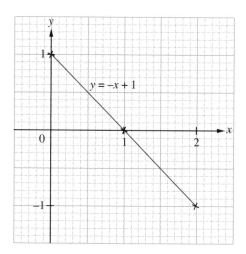

(b) (i) For the line $y = \dfrac{1}{2}x + 1$,

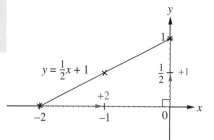

$$\text{Gradient} = \frac{+1}{+2}$$

$$= \frac{1}{2}$$

Alternative method:

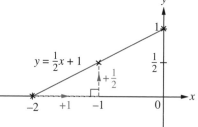

$$\text{Gradient} = \frac{+\dfrac{1}{2}}{+1}$$

$$= \frac{1}{2}$$

(ii) For the line $y = -x + 1$,

Alternative method:

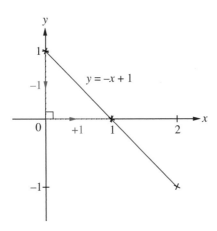

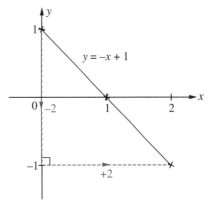

$$\text{Gradient} = \frac{-1}{+1}$$
$$= -1$$

$$\text{Gradient} = \frac{-2}{+2}$$
$$= -1$$

Positive or Negative?

Based on the results of Examples 11 to 13, state whether the gradients are positive or negative for lines

(a) sloping up to the right,

(b) sloping down to the right.

3.3.2 Gradients of Horizontal and Vertical Lines

In the previous section, we have learned how to find the gradient of a straight line graph. We have also seen that gradients can be positive or negative. Let us now take a look at the gradients of horizontal and vertical lines.

Consider the points $A(-1, 1)$ and $B(3, 1)$ on the horizontal straight line as shown.

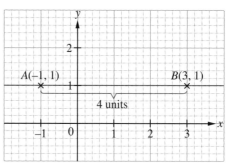

> **note**
>
> The vertical change for any horizontal line is always zero.

Gradient of $AB = \dfrac{\text{vertical change}}{\text{horizontal change}}$

$$= \frac{0}{4} = 0$$

Therefore, the gradient of the horizontal line is 0.

Next, consider the points $C(1, -1)$ and $D(1, 3)$ on the vertical line as shown.

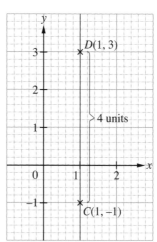

> **note**
>
> The horizontal change for any vertical line is always zero.

Gradient of $CD = \dfrac{\text{vertical change}}{\text{horizontal change}}$

$$= \frac{4}{0} \text{ which is undefined}$$

Therefore, the gradient of the vertical line is undefined.

Try finding the gradients of other horizontal and vertical lines. What do you notice?

1. Find the gradient of the line joining the points A and B in each of the following.

(a)

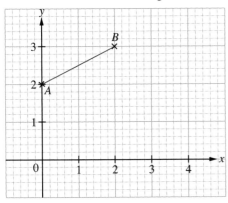

(b)

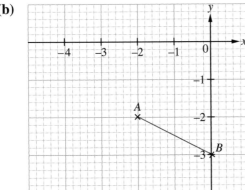

2. Find the gradient of the line joining the points
   (a) A and B,
   (b) C and D.

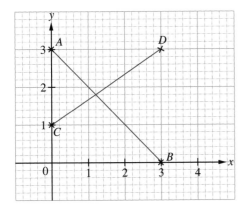

3. Find the gradients of the sides of △ABC.

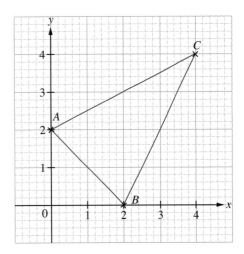

4. Find the gradient of the line joining each pair of points shown.

(a)

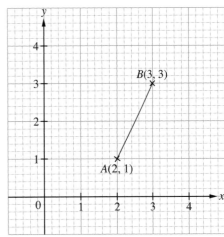

(b)

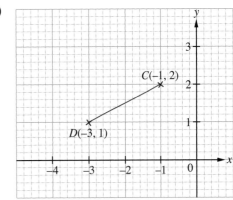

(c)

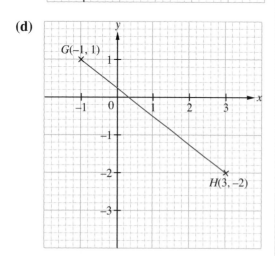

(d)

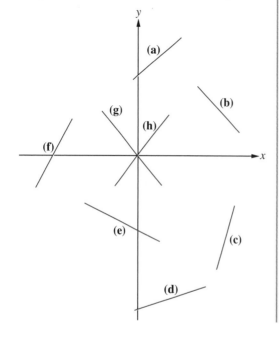

5. State the sign (i.e. positive or negative) of the gradients of each of the following lines.

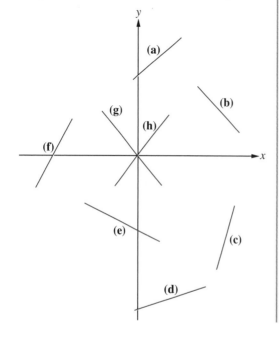

6. For each of the following pairs of points, draw the line joining them and find its gradient.
  (a) $O(0, 0)$ and $P(2, 6)$
  (b) $A(-1, 2)$ and $B(3, 4)$
  (c) $C(1, -2)$ and $D(3, 5)$
  (d) $E(1, 2)$ and $F(-3, 5)$
  (e) $G(1, 2)$ and $H(3, -5)$
  (f) $M(2, 2)$ and $N(-2, -4)$

7. Find the gradient of each of the following lines.

(a)

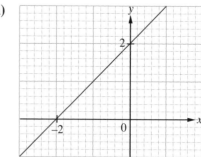

(b)

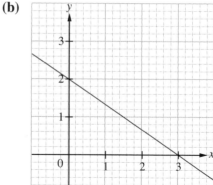

(c)

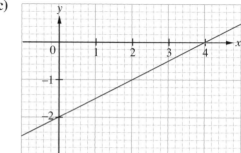

(d)

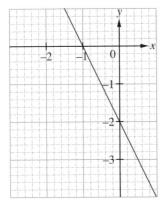

(e)

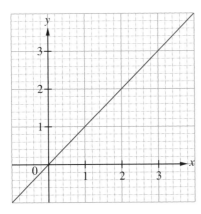

(f)

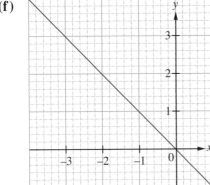

8. Using a scale of 2 cm to represent 1 unit on each axis, draw the graph of each of the following lines and find its gradient.

(a) $y = 2x - 3$ for $0 \le x \le 2$,

(b) $y = 3x + 2$ for $-1 \le x \le 1$,

(c) $y = -\dfrac{1}{2}x + 1$ for $0 \le x \le 2$,

(d) $y = -x + \dfrac{1}{2}$ for $0 \le x \le 2$.

9. (a) Is the x-axis a horizontal or vertical line? State the gradient of the x-axis.

(b) Is the y-axis a horizontal or vertical line? State the gradient of the y-axis.

10. State the gradient of each of the lines in the Cartesian plane shown below.

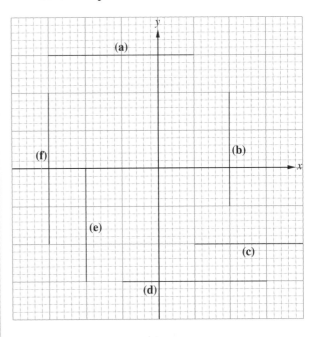

11. The amount C, in cents, charged by a telecommunications company is given by the equation

$$C = 30 + 5t$$

where t represents the call duration in minutes.

The graph of $C = 30 + 5t$ for $0 \le t \le 30$ is shown below.

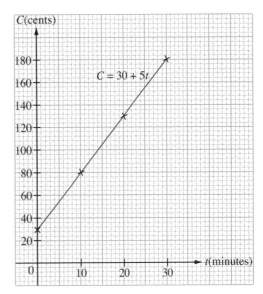

(a) Use the graph to find the basic connection fee that the company charges.

(b) From the graph, find the amount charged for a
   (i) 6-minute call,
   (ii) 22-minute call.

(c) Find the gradient of the graph.

(d)  State briefly what this gradient represents.

12. The value, $V, of an article over a period of 10 years is given by the equation

$$V = 3\,000 - 200t$$

where t represents the number of years passed.

The graph of $V = 3\,000 - 200t$ for $0 \leq t \leq 10$ is shown.

(a) From the graph, find the value of the article at the beginning of the 10-year period.

(b) From the graph, find the value of the article after
   (i) 3 years, **(ii)** 7 years.

(c) Find the gradient of the graph.

(d) 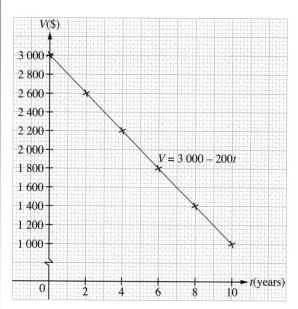 State briefly what this gradient represents.

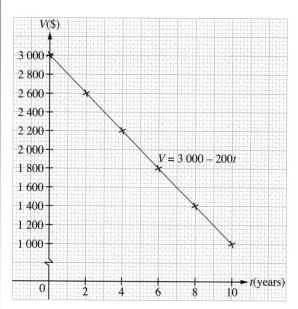

SUMMARY

1. The Cartesian coordinate system:

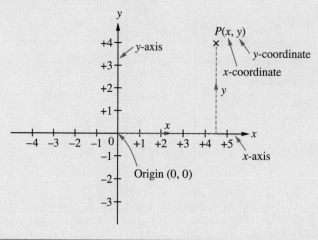

2. Plotting the graphs of linear equations:
   (a) First, draw a table of values for a few different values of x.
   (b) Then, substitute these x-values into the equation to obtain the corresponding y-values.
   (c) Finally, use these pairs of coordinates for plotting the straight line graph.

3. (a) Equation of horizontal lines:

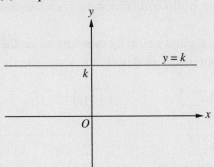

   (b) Equation of vertical lines:

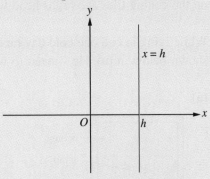

4. Gradient $= \dfrac{\text{vertical change}}{\text{horizontal change}}$

5. (a) A line sloping up to the right has a positive gradient.

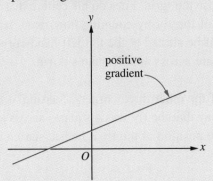

   (b) A line sloping down to the right has a negative gradient.

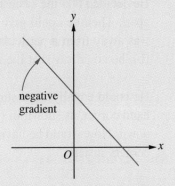

6. (a) All horizontal lines have a zero gradient.

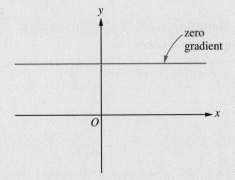

   (b) All vertical lines have an undefined gradient.

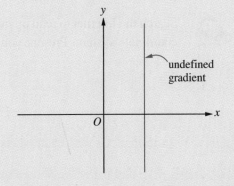

Descartes and the Fly

There is a story that René Descartes, the famous French mathematician, who lived from 1596 to 1650, invented the Cartesian coordinate system while watching a fly crawl around on the ceiling tiles above his head while he lay in bed. The story goes like this:

While lying in bed one cold day he looked up and saw a fly crawling along the ceiling as shown below in **(a)**. He wanted to work out a way of describing where the fly was.

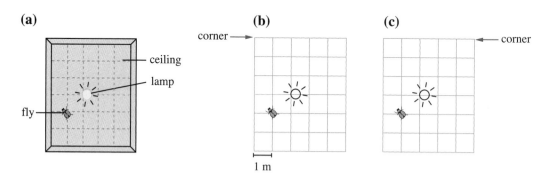

He decided that the easiest way was to use the 'grid' lines on his ceiling that were 1 metre apart. Then he could give the position of the fly by counting how many squares the fly was away from a particular corner. So if he started at the top left-hand corner marked in **(b)**, he could say that the fly was 1 square across and 4 squares down.

He could equally have started at any of the other three corners. Starting at the top right-hand corner, as shown in **(c)**, he could say that the fly was 4 squares across and 4 squares down. How would he have described the position of the fly if he had started at the bottom corners instead?

Due to the different possible ways of describing the position of the fly, he decided to make a rule about where to start counting from. From your knowledge of the Cartesian coordinate system, what rule do you think he came up with?

 Search the Internet to read up more about René Descartes and his invention of the Cartesian coordinate system. Present your findings to your class.

You have 10 minutes to answer the following questions.
Choose the most appropriate answer.

MINUTES

CONCEPT CHECK

3.1 **1.** The coordinates of point P are
    A $(-1, 2)$.
    B $(2, -1)$.
    C $(1, -2)$.
    D $(-2, 1)$.

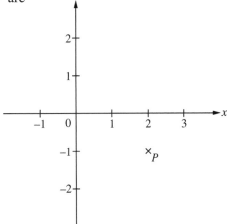

3.2 **2.** The line $y = 2x - 3$ passes through all the following points except
    A $(2, 1)$.
    B $(0, -3)$.

    C $(-1, -4)$.

    D $\left(\dfrac{1}{2}, -2\right)$.

3.2 **3.** Which of the following lines correctly shows the graph of $y = x + 1$?

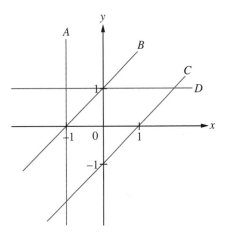

4. Which of the following lines correctly shows the graph of $2x + y = -1$?

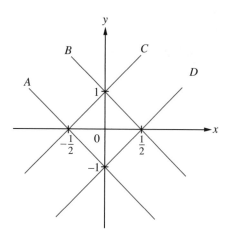

5. The equation of the horizontal line shown is

A $y = 5$. **B** $x = 5$.

C $y = x + 5$. **D** $x = y + 5$.

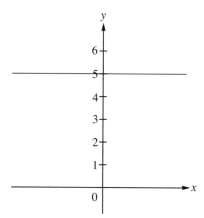

6. The equation of the vertical line shown is

A $x + y = -2$. **B** $y = -2$.

C $x = -2$. **D** $y = x - 2$.

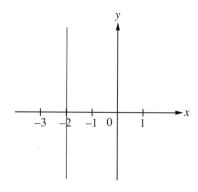

7. The gradient of the line shown is

A   2.

B $\dfrac{1}{2}$.

C   −2.

D $-\dfrac{1}{2}$.

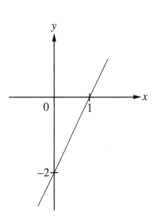

8. The gradient of the line shown is

A   2.

B $\dfrac{1}{2}$.

C   −2.

D $-\dfrac{1}{2}$.

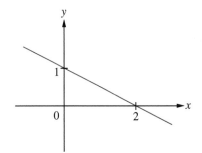

9. The gradient of the horizontal line shown is

A   −1.

B   0.

C   1.

D   undefined.

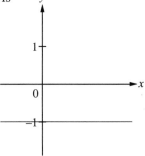

10. The gradient of the vertical line shown is

A   −1.

B   0.

C   1.

D   undefined.

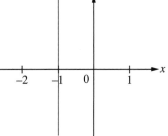

SECTION A

1. Write down the coordinates of the points A, B, C and D.

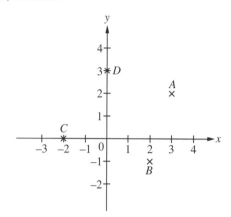

2. Plot the points $P(3, 2)$, $Q(0, -1)$ and $R(-2, 4)$ on a piece of graph paper. Join P to Q, Q to R and R to P. Identify the type of triangle formed.

3. Plot the points $E(5, 1)$, $F(1, 4)$ and $G(-2, 0)$. If these are the three corners of a square, mark the fourth corner and write down its coordinates.

4. A letter T is drawn by joining the points $(-1, -1)$ to $(1, 1)$ and $(1, 3)$ to $(3, 1)$, and by extending one line to touch the other line. By plotting the points, form the required letter T and state the coordinates of the point where one line touches the other line.

SECTION B

5. Copy and complete the following table of values for $y = 2x - 4$.

x	-2	0	2
$y = 2x - 4$			0

State the coordinates of the point where the graph cuts the y-axis.

6. Match the graphs **(a)** – **(e)** sketched below with the equations from the following list **(i)** – **(v)**:

(i) $x = 2$
(ii) $y = x$
(iii) $y = -x$
(iv) $y = x + 2$
(v) $y = 2$

(a)

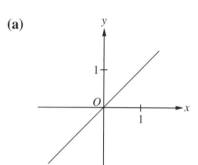

(b)

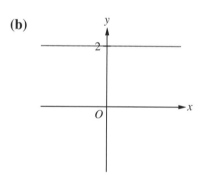

(c)

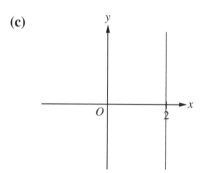

(d)

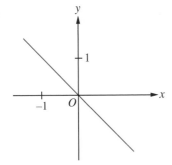

(e)

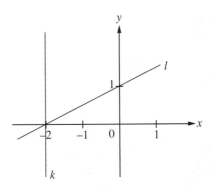

7. **(a)** Find the gradient of the
   (i) line k, **(ii)** line l.

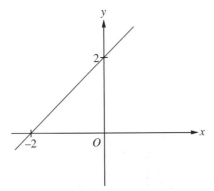

(b) Draw the line joining the points $A(2, -3)$ and $B(1, -1)$. Then, find its gradient.

8. **(a)** Find the gradient of the
   (i) line m, **(ii)** line n.

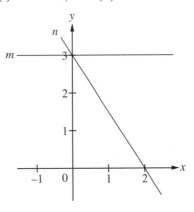

(b) Draw the line joining the points $C(-1, 6)$ and $D(-3, -2)$. Then, find its gradient.

SECTION C

9. Using 2 cm to represent 1 unit on both axes, draw the graphs of

   (a) $x = 3$, **(b)** $y = \dfrac{1}{2}x$,

   (c) $y = \dfrac{1}{2}x + 2$, **(d)** $x = 0$.

   for $0 \le x \le 3$ and $0 \le y \le 4$ on the same Cartesian plane. State the type of quadrilateral enclosed by the four lines.

10. The amount, $\$y$, charged by a mobile phone company is given by the equation

$$y = 0.1t + 20$$

   where t is the talk time in a month in minutes.

   (a) Draw the graph of $y = 0.1t + 20$ for $0 \le t \le 400$. Use a scale of 2 cm to represent 100 minutes on the horizontal axis and 2 cm to represent $\$10$ on the vertical axis.

   (b) Use your graph to find
   (i) the basic amount charged,
   (ii) the gradient of the line graph.

   (c) State briefly what this gradient represents.

Proportions and Map Scales

Maps help us find our way in unfamiliar places. We can also find the distance between two places by taking measurements on a map that shows these places and then using the scale found on it to determine the actual distance.

Using the scale found on a map is an application of direct proportion. In this chapter, you will learn how to solve problems involving direct proportion and inverse proportion and how they can be used to solve real-life problems.

4.1.1 Real-Life Problems Involving Direct Proportion

A man wishes to buy some fried chicken drumsticks. The table below shows the amount of money he needs to spend if he buys a certain number of chicken drumsticks.

$2 per drumstick

No. of chicken drumsticks bought	Price
1	$2
2	$4
3	$6
4	$8
5	$10

increasing number | | increasing amount

Notice that if the number of chicken drumsticks bought increases by 1, the corresponding price increases by $2. To understand the relationship between these two quantities better, let us now compare their ratios.

2 drumsticks : 4 drumsticks = 2 : 4 = 1 : 2
$4 : $8 = 4 : 8 = 1 : 2

3 drumsticks : 4 drumsticks = 3 : 4
$6 : $8 = 6 : 8 = 3 : 4

In both cases above, the number of drumsticks bought increases in the same ratio as the increase in price. For example, when the number of drumsticks is doubled, the price is also doubled. In this case, we say that the number of chicken drumsticks increases **proportionately** to the price.

In general,

Quantities that increase or decrease in the same ratio are said to be in **direct proportion**.

The examples below show real-life problems involving quantities that are usually in direct proportion.

note

Normally, we can assume that the rate of consumption of fuel is constant even though it is not stated in the question.

Example 1

A hybrid car requires 21 litres of petrol to travel 320 km. How much petrol is needed to travel 80 km?

Solution

The amount of petrol needed is directly proportional to the distance travelled by the car. Let the amount of petrol needed be n litres.

note

To simplify your calculations in the main method shown, write the unknown first on the LHS. Take note of the order of the ratios.

n litres : 21 litres = 80 km : 320 km

$$\frac{n}{21} = \frac{80}{320}$$

$$n = \frac{80}{320} \times 21$$

$$n = 5.25$$

Alternative method:

21 litres for 320 km

n litres for 80 km

$$\therefore \quad \frac{n}{80} = \frac{21}{320}$$

$$n = \frac{21}{320} \times 80$$

$$= 5.25$$

Therefore, 5.25 litres of petrol is needed to travel 80 km.

Example 2

If 0.8 kg of grapes costs $6.40, how many kilograms of grapes can be bought with $9.60?

Solution

The mass of grapes bought is directly proportional to the cost. Let the mass of grapes that can be bought be x kg.

note

The unitary method can also be used to solve these problems. In Example 2, we can first find the mass of grapes that can be bought with $1.00.

x kg : 0.8 kg = $9.60 : $6.40

$$\frac{x}{0.8} = \frac{9.60}{6.40}$$

$$x = \frac{9.60}{6.40} \times 0.8$$

$$x = 1.2$$

Alternative method:

0.8 kg costs $6.40

x kg costs $9.60

$$\therefore \quad \frac{x}{9.60} = \frac{0.8}{6.40}$$

$$x = \frac{0.8}{6.40} \times 9.60$$

$$= 1.2$$

Therefore, 1.2 kg of grapes can be bought with $9.60.

1. A car requires 15 litres of petrol to travel 200 km. How much petrol is needed to travel 120 km?

2. If the mass of 9 chocolate bars is 540 g, find the mass of 6 such chocolate bars.

3. If 500 g of grapes cost $2.80, find the cost of 1.2 kg of grapes.

4. A cyclist travels 3 km in 6 minutes. How far does he travel in 30 seconds?

5. The cost of 8 kg of bananas is $12.
   (a) Calculate the cost of 12 kg of bananas.
   (b) How many kilograms of bananas can be bought for $15?

6. A man works 40 hours in order to earn $210. Assuming that he works at this payment rate,
   (a) how much will he earn if he works 12 hours?
   (b) how many hours will he have to work in order to earn $126?

7. A hotel charges $910 per week for a room. The room rate for each day of the week is the same.

   (a) What would be the charge for 5 days for a similar room?
   (b) If a tourist has only $390, how many days can he stay in the hotel?

8. A car travels 85 km in 51 minutes.
   (a) How far does it travel in 1 hour at the same speed?
   (b) How many seconds does it take to travel 510 m?

9. 100 g of fish cost 70¢.
   (a) Calculate the cost of 180 g.
   (b) Mr Tan paid $2.45 for some fish. How many grams of fish did he buy?
   [N/91/P1]

10. A car travels 30 kilometres in 1 hour.
    (a) How many kilometres does the car travel in 5 minutes?
    (b) How many metres does it travel in 1 minute? [N/88/P1]

4.1.2 Tabular, Algebraic and Graphical Approach in Direct Proportion

The costs of certain amounts of rice are shown in the table below.

Amount of rice (A kg)	4	8	12	16	20
Cost (C)	6	12	18	24	30

As the amount of rice increases, the total cost also increases. Furthermore, for each pair of values in the above table, the rate of cost per unit amount of rice is the same, i.e.,

$$\frac{C}{A} = \frac{6}{4} = \frac{12}{8} = \frac{18}{12} = \frac{24}{16} = \frac{30}{20} = \frac{3}{2}$$

$$\therefore \quad \frac{C}{A} = \frac{3}{2} \Rightarrow C = \frac{3}{2}A$$

$C = \frac{3}{2}A = 1.5A$

Thus, each kilogram of rice costs $1.50.

Thus, we have obtained an algebraic relationship between C and A.

In the previous chapter, we have learned how to plot linear graphs from a table of values. We can use the above table to plot the following graph.

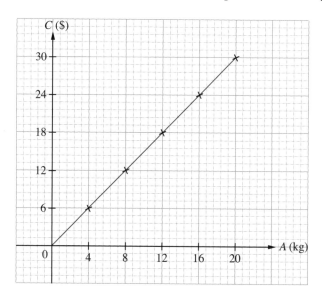

The graph is a straight line passing though the origin. It can be seen that if the amount of rice is doubled, the cost is doubled; if the amount of rice is trebled, the cost is trebled; and so on.

Now consider the costs of certain amounts of sugar as shown in the table below.

Amount of sugar (A kg)	2	4	6	8	10
Cost ($\$C$)	4	8	12	16	20

We can calculate the rate of cost per unit amount of sugar as shown below.

$$\frac{C}{A} = \frac{4}{2} = \frac{8}{4} = \frac{12}{6} = \frac{16}{8} = \frac{20}{10} = 2$$

$$\therefore \quad \frac{C}{A} = 2 \Rightarrow C = 2A$$

Therefore, we get an algebraic relationship between C and A using a similar method as shown on the previous page.

From the above table, if we plot the graph of C against A, we will get the following graph.

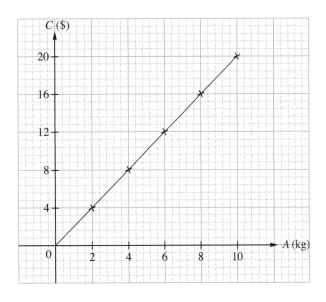

Notice that we get a straight line passing through the origin again.

We say that one variable is **directly proportional** to the other variable when the rate of increase of the two variables is a constant. Thus, in both cases shown earlier, C is directly proportional to A. This can be written as:

$$\frac{C}{A} = k \quad \text{or} \quad C = kA, \qquad \text{where } k \text{ is a constant.}$$

In general,

If y is **directly proportional** to x,

(a) then $\dfrac{y}{x} = k$ or $y = kx$, where k is a constant.

(b) a graph of y against x will give a straight line passing through the origin.

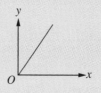

Example 3

For each table, determine whether y is directly proportional to x, and if so, find an equation relating y and x.

(a)

x	2	4	7
y	8	16	28

(b)

x	1	3	4
y	2	6	12

Solution

(a) Considering $\dfrac{y}{x}$, we have

$$\frac{8}{2} = 4, \qquad \frac{16}{4} = 4, \qquad \frac{28}{7} = 4$$

$\therefore \quad \dfrac{y}{x} = 4$ ⟵ Constant $k = 4$

Therefore, y is directly proportional to x. The equation relating y and x is $y = 4x$.

(b) Considering $\dfrac{y}{x}$, we have

$$\frac{2}{1} = 2, \qquad \frac{6}{3} = 2, \qquad \frac{12}{4} = 3$$

$\therefore \quad \dfrac{y}{x} \neq$ constant

Therefore, y is not directly proportional to x.

Example 4

If d is directly proportional to t, and $d = 120$ when $t = 2$,

(a) find an equation relating d and t,

(b) find the value of d when $t = 6$,

(c) find the value of t when $d = 60$.

Solution

(a) Since d is directly proportional to t,
$$d = kt, \quad \text{where } k \text{ is a constant.}$$

Substitute the values of d and t into $d = kt$ to find k.

Given $d = 120$ when $t = 2$,
$$120 = k(2)$$
$$k = \frac{120}{2}$$
$$= 60$$
$\therefore$ the equation is $d = 60t$.

Substitute $t = 6$ into $d = 60t$.

(b) When $t = 6$,
$$d = 60(6)$$
$$= 360$$

Substitute $d = 60$ into $d = 60t$.

(c) When $d = 60$,
$$60 = 60t$$
$$t = \frac{60}{60}$$
$$= 1$$

Example 5

In the following table, b is directly proportional to a.

a	1	2	3		7.5
b	7	14		49	

(a) Find an equation relating b and a.

(b) Find the missing values in the table.

Solution

(a) $\dfrac{b}{a} = \dfrac{7}{1} = \dfrac{14}{2} = 7$

$\therefore \quad b = 7a$

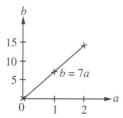

The graph of b against a gives a straight line passing through the origin.

Alternative method:

Since b is directly proportional to a,
$$b = ka, \quad \text{where } k \text{ is a constant.}$$

Given $a = 1$ when $b = 7$,
$$7 = k(1)$$
$$k = 7$$

$\therefore$ the equation is $b = 7a$.

Substitute $a = 3$ into $b = 7a$.

(b) When $a = 3$,
$$b = 7(3)$$
$$= 21$$

Substitute $b = 49$ into $b = 7a$.

When $b = 49$,
$$49 = 7a$$
$$a = \frac{49}{7}$$
$$= 7$$

Substitute $a = 7.5$ into $b = 7a$.

When $a = 7.5$,
$$b = 7(7.5)$$
$$= 52.5$$

Exercise 4B

1. For each table, determine whether y is directly proportional to x, and if so, find an equation relating y and x.

    (a)

x	3	7	9
y	9	21	27

    (b)

x	2	5	10
y	1	$2\frac{1}{2}$	5

    (c)

x	2	3	4
y	3	4	5

    (d)

x	1	2	3
y	2	8	18

2. Draw the graph of y against x for each of the tables in Question 1.
    (a) Which graphs are straight lines?
    (b) Which graphs pass through the origin?
    (c) Which tables contain variables that are in direct proportion?
    (d) What can you conclude about the graph of two variables that are in direct proportion?

3. State if the variables are in direct proportion in each of the following cases.

    (a) 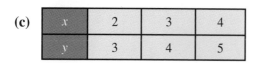   **(b)**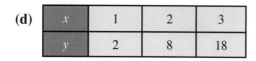

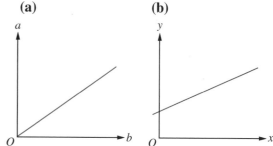

(c)

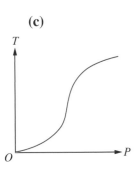

(d)

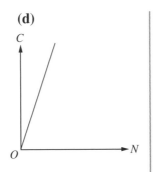

(e)

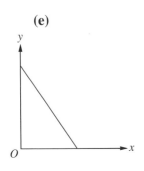

(f)

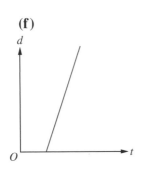

4. Rewrite each of the following statements as an equation with a constant k. The first one has been done for you.

(a) a and b are in direct proportion.
$\Rightarrow a = kb$, where k is a constant.

(b) y and x are in direct proportion.

(c) c is directly proportional to d.

(d) v is directly proportional to t.

5. If y is directly proportional to x, and $y = 2$ when $x = 4$,

(a) find an equation relating y and x,

(b) find the value of y when $x = 6$,

(c) find the value of x when $y = 4$.

6. If P is directly proportional to T, and $P = 9$ when $T = 3$,

(a) express P in terms of T,

(b) find the value of P when $T = 10$,

(c) find the value of T when $P = 10$.

7. If V and h are in direct proportion, and $V = 25$ when $h = 2.5$,

(a) find the value of V when $h = 5.2$,

(b) find the value of h when $V = 100$.

8. Given that V is directly proportional to T, copy and complete the following table.

T	10	40	
V		200	250

9. In the following table, y is directly proportional to x.

x	2	4	
y	9		81

(a) Find an equation relating y and x.

(b) Find the missing values in the table.

10. In the following table, P and T are in direct proportion.

P		51	81
T	2		54

(a) Express P in terms of T.

(b) Find the missing values in the table.

11. The time taken to complete a Mathematics trail is directly proportional to the number of activities in the trail. If it takes 3 hours to complete 6 activities, how long does it take to complete a Mathematics trail that contains 9 activities?

12. The amount of petrol and the distance that a car can travel are in direct proportion. A car with a full tank of 60 litres of petrol can travel 720 km. Find

(a) how far the car can travel if it has 15 litres of petrol,

(b) how much petrol the car must have to travel 156 km,

(c) how far the car can travel if it has x litres of petrol,

(d) how much petrol the car must have to travel m km.

Is There Direct Proportion?

Study the table below.

x	0	1	2	3	4
y	6	9	12	15	18

Adam says that there is no proportionality between the variables x and y as $\dfrac{9}{1} \neq \dfrac{12}{2} \neq \dfrac{15}{3}$.

Bala agrees with Adam but also says that the two variables will be in a direct proportion if 2 is added to every value of x.

 Discuss whether Bala is correct. Assuming that Bala is correct, express y in terms of x for the values in the table above.

4.2 Inverse Proportion

4.2.1 Real-Life Problems Involving Inverse Proportion

A building maintenance company is going to start repainting the walls of a cluster of HDB blocks. It needs to plan the amount of time it will take to complete this task. The project manager draws up a table to show the relationship between the number of workers that could be assigned to this task and the corresponding time it will take to complete the task.

No. of workers	Time taken
2	30 hours
3	20 hours
4	15 hours
5	12 hours
6	10 hours

increasing number → (left)   decreasing amount → (right)

As can be seen from the table above, if the company assigns more workers for this task, it will take a shorter time to complete it. Notice that if the number of workers is doubled, the time taken to complete the task is halved.

E.g.

No. of workers	Time taken
2	30 hours
4	15 hours

doubled (...) halved

Similarly, if the number of workers is tripled, the time taken to complete the task is $\frac{1}{3}$ of its original value.

E.g.

No. of workers	Time taken
2	30 hours
6	10 hours

×3 (...) ×$\frac{1}{3}$

In general,

> If one quantity decreases in the same ratio as another quantity increases, the two quantities are said to be in **inverse proportion**.

Example 6

A motorist takes 18 minutes to travel a certain stretch of road at a speed of 50 km/h. At what speed must he travel the same stretch of road if the journey is to take only 15 minutes?

Solution

The motorist will need to travel faster (i.e., at a greater speed) to achieve a shorter travel time, implying an inverse proportion relationship. Let the required speed be v km/h.

	First quantity		Second quantity
He travels	v km/h	in	15 minutes,
and	50 km/h	in	18 minutes.

$$\therefore \quad v \text{ km/h} : 50 \text{ km/h} = 18 \text{ minutes} : 15 \text{ minutes}$$

$$\frac{v}{50} = \frac{18}{15}$$

$$v = \frac{18}{15} \times 50$$

$$= 60$$

Therefore, the motorist has to travel at a speed of 60 km/h if the journey is to take only 15 minutes.

Example 7

If an emergency pack of food for 30 men can last 32 days, how long would the food last if there are 40 men instead?

Solution

The food will last a shorter time if there are more men, implying an inverse proportion relationship. Let the number of days that the food can last for 40 men be d.

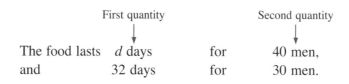

	First quantity		Second quantity
The food lasts	d days	for	40 men,
and	32 days	for	30 men.

For inverse proportion, reverse the ratio of the second quantity.

$$\therefore \quad d \text{ days} : 32 \text{ days} = 30 \text{ men} : 40 \text{ men}$$
$$\frac{d}{32} = \frac{30}{40}$$
$$d = \frac{30}{40} \times 32$$
$$= 24$$

Alternative method:

Amount of food = Number of men × Number of days

$$\therefore \quad 40 \times d = 30 \times 32$$
$$d = \frac{30 \times 32}{40}$$
$$= 24$$

Therefore, the emergency pack of food can last 24 days if there are 40 men.

Exercise 4C

1. If 8 soldiers can build a bridge in 5 hours, how many soldiers are needed to build the same bridge in 4 hours?

2. A cyclist takes 12 minutes to travel a certain stretch of road at a speed of 12 km/h. At what speed must he travel the same stretch of road if he is to take only 10 minutes?

3. A rope can be cut into 12 pieces, each 45 cm long. How many pieces can the rope be cut into if each piece is 0.3 m long?

4. 3 carpenters can build a boat in 2 weeks. How many carpenters are needed to build the same boat in 6 days?

5. A task can be completed in 25 days by 24 men. Assuming that they work at the same rate,
  (a) how long will it take 15 men to finish the same job,
  (b) how many men would be required to finish the job in 10 days?

6. If 5 farmers take 16 days to harvest a plantation,
  (a) how many days would 8 farmers take,
  (b) how many farmers would be needed to harvest the plantation in 4 days?

7. A farmer has enough grains to feed 90 sheep for 40 days. How many sheep does he have to sell so that the grains can feed the remaining sheep for 60 days?

8. 8 men are able to build a fence in 8 hours. If 2 of the men were absent, how much more time would the rest of the men take to build the same fence?

9. A holiday is planned for a group of 20 children and food is bought to last for 15 days. If the number of children were to increase to 25, how long would you expect the same amount of food to last? [O/Nov 94/P1]

10. If 6 men take 6 days to complete a task,
  (a) how many days would 3 men take,
  (b) how many men would be needed to complete the task in 2 days? [N/90/P1]

4.2.2 Tabular, Algebraic and Graphical Approach in Inverse Proportion

Activity

To study the tabular approach in inverse proportion.

 (A) Using a Spreadsheet Programme

Step   Action

1   Open a new worksheet and type in the headings and data as they are shown in the table below. The data shows the flying times for aeroplanes travelling at various speeds between two airports 3 000 km apart.

		A	B	C	D
	1	**Average speed in km/h** (v)	**Time in hours** (t)	v/t	$v \times t$
	2	200	15		
	3	300	10		
	4	400	7.5		
	5	500	6		
	6	1000	3		

2   In **Column C Row 2** cell, key in =A2/B2 and press *Enter*. (The value of $200 \div 15$ will be shown in this cell.)

3   Select **Column C Row 2** cell and click on **Edit** menu. Then click on **Copy**.

4   Select **Column C Row 3** till **Column C Row 6** cells. Click on **Edit** menu again and then click on **Paste**.

5   In **Column D Row 2** cell, key in =A2*B2 and press *Enter*. (The value of 200×15 will be shown in this cell.)

6   Select **Column D Row 2** cell and click on **Edit** menu. Then click on **Copy**.

7   Select **Column D Row 3** till **Column D Row 6** cells. Click on **Edit** menu again and then click on **Paste**.

8   Using your results, answer the following questions.
   (a) Is v directly proportional to t? Why?
   (b) Is $v \times t =$ constant? Hence, find a relationship between v and t.

(B) Using a Calculator

a	b	$\dfrac{a}{b}$	$a \times b$
1	12		
2	6		
3	4		
4	3		

Step   *Action*

1   Copy and complete the above table.

2   Using the above table, answer the following questions.
   (a) Is a directly proportional to b? Why?
   (b) Is $a \times b =$ constant? Hence, find a relationship between a and b.

In the previous activity, it can be seen that **as one quantity increases, the other decreases**. In fact, if one quantity is doubled, the other is halved; if one quantity increases by 3 times, the other quantity decreases by 3 times. Notice that for each pair of values, the product is a constant. For example, in part B of the previous activity,

$$1 \times 12 = 2 \times 6 = 3 \times 4 = 4 \times 3 = 12$$

i.e. $$a \times b = 12$$

So, $a \times b$ is constant. When written in the general form, we have:

$$a \times b = k$$

or $\qquad b = \dfrac{k}{a}$

i.e. $\qquad b = k\left(\dfrac{1}{a}\right),$ $\qquad$ where k is a constant.

Recall from Section 4.1.2 that y is directly proportional to x implies that $y = kx$. Conversely, $y = kx$ implies that y is directly proportional to x.

$$\therefore \quad b = k\left(\dfrac{1}{a}\right) \quad \Rightarrow \quad b \text{ is directly proportional to } \dfrac{1}{a}$$

Thus, we say that b is **inversely proportional** to a.

Let us draw the graph for part B of the previous activity by plotting b against a. The table of values is as follows:

a	1	2	3	4
b	12	6	4	3

When we plot the graph of b against a, we obtain a curve as shown below.

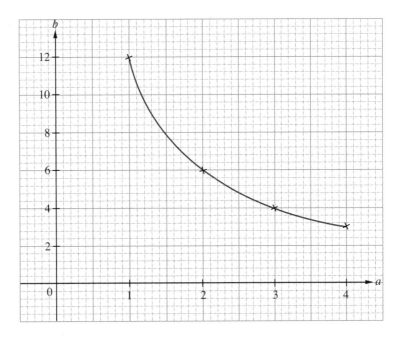

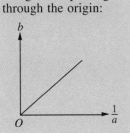
Notice that as the value of a becomes bigger, the value of b becomes smaller.

In general,

note

If y is inversely proportional to x, then x is also inversely proportional to y.

If y is **inversely proportional** to x,

(a) then $yx = k$ or $y = \dfrac{k}{x}$, where k is a constant.

(b) a graph of y against x will give a curve (as shown).

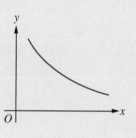

Example 8

For each table, determine whether y is inversely proportional to x, and if so, find an equation relating y and x.

(a)

x	2	4	8
y	24	12	6

(b)

x	1	3	5
y	6	2	1

Solution

note

If $y \times x = k$ where k is a constant, then y is inversely proportional to x.

(a) Considering $y \times x$, we have

$$24 \times 2 = 48, \qquad 12 \times 4 = 48, \qquad 6 \times 8 = 48$$

$$\therefore \quad y \times x = 48 \quad \longleftarrow \text{Constant } k = 48$$

Therefore, y is inversely proportional to x. The equation relating y and x is $y = \dfrac{48}{x}$.

note

Check all pairs of values.

(b) Considering $y \times x$, we have

$$6 \times 1 = 6, \qquad 2 \times 3 = 6, \qquad 1 \times 5 = 5$$

$$\therefore \quad y \times x \neq \text{constant}$$

Therefore, y is not inversely proportional to x.

Example 9

Given that P is inversely proportional to V and that $P = 4$ when $V = 2$,
(a) express P in terms of V,
(b) calculate the value of P when $V = 4$,
(c) calculate the value of V when $P = 6$.

Solution

(a) Since P is inversely proportional to V,

$$P = \frac{k}{V}, \qquad \text{where } k \text{ is a constant.}$$

Given $P = 4$ when $V = 2$,
$$4 = \frac{k}{2}$$
$$k = 4 \times 2$$
$$= 8$$
$$\therefore \quad P = \frac{8}{V}$$

(b) When $V = 4$,
$$P = \frac{8}{4} = 2$$

(c) When $P = 6$,
$$6 = \frac{8}{V}$$
$$V = \frac{8}{6} = \frac{4}{3}$$

$6 = \dfrac{8}{V}$
$6V = 8$
$V = \dfrac{8}{6}$

Example 10

In the following table, n is inversely proportional to m.

m	2	3	4	
n	6	4		2

(a) Find an equation relating m and n.
(b) Find the missing values in the table.

Solution

(a) $n \times m = 6 \times 2 = 4 \times 3 = 12$
$$\therefore \quad n = \frac{12}{m}$$

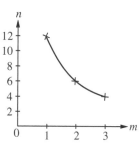

The graph of n against m gives a curve as shown above.

Alternative method:

Since n is inversely proportional to m,

$$n = \frac{k}{m}, \qquad \text{where } k \text{ is a constant.}$$

Given $m = 2$ when $n = 6$,

$$6 = \frac{k}{2}$$
$$k = 6 \times 2$$
$$= 12$$

$$\therefore \quad \text{the equation is } n = \frac{12}{m}.$$

Substitute $m = 4$ into $n = \frac{12}{m}$.

(b) When $m = 4$,

$$n = \frac{12}{4}$$
$$= 3$$

When $n = 2$,

$$2 = \frac{12}{m}$$

Substitute $n = 2$ into $n = \frac{12}{m}$.

$$m = \frac{12}{2}$$
$$= 6$$

Exercise 4D

1. For each table, determine whether y is inversely proportional to x, and if so, find an equation relating y and x.

   (a)

x	1	2	4	5
y	20	10	5	4

   (b)

x	1	2	3	4
y	10	9	8	7

   (c)

x	2	3	4	5
y	30	20	15	12

   (d)

x	3	4	8	10
y	32	24	12	9.6

2. Rewrite each of the following statements as an equation with a constant k. The first one has been done for you.

   (a) y and x are in inverse proportion.

   $$\Rightarrow y = \frac{k}{x}, \text{ where } k \text{ is a constant.}$$

   (b) p and q are in inverse proportion.

   (c) m is inversely proportional to n.

   (d) a is inversely proportional to b.

3. If y is inversely proportional to x, and $y = 10$ when $x = 6$,
   (a) express y in terms of x,
   (b) find the value of y when $x = 4$,
   (c) find the value of x when $y = \dfrac{1}{2}$.

4. If a and b are in inverse proportion, and $a = 5$ when $b = 4$,
   (a) find the value of a when $b = 10$,
   (b) find the value of b when $a = 7$.

5. The variables x and y are related by the equation $xy = $ constant. Copy and complete the following table.

x	2	3	
y	9		5

6. In the following table, y is inversely proportional to x.

x	2	3		9
y	18	12	6	

   (a) Find an equation relating x and y.
   (b) Find the missing values in the table.

7. In the following table, P and Q are in inverse proportion.

P	0.25	0.5	1	
Q		1	0.5	0.4

   (a) Express Q in terms of P.
   (b) Find the missing values in the table.

8. When the temperature is constant, the pressure of a given mass of gas is inversely proportional to its volume. Given that the pressure is 75 cm of mercury when the volume is 150 cm^3, find the pressure when the volume is 100 cm^3.

9. The time taken to travel a journey and the speed for the journey are in inverse proportion. If it takes 5 h to complete a journey when the speed is 80 km/h, how long would the same journey take if the speed was increased by 20 km/h?

10. Mrs Wang and her friends would like to charter a bus for a shopping trip to Johor Bahru. The cost per person is inversely proportional to the number of people going for the trip. It costs $32 per person when 10 people are taking the chartered bus. Find
   (a) the total cost of chartering the bus,
   (b) the cost per person when 16 people are taking the bus,
   (c) the number of people required for the trip if they would like to reduce the cost to $8 per person,
   (d) the cost per person if x people are taking the bus,
   (e) the number of people required for the trip if the cost per person is M.

★11. A chemical experiment was carried out at a temperature of 20°C. If the temperature was increased by 10°C, the time taken for the chemical reaction to occur would be 3 minutes faster. Given that the time taken for the chemical reaction to occur is inversely proportional to the temperature, how much should the temperature be increased by in order for the chemical reaction to occur 5 minutes faster?

Cat and Mouse

Gerald and Melanie were given the following problem to solve:

*If 4 cats can catch 4 mice in 4 days, how many days
would it take for 2 cats to catch 2 mice?*

Gerald uses direct proportion to solve the problem and get an answer of
2 days. Melanie thinks Gerald is wrong and uses inverse proportion instead
to get an answer of 8 days.

 Discuss with your classmates and explain in your Mathematics Journal who is
right or wrong. Show the correct working in your Mathematics Journal.

In order to be useful, a map cannot be of the same size as the region it represents. Things such as ground area, rivers and distances between places must be shown proportionately smaller than they really are, so as to fit on the available paper or screen. We can use a scale to show this proportion.

The figure that follows shows the map of the countries in Southeast Asia. The **scale** shown on the map gives a measure of the ratio of the distance on the map to the actual distance on the ground.

note

Different maps may use different scales. Do not assume that the scale used in one map is the same as that used in another.

The map scale above shows that 1 cm on the map represents an actual length of 500 km on the ground. This scale can be expressed in a ratio form.

1 km = 1 000 m
1 m = 100 cm

$$1 \text{ cm} : 500 \text{ km} = 1 \text{ cm} : 500\ 000 \text{ m}$$
$$= 1 \text{ cm} : 50\ 000\ 000 \text{ cm}$$
$$= 1 : 50\ 000\ 000$$

Did you know?

Maps are sometimes referred to as being 'small-scale' or 'large-scale'. Small-scale maps (e.g. maps with a scale of 1 : 500 000) show a larger area but with less detail. Large-scale maps (e.g. maps with a scale of 1 : 10 000) show a smaller area but with greater detail.

The above scale of 1 : 50 000 000 means that 1 cm on the map represents 50 000 000 cm on the ground. Using this scale, we can see that:

2 cm on the map represents 1 000 km or 100 000 000 cm on the ground,

and

4 cm on the map represents 2 000 km or 200 000 000 cm on the ground.

In general,

> A **map scale** is usually expressed in the form $1 : n$, where n is a whole number.
> E.g. $1 : 50\ 000\ 000$ means 1 cm represents $50\ 000\ 000$ cm,
> i.e. $500\ 000$ m,
> i.e. 500 km.

Example 11

Express the scale of 2 cm representing 5 km in the form of $1 : n$, where n is a whole number.

Solution

Change to the same unit. Then, remove the units and simplify the ratio.

$$2 \text{ cm} : 5 \text{ km} = 2 \text{ cm} : 5\ 000 \text{ m}$$
$$= 2 \text{ cm} : 500\ 000 \text{ cm}$$
$$= 2 : 500\ 000$$
$$= 1 : 250\ 000$$

Example 12

On the map of Southeast Asia given on the previous page, the distance between Singapore and Phnom Penh is 2.3 cm. Find the actual distance (on the ground) between the two cities. (1 cm on the map represents 500 km on the ground.)

Solution

1 cm represents 500 km.
$\therefore$ 2.3 cm represents $2.3 \times 500 = 1\ 150$ km

note

The distance on the map is directly proportional to the distance on the ground.

Alternative method:
Let the actual distance on the ground be x km.
$\therefore$ x km is represented by 2.3 cm
and   500 km is represented by 1 cm.

$\therefore$ $x : 500 = 2.3 : 1$
$$\frac{x}{500} = \frac{2.3}{1}$$
$$x = 2.3 \times 500$$
$$= 1\ 150$$

Therefore, the actual distance between the two cities is 1 150 km.

Example 13

The actual distance between Singapore and Jakarta is 900 km. On a particular map, 1 cm on the map represents 500 km on the ground. What length on the map represents the distance between the two cities?

Solution

500 km is represented by 1 cm.

$\therefore$ 900 km is represented by $\dfrac{1}{500} \times 900 = 1.8$ cm

Alternative method:

Let x cm on the map represents 900 km on the ground.

$\therefore$ $\quad x$ cm represents 900 km

and $\quad$ 1 cm represents 500 km.

$\therefore$ $\quad x : 1 = 900 : 500$

$$\dfrac{x}{1} = \dfrac{900}{500}$$

$$x = 1.8$$

Therefore, 1.8 cm on the map represents the distance between the two cities.

To access an online map of Singapore, visit http://www.streetdirectory.com. To view satellite maps of any country in the world, visit http://www.google.com/maps.

Example 14

A map has a scale of 1 : 40 000. A rectangular swimming lagoon measures 1.4 cm by 0.35 cm on the map. Find the actual length and breadth of the lagoon in metres. What is the actual area of the lagoon in hectares? (1 ha = 10 000 m^2)

Solution

1 m = 100 cm

The scale is 1 : 40 000.

i.e. 1 cm : 40 000 cm = 1 cm : 400 m.

$\therefore$ $\quad$ Actual length of the lagoon $= 1.4 \times 400$

$= 560$ m

Actual breadth of the lagoon $= 0.35 \times 400$

$= 140$ m

$\therefore$ $\quad$ Area of the lagoon $= 560 \times 140$

$= 78\ 400$ m^2

$= \dfrac{78\ 400}{10\ 000}$ ha

$= 7.84$ ha

Example 15

A map is drawn to a scale of 1 : 200 000.
(a) Find the actual distance, in kilometres, represented by 6 cm on the map.
(b) An island shown on this map has an actual area of 600 square kilometres. Find, in square centimetres, the area representing the island on this map.

Solution

(a) The scale is 1 : 200 000.

1 m = 100 cm
1 km = 1 000 m

i.e. 1 cm : 200 000 cm = 1 cm : 2 000 m
$$= 1 \text{ cm} : 2 \text{ km}$$

1 cm represents 2 km.
$\therefore$ 6 cm represents $6 \times 2 = 12$ km.

Therefore, 6 cm on the map represents an actual distance of 12 km.

(b)   1 cm represents 2 km.
$\therefore$ $(1 \text{ cm})^2$ represents $(2 \text{ km})^2$.
i.e. 1 cm^2 represents 4 km^2.
Let x cm^2 represents 600 km^2.
$$\therefore \quad \frac{x}{1} = \frac{600}{4}$$
$$x = 150$$

Therefore, the area representing the island on this map is 150 cm^2.

Exercise 4E

1. Write the following scales in the form of $1 : n$, where n is a whole number.
(a) 4 cm represents 5 m
(b) 5 cm represents 4 m
(c) 5 cm represents 4 km
(d) 4 cm represents 5 km

2. A length of 5 cm on a map represents a distance of 2 km on the ground. What length on the map represents an actual distance of 1 800 m?

3. A map has a scale of 1 : 125 000. What length on the map represents an MRT track that is 10 km long?

4. A map has a scale of 1 : 40 000. A rectangular lagoon measures 1.5 cm by 0.32 cm on the map.
(a) Find the actual length and breadth of the lagoon in metres.
(b) What is the actual area of the lagoon in hectares? (1 ha = 10 000 m^2)

5. A map is drawn to a scale of 1 : 20 000.
(a) The perimeter of a lake is 2.5 km. Find, in cm, the perimeter of the lake on the map.
(b) The area of the lake on the map is 12.5 cm^2. Find, in km^2, the actual area of the lake.

6. A map is drawn to a scale of 1 : 500 000.
   (a) Find, in km, the actual distance of a railway track that is represented by a 40 cm track on the map.
   (b) A country has an area of 40 000 km². Find, in cm², the area representing the country on the map.

7. Study the map below.

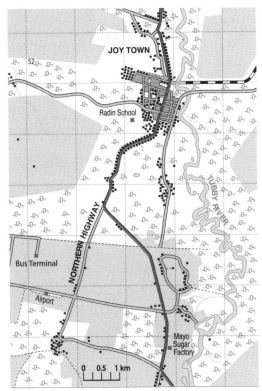

   (a) Measure the following distances (along a straight line) on the map.
      (i) Between the Bus Terminal and Mayo Sugar Factory.
      (ii) Between the Bus Terminal and Radin School.
      (iii) Between the Airport and Mayo Sugar Factory.
   (b) For each of (i) – (iii) above, find the actual distance between the two places using the scale shown. Give your answers correct to 3 significant figures.

8. The plans of a house are drawn to a scale of 1 : 50.
   (a) Find the actual length, in metres, represented by 14 cm on the plan.
   (b) What length, in centimetres, on the plan represents an actual length of 11 metres? [N/85/P1]

9. The straight line on the map below represents the Cable Car System from Mount Faber station to Sentosa station, passing through the World Trade Centre station. The actual distance from the World Trade Centre station to Sentosa station is 1 km.
   (a) What actual distance, in metres, is represented by 1 cm on the map?
   (b) Find the scale of the map in the form of 1 : *n*.
   (c) What is the actual distance, in metres, from Mount Faber station to the World Trade Centre station?

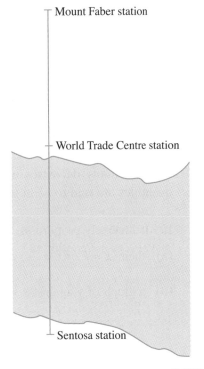

[N/89/P1]

10. If triangle *POQ* (not drawn to scale) is represented on a map of scale 1 : 50 000, calculate

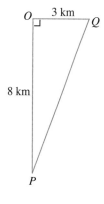

(a) the length, in cm, of the line on the map representing *OP*,

(b) the area, in cm², of the triangle on the map representing triangle *POQ*.

[N/86/P2]

11. Give your answers to this question in metres correct to 1 decimal place.

The diagram is a plan of a room, drawn to a scale of 1 : 100.

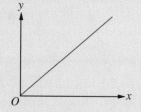

(a) What is the actual length of the wall represented by *AB*?

(b) What is the actual perimeter of the room? [N/90/P1]

SUMMARY

1. Quantities that increase in the same ratio are said to be in **direct proportion**.

2. If *y* is directly proportional to *x*,

(a) then $\frac{y}{x} = k$ or $y = kx$, where *k* is a constant.

(b) a graph of *y* against *x* will give a straight line passing through the origin.

3. If one quantity decreases in the same ratio as another quantity increases, the two quantities are said to be in **inverse proportion**.

4. If *y* is inversely proportional to *x*,

(a) then $yx = k$ or $y = \frac{k}{x}$, where *k* is a constant.

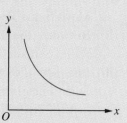

(b) a graph of *y* against *x* will give a curve (as shown).

5. A map scale is usually expressed in the form 1 : *n*, where *n* is a whole number.
E.g. 1 : 50 000 000 means 1 cm represents 50 000 000 cm,

i.e. 500 000 m,

i.e. 500 km.

A Full Tank

An empty tank is to be filled with water from either Tap *A* or Tap *B*.

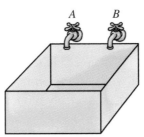

(a) If Tap *A* is fully turned on and Tap *B* is turned off, it takes 12 minutes to fill up the tank. What fraction of the whole tank can be filled by Tap *A* alone in 1 minute?

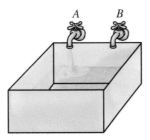

(b) If Tap *B* is fully turned on and Tap *A* is turned off, it takes 8 minutes to fill up the tank. What fraction of the whole tank can be filled by Tap *B* alone in 1 minute?

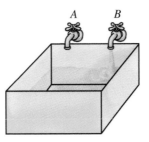

(c) Find the time it takes to fill up the tank if both Tap *A* and Tap *B* are fully turned on. Discuss in pairs the methods that can be used to solve this problem.

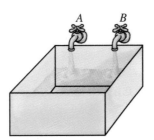

You have 10 minutes to answer the following questions.
Choose the most appropriate answer.

4.1 **1.** If 9 apples cost $3, how many apples can you buy if you have $9?

    A 3   **B** 18   **C** 27   **D** 81

4.1 **2.** If X doubles when Y doubles, then

    A X is directly proportional to Y.

    B X is inversely proportional to Y.

    C X is not proportional to Y.

    D Y is inversely proportional to X.

4.1 **3.** Which one of the following graphs represents two quantities that are in direct proportion?

A    **B**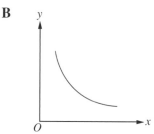

C 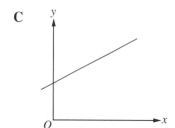   **D**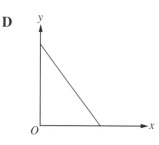

4.1 **4.** If $\dfrac{y}{x} = 2$, then

    A y is inversely proportional to x.

    B y is directly proportional to x.

    C y is not directly proportional to x.

    D y is proportional to 2.

4.2 **5.** If 4 taps that are fully turned on can fill a tank in 6 hours, how long does it take to fill the tank using 3 identical taps that are fully turned on?

    A 2 hours   **B** 4.5 hours

    C 6 hours   **D** 8 hours

4.2　**6.** If quantity Q doubles when R is halved, then

    A R is proportional to Q.

    B Q is directly proportional to R.

    C Q is not proportional to R.

    D Q is inversely proportional to R.

4.2　**7.** Which one of the following graphs represents two quantities that are in inverse proportion?

A 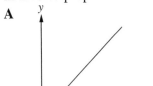　　**B**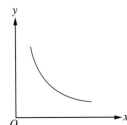

C 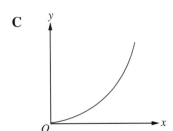　　**D**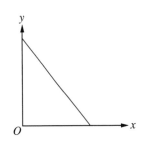

4.2　**8.** If $xy = 10$, then

    A y is inversely proportional to x.

    B y is directly proportional to x.

    C y is directly proportional to 10.

    D y is proportional to x.

4.3　**9.** Write the scale 4 cm to 500 m in the form of $1 : n$, where n is a whole number.

    A $1 : 125$ **B** $1 : 1\ 250$

    C $1 : 12\ 500$ **D** $1 : 125\ 000$

4.3　**10.** If a scale on a map is $1 : 50\ 000$, then 0.5 cm^2 on the map represents

    A   0.5 km^2.   **B**   0.25 km^2.

    C   0.125 km^2.   **D**   0.062 5 km^2.

SECTION A

1. Rewrite each statement as an equation.
   (a) U is directly proportional to v.
   (b) S is directly proportional to $\dfrac{1}{T}$.
   (c) Y is inversely proportional to x.

2. If 6 kg of sugar costs $6.30,
   (a) what is the cost of 9 kg of sugar?
   (b) how much sugar can be bought for $4.20?

3. State whether direct proportion exists in each of the following cases.
   (a)
   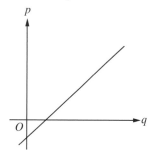
   (b)

   (c)
   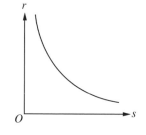

(d)
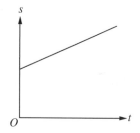

4. A task can be completed in 24 days by 15 men. Assuming that they work at the same rate,
   (a) how long will it take 18 men to finish the same task,
   (b) how many men can complete the task in 8 days?

SECTION B

5. If m is directly proportional to n, and $m = 60$ when $n = 4$,
   (a) find an equation, expressing m in terms of n,
   (b) find the value of m when $n = 3$,
   (c) find the value of n when $m = 90$.

6. Given that V is inversely proportional to I and that $V = 250$ when $I = 4$,
   (a) express V in terms of I,
   (b) calculate the value of V when $I = 5$,
   (c) calculate the value of I when $V = 125$.

7. A length of 5 cm on a map represents a distance of 4 km on the ground.
   (a) What distance is represented by a length of 12.5 cm on the map?
   (b) What length on the map represents a distance of 1 600 m?

8. A map has a scale of 1 : 50 000.
   (a) Find the actual length of an expressway that is 38 cm long on the map.
   (b) What length on the map represents a river that is 18 km long?

SECTION C

9. For each table, determine whether y is directly or inversely proportional to x, and if so, find an equation relating y and x.

(a)

x	2	3	4
y	1	3	5

(b)

x	2	3	4
y	18	27	36

(c)

x	2	3	4
y	150	100	75

10. (a) Write the following scales in the form of $1 : n$, where n is a whole number.
   (i) 2 cm represents 500 m
   (ii) 1 cm represents 20 km

   (b) On a map of Peninsular Malaysia using a scale of 1 : 1 000 000, the distance between Johor Bahru and Kluang is 11 cm. What is the actual distance on the ground in km?

   (c) On a map of Singapore using a scale of 1 : 180 000, the area of Sentosa Island is 1.6 cm^2. What is its actual area in km^2?

Review Paper 1

SECTION A

1. **(a)** Expand the following.
    (i) $7(5a + 3)$
    (ii) $-6(3b + 2)$
    (b) Factorise the following.
    (i) $2 - 4m$
    (ii) $-9n + 21$

2. **(a)** Expand the following.
    (i) $2(3c + d)$
    (ii) $-3e(e + f)$
    (b) Factorise the following.
    (i) $2p^2 - 6p$
    (ii) $-3qr^2 - 6r$

3. **(a)** Expand the following.
    (i) $6u(v - 8u)$
    (ii) $-5t(t + s)$
    (b) Factorise the following.
    (i) $2c^2 + 10ce$
    (ii) $-f^2g - fg^2$

4. **(a)** Simplify the following.
    (i) $\dfrac{3u}{vw} \times \dfrac{5v}{6u}$
    (ii) $\dfrac{2x}{3} \div \dfrac{8y}{5}$
    (b) Solve the following equations.
    (i) $2(g - 3) = 5$
    (ii) $3(2 - h) = 7$

5. **(a)** Solve the following equations.
    (i) $x - 2(3x - 4) = 5$
    (ii) $5(y + 4) - 6(5 - 2y) = 3$
    (b) Solve the following equations.
    (i) $\dfrac{7k}{9} = \dfrac{3}{5}$
    (ii) $2 - \dfrac{2m}{3} = \dfrac{1}{4}$

6. **(a)** Write down the coordinates of the points A, B and C.

    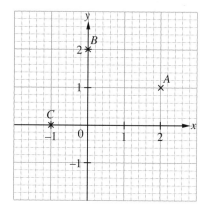

    (b) If the points above are the three corners of a square $ABCD$, mark the fourth corner and write down its coordinates.

7. If 7 kg of flour costs \$5.60,
    (a) what is the cost of 9 kg of flour?
    (b) how much flour can be bought with \$4.40?

8. Rewrite each of the following statements as an equation with a constant k.
    (a) c is directly proportional to d.
    (b) a is inversely proportional to b.

SECTION B

9. Expand the following.
    (a) $(a + 2)(3a + 4)$
    (b) $(2b + 3)(4b - 5)$
    (c) $(3c - 4)(5c - 6)$
    (d) $(a + 2b)(c - 3)$

10. Factorise the following.
    (a) $3uw - 4u + 6vw - 8v$
    (b) $3hx - 4kx - 6hy + 8ky$

11. Factorise the following.
  (a) $y^2 + 5y - 6$
  (b) $3b^2 - 25b + 28$

12. (a) A woman's age is five times her son's age. If the sum of their ages is 42 years, form an equation and find their ages.
  (b) A man's age is four times his daughter's age. How old is his daughter if he is presently 39 years older than her?

13. Using 1 cm to represent 1 unit on both axes, draw the graph of $y = 2x - 3$ for $-2 \leq x \leq 4$.
State the coordinates of the point where the graph cuts
  (a) the x-axis,
  (b) the y-axis.

14. (a) Find the gradient of the
    (i) line l,
    (ii) line m.

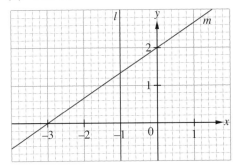

  (b) Draw the line joining the points $P(-1, -2)$ and $Q(-3, -5)$. Then, find its gradient.

15. If y is directly proportional to x, and $y = 15$ when $x = 3$,
  (a) find an equation, expressing y in terms of x,
  (b) find the value of y when $x = 9$,
  (c) find the value of x when $y = 10$.

16. (a) Write the scale 1 cm to 20 m in the form of $1 : n$, where n is a whole number.

  (b) A map has a scale of $1 : 500\ 000$. What length on the map represents a highway that is 40 km long?

SECTION C

17. Evaluate the following using the special result $a^2 - b^2 = (a + b)(a - b)$.
  (a) $8.1^2 - 1.9^2$
  (b) $\sqrt[3]{11.25^2 - 1.25^2}$
  (c) $\sqrt{\dfrac{20(60^2 - 40^2)}{25^2 - 15^2}}$

18. In a hostel, the rate for a room is $56 per week inclusive of weekends.
  (a) If two students shared a room for 30 days, how much would each of them have to pay?
  (b) If two students have $500 altogether,
    (i) form an inequality in d, where d represents the number of days they can afford to stay in the hostel.
    (ii) Hence, find the maximum number of days they can afford to stay in the hostel.

19. The amount, y, charged by a technician is given by the equation

$$y = 8x + 40$$

where x represents the number of hours he spent on repair work.
  (a) Draw the graph of $y = 8x + 40$ for $0 \leq x \leq 8$. Use a scale of 2 cm to represent 1 hour on the horizontal axis and 2 cm to represent $10 on the vertical axis.
  (b) Use your graph to find
    (i) the basic fee charged by the technician,
    (ii) the total charges for a repair lasting $2\dfrac{1}{4}$ hours,
    (iii) the time taken for a repair if the technician charged $93.50.

20. For each table, determine whether y is directly or inversely proportional to x, and if so, find an equation relating y and x.

(a)

x	3	5	6
y	18	30	42

(b)

x	3	5	6
y	20	12	10

(c)

x	3	5	6
y	21	35	42

Review Paper 2

SECTION A

1. **(a)** Expand the following.
   (i) $5(3b - 1)$
   (ii) $-5(4y - 3)$
   (b) Factorise the following.
   (i) $15c + 20$
   (ii) $-12x + 8$

2. **(a)** Expand the following.
   (i) $4(3b + 2c)$
   (ii) $-3x(2 - y)$
   (b) Factorise the following.
   (i) $9x - 6y$
   (ii) $-3x - 12xy$

3. **(a)** Expand the following.
   (i) $2c(3 + 4c)$
   (ii) $-3y(2y - 1)$
   (b) Factorise the following.
   (i) $6x^2 - 3x$
   (ii) $-27x^2 + 12$

4. Simplify the following inequalities.
   (a) $4p < -20$
   (b) $\dfrac{q}{3} > -12$
   (c) $\dfrac{3r}{5} \geq 3\dfrac{1}{5}$

5. A letter X is drawn by joining the points $(-1, -1)$ to $(3, 3)$ and $(-1, 3)$ to $(3, -1)$. By plotting the points on a piece of graph paper, form the required letter X and state the coordinates of the point where the two lines intersect each other.

6. Plot the points $A(-2, 2)$ and $B(3, -1)$ on a piece of graph paper. A and B are opposite corners of a rectangle with sides that are parallel to the axes. State the coordinates of the other two corners.

7. A car travels 280 km on 20 litres of petrol.
   (a) How far can it travel on 14 litres of petrol?
   (b) How much petrol is needed to travel 420 km?

8. If 10 soldiers can assemble a bridge in 3 hours,
   (a) how many soldiers are required to assemble the bridge in 2 hours,
   (b) how long would it take to assemble the bridge if 4 soldiers were injured and could not work?

SECTION B

9. Expand the following.
   (a) $(x - 5)(x + 10)$
   (b) $(2x - 3)(2x + 3)$
   (c) $(5x + 1)^2$
   (d) $(3x - 2y)^2$

10. Factorise the following.
    (a) $y^2 + 6y + 9$
    (b) $9y^2 - 6y + 1$
    (c) $4y^2 - 49$
    (d) $8m^2 - 10mn + 3n^2$

11. Simplify the following.
    (a) $\dfrac{(5p - 2q)(5p + 2q)}{4q} \times \dfrac{2}{3(5p + 2q)}$
    (b) $\dfrac{(w - 6)(w + 1)}{w + 6} \div \dfrac{2(w - 6)}{w + 6}$

12. Solve the following equations.
    (a) $\dfrac{w}{3} - \dfrac{w - 5}{8} = 5$
    (b) $\dfrac{13r - 8}{5} - \dfrac{2r - 1}{3} = 1$

13. Jasmine has $50. She can buy x number of hairclips at $3 each.
    (a) Form an inequality in x.
    (b) Solve the inequality and hence, find the maximum number of hairclips that Jasmine can buy.

14. **(a)** Find the gradient of the
       (i) line l,
       (ii) line m.

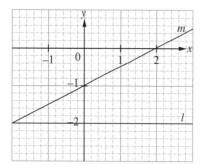

    (b) Draw the line joining the points $P(2, -6)$ and $Q(-5, 1)$. Then, find its gradient.

15. A length of 4 cm on a map represents a distance of 5 km on the ground.
    (a) What distance is represented by a length of 10 cm on the map?
    (b) What length on the map represents an actual distance of 1 500 m?

16. The wavelength (l m) of radio waves is inversely proportional to the frequency (f MHz).

The table below shows some radio stations with their wavelengths and frequencies.

Station	Wavelength (l m)	Frequency (f MHz)
TV mobile	3.36	89.30
Newsradio		93.80
BBC World Services	3.375	

    (a) Find the equation connecting l and f.
    (b) Using your equation, calculate

       (i) the wavelength of Newsradio,
      (ii) the frequency of BBC World Services.

SECTION C

17. **(a)** Factorise the following.
       (i) $18x^2 - 50y^2$
      (ii) $3a + 6 - 5ab - 10b$
    (b) Given that $x^2 + 4y^2 = 40$ and $xy = 6$, find the value of
       (i) $(x + 2y)^2$,
      (ii) $(x - 2y)^2$,
     (iii) $(x + 2y)(x - 2y)$.

18. **(a)** The sum of three odd consecutive numbers is 87. If the smallest number is x, form an equation in x and find the numbers.
    (b) Miss Teng, a school teacher, usually walks at a speed of 0.5 m/s for y km to reach her school on time. On one cloudy day, she decided to walk the y km at a faster speed of 1 m/s in case it rained. If she reached her school 5 minutes earlier than usual, calculate y.

19. A temperature that is measured in degrees Fahrenheit can be converted to degrees Celsius by using the following formula

$$C = \frac{5}{9}(F - 32)$$

where C is the temperature in degrees Celsius, and F is the temperature in degrees Fahrenheit.
    (a) Draw the graph of $C = \frac{5}{9}(F - 32)$ for $0 \leq F \leq 250$. Use a scale of 2 cm to represent 50 degrees Fahrenheit on the horizontal axis and 2 cm to represent 20 degrees Celsius on the vertical axis.
    (b) Use your graph to find the value of
       (i) F when $C = 0$,
      (ii) F when $C = 100$.

(c) Find the gradient of the graph.

(d) State briefly what this gradient represents.

20. **(a)** Write the following scales in the form of $1 : n$, where n is a whole number.
    (i) 4 cm represents 500 m
    (ii) 2 cm represents 5 km

(b) On a map with a scale of 1 : 500 000, the distance between Town *A* and Town *B* is 20 cm. What is the actual distance on the ground in km?

(c) On a map with a scale of 1 : 80 000, the area of Town *C* is 25 cm². Find, in km², the actual area of Town *C*.

Simultaneous Linear Equations

In primary school, you have learned how to solve problems of the type shown below using the model method. We can also solve problems of this type by translating the problem into a pair of simultaneous linear equations and then solving it algebraically.

The problem above, for example, can first be translated into the following pair of simultaneous linear equations and then solved algebraically:

$$3c + 4d = 50$$
$$2c + 3d = 36$$

where c is the cost of 1 chicken and d is the cost of 1 duck.

Simultaneous linear equations are used in many occupational fields to model the world around us. For example, a biologist may need to solve simultaneous linear equations to get an idea of how a population of animals may change over time. A chemical engineer working in an oil refinery may need to use simultaneous linear equations to help determine how much of each type of crude oil to use.

In this chapter, you will learn how to solve simultaneous linear equations using different methods as well as how to formulate simultaneous linear equations in two unknowns in order to solve word problems.

If we use the model method learned in primary school to solve the problem shown on the previous page, we have the following:

Recall problem on previous page:

3 chickens and 4 ducks cost $50.
2 chickens and 3 ducks cost $36.
Find the cost of 1 duck.

Model 1: | C | C | C | = 50
DDDD

Model 2: | C | C | = 36
DDD

Using **Model 1 – Model 2**, we have:

CCC − CC = 50 − 36
DDDD   DDD

⇒ | C | = 14
    D

Model 3: ∴ | C | C | = 2 × 14 = 28
              DD

Next, using **Model 2 – Model 3**, we have:

CC − CC = 36 − 28
DDD   DD

⇒ | D | = 8

Therefore, each duck costs $8.

We can also use algebraic methods to solve problems of the type shown above. Using these methods may be less tedious than using the model method in some cases. Let us now explore the concept of solving such problems algebraically.

Consider first the linear equation $x + y = 6$ which contains two unknowns. There are many pairs of values of x and y that will satisfy this equation as shown below.

For example, in $x + y = 6$,

$x = 5, y = 1$	gives	$5 + 1 = 6$
$x = 4, y = 2$	gives	$4 + 2 = 6$
$x = 2, y = 4$	gives	$2 + 4 = 6$
$x = -3, y = 9$	gives	$-3 + 9 = 6$
$x = 1\frac{1}{2}, y = 4\frac{1}{2}$	gives	$1\frac{1}{2} + 4\frac{1}{2} = 6$

and so on.

Therefore, a linear equation containing two unknowns will have infinitely many pairs of solutions for x and y.

Now consider another linear equation $x - y = 4$ which also contains two unknowns. Similarly, there are many pairs of values of x and y that will satisfy this equation.

For example, in $x - y = 4$,

$x = 5, y = 1$	gives	$5 - 1 = 4$
$x = 6, y = 2$	gives	$6 - 2 = 4$
$x = 7, y = 3$	gives	$7 - 3 = 4$
$x = -3, y = -7$	gives	$-3 - (-7) = 4$
$x = -\frac{1}{2}, y = -4\frac{1}{2}$	gives	$-\frac{1}{2} - \left(-4\frac{1}{2}\right) = 4$

and so on.

note

Doing two things 'simultaneously' means doing both of them at the same time. Thus, **solving simultaneous linear equations** means solving both equations at the same time to get a common solution.

What if we want to find the values of x and y that satisfy **both** $x + y = 6$ and $x - y = 4$? When we do this, we are said to be solving **simultaneous linear equations**.

From the above list of values of x and y, we can easily see that $x = 5$ and $y = 1$ satisfy both equations. Therefore, the solution for the simultaneous linear equations $x + y = 6$ and $x - y = 4$ is $x = 5$ and $y = 1$.

It is usually tedious to obtain the solution by listing possible values as what we have done above. In the following sections, we will learn about other ways of solving simultaneous linear equations using methods involving algebra and graphs.

5.2 Algebraic Method of Solving Simultaneous Linear Equations

There are two algebraic methods of solving simultaneous linear equations:

(a) substitution method
(b) elimination method

5.2.1 Substitution Method

The method of **substitution** is especially useful when at least one equation is given in the form '$y = \dots$' or '$x = \dots$'. We can then substitute the expression given on the right hand side directly into the other equation to obtain a linear equation in one unknown.

Example 1

Solve the simultaneous linear equations

$$y = 3x - 5,$$
$$y = 2x + 3.$$

Solution

$$y = 3x - 5 \dots\dots\dots\dots\dots (1)$$
$$y = 2x + 3 \dots\dots\dots\dots\dots (2)$$

Substitute y from (1) into (2):

$$y = 2x + 3$$
$$3x - 5 = 2x + 3$$

Substitute (1) into (2),
$$3x - 5 = 2x + 3$$
$$3x - 2x = 3 + 5$$
$$x = 8$$

We can also substitute $x = 8$ into (2) to get the answer for y.

Substitute $x = 8$ into (1),
$$y = 3(8) - 5$$
$$= 19$$

$\therefore$ the solution is $x = 8$ and $y = 19$.

note

If we substituted $x = 8$ into (2) earlier, we have to use (1) instead to check our answers.
If LHS $\neq$ RHS, the solution is wrong. Check your working again.

Check: Substitute $x = 8$ and $y = 19$ into (2),
$$\text{LHS} = y = 19$$
$$\text{RHS} = 2x + 3$$
$$= 2(8) + 3$$
$$= 19$$
$$\therefore \quad \text{LHS} = \text{RHS}$$

Example 2

Solve the simultaneous linear equations

$$2x + 3y = 4,$$
$$y = 3x + 5.$$

Solution

$$2x + 3y = 4 \quad\text{........................} \quad (1)$$
$$y = 3x + 5 \quad\text{..........................} \quad (2)$$

Substitute *(2)* into *(1)*,
$$2x + 3(3x + 5) = 4$$
$$2x + 9x + 15 = 4$$
$$11x = 4 - 15$$
$$= -11$$
$$x = -1$$

Substitute $x = -1$ into *(2)*,
$$y = 3(-1) + 5$$
$$= 2$$

$\therefore$ the solution is $x = -1$ and $y = 2$.

Check: Substitute $x = -1$ and $y = 2$ into *(1)*,
$$\text{LHS} = 2x + 3y$$
$$= 2(-1) + 3(2)$$
$$= 4$$
$$\text{RHS} = 4$$
$$\therefore \quad \text{LHS} = \text{RHS}$$

Example 3

Solve the simultaneous linear equations

$$2x = 5y - 1,$$
$$2x = 3y + 1.$$

Solution

$$2x = 5y - 1 \quad\text{........................} \quad (1)$$
$$2x = 3y + 1 \quad\text{........................} \quad (2)$$

Substitute $2x$ from *(1)* into *(2)*:
$$2x = 3y + 1$$
$$5y - 1 = 3y + 1$$

Substitute *(1)* into *(2)*,
$$5y - 1 = 3y + 1$$
$$5y - 3y = 1 + 1$$
$$2y = 2$$
$$y = 1$$

Substitute $y = 1$ into *(1)*,
$$2x = 5(1) - 1$$
$$= 4$$
$$x = 2$$

Remember to check your answers.

$\therefore$ the solution is $x = 2$ and $y = 1$.

Example 4

Solve the simultaneous linear equations

$$3x + 2y = 13,$$
$$2x + 3y = 12.$$

Solution

$$3x + 2y = 13 \dots\dots\dots\dots\dots\dots\dots (1)$$
$$2x + 3y = 12 \dots\dots\dots\dots\dots\dots\dots (2)$$

Manipulate *(1)* to make x alone on the left hand side of the equation.

From *(1)*,
$$3x = 13 - 2y$$
$$x = \frac{13 - 2y}{3} \dots\dots\dots\dots\dots\dots\dots (3)$$

Substitute *(3)* into *(2)*,

$$2\left(\frac{13 - 2y}{3}\right) + 3y = 12$$
$$\frac{26 - 4y}{3} + 3y = 12$$
$$26 - 4y + 9y = 36$$
$$5y = 36 - 26$$
$$= 10$$
$$y = 2$$

note

Alternatively, we can substitute $y = 2$ into *(1)* or *(2)* to obtain the same answer for x.

We cannot check the answer by substituting the solution into *(1)* as *(1)* and *(3)* are essentially the same equation.

Substitute $y = 2$ into *(3)*,

$$x = \frac{13 - 2(2)}{3}$$
$$= 3$$

$\therefore$ the solution is $x = 3$ and $y = 2$.

1. Use the substitution method to solve the following pairs of simultaneous linear equations.

   (a) $y = 2x + 1$
   $y = x - 1$

   (b) $x = 3y - 1$
   $x = 2y + 1$

   (c) $3x + 4y = 11$
   $y = 9 - 2x$

   (d) $y = 3 - 4x$
   $6x - 5y = -2$

   (e) $2x = 3y + 4$
   $2x = 5y + 8$

   (f) $3y = 2x + 1$
   $3y = 3x + 4$

   (g) $3x - 4y = 2$
   $3x = 7y - 1$

   (h) $5y - 3x = 2$
   $5y = 8x - 3$

2. Use the substitution method to solve the following pairs of simultaneous linear equations.

   (a) $5x + 2y = -1$
   $x - 3y = -7$

   (b) $3x + 7y = 4$
   $2x + y = -1$

   (c) $4x + 5y = 1$
   $4x - y = -5$

   (d) $5y + 3x = 20$
   $-x + 6y = 24$

   (e) $5y - 7 = 3x$
   $5y - 17x = -7$

   (f) $7x - 2y = 8$
   $3y + 7x = 23$

3. Use the substitution method to solve the following pairs of simultaneous linear equations.

   (a) $2x + 3y = -3$
   $3x - 4y = 4$

   (b) $5x + 4y = 5$
   $7x - 3y = 50$

   (c) $2x + 2y = 3$
   $8x - 3y = 1$

   (d) $5x = 1 + 4y$
   $2y = 1 + 4x$

   (e) $3x + 2y = -10$
   $4x + 9y = -7$

   (f) $5x - 4y = 35$
   $6y + 13x = 9$

   (g) $2x - 3y = 7$
   $5x - 7y = 18$

   (h) $2x + \dfrac{1}{2}y = 16$
   $3x - 2y = 13$

Spot the Mistakes

Anthony was given a pair of simultaneous linear equations to solve.

$y = x - 1$ .... (1)
$2x - 3y = 4$ .... (2)

His solution is shown below.

Substitute (1) into (2),
$$2x - 3(x - 1) = 4$$
$$2x - 3x - 3 = 4$$
$$-x = 4 + 3$$
$$x = -7$$

Substitute $x = -7$ into (1),
$$y = -7 - 1$$
$$= -8$$

∴ the solution is $x = -7$ and $y = -8$.

Check: Substitute $x = -7$ and $y = -8$ into **(1)**,

$$\text{LHS} = y = -8$$
$$\text{RHS} = x - 1$$
$$= -7 - 1$$
$$= -8$$
$$\therefore \quad \text{LHS} = \text{RHS}$$

Anthony was happy that he has found the solution and he has checked to ensure that his solution is correct. However, his teacher said that Anthony's solution and method of checking is wrong.

Discuss with your classmates and explain in your Mathematics Journal why Anthony's solution is wrong. How would you advise Anthony to check his solution?

5.2.2 Elimination Method

We have seen how we can use the substitution method to solve a pair of simultaneous linear equations. In this section, we will learn about the **elimination** method. Sometimes, it is more convenient to use the elimination method to solve a pair of simultaneous linear equations as compared to using the substitution method.

To use this method, we either add or subtract the two equations to eliminate one of the unknowns and obtain an equation in only one unknown.

Example 5

Solve the simultaneous linear equations

$$2x + y = 5,$$
$$5x - y = 9.$$

Solution

$$2x + y = 5 \quad \dots\dots\dots\dots\dots\dots \textbf{(1)}$$
$$5x - y = 9 \quad \dots\dots\dots\dots\dots\dots \textbf{(2)}$$

Adding the LHS of **(1)** and the LHS of **(2)** eliminates the terms in y, leaving only one unknown, i.e., x.

(1) + (2),
$$(2x + y) + (5x - y) = 5 + 9$$
$$7x = 14 \quad \longleftarrow \quad y \text{ is eliminated}$$
$$x = 2$$

Substitute $x = 2$ into **(1)**,

$$2(2) + y = 5$$
$$4 + y = 5$$
$$y = 5 - 4$$
$$= 1$$

$\therefore$ the solution is $x = 2$ and $y = 1$.

Check: Substitute $x = 2$ and $y = 1$ into **(2)**,

$$\text{LHS} = 5x - y$$
$$= 5(2) - 1$$
$$= 9$$
$$\text{RHS} = 9$$
$$\therefore \quad \text{LHS} = \text{RHS}$$

Example 6

Solve the simultaneous linear equations

$$x + y = 0,$$
$$x - 2y = -6.$$

Solution

$$x + y = 0 \quad \text{................................} \quad \textbf{(1)}$$
$$x - 2y = -6 \quad \text{.............................} \quad \textbf{(2)}$$

Eliminate x by subtracting each side of **(2)** from the respective sides of **(1)**. Alternatively, we can subtract **(1)** from **(2)** to eliminate x.

(1) − (2),

$$(x + y) - (x - 2y) = 0 - (-6)$$
$$x + y - x + 2y = 0 + 6$$
$$3y = 6 \quad \longleftarrow \quad x \text{ is eliminated}$$
$$y = 2$$

Substitute $y = 2$ into **(1)**,

$$x + 2 = 0$$
$$x = 0 - 2$$
$$= -2$$

$\therefore$ the solution is $x = -2$ and $y = 2$.

Check: Substitute $x = -2$ and $y = 2$ into **(2)**,

$$\text{LHS} = x - 2y$$
$$= -2 - 2(2)$$
$$= -6$$
$$\text{RHS} = -6$$
$$\therefore \quad \text{LHS} = \text{RHS}$$

Example 7

Solve the simultaneous linear equations

$$2x + y = -1,$$
$$3x - 4y = 4.$$

Solution

$$2x + y = -1 \quad\text{.............................. } (1)$$
$$3x - 4y = 4 \quad\text{.............................. } (2)$$

We multiply (1) by 4 to obtain the same numerical coefficient of y (disregard the sign) as in (2).

(1) × 4,
$$(2x + y) \times 4 = (-1) \times 4$$
$$8x + 4y = -4 \quad\text{.....................}(3)$$

Add (2) and (3) to eliminate y.

(2) + (3),
$$(3x - 4y) + (8x + 4y) = 4 + (-4)$$
$$11x = 0$$
$$x = 0$$

Substitute $x = 0$ into (1),
$$2(0) + y = -1$$
$$y = -1$$

Remember to check your answers.

$\therefore$ the solution is $x = 0$ and $y = -1$.

> In the above example, you may wish to eliminate x instead of y. In this case, to obtain the same coefficient of x in both equations, we have to multiply (1) by 3 and (2) by 2 to obtain a common coefficient of 6. Which is easier to eliminate in the above example, x or y?

Test your understanding of solving simultaneous linear equations at http://www.quia.com/pp/11581.html. You will be in for a surprise!

Example 8

Solve the simultaneous linear equations

$$5x - 4y = 2,$$
$$2x + 3y = 10.$$

Solution

$$5x - 4y = 2 \quad\text{.............................. } (1)$$
$$2x + 3y = 10 \quad\text{........................... } (2)$$

We multiply (1) by 3 and (2) by 4 so that the numerical coefficients of y (disregard the sign) are the same. The L.C.M. of 4 and 3 is 12.

(1) × 3,
$$15x - 12y = 6 \quad\text{.........................}(3)$$

(2) × 4,
$$8x + 12y = 40 \quad\text{.........................}(4)$$

(3) + (4),
$$(15x - 12y) + (8x + 12y) = 6 + 40$$
$$23x = 46$$
$$x = 2$$

Substitute $x = 2$ into **(1)**,
$$5(2) - 4y = 2$$
$$10 - 4y = 2$$
$$-4y = 2 - 10$$
$$-4y = -8$$
$$y = \frac{-8}{-4}$$
$$= 2$$

$\therefore$ the solution is $x = 2$ and $y = 2$.

Exercise 5B

1. Use the elimination method to solve the following pairs of simultaneous linear equations.

   (a) $x + y = 3$
   $x - y = 1$

   (b) $2a + b = 8$
   $3a - b = 17$

   (c) $4p + 2q = 24$
   $p - 2q = 1$

   (d) $x + y = -1$
   $3x + y = 1$

   (e) $f - 2g = 5$
   $3f - 2g = 3$

   (f) $2c - 3d = 11$
   $7c - 3d = 1$

2. Use the elimination method to solve the following pairs of simultaneous linear equations.

   (a) $5x - 2y = 11$
   $x + y = 5$

   (b) $4p - q = -2$
   $3p + 2q = -7$

   (c) $4e + 3f = 9$
   $e + f = 2$

   (d) $2r + 7s = 26$
   $r + s = 3$

   (e) $2j - 3k = 3$
   $3j - k = -13$

   (f) $7w - v = -29$
   $2w - 3v = -11$

3. Use the elimination method to solve the following pairs of simultaneous linear equations.

   (a) $4a + 3b = 0$
   $7a - 2b = -29$

   (b) $2c - 5d = 21$
   $7c + 3d = 12$

   (c) $3x + 2y = 6$
   $5x + 3y = 11$

   (d) $5x - 4y = -1$
   $2x - 3y = 1$

   (e) $3x - 8y = 5$
   $4x + 5y = 38$

   (f) $7x + 2y = 3$
   $2x - 9y = -47$

4. Use the elimination method to solve the following pairs of simultaneous linear equations.

   (a) $-3c + 4d = 4$
   $9c - 2d = 3$

   (b) $2m + 3n = -2$
   $8m - 9n = -1$

   (c) $x + \frac{1}{2}y = 4$
   $\frac{1}{2}x - \frac{1}{2}y = \frac{1}{2}$

   (d) $\frac{x}{2} + \frac{y}{3} = 3$
   $\frac{x}{4} + \frac{2y}{3} = 3$

5. Use a **suitable method** to solve the following pairs of simultaneous linear equations.

   (a) $5a - 3b = 6$
   $5a - 4b = 8$

   (b) $c + d = \frac{1}{2}$
   $c - d = \frac{1}{4}$

   (c) $2e - 4f = 9$
   $2e - 2f = 5$

   (d) $x + 2y = 5$
   $3x + 4y = 11$

   (e) $3x + 4y = -14$
   $x - 3y = 17$

   (f) $3x + 2y = 10$
   $x - y = 2.5$

   (g) $3x + 2y = 5$
   $2x - 3y = 12$

   (h) $3x - 2y = 0$
   $2x + 3y = 13$

   (i) $2x + 3y = 19$
   $5x + 2y = -2$

   (j) $3x - 4y = 2$
   $2x - 6y = -7$

Graphical Method of Solving Simultaneous Linear Equations

5.3

We have seen how we can use the two basic algebraic methods to solve simultaneous linear equations. What is the significance of the solution of a pair of simultaneous linear equations?

To find out, let us draw the **graphs** of the two equations in Example 7 on the same Cartesian plane. The pair of simultaneous linear equations in Example 7 are $2x + y = -1$ and $3x - 4y = 4$.

For the equation $2x + y = -1$, when $x = -2$,

$$2x + y = -1$$
$$2(-2) + y = -1$$
$$y = = -1 + 4$$
$$\therefore \quad y = 3$$
$$\Rightarrow (-2, 3)$$

Continuing in this way for $x = 0$ and $x = 2$, we will get the points $(0, -1)$ and $(2, -5)$. Hence, the table of values for **$2x + y = -1$** is:

x	−2	0	2
y	3	−1	−5

> **note**
> Plotting any two points is sufficient to draw a straight line graph. However, we plot a third point as a check to make sure that there is no error.

Similarly, by substituting $x = -2$, 0 and 2 into the equation **$3x - 4y = 4$**, we will get the following table of values:

x	−2	0	2
y	−2.5	−1	0.5

Alternatively, for each of the above equations, we can express y in terms of x first and then use this equation to directly calculate the values of y. For example, for the equation $3x - 4y = 4$,

$$3x - 4y = 4$$
$$3x - 4 = 4y$$
$$\frac{3x - 4}{4} = y$$
$$\therefore \quad y = \frac{3}{4}x - 1$$

If the same values of x are chosen, the table of values for $y = \frac{3}{4}x - 1$ will be the same as that for $3x - 4y = 4$.

Next, plot the points in the table of values and draw the lines on a piece of graph paper as shown below.

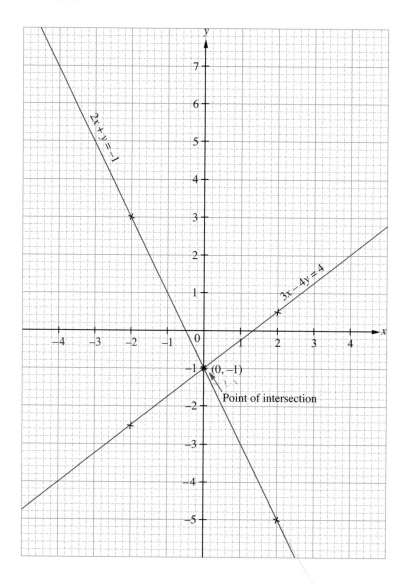

Notice that the two lines intersect at the point $(0, -1)$. The solution we obtained using the algebraic method in Example 7 was $x = 0$ and $y = -1$.

> The **point of intersection** of the two graphs representing the pair of simultaneous linear equations is its **solution**.

Example 9

Solve the following pair of simultaneous equations using the graphical method.

$$x - y = 2$$
$$2x + y = 10$$

Solution

Table of values for **x − y = 2**:

x	−2	0	2
y	−4	−2	0

Table of values for **2x + y = 10**:

x	−2	0	2
y	14	10	6

Drawing the two graphs on a piece of graph paper, we get:

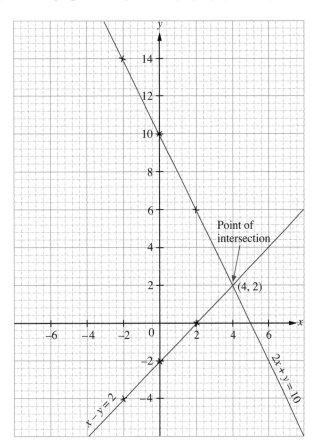

note

Substitute the solution into both linear equations to check your answer, similar to what you have done in Section 5.2.

From the graph, the coordinates of the point of intersection are (4, 2). Therefore, the solution is $x = 4$ and $y = 2$.

1. Solve the following pairs of simultaneous linear equations graphically.

   (a) $y = x - 2$
   $y = -2x + 4$

   (b) $y = 3x - 1$
   $y = 2x + 1$

   (c) $y = 3x$
   $y = x - 6$

   (d) $y = -2x$
   $y = -x + 5$

   (e) $y = \dfrac{5}{2}x$
   $y = 6x + 7$

   (f) $y = -\dfrac{1}{2}x + 3$
   $y = \dfrac{3}{2}x + 1$

2. Find the solutions to the following pairs of simultaneous linear equations by drawing their graphs.

   (a) $y = x - 4$
   $x + y = 6$

   (b) $y = x - 2$
   $3x + y = 6$

   (c) $x + y = 2$
   $2x - y = -5$

   (d) $x + y = 4$
   $4x - y = 1$

   (e) $x = 3$
   $x - y = 5$

   (f) $y = 5$
   $3x + y = -4$

   (g) $2x - y = 3$
   $3x + 2y = 1$

   (h) $x - 2y = -1$
   $x - y = -2$

TIME-OUT ACTIVITY

Comparing the Graphical Method and the Algebraic Method

Let us try to use both the graphical method and the algebraic method to solve the following simultaneous linear equations:

$$x + 4y = 14$$
$$2x + y = 4$$

(a) Firstly, draw the graphs for the above equations for $-2 \le x \le 2$.

(b) Then, use your graphs to solve the simultaneous linear equations. What is your solution?

(c) Now, use either the substitution method or the elimination method to solve the same pair of simultaneous linear equations. Compare your solution with the one obtained in **(b)**. Are the solutions the same?

 (d) Discuss with your classmates and explain in your Mathematics Journal what you can conclude from this activity. Is there any difference between using the graphical method and the algebraic method?

No Solution and Infinitely Many Solutions

Activity

To study cases of simultaneous linear equations with no solution and infinitely many solutions.

1. **(a)** Try solving the following simultaneous linear equations using either the substitution or the elimination method.

    $$x + y = 3$$
    $$x + y = 6$$

    What do you notice?

    (b) Next, draw the graphs of the two equations above on the same Cartesian plane. Which one of the three graphs below is the correct graph? Do the lines intersect each other?

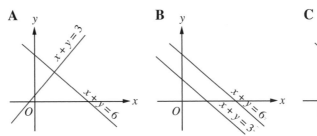

2. **(a)** Now, try solving this pair of simultaneous linear equations algebraically.

    $$x - 2y = 2$$
    $$y = \frac{1}{2}x - 1$$

    What do you notice?

    (b) Next, draw the two lines on the same Cartesian plane. Which one of the three graphs below is the correct graph? How many points of intersections are there?

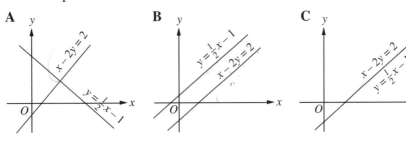

Most pairs of simultaneous linear equations have only one solution each. This can be shown by the single point of intersection when the graphs of the two equations are drawn.

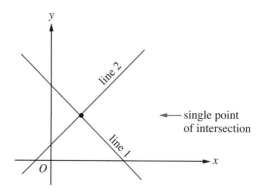

In Question 1 of the activity on the previous page, we notice that the pair of simultaneous linear equations have **no solution**. This can be seen graphically as the two lines representing the equations are parallel and thus **do not intersect**.

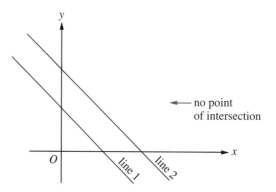

In Question 2 of the activity, we can see an example of a pair of simultaneous linear equations that have **infinitely many solutions** (countless solutions). This can be seen graphically as the two lines representing the equations **overlap each other completely**.

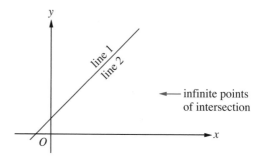

Problem Solving Using Simultaneous Linear Equations

Many problems in everyday life involve more than one unknown quantity. Simultaneous equations can often be used to find the required values of these quantities. In this section, problems involving two unknowns will be discussed.

In such problems, firstly, the **unknown quantities** must be given appropriate letters to represent **variables**. The given information is then translated into **equations**. If there are two unknowns, there must be at least two pieces of information leading to two equations before the problem can be solved.

Example 10

The sum of two numbers is 20 and their difference is 2. Find the numbers.

Solution

Let the larger number be x and the smaller number be y.

The sum of the two numbers is 20.

i.e. $x + y = 20$ ....**(1)**

The difference of the numbers is 2.

We write $x - y = 2$ and not $y - x = 2$ as $x > y$.

i.e. $x - y = 2$ ....**(2)**

(1) + (2),
$$(x + y) + (x - y) = 20 + 2$$
$$2x = 22$$
$$x = 11$$

> **note**
> The solutions must be translated back into the context of the original question and a final statement must be written to answer the question.

Substitute $x = 11$ into **(1)**,
$$11 + y = 20$$
$$y = 9$$

Therefore, the numbers are 11 and 9.

Example 11

The total cost of the tickets to a show for 2 adults and 3 children is $16 while the cost for 3 adults and 2 children is $19. Find the cost of an adult's ticket and that of a child's ticket.

Solution

Let the cost of an adult's ticket be a and that of a child's ticket be c.

$$2a + 3c = 16 .... (1)$$
$$3a + 2c = 19 .... (2)$$

$(1) \times 2,$ $4a + 6c = 32 .... (3)$
$(2) \times 3,$ $9a + 6c = 57 .... (4)$

$(4) - (3),$ $5a = 25$
                        $a = 5$

Remember to check your answer. You can do this by substituting the solution into (2).

Substitute $a = 5$ into $(1),$
$$2(5) + 3c = 16$$
$$10 + 3c = 16$$
$$3c = 6$$
$$c = 2$$

Therefore, an adult's ticket costs $5 and a child's ticket costs $2.

Example 12

Five years ago, Mrs Wen was three times as old as her son, Shaohong. Five years from now, Mrs Wen's age will be twice her son's age. Find their present ages.

Solution

Let Mrs Wen's present age be x years and Shaohong's present age be y years.

Five years ago:
Mrs Wen's age was $(x - 5)$ years
and Shaohong's age was $(y - 5)$ years.
$$\therefore \quad x - 5 = 3(y - 5)$$
$$= 3y - 15$$
$$x = 3y - 10 .... (1)$$

Five years from now:

Mrs Wen's age will be $(x + 5)$ years

and Shaohong's age will be $(y + 5)$ years.

$$\therefore \quad x + 5 = 2(y + 5)$$
$$= 2y + 10$$
$$x = 2y + 5 \dots\dots\dots\dots\dots(2)$$

Substitute (1) into (2),

$$3y - 10 = 2y + 5$$
$$3y - 2y = 5 + 10$$
$$y = 15$$

Substitute $y = 15$ into (2),

$$x = 2(15) + 5$$
$$= 30 + 5$$
$$= 35$$

Therefore, Mrs Wen's present age is 35 years and Shaohong's present age is 15 years.

Exercise 5D

1. The sum of two numbers is 15 and their difference is 1. Find the numbers.

2. The sum of two numbers is 7. The difference between two times the larger number and the smaller one is 5. Find the two numbers.

3. Sam's Science mark is 15 less than his Maths mark. The total of his two marks is 145. Find Sam's mark for each subject.

4. The length of a rectangular label is 2 cm more than its width. If the perimeter of the label is 68 cm, find the length and the width.

5. The cost of 3 English books and 4 Maths books is $78 while the cost of 2 English books and 3 Maths books is $56. Find the cost of an English book and that of a Maths book.

6. In a farm, there are some cows and some chickens. If the animals have a total of 35 heads and 96 legs, how many cows and chickens are there respectively?

7. Four years ago, Ahmad was three times as old as Weihui. Four years from now, Ahmad will be only twice as old as Weihui. Find their present ages.

8. Five years ago, Ganesh was four times as old as his grandson, Ajit. Five years from now, Ganesh will be three times as old as Ajit. Find their present ages.

9. *ABC* is an equilateral triangle.

   (a) Find the values of *x* and *y*.

   (b) Hence, find its perimeter.

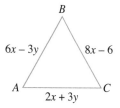

10. A shirt costs $*s* and a pair of trousers costs $*t*.

It is given that $2s + t = 115$.

   (a) Given also that three shirts and two pairs of trousers cost a total of $200, write a second equation in *s* and *t*.

   (b) Solve the two simultaneous equations to find the value of *s* and the value of *t*.

                                  [N/92/P2]

TIME-OUT ACTIVITY

A Heavy Load

A pony and a donkey were carrying some bundles of cloth for a cloth merchant. On the way, the donkey said to the pony, "If I give you one bundle, my load will be half of yours." In an angry mood, the pony retorted, "Why don't you take one bundle from me, then my load will be half of yours!"

Assuming that the bundles are of equal weight, how many bundles did the pony and the donkey each carry?

SUMMARY

1. The pair of numbers which satisfy a pair of simultaneous linear equations is called the solution of the equations.

2. The two algebraic methods commonly used in solving simultaneous linear equations are
   (a) the substitution method,
   (b) the elimination method.

3. The graphical method can also be used to solve simultaneous linear equations. The point of intersection of the two lines representing the pair of equations is its solution.

A Business Graph

Chong Ming plans to set up a stall selling T-shirts during a special fair at the community centre near his home. The stall rental is fixed at $100 per day. Each T-shirt costs him $5 and he intends to sell each for $8. It is assumed that Chong Ming is able to sell off all the T-shirts he had bought.

The graph below shows the relationship between Chong Ming's total expenses and the number of T-shirts he buys.

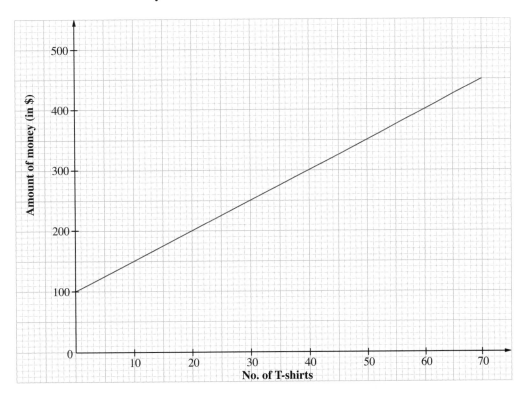

(a) By letting the total expenses be Y and the number of T-shirts bought by Chong Ming be X, show that the equation represented by the above graph is

$$Y = 5X + 100$$

(b) By letting the revenue from the sales of T-shirts be y and the number of T-shirts sold by Chong Ming be x, form another equation that relates the revenue and the number of T-shirts sold.

(c) Copy the above graph on a graph paper. Then, draw the line that represents the equation in **(b)** on the same axes.

(d) Deduce the minimum number of T-shirts that he must sell in order to break even.

(e) Deduce the number of T-shirts he must sell in order to earn a profit of $140. (Profit = revenue − expenses)

You have 10 minutes to answer the following questions.
Choose the most appropriate answer.

5.1 **1.** Which one of the following satisfies both linear equations $2x + y = 5$ and $x - y = -2$?

   A $x = 0, y = 5$ **B** $x = 2, y = 4$

   C $x = 1, y = 3$ **D** $x = 5, y = 3$

5.2 **2.** Use the substitution method to solve the simultaneous linear equations

$$x + 2y = 4,$$
$$x = 2y.$$

   A $x = 0, y = 2$ **B** $x = 4, y = 2$

   C $x = 2, y = 1$ **D** $x = 1, y = 2$

5.2 **3.** Use the elimination method to solve the simultaneous linear equations

$$3x + 2y = 10,$$
$$5x - 2y = 6.$$

   A $x = 2, y = -2$ **B** $x = 2, y = 2$

   C $x = 4, y = -2$ **D** $x = -2, y = 8$

5.2 **4.** Solve the simultaneous linear equations

$$2y = x + 3,$$
$$y = x + 2.$$

   A $x = -1, y = 1$ **B** $x = 1, y = 3$

   C $x = 1, y = 2$ **D** $x = 1, y = -1$

5.2/5.3 **5.** Which is the most suitable method to solve the following simultaneous linear equations?

$$x = 5 - 2y$$
$$3x - y = -1$$

   A   Substitution method   **B**   Elimination method

   C   Graphical method   **D**   Trial and error

5.3/5.4   **6.**   Which of the following statements is true about the graphs that represent the simultaneous linear equations $x + y = 4$ and $x - y = 2$?
A   The graphs intersect at one point to give only one solution.
B   The graphs intersect at two points to give two solutions.
C   The graphs do not intersect and thus the equations have no solution.
D   The graphs overlap completely to give an infinite number of solutions.

5.3/5.4   **7.**   Which of the following statements is true about the graphs that represent the simultaneous linear equations $x + y = 1$ and $x + y = 5$?
A   The graphs intersect at one point to give only one solution.
B   The graphs intersect at two points to give two solutions.
C   The graphs do not intersect and thus the equations have no solution.
D   The graphs overlap completely to give an infinite number of solutions.

5.3/5.4   **8.**   Which of the following statements is true about the graphs that represent simultaneous linear equations $x + 2y = 4$ and $2x + 4y = 8$?
A   The graphs intersect at one point to give only one solution.
B   The graphs intersect at two points to give two solutions.
C   The graphs do not intersect and thus the equations have no solution.
D   The graphs overlap completely to give an infinite number of solutions.

5.5   **9.**   The sum of two numbers is 16. The difference between three times the larger number and the smaller one is 20. Find the two numbers.
A   −1, 17   B   2, 14
C   7, 9   D   18, −2

5.5   **10.**   The cost of 3 pens and 4 pencils is $5 while the cost of 2 pens and 2 pencils is $3. What is the cost of a pen?
A $0.50   B $1.00
C $1.50   D $2.00

SECTION A

1. Solve the simultaneous linear equations
$$5y = 3x + 4,$$
$$5y = 4x - 3.$$

2. Solve the simultaneous linear equations
$$3x + 4y = 5,$$
$$y = x - 4.$$

3. Solve the simultaneous linear equations
$$x + y = 4,$$
$$x - y = -2.$$

4. Solve the simultaneous linear equations
$$3x + y = 22,$$
$$2x + y = 17.$$

SECTION B

5. Solve the simultaneous linear equations
$$5x + 2y = 16,$$
$$7x - 3y = 5.$$

6. The sum of two numbers is 30 and their difference is 4. Form a pair of simultaneous linear equations and find the numbers.

7. 6 kg of mutton and 1 chicken cost $60 while 8 kg of mutton and 5 chickens cost $124. Find the cost of 1 kg of mutton and 1 chicken respectively.

8. (a) Copy and complete the table of values for $y = 4x - 3$ and $y = -2x + 3$.
   (i) Table of values for $y = 4x - 3$:

x	0	2	4
y	-3		

   (ii) Table of values for $y = -2x + 3$:

x	0	2	4
y		-1	

   (b) Using a scale of 2 cm to represent 1 unit on the x-axis and 1 cm to represent 1 unit on the y-axis, draw the graphs of $y = 4x - 3$ and $y = -2x + 3$ for $0 \le x \le 4$.

   (c) Use your graphs to solve the simultaneous linear equations
$$y = 4x - 3,$$
$$y = -2x + 3.$$

SECTION C

9. Two years ago, Liza was three times as old as Petrina. Three years from now, Liza will only be twice as old as Petrina. Form a pair of simultaneous equations and find their present ages.

10. $ABCD$ is a rectangle.

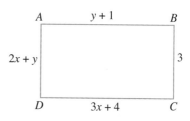

   (a) Find the values of x and y.
   (b) Hence, find the area of the rectangle.

6

Triangles, Polygons and Congruence

DISCOVER !

How to:

- construct simple geometrical figures

- classify triangles and special quadrilaterals according to their properties

- apply properties of triangles and special quadrilaterals to calculate unknown angles

- construct various types of triangles and quadrilaterals

- find the angle sum of the interior and exterior angles of any convex polygon

- recognise congruent figures

- match sides and angles of two congruent polygons

Take a look at the design of buildings around you. Are they always rectangular or round? Can you find buildings that take the form of other shapes?

Dear, look at that octagonal building! It's so interesting! Let's take some photos of it!

No time for that, dear! Our tour group's leaving for the airport in 1 minute's time!

The tall building shown in the picture above is in the form of an octagon which is an eight-sided plane figure. Octagons belong to a group of geometric figures called polygons. Polygons, by definition, are plane figures that have three or more line segments as their sides. They are named according to the number of sides that they have; triangles being the simplest type of polygons. Eight-sided polygons are thus named 'octagons' as the prefix 'octa' stands for eight. Octagons are especially favoured by the Chinese in the design of buildings. Do you know why?

In this chapter, you will learn more about different types of polygons and their properties.

6.1.1   Angle Bisectors

In Book 1, we have seen how an **angle** is formed when two line segments or rays meet at a point. An additional line segment or ray can be drawn to **bisect an angle** (i.e., divide an angle into two equal parts). Let us explore how we can bisect any angle using a pair of compasses and a ruler.

Activity

> *To bisect an angle using a pair of compasses and a ruler and to explore its properties.*

Step	Action

1   Construct an acute angle and label it as $\angle ABC$.

2   With the compass point at vertex B and a suitable radius, draw an arc to cut the two rays of the angle. Label these points as P and Q.

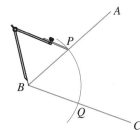

> **note**
>
> An **arc** is a part of the circumference of a circle.
>
>

3   Next, draw two more arcs with the same radius, using P and Q as the centres as shown in the diagrams below. Label the point where the two arcs intersect as M.

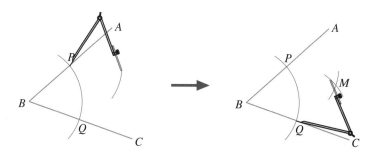

> **note**
>
> Use a sharp pencil to do any construction and to draw lines. All construction lines and arcs must be clearly and neatly shown and must not be erased away.

4   Join BM.

5   Use a protractor to measure $\angle ABM$ and $\angle CBM$. Are the two angles equal?

6   Repeat steps 1–5 with an obtuse angle.

From the activity on the previous page, we can see the following:

$$\angle ABM = \angle CBM = \frac{1}{2}\angle ABC.$$

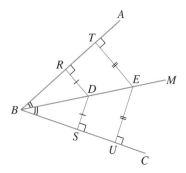

We can thus say that the line BM bisects $\angle ABC$. We call this line the **angle bisector** of $\angle ABC$.

Notice also, from the diagram shown below, that if we mark a point D on the angle bisector and draw a perpendicular line from point D to each of the arms of the angle and label them R and S respectively, then $DR = DS$.

The same can be observed if we take another point E on the angle bisector. In this case, $ET = EU$, as can be seen on the diagram shown above. We say that the points D and E are equidistant from the arms of the angle.

Try this with the diagram that you have drawn in the previous activity. Does this hold true for any point on the angle bisector?

In general,

1. The **angle bisector** of an angle is the line segment or ray that bisects the angle.
2. We can construct an angle bisector using a pair of compasses and a ruler.
3. Any point on the angle bisector of an angle is **equidistant** from the arms of the angle.

6.1.2 Perpendicular Bisectors

We have just learned how to bisect an angle using a pair of compasses and a ruler. We can also use a pair of compasses and a ruler to bisect a line segment.

Activity

> **To bisect a line segment using a pair of compasses and a ruler and to explore its properties.**

Step   Action

1   Draw a line and label its end-points *A* and *B* respectively. (The line segment that you draw should preferably be at least 4 cm long.)

2   With *A* as the centre and a radius that is slightly more than half of the length of the line *AB*, draw an arc as shown in the diagram below.

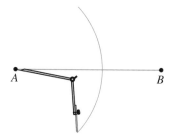

3   With *B* as the centre and the same radius as in step 2, draw an arc to intersect the first arc at two points. Label these points as *P* and *Q*.

4   Join *PQ* and label the point where *PQ* cuts *AB* as *M*.

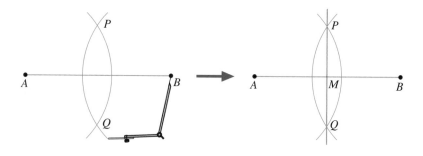

5   Measure *AM* and *MB*. Are the line segments *AM* and *MB* of the same length?

6   Use a protractor to measure ∠*AMP* and ∠*BMP*. What can you say about ∠*AMP* and ∠*BMP*?

From the activity on the previous page, we can see the following:

$$AM = MB = \frac{1}{2} AB$$
$$\angle AMP = \angle BMP = 90°$$

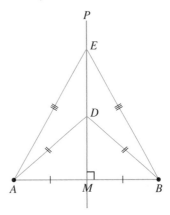

We can thus say that the line PQ bisects the line AB at right angles. We call this line the **perpendicular bisector** of the line AB.

Notice also, from the diagram shown below, that if we mark a point D on the perpendicular bisector and draw a line from it to each of the end-points of the line segment AB, then $AD = BD$.

The same can be observed if we take another point E on the perpendicular bisector. In this case, $AE = BE$ as can be seen on the diagram shown above. We say that the points D and E are equidistant from the two end-points of the line segment.

Try this with the diagram that you have drawn in the previous activity. Does this hold true for any point on the perpendicular bisector?

In general,

1. The **perpendicular bisector** of a line segment is the line that bisects the line segment and is perpendicular to it.
2. We can construct a perpendicular bisector using a pair of compasses and a ruler.
3. Any point on the perpendicular bisector of a line segment is **equidistant** from the two end-points of the line segment.

Construct Us!

You have learned how an angle bisector and a perpendicular bisector can each be constructed using a pair of compasses and a ruler. Try constructing each of them in another way. (For example, try using a protractor and a ruler instead to construct them. You can also try using the GSP software to do this.) Explain the method you use and the steps in detail in your Mathematics Journal.

Exercise 6A

1. **(a)** Use a protractor to draw angles of following sizes.
   (i) 45°   **(ii)** 120°
   (b) Bisect each angle using only a pair of compasses and a ruler. Check the angles in the two halves with a protractor.

2. **(a)** Draw the reflex angle *PQR* given below.

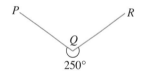

250°

(b) Construct its angle bisector using a pair of compasses and a ruler. Check the angles in the two halves with a protractor.

3. **(a)** Draw lines of the following lengths.
   (i) 8 cm   **(ii)** 10.4 cm
   (b) Bisect each line using only a pair of compasses and ruler. Check the lengths of the two halves.

6.2 Triangles and Their Properties

6.2.1 Types of Triangles

As you have learned before, a **triangle** is a closed plane figure with three sides.

Look at the triangle shown on the right. The points *A*, *B* and *C* are called the **vertices** (singular: **vertex**) of the triangle.

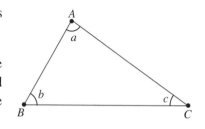

We can refer to the given triangle as triangle *ABC* or △*ABC* where '△' stands for 'triangle'.

The angles, *a*, *b* and *c*, which lie inside the triangle *ABC* are known as its **interior angles**.

Triangles can be classified according to the lengths of their sides or the sizes of their angles.

Classifying by sides:

1. A triangle with all sides of equal length is known as an **equilateral triangle**. All its angles are equal.

2. A triangle with two sides of equal length is known as an **isosceles triangle**. Its base angles, which are the two angles opposite the equal sides, are equal.

3. A triangle with all sides of different lengths is known as a **scalene triangle**. All its angles are different.

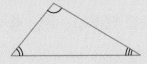

We have seen that we can identify the different types of triangles by measuring the lengths of their sides. In some triangles, however, the sides are already marked with the following symbols: ⊢, ⊬ or ⊧. Sides which are of equal length are marked with the same symbol. Thus, in such cases, we do not need to measure the lengths of the sides in order to identify the type of triangle.

E.g.

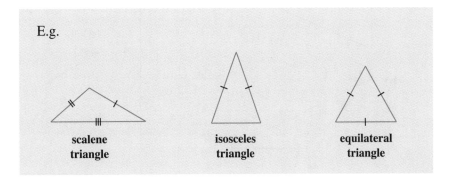

| scalene triangle | isosceles triangle | equilateral triangle |

Classifying by angles:

1. A triangle with all angles measuring less than 90° is called an **acute-angled triangle**.

   E.g.

2. A triangle with one angle measuring exactly 90° is called a **right-angled triangle**.

   E.g.

   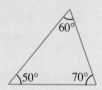

3. A triangle with one angle measuring greater than 90° is called an **obtuse-angled triangle**.

   E.g.

   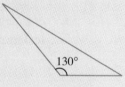

Exercise 6B

1. Name each of the following triangles according to
   (i) the lengths of its sides,
   (ii) the sizes of its angles.

   (a)

   (b)

   (c)

   (d)

(e)

(f)

Name Us!

Study the three triangles below.

(i)

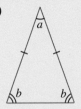

(ii)

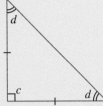

(iii)

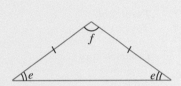

(a) Give an appropriate name to each of the triangles above such that each triangle is classified both by its side properties and angle properties. Can you pick out the common property that the three triangles have?

(b) Is it possible to have equilateral triangles named in three different ways as you have seen in **(a)**? Explain your reasons.

6.2.2 Sum of the Angles of a Triangle

Draw a triangle and label each angle with a letter. Next, tear off each corner and place them side by side with their vertices together.

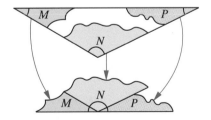

Notice that all three angles, when placed side by side, will lie on a straight line. Since adjacent angles on a straight line add up to 180°, we can deduce that the sum of the angles in the triangle is 180°.

Let us use the Geometer's Sketchpad (GSP) to investigate whether the above property applies to all triangles.

Activity

> *To study the property relating to the sum of the angles in a triangle using Geometer's Sketchpad (GSP).*

The GSP is a powerful IT tool for geometrical construction.

A quick guide of the basic tools in GSP is given below.

 Selection Arrow tool
To select a point or line.

 Point tool
To draw a point.

 Compass tool
To draw a circle.

 Straightedge tool
To draw a straight line.

 Text tool
To label a point, line, etc.

Step	*Action*
1	To access the program, double-click on the GSP icon on the desktop.
2	Click on the *Straightedge tool* and drag right to choose the *Line Segment tool*.
3	Draw three line segments in succession to form a triangle.
4	Click on the *Text tool* to label the vertices of the triangle as *A*, *B* and *C*.

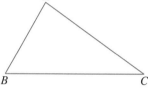

Step 5 — Click on the *Selection Arrow tool*. Holding the *Shift* key down, click on the points *C*, *A* and *B* in succession before releasing the *Shift* key.

Step 6 — Click on *Measure* from the *Menu Bar* and choose *Angle*. (Note: The angle *CAB* will be displayed on the screen as '$m\angle CAB = $ ')

Step 7 — Repeat steps 5 and 6 for the points *A*, *B* and *C*. (Note: The angle *ABC* will be displayed on the screen as '$m\angle ABC = $ ')

Step 8 — Repeat steps 5 and 6 for the points *B*, *C* and *A*. (Note: The angle *BCA* will be displayed on the screen as '$m\angle BCA = $ ')

Step 9 — Click on *Measure* from the *Menu Bar* and choose *Calculate*. (A calculator will be shown on the screen.)

Step 10 — Click on:
'$m\angle CAB = $ ' (on the main screen), '+' (on the calculator screen),
'$m\angle ABC = $ ' (on the main screen), '+' (on the calculator screen),
'$m\angle BCA = $ ' (on the calculator screen) and then *OK* (on the calculator screen).

What can you observe about the value of '$m\angle CAB + m\angle ABC + m\angle BCA$'?

Step 11 — Use the *Selection Arrow tool* to change the sizes of the angles by dragging any one of the vertices of the triangle.

Step 12 — Click on *File* and choose the *Save As* command from the *Menu Bar*. Enter the filename as 'TriSum.gsp' in the *Save As* window and then click on *Save*.

Does your earlier observation hold true even when the values of the angles are changed?

By induction, the results of the activity on the previous page can be generalised as follows:

Generalising by induction

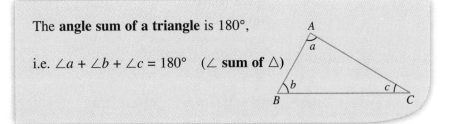

The **angle sum of a triangle** is 180°,

i.e. $\angle a + \angle b + \angle c = 180°$ ($\angle$ **sum of** $\triangle$)

Example 1

Find the value of $\angle a$ in the figure shown below.

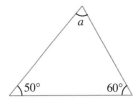

Solution

$$\angle a + 50° + 60° = 180° \quad (\angle \text{ sum of } \triangle)$$
$$\therefore \quad \angle a = 180° - (50° + 60°)$$
$$= 180° - 110°$$
$$= 70°$$

Example 2

Find the value of b in the figure shown below.

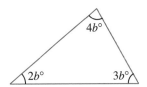

Solution

$$2b° + 3b° + 4b° = 180° \quad (\angle \text{ sum of } \triangle)$$
$$9b° = 180°$$
$$\frac{9b°}{9} = \frac{180°}{9}$$
$$b° = 20°$$
$$\Rightarrow b = 20$$

Example 3

Find the value of the unknown angle marked in each of the triangles given below.

(a)

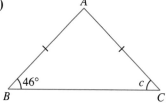

(b)

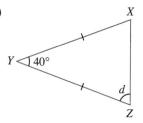

Solution

(a) $\triangle ABC$ is an isosceles triangle,

$$\therefore \quad \angle c = 46° \quad \text{(base } \angle\text{s of isos. } \triangle ABC)$$

(b) $\triangle XYZ$ is an isosceles triangle,

$$\therefore \quad \angle d = \frac{180° - 40°}{2} \quad \text{(base } \angle\text{s of isos. } \triangle XYZ)$$

$$= \frac{140°}{2}$$

$$= 70°$$

Exercise 6C

1. Find the value of the unknown angle(s) marked in each of the following figures. The figures shown are not drawn to scale.

(a)

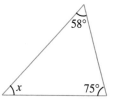

(b)

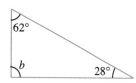

(c)

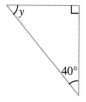

(d)

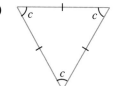

(e)

(f)

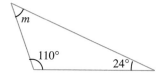

2. Find the value of x in each of the following figures. The figures shown are not drawn to scale.

(a)

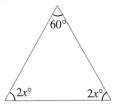

(b)

(c)

(d)

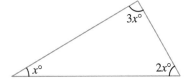

(e)

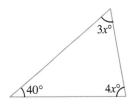

3. PQR is an isosceles triangle in which $PQ = PR$ and $\angle QPR = 48°$. PS is parallel to QR and TPR is a straight line. Calculate

(a) $\angle QRP$,

(b) $\angle TPS$.

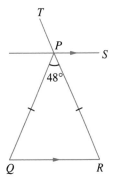

6.2.3   Exterior Angle of a Triangle

When a side of a triangle is **produced** (extended), an angle is formed between the produced side and one of the sides of the triangle. We call such an angle an **exterior angle**. In the diagram given below, $\angle ACD$ is an exterior angle of $\triangle ABC$.

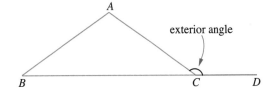

Besides $\angle ACD$, triangle ABC can have several other exterior angles. Can you draw and name some of them?

Recall that angles that lie within a triangle are known as its **interior angles**.

In the diagram shown below, the interior angles are marked *a*, *b* and *c*. Notice that two of the interior angles, $\angle a$ and $\angle b$, lie opposite the exterior angle, $\angle e$. They are called the **interior opposite angles** with respect to $\angle e$. The remaining interior angle, $\angle c$, is adjacent to the exterior angle, $\angle e$.

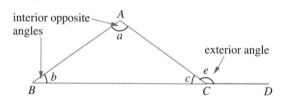

Let us now explore the relationship between an exterior angle of a triangle and its two interior opposite angles.

Draw a triangle and label each angle with a letter. Next, produce one of it sides. Tear off the corners at *A* and *B* and place them along the produced side next to $\angle c$, as shown in the second diagram below.

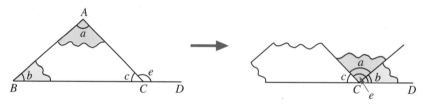

You will see that the two angles, $\angle a$ and $\angle b$, add up to give the exterior angle, $\angle e$. We can thus deduce that an exterior angle of a triangle is equal to the sum of its two interior opposite angles.

We shall next use the Geometer's Sketchpad (GSP) to investigate whether the above property applies to all triangles.

note

Another way of deducing the relationship between the exterior angle of a triangle and its two interior opposite angles:

$\angle a + \angle b + \angle c$
$= 180°$ ($\angle$ sum of $\triangle$)
and
$\angle e + \angle c$
$= 180°$ (adj. $\angle$s on a str. line)

$\therefore \angle e = \angle a + \angle b$
(ext. $\angle$ of $\triangle$)

Activity

> ***To study the relationship between an exterior angle of a triangle and its two interior opposite angles using Geometer's Sketchpad (GSP).***

Step	*Action*
1	Open the GSP file [TriSum.gsp] that you have saved from the previous activity on page 182.
2	Click on the *Selection Arrow tool*. Holding the *Shift* key down, click on the points *B* and *C* in succession before releasing the *Shift* key.
3	Click on *Transform* from the *Menu Bar* and choose *Mark <u>V</u>ector 'B->C'*.

4   Holding the *Shift* key down, click on the line segment *BC* before releasing the *Shift* key.

5   Click on *Transform* from the *Menu Bar* and choose *Translate*. Then, click *OK* and relabel the point *C'* as *D*.

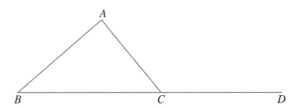

6   Holding the *Shift* key down, click at the points *A, C* and *D* in succession before releasing the *Shift* key.

7   Click on *Measure* from the *Menu Bar* and choose *Angle*. (Note: The angle *ACD* will be displayed on the screen as '*m∠ACD* =   ')

8   Repeat steps 6 and 7 for *A, B* and *C*. (Note: The angle *ABC* will be displayed on the screen as '*m∠ABC* =   ')

9   Repeat steps 6 and 7 for *C, A* and *B*. (Note: The angle *CAB* will be displayed on the screen as '*m∠CAB* =   ')

10   Click on *Measure* from the *Menu Bar* and choose *Calculate*. (A calculator is shown on the screen.)

11   Click on:
'*m∠ABC* =   ' (on the main screen), '+' (on the calculator screen), '*m∠CAB* =   ' (on the main screen) and then *OK* (on the calculator screen).

What can you observe about the value of '*m∠ABC* + *m∠CAB* =   ' and the value of '*m∠ACD* =   '?

12   Use the *Selection Arrow tool* to change the sizes of the angles by dragging any one of the vertices of the triangle.

Does your earlier observation hold true even when the values of the angles are changed?

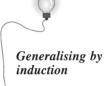

Generalising by induction

By induction, the results of the above activity can be generalised as follows:

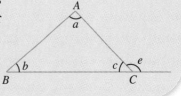

An **exterior angle of a triangle** is equal to the sum of the two interior opposite angles,

i.e. $\angle e = \angle a + \angle b$ (**ext. ∠ of △**)

Example 4

Find the value of the unknown angle marked in each of the figures given below.

(a)
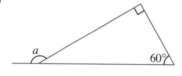

(b)
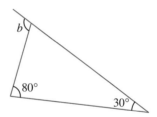

Solution

(a) $\angle a = 90° + 60°$ (ext. $\angle$ of $\triangle$)
       $= 150°$

(b) $\angle b = 80° + 30°$ (ext. $\angle$ of $\triangle$)
       $= 110°$

Example 5

Find the value of $\angle c$ in the figure shown on the right.

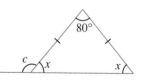

Solution

Let the base angles of the triangle be x.

> **note**
>
> Since $\angle c$ and $\angle x$ lie on a straight line. We can also find $\angle c$ in the following way:
> $\angle c + \angle x = 180°$ (adj. $\angle$s on a str. line)
> $\therefore \angle c = 180° - \angle x$
> $= 180° - 50°$
> $= 130°$

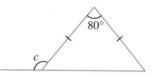

$$\angle x = \frac{180° - 80°}{2} \quad \text{(base } \angle\text{s of isos. } \triangle)$$
$$= \frac{100°}{2}$$
$$= 50°$$

$\therefore \quad \angle c = 80° + 50°$ (ext. $\angle$ of $\triangle$)
       $= 130°$

Example 6

Find the value of $\angle d$ in the figure shown on the right.

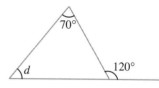

Solution

$$120° = 70° + \angle d \quad \text{(ext. } \angle \text{ of } \triangle)$$
$$\therefore \quad \angle d = 120° - 70°$$
$$= 50°$$

1. Find the value of the unknown angle marked in each of the following figures.

   (a)

   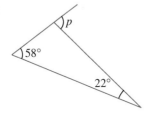

   (b)

   (c)

   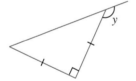

   (d)

   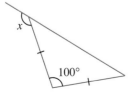

   (e)

   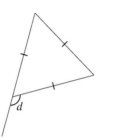

   (f)

   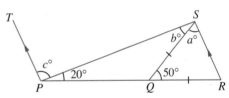

   (g)

   (h)

   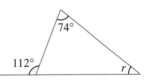

2. Find the size of the angle labelled *u* in the following figure.

   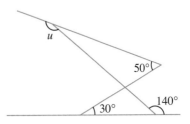

3. In the diagram given below, *PQR* is a straight line, *QR* = *QS* and *TP* is parallel to *SR*. ∠*RQS* = 50° and ∠*QPS* = 20°. Find the values of

   (a) *a*,　　　　**(b)** *b*,　　　　**(c)** *c*.

4. The lines *AB* and *CDEF* are parallel. Angle *CDB* = 115° and angle *DBE* = 70°. Calculate

   (a) angle *GDE*,

   (b) angle *ABD*,

   (c) angle *BEF*.

   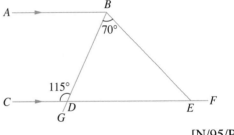

   [N/95/P1]

In this section, you will learn how to construct triangles when given certain measurements.

A triangle can be constructed if we are given any one of the following:

(i) the lengths of all its three sides; or

(ii) two angles and an included side; or

(iii) the lengths of two sides and any angle.

> **note**
>
> An '**included side**' is a side that is a common arm of the two given angles.

Let us take a look at some examples of how we can construct triangles with given measurements using some of these tools: a pair of compasses, a ruler and/or a protractor.

Example 7

(To construct a triangle given the lengths of all its three sides)

Construct $\triangle ABC$ in which $AB = 5$ cm, $BC = 4$ cm and $CA = 2$ cm.

> **note**
>
> Drawing a sketch before constructing the actual figure is very useful as it helps you check your final construction.

Solution

Step 1   Draw a line 5 cm long. Label it AB.

Step 2   With centre A and radius 2 cm, draw an arc.

Sketch:

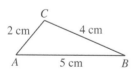

Step 3   With centre B and radius 4 cm, draw another arc to cut the first arc. Label this point of intersection as C.

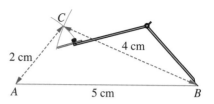

Step 4   Join A to C and B to C.

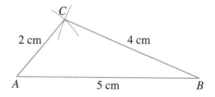

Example 8

(To construct a triangle given two angles and an included side)

Construct $\triangle ABC$ in which $AB = 4$ cm, $\angle CAB = 80°$ and $\angle CBA = 30°$.

Solution

Sketch:

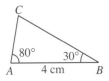

Step 1 Draw a line 4 cm long. Label it AB.

Step 2 Use a protractor to draw an angle of 80° at A and an angle of 30° at B.

Step 3 Produce the ray at B to cut the ray at A. Label this point of intersection as C.

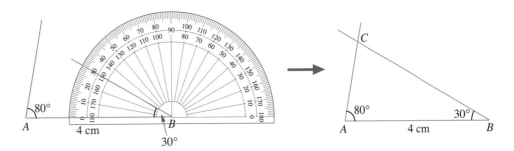

note

An 'included angle' is an angle whose arms are the two given sides.

Example 9

(To construct a triangle given the lengths of two sides and an included angle.)

Construct $\triangle ABC$ in which $AB = 3$ cm, $AC = 2$ cm and $\angle BAC = 80°$.

Solution

Sketch:

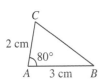

Step 1 Draw a line 3 cm long. Label it AB.

Step 2 Use a protractor to draw an angle of 80° at A.

Step 3 With centre A and radius 2 cm, draw an arc to cut this ray. Label this point of intersection as C.

Step 4 Join B to C.

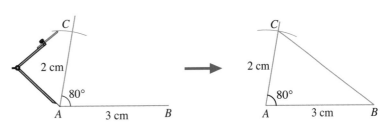

Example 10

(To construct a triangle given the lengths of two sides and a non-included angle.)

Construct $\triangle ABC$ in which $AB = 3$ cm, $AC = 5$ cm and $\angle ABC = 50°$.

Solution

Sketch:

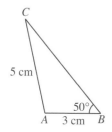

Step 1 Draw a line 3 cm long. Label it AB.
Step 2 Use a protractor to draw an angle of 50° at B.
Step 3 With centre A and radius 5 cm, draw an arc to cut this ray. Label this point of intersection as C.
Step 4 Join A to C.

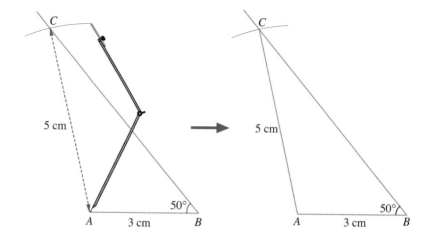

note

Remember to add to your final construction all the dimensions given in the question. Do not erase the construction lines, such as the arcs, from your final drawing.

Exercise 6E

1. Construct $\triangle ABC$ in which
    (a) $AB = 3$ cm, $BC = 5$ cm and $AC = 7$ cm;
    (b) $AB = 6$ cm, $BC = 4$ cm and $AC = 5$ cm.

2. Construct $\triangle DEF$ in which
    (a) $DE = 6$ cm, $\angle FDE = 40°$ and $\angle FED = 60°$;
    (b) $DE = 5$ cm, $\angle FDE = 30°$ and $\angle FED = 50°$.

3. Construct $\triangle LMN$ in which
    (a) $LM = 4$ cm, $LN = 6$ cm and $\angle MLN = 50°$;
    (b) $LM = 5$ cm, $LN = 4$ cm and $\angle MLN = 60°$.

4. Construct $\triangle XYZ$ in which
    (a) $XY = 5$ cm, $XZ = 6$ cm and $\angle XYZ = 35°$;
    (b) $XY = 6$ cm, $XZ = 4$ cm and $\angle XYZ = 40°$.

5. Use triangle *PQR* to do the following.

    (a) Measure and write down, correct to the nearest mm, the length *QR*.

    (b) Measure and write down, correct to the nearest degree, the angle *QPR*.

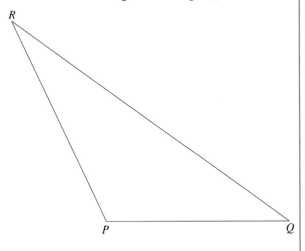

(c) *X* is the point inside the triangle such that ∠*QPX* = 90° and ∠*PQX* = 25°. Using your protractor, or otherwise, construct accurately and label clearly the position of *X*.

6.   **(a)** Construct accurately the triangle *LMN* where *LM* = 9 cm, *LN* = 5 cm and *MN* = 6.6 cm.

    (b) On the same diagram, draw

        (i) the angle bisector of angle *MLN*,

        (ii) the perpendicular bisector of *LM*.

Possible Triangles

Try constructing a triangle with each of the following sets of measurements.

  (a) 3 cm, 4 cm and 6 cm;   **(d)** 4 cm, 5 cm and 8 cm;

  (b) 3 cm, 4 cm and 7 cm;   **(e)** 4 cm, 5 cm and 9 cm;

  (c) 3 cm, 4 cm and 8 cm.   **(f)** 4 cm, 5 cm and 10 cm;

Which are the sets of measurements that you could construct a triangle with? Which are the sets of measurements that you could not construct a triangle with?

Discuss in groups and try to deduce a relationship between the sum of the lengths of the shorter sides of a triangle and the length of its longest side.

6.4 Quadrilaterals and Their Properties

A **quadrilateral** is a closed plane figure with four sides joined by four **vertices**. Thus, a quadrilateral has four interior angles.

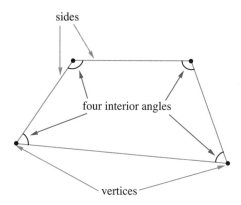

Some examples of quadrilaterals, which you may have already come across before, are the parallelogram, rectangle, rhombus, square and trapezium.

6.4.1   Sum of the Angles of a Quadrilateral

We can find the sum of the angles of a quadrilateral in the same way as we did for a triangle in Section 6.2.2.

By labelling each angle of the quadrilateral with a letter, tearing off each corner and then placing their vertices together, we can observe that the four angles form a full turn, i.e., 360°.

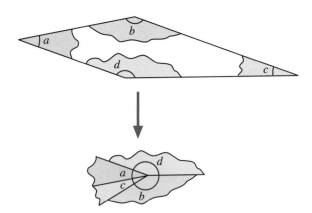

Therefore, the sum of the angles of a quadrilateral is 360°.

Alternatively, if we draw a line from one vertex to the opposite vertex in the quadrilateral, we will obtain two triangles as shown below.

A line segment that joins two opposite vertices of the quadrilateral together is called a **diagonal**. Since a quadrilateral has two pairs of opposite vertices, there are two diagonals in a quadrilateral. You will learn more about the properties of diagonals in special quadrilaterals in the next section.

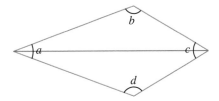

Since we know that the sum of the angles of a triangle is 180°, we can deduce that the sum of the angles of a quadrilateral is $2 \times 180° = 360°$.

The **sum of the angles of a quadrilateral** is 360°,

i.e. $\angle a + \angle b + \angle c + \angle d = 360°$ ($\angle$ **sum of quad.**)

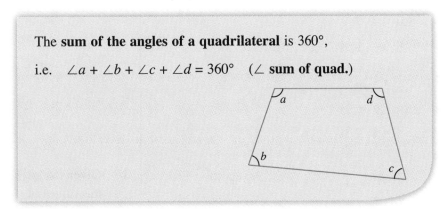

Example 11

Find the unknown angle marked in the quadrilateral given below.

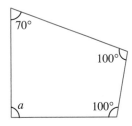

Solution

$$\angle a = 360° - (70° + 100° + 100°) \quad (\angle \text{ sum of quad.})$$
$$= 360° - 270°$$
$$= 90°$$

1. Find the value of the unknown angle marked in each of the following quadrilaterals. The figures shown are not drawn to scale.

(a)

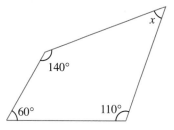

(b)

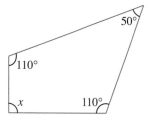

(c)

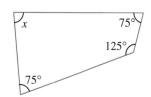

(d)

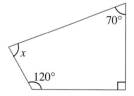

(e)

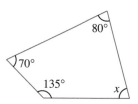

(f)

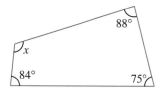

(g)

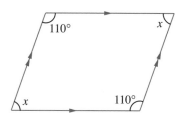

(h)

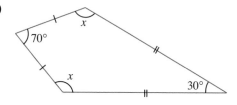

2. Find the value of x.

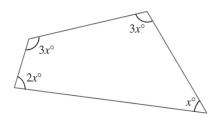

3. Given the angles shown in the diagram, find the values of
   (a) x,
   (b) y.

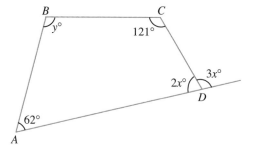

6.4.2 Properties of Special Quadrilaterals

In this section, we will be studying more about the properties of the six special types of quadrilaterals shown below.

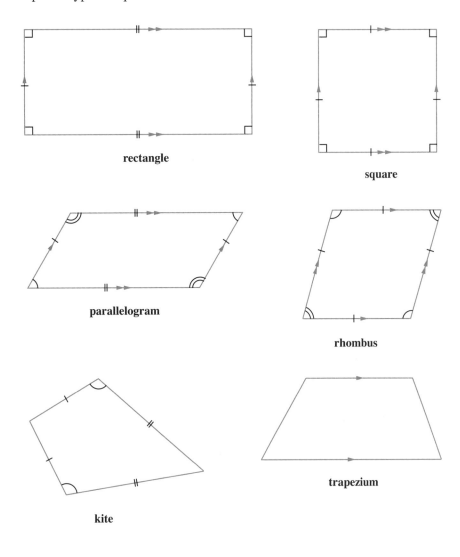

rectangle

square

parallelogram

rhombus

kite

trapezium

Activity

To study the properties of special quadrilaterals.

1. Study the quadrilaterals shown above. Then, copy and complete the following chart with the names of the quadrilaterals that satisfy the given **side properties**.

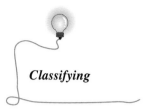

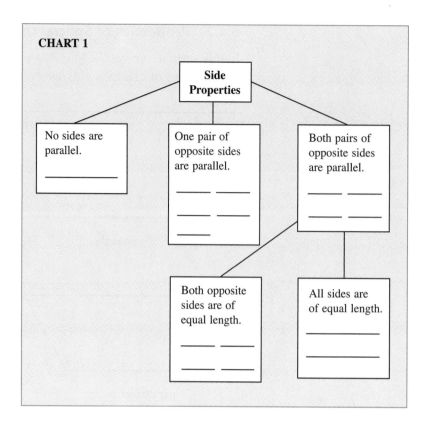

CHART 1

Side Properties

No sides are parallel.

One pair of opposite sides are parallel.

Both pairs of opposite sides are parallel.

Both opposite sides are of equal length.

All sides are of equal length.

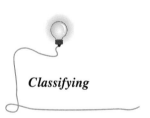

Classifying

2. Study the quadrilaterals shown on the previous page. Then, copy and complete the following chart with the names of the quadrilaterals that satisfy the given **angle properties**.

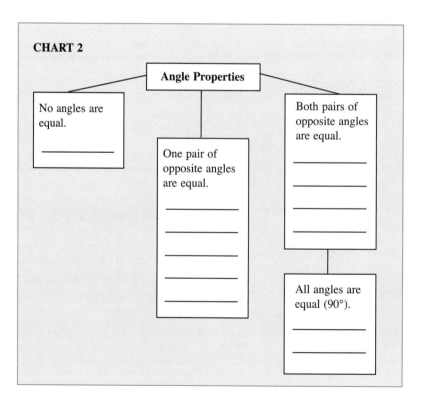

CHART 2

Angle Properties

No angles are equal.

One pair of opposite angles are equal.

Both pairs of opposite angles are equal.

All angles are equal (90°).

3. **(a)** Trace all the six quadrilaterals on page 197 onto a piece of paper.

(b) For each quadrilateral, draw its two diagonals.

Study the diagonals formed in each of the quadrilaterals. Then, copy and complete the following chart with the names of the quadrilaterals that satisfy the given **diagonal properties**.

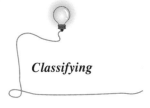

Classifying

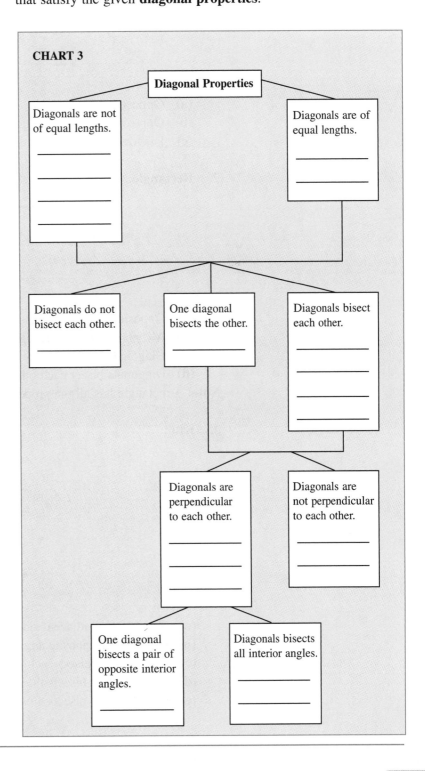

The properties of the six types of special quadrilaterals can be summarised as follows:

1. **Parallelogram:**

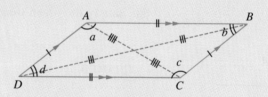

   (a) Opposite sides are equal and parallel.
   (b) Opposite angles are equal.
   (c) Diagonals bisect each other.

2. **Rectangle:**

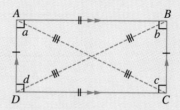

   (a) Opposite sides are equal and parallel.
   (b) All interior angles are right angles.
   (c) Diagonals are equal.
   (d) Diagonals bisect each other.

Note: A rectangle has all the properties of a parallelogram.

3. **Kite:**

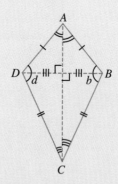

   (a) Two pairs of adjacent sides are equal.
   (b) One pair of opposite angles are equal.
   (c) Diagonals intersect each other at right angles.
   (d) One diagonal bisects the other.
   (e) One diagonal bisects a pair of opposite angles.

4. Rhombus:

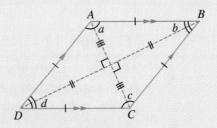

(a) All sides are equal.

(b) Opposite sides are parallel.

(c) Opposite angles are equal.

(d) Diagonals bisect each other at right angles.

(e) Diagonals bisect all interior angles.

Note: A rhombus has all the properties of a parallelogram.

5. Square:

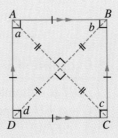

(a) All sides are equal.

(b) Opposite sides are parallel.

(c) All interior angles are right angles.

(d) Diagonals are equal.

(e) Diagonals bisect each other at right angles.

(f) Diagonals bisect all interior angles.

Note: A square has all the properties of both a parallelogram and a rhombus.

6. Trapezium:

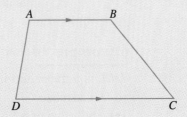

One pair of opposite sides are parallel.

With the properties of special quadrilaterals that we have just learned, we can solve some problems involving angles in such quadrilaterals.

Example 12

ABCD is a parallelogram. *P* is a point on *AB* such that $\angle PAD = 110°$ and $PC = BC$. Calculate

(a) $\angle ABC$,

(b) $\angle DCP$.

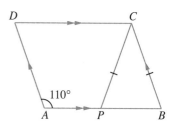

Solution

(a) $\angle ABC = 180° - 100°$ (int. ∠s, // lines)

          $= 70°$

(b) $\angle BPC = 70°$ (base ∠s of isos. △)

    $\angle DCP = \angle BPC$ (alt. ∠s, // lines)

          $= 70°$

Example 13

EFGH is a rhombus in which the diagonals *EG* and *FH* intersect at *M*. Find

(a) $\angle FEM$,

(b) $\angle EFM$.

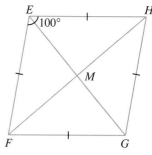

Solution

(a) $\angle FEM = \dfrac{100°}{2}$ (Diagonal *EG* bisects $\angle FEH$)

        $= 50°$

Can you find $\angle EFM$ by another method? Try it on your own.

(b) $\angle EMF = 90°$ (diagonals of a rhombus bisect each other at rt. ∠s)

    ∴ $\angle EFM = 180° - 90° - 50°$ (∠ sum of △)

          $= 40°$

Example 14

IJKL is a trapezium in which *LK* is parallel to *IJ*. Calculate

(a) the value of *x*,

(b) $\angle IJK$.

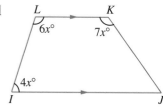

Solution

(a) $4x° + 6x° = 180°$ (int. $\angle$s, // lines)

$$10x° = 180°$$

$$x° = \frac{180°}{10}$$

$$x° = 18°$$

$$\therefore \quad x = 18$$

(b) $\angle JKL = 7x°$

$$= 7 \times 18°$$

$$= 126°$$

$$\therefore \quad \angle IJK = 180° - 126° \quad \text{(int. } \angle\text{s, // lines)}$$

$$= 54°$$

Exercise 6G

1. For each of the rectangles given below, calculate the unknown angles marked x and y.

(a)

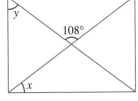

(b)

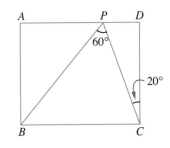

2. $ABCD$ is a rectangle in which $\angle BPC = 60°$ and $\angle PCD = 20°$.

Calculate

(a) $\angle CPD$,

(b) $\angle ABP$.

3. For each of the squares given below, calculate the unknown angles marked x and y.

(a)

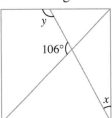

(b)

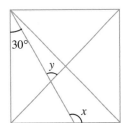

4. $EFGH$ is a square in which the diagonals intersect at M. Q is a point on EH such that $HQ = HM$. Calculate

(a) $\angle HQM$,

(b) $\angle EMQ$.

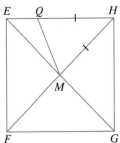

5. For each of the parallelograms given below, calculate the values of x and y.

(a)

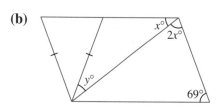

(b)

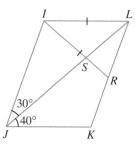

6. *IJKL* is a parallelogram in which R is a point on *LK* such that $IR = IL$. *IR* intersects the diagonal *JL* at S. Given that $\angle IJL = 30°$ and $\angle KJL = 40°$, calculate

(a) $\angle IRL$,

(b) $\angle JSR$.

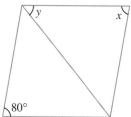

7. For each of the rhombuses given below, calculate the unknown angles marked x and y.

(a)

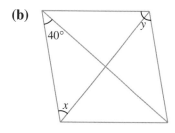

(b)

8. *OPQR* is a rhombus in which the diagonals intersect at M. N is a point on *OP* such that $QN = QP$. Given that $\angle ORP = 35°$, calculate

(a) $\angle OPQ$, **(b)** $\angle ONQ$.

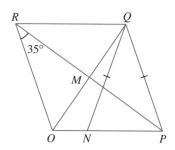

9. For each of the kites given below, calculate the unknown angles marked x and y.

(a)

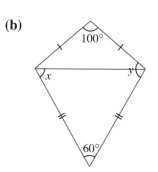

(b)

10. *STUV* is a kite in which the diagonals intersect at N. Calculate

(a) $\angle STN$, **(b)** $\angle SVU$.

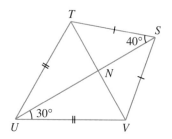

11. For each of the trapeziums given below, calculate the unknown angles marked x and y.

(a)

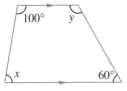

(b)

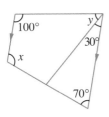

12. *WXZ* and *XYZ* are isosceles triangles in which *WX* = *YX* = *ZX* and $\angle WZX = \angle YXZ = 70°$.

(a) Calculate
  (i) $\angle WXZ$,
  (ii) $\angle XYZ$.

(b) State the name of this special type of quadrilateral.

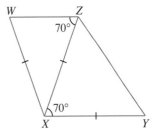

6.5 **Constructing Quadrilaterals**

In this section, you will learn how to construct quadrilaterals when given certain measurements.

Let us take a look at some examples of how we can construct quadrilaterals with given measurements using some of these tools: a pair of compasses, a ruler, a set-square and/or a protractor.

Example 15 ─────────────────────────

Construct a parallelogram *ABCD* in which $\angle DAB = 50°$, *AB* = 4.5 cm and *AD* = 4 cm.

Sketch:

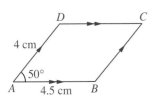

Solution

Step 1   Draw a line 4.5 cm long. Label it *AB*.
Step 2   At *A*, use a protractor to draw an angle of 50°.
Step 3   With centre *A* and radius 4 cm, draw an arc to cut this ray. Label this point of intersection as *D*.

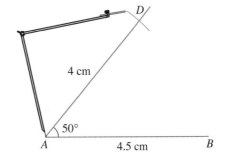

Since *ABCD* is a parallelogram, *BC* must be equal to *AD*.

Step 4   With centre *B* and radius 4 cm, draw an arc above *B*.

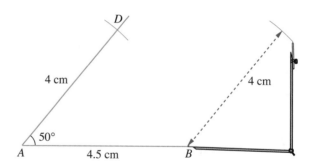

Since *ABCD* is a parallelogram, *DC* must be equal to *AB*.

Step 5   With centre *D* and radius 4.5 cm, draw another arc to cut the arc above *B*. Label their point of intersection as *C*.

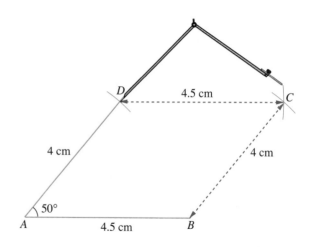

Step 6   Join *B* to *C* and *D* to *C*.

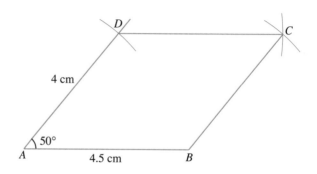

Example 16

Construct a quadrilateral *ABCD* in which *DC* is parallel to *AB*. It is also given that *AB* = 4 cm, $\angle DAB = 90°$, *AD* = 3 cm and $\angle ABC = 110°$.

Sketch:

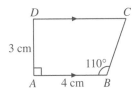

Solution

Step 1 Draw a line 4 cm long. Label it *AB*.

Step 2 At *A*, construct a perpendicular line.

Step 3 With centre *A* and radius 3 cm, draw an arc to cut this perpendicular line. Label this point of intersection as *D*.

Step 4 At *B*, use a protractor to draw an angle of 110°.

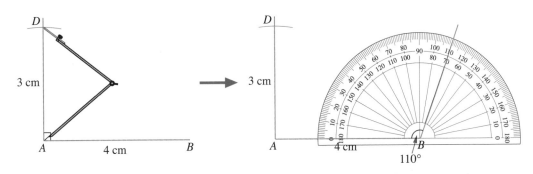

Step 5 Placing one edge of the set-square along *AB* with the ruler against the other edge of the set-square, slide the set-square up along the ruler, stopping when the horizontal edge touches *D*.

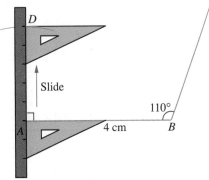

Step 6 Using the edge of the set-square, draw a line from *D* to cut the ray at *B*. Label this point of intersection as *C*.

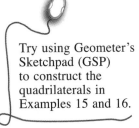

Try using Geometer's Sketchpad (GSP) to construct the quadrilaterals in Examples 15 and 16.

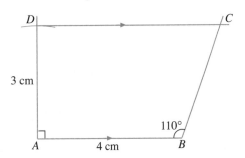

1. Construct a rectangle *EFGH* such that *EF* = 5.5 cm and *FG* = 3.3 cm.

2. Construct a square of side 4 cm.

3. Construct a parallelogram *IJKL* such that *IJ* = 6 cm, *JK* = 5 cm and ∠*IJK* = 70°.

4. Construct a rhombus *MNOP* of sides 5 cm such that ∠*MNO* = 50°.

5. Construct a trapezium *PQRS* in which *PQ* is parallel to *SR*, *PQ* = 5.5 cm, *QR* = 6 cm, *PS* = 4.5 cm and ∠*SPQ* = 90°.

6. Construct a quadrilateral *STUV* in which *ST* = *SV* = 3 cm, *TU* = *VU* = 6 cm and *SU* = 7 cm. Measure the angles of the quadrilateral. What type of quadrilateral is *STUV*?

7. Construct a quadrilateral *QRST* in which *QR* = 6 cm, ∠*TQR* = 90°, *QT* = 5 cm, ∠*QRS* = 70°, *ST* = 4 cm and *RS* < 6 cm. Measure and write down ∠*RST*.

8. Construct a quadrilateral *UVWX* in which *XW* is parallel to *UV*. It is also given that *UV* = 5 cm, ∠*XUV* = 56°, *XU* = 3.4 cm and *XW* = 4 cm. Measure and write down the length of *VW*.

9. Construct a parallelogram *ABCD* in which *AB* = 4 cm, *BC* = 5 cm and ∠*DAB* = 67°.
   (a) Measure and write down the length of *AC*.
   (b) Construct the perpendicular bisector of *AB*.
   (c) Measure and write down the perpendicular distance between the lines *AB* and *DC*.

10. Construct accurately the quadrilateral *WXYZ* in which *WX* = 8 cm, ∠*WXY* = 89°, *XY* = 3.4 cm, ∠*XWZ* = 95° and *WZ* = 5.5 cm.
    (a) Construct the angle bisector of ∠*XYZ*.
    (b) Extend the angle bisector of ∠*XYZ* to cut *WX*. Mark this point as *V*. Measure and write down
       (i) ∠*XVY*,
       (ii) the length of *VY*.

6.6 Polygons and Their Properties

6.6.1 Types of Polygons

A **polygon** is a closed plane figure formed by three or more line segments.

Polygons are named according to the number of sides that they have. For example, a three-sided polygon is called a triangle while a four-sided polygon is called a quadrilateral. ('tri' means 'three' and 'quad' means 'four' in Greek.)

Did you know?

The ancient Greeks called a three-sided polygon a 'trigon'.

We can name other polygons by adding a prefix, that indicates the number of sides it has, to the word 'gon' (which means 'corner' or 'angle' in Greek). For example, a polygon with five sides is called a '*penta*gon' while a polygon with six sides is called a '*hexa*gon'. ('penta' means 'five' and 'hexa' means 'six' in Greek.)

The following table shows some polygons with up to 10 sides and their corresponding names.

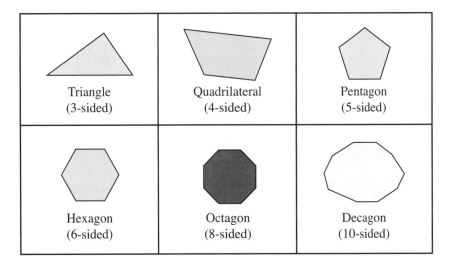

| Triangle (3-sided) | Quadrilateral (4-sided) | Pentagon (5-sided) |
| Hexagon (6-sided) | Octagon (8-sided) | Decagon (10-sided) |

For polygons with more than 10 sides, we can simply write down the numeral that represents the number of sides the polygon has followed by the word 'gon'. For example, we can call a polygon with 11 sides an 11-gon and a polygon with 15 sides a 15-gon. In general, an n-sided polygon (where $n > 10$) can be simply called an **n-gon**.

Having learned the naming of polygons, let us now look at some terms associated with a polygon in general.

For any general polygon:
* any point at which two sides meet is called a **vertex**.
* any angle that lie inside the polygon at the vertex is called an **interior angle**.
* any line segment that joins two non-adjacent vertices together is called a **diagonal**.

In the pentagon shown below for example, A, B, C, D and E are the vertices; a, b, c, d and e are the interior angles and AC, AD, BE, BD and CE are the diagonals.

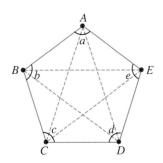

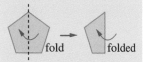
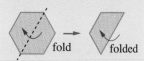
Based on the properties of their sides and interior angles, polygons can be classified into two groups — regular polygons and irregular polygons. Polygons which have equal sides and equal interior angles are known as **regular polygons**. All other polygons are **irregular polygons**.

Some examples of regular and irregular polygons are shown below.

Regular polygons:

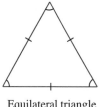
Equilateral triangle

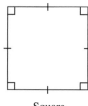
Square

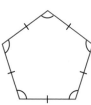
Regular pentagon

Regular hexagon

Regular octagon

Regular decagon

Irregular polygons:

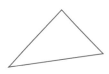
Triangle

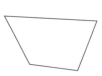
Quadrilateral

Pentagon

Hexagon

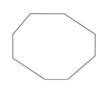
Octagon

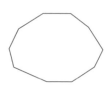
Decagon

1. Name all the different polygons you can find in the plane figure given below.

2. The regular hexagon given below has all its diagonals intersecting at the centre O with $OP = OQ = OR = OS = OT = OU$.

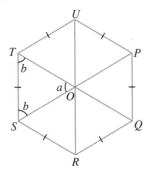

(a) Calculate
   (i) angle a, (ii) angle b.
(b) What type of triangle is $\triangle OPQ$? (according to the lengths of its sides or angles)
(c) What type of quadrilateral is $PQRS$?

3. The regular octagon given below has the diagonals BF and HD intersecting at O with $OB = OD = OF = OH$.

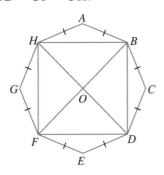

(a) (i) What type of triangle is $\triangle ABH$? (according to the lengths of its sides)
   (ii) What type of triangle is $\triangle BOH$? (according to the sizes of its angles)
(b) What type of quadrilateral is
   (i) $ABOH$, (ii) $BDFH$?

4. (a) (i) Write down all the diagonals of the quadrilateral $ABCD$ shown below.
   (ii) How many diagonals are there?

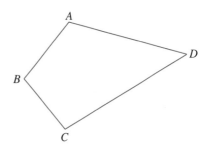

(b) (i) Write down all the diagonals of the pentagon $ABCDE$ shown below.
   (ii) How many diagonals are there?

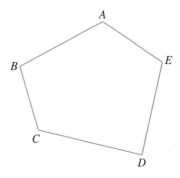

(c) How many diagonals can you obtain from a polygon of 50 sides?

6.6.2 Sum of the Interior Angles of a Polygon

Since we know that the sum of the angles of a triangle is 180°, we can calculate the sum of the interior angles of a polygon by considering the number of triangles it can be divided into.

No. of Sides	Polygon	No. of triangles	Sum of interior angles
3		1	180°
4		2	$2 \times 180° = 360°$
5		3	$3 \times 180° = 540°$
6		4	$4 \times 180° = 720°$
⋮		⋮	⋮
n		$n - 2$	$(n - 2) \times 180°$

Looking for a pattern

In general,

> The **sum of the interior angles of a polygon** is $(n - 2) \times 180°$, where n = number of sides.

Example 17

Find the sum of the interior angles of an octagon.

Solution

Since an octagon has 8 sides,

Sum of interior angles
$= (n - 2) \times 180°$

∴   Sum of interior angles of octagon $= (8 - 2) \times 180°$
$$= 6 \times 180°$$
$$= 1\,080°$$

All the interior angles of a regular polygon are equal.

The number of interior angles a polygon has corresponds to its number of sides. Thus, a 9-sided polygon has 9 interior angles, i.e., $n = 9$.

Example 18

Find the value of each interior angle of a regular 9-sided polygon.

Solution

$\therefore$ Sum of interior angles of a 9-sided polygon $= (9 - 2) \times 180°$

$$= 7 \times 180°$$

$\therefore$ Each interior angle $= \dfrac{7 \times \overset{20°}{\cancel{180°}}}{\underset{1}{\cancel{9}}}$

$$= 140°$$

Example 19

The sum of the interior angles of a polygon is 1 440°. How many sides does the polygon have? What is the name given to this type of polygon?

Solution

Let the number of sides the polygon has be n.

$$\text{Sum of interior angles of polygon} = 1\,440°$$
$$\therefore \quad (n - 2) \times 180° = 1\,440°$$
$$n - 2 = \frac{1\,440°}{180°}$$
$$n - 2 = 8$$
$$\therefore \quad n = 8 + 2 = 10$$

$\therefore$ the polygon has 10 sides. Thus, it is a decagon.

Example 20

Five of the interior angles of an irregular hexagon are each 110°. Calculate the sixth angle.

Solution

Let the sixth angle be $\angle x$.

$$\text{Sum of interior angles} = (n - 2) \times 180°$$
$$5(110)° + \angle x = (6 - 2) \times 180°$$
$$550° + \angle x = 4 \times 180°$$
$$550° + \angle x = 720°$$
$$\therefore \quad \angle x = 720° - 550°$$
$$= 170°$$

6.6.3 Sum of the Exterior Angles of a Polygon

In the pentagon shown below, $\angle p$, $\angle q$, $\angle r$, $\angle s$, and $\angle t$ are **interior angles** while $\angle a$, $\angle b$, $\angle c$, $\angle d$, and $\angle e$ are the **exterior angles** of the polygon.

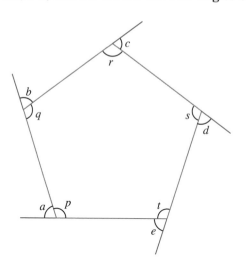

If we cut out the exterior angles and place them side by side as shown on the right, they would form a full turn, i.e. 360°. Therefore, the exterior angles in a pentagon add up to 360°.

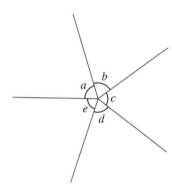

Generalising by induction

Repeat this procedure with a hexagon and a heptagon. For each of these polygons, what is the sum of their exterior angles?

> The **sum of the exterior angles of any polygon** is 360°.

Example 21

Find the value of an exterior angle of a regular decagon.

Solution

A decagon has 10 sides.

$$\text{Sum of exterior angles of a decagon} = 360°$$
$$\therefore \quad \text{Sum of 10 exterior angles} = 360°$$
$$\therefore \quad \text{Each exterior angle} = \frac{360°}{10}$$
$$= 36°$$

note

Interior angle +
Exterior angle
= 180°

interior
angle   exterior
               angle

Example 22

Given that each interior angle of a regular polygon is 135°, find the number of sides the polygon has.

Solution

Each interior angle = 135°

∴   Each exterior angle = 180° − 135° = 45°   (adj. ∠s on a str. line)

Sum of exterior angles = 360°

∴   Number of sides = $\dfrac{360°}{45°}$ = 8

Exercise 6J

1. Find the sum of the interior angles of a polygon with each of the following number of sides.

    (a) 6   **(b)** 9

2. Find the value of each interior angle of

    (a) a regular pentagon,

    (b) a regular octagon.

3. How many sides does a polygon have if the sum of its interior angles is

    (a) 900°,   **(b)** 360°?

4. How many sides does a regular polygon have if each of its interior angles is

    (a) 150°,   **(b)** 144°?

5. Four of the interior angles of a pentagon are each 110°. Calculate the fifth angle.

6. Five of the interior angles of a hexagon are 99°, 111°, 123°, 135° and 144°. Find the size of the remaining interior angle.

7. If the sum of the interior angles of a polygon is equivalent to 12 right angles, find the number of sides that it has.

8. The interior angles of a hexagon are 90°, $2x°$, 110°, 120°, $3x°$ and $3x°$. Find the value of x.

9. In the diagram shown below, *DEFGH* is a regular pentagon. Find the values of the unknown angles, *a* and *b*.

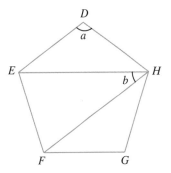

★10. In the diagram shown below, *ABCDEF* is a regular hexagon. Find the values of the unknown angles *x*, *y* and *z*.

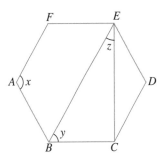

11. Find the value of an exterior angle of
   (a) a regular 12-gon,
   (b) a regular triangle.

12. Given that the exterior angles of a pentagon are $x°$, $2x°$, $3x°$, $4x°$ and $5x°$, find the value of x.

13. Given that the size of each interior angle of a regular polygon is 8 times the size of each exterior angle, find
   (a) the value of each exterior angle,
   (b) the number of sides the polygon has.

14.

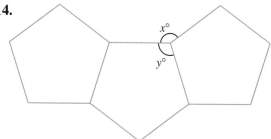

The given diagram shows three regular pentagons placed next to each other.
   (a) Find the value of
      (i) x,   (ii) y.
   ★(b) Additional pentagons are added to these three to form a closed ring surrounding a regular polygon. What is the total number of pentagons which form the ring?

6.7 **Congruence**

6.7.1 Congruent Figures

Look at the three stars shown below.

A B C

It is easy to see that star B is the smallest but not easy to see that star A and star C are the same in shape and size. An easy way, however, to compare star A and star C would be to cut out one figure and place it on top of the other. We would then find that star A and star C are exactly the same in shape and size. We say they are **congruent**.

For more practice on identifying congruent figures, visit the following website: http://www.learner. org/channel/courses/ teachingmath/grades3_ 5/session_02/section_ 02_b.html

> Two geometrical figures are **congruent** if they have exactly the same shape and size.

6.7.2 Congruent Polygons

Consider the three triangles given below.

First triangle

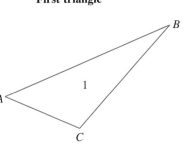

Second triangle

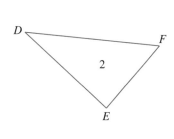

Third triangle

$AB = 49$ mm
$BC = 37$ mm
$AC = 22$ mm

$DE = 30$ mm
$DF = 37$ mm
$EF = 22$ mm

$GH = 37$ mm
$GI = 49$ mm
$HI = 22$ mm

If we compare the lengths of the sides in the first triangle with those in the second, we will see that

$$AC = EF \text{ and } BC = DF \text{ but } AB \neq DE$$

However, when we compare the lengths of the sides of the first triangle with those of the third triangle, we will find that

$$AB = GI, BC = GH \text{ and } AC = HI$$

This means that each side of the first triangle matches with or **corresponds** to a side of equal length in the third triangle. We call the first triangle and the third triangle **congruent triangles**.

In symbol, we write $\triangle ABC \equiv \triangle IGH$ where '$\equiv$' means 'is congruent to'. The corresponding vertices must be correctly paired when writing this congruency statement.

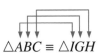

$$\triangle ABC \equiv \triangle IGH$$

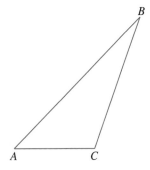

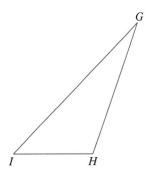

Activity

To study the properties of congruent polygons.

(a) Trace the quadrilateral *ABCD*, cut it out and label it correctly.

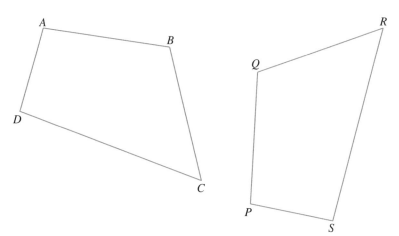

(b) Place your cut-out figure onto the quadrilateral *PQRS*? Do they match exactly?

(c) Next, look at the statements below. Which are the angles and sides in quadrilateral *PQRS* that correspond to the angles and sides shown below?

$\angle A = \angle$ _____ $AB =$ _____

$\angle B = \angle$ _____ $BC =$ _____

$\angle C = \angle$ _____ $CD =$ _____

$\angle D = \angle$ _____ $DA =$ _____

Deduction

(d) The two quadrilaterals *ABCD* and *PQRS* are _____.

   (i) Their corresponding angles are _____.

   (ii) Their corresponding sides are _____ .

In general,

> **Congruent polygons** have identical shapes and sizes. For congruent polygons, their
> • corresponding angles are equal,
> • corresponding sides are equal.
> The converse is also true, i.e., when the corresponding sides and angles of two polygons are equal, they are said to be congruent.

Example 23

For the pair of congruent triangles shown below, find the lengths of the unknown sides *a* and *b*.

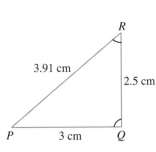
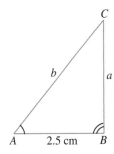

Solution

We can flip and turn $\triangle ABC$ such that its angles and sides matches with the corresponding angles and sides of $\triangle RQP$.

note

Moving, flipping and turning a plane figure does not change its shape and size.

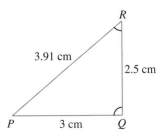
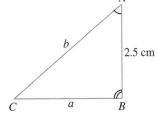

$\triangle ABC \equiv \triangle RQP$

$\therefore$ $BC = QP$ and $AC = RP$.

$\therefore$ $a = 3$ cm and $b = 3.91$ cm.

Example 24

Triangle *PQR* and triangle *FED* are congruent. Find the unknown angle, *f*, marked in triangle *FED* shown below.

We can turn $\triangle FED$ and then compare it with $\triangle PQR$ as shown below:

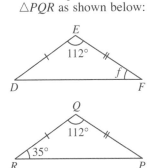

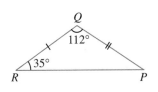
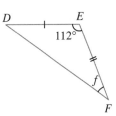

Solution

Given that $\triangle FED \equiv \triangle PQR$,

$\therefore$ $\angle F = \angle P$

i.e. $\angle f = 180° - 35° - 112°$ ($\angle$ sum of $\triangle PQR$)

    $= 33°$

Example 25

Triangle *ABC* and triangle *ADC* are congruent. Find the unknown angles marked in the diagram.

We can flip △*ADC* and then compare it with △*ABC* as shown below:

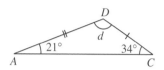

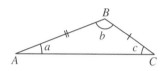

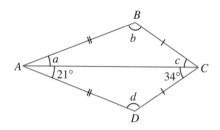

Solution

$\angle d = 180° - 21° - 34°$ ($\angle$ sum of △)
$\quad = 125°$

$$\triangle ABC \equiv \triangle ADC$$
$$\therefore \quad \angle a = 21°$$
$$\angle b = 125°$$
$$\angle c = 34°$$

Example 26

Triangle *ABC* and triangle *EDC* are congruent. Find the unknown angle and side marked in the diagram, given that *BCD* and *ACE* are straight lines.

We can rotate △*EDC* and then compare it with △*ABC* as shown below:

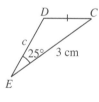

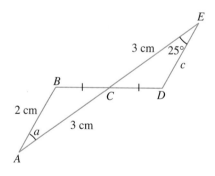

Solution

Given that $\triangle ABC \equiv \triangle EDC$,
$$\therefore \quad \angle A = \angle E$$
$$= 25°$$
Since $\quad ED = AB,$
$$\therefore \quad c = 2 \text{ cm}$$

Example 27

Quadrilaterals *ABCD* and *PQRS* are congruent.
Find the unknown sides x and y and the unknown angle z.

We can flip *PQRS* and then compare it with *ABCD* as shown below:

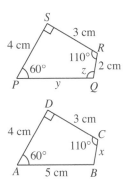

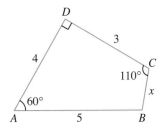

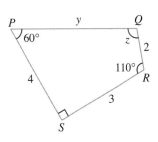

| Solution

Given that $ABCD \equiv PQRS$,

$$\therefore \quad \angle Q = \angle B$$
$$\angle z = 360° - 110° - 90° - 60° \quad (\angle \text{ sum of quad.})$$
$$= 100°$$

Since $BC = QR$ and $PQ = AB$,
we have $x = 2$ cm and $y = 5$ cm.

Exercise 6K

1. For each of the following pairs of figures, trace one of them on a transparency and place it over the other to deduce whether they are congruent.

    (a)

    (b)

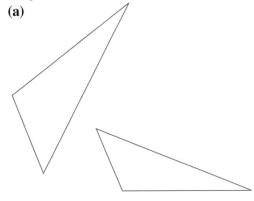

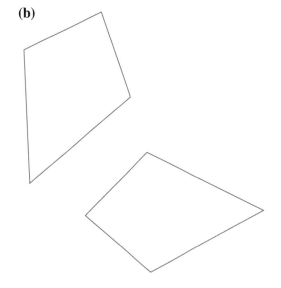

2. Measure the lengths of the sides of the figures in each of the following groups. Then, state which of the figures in each group are congruent.

(a)

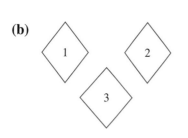

(b)

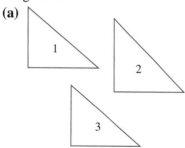

(c)

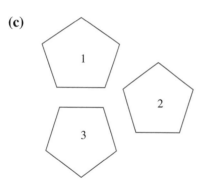

3. For each of the following pairs of congruent polygons, find the side corresponding to *AB* and the angle corresponding to ∠*A*.

(a)

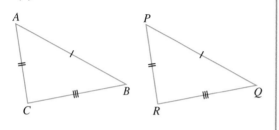

(b)

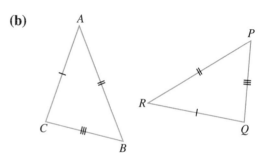

(c)

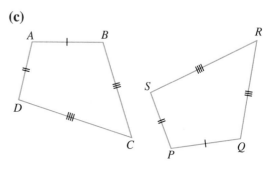

4. Find the values of all the unknown angles and the lengths of the sides marked with a letter in each of the following pairs of congruent polygons. All the sides are measured in cm.

(a)

(b)

(c)

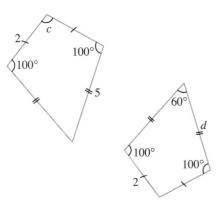

(d)

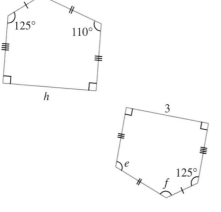

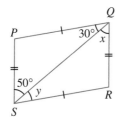

5. Each of the following diagrams are made up of two congruent triangles. Find the values of the unknown angles and sides marked in these diagrams. All the sides are measured in cm.

(a)

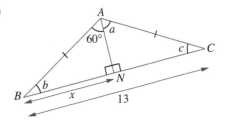

(b)

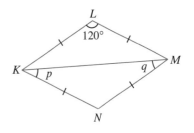

(c)

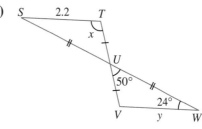

TUV and *SUW* are straight lines.

(d)

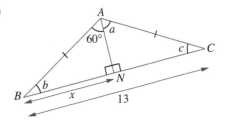

BNC is a straight line.

1. (a) The angle bisector of an angle is the line segment or ray that bisects the angle.

   (b) We can construct an angle bisector using a pair of compasses and a ruler.

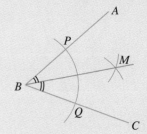

2. (a) The perpendicular bisector of a line segment is the line that bisects the line segment and is perpendicular to it.

   (b) We can construct a perpendicular bisector using a pair of compasses and a ruler.

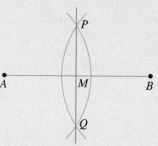

3. Triangles

   (a) A triangle is a closed plane figure that has three sides.

   (b) Types of triangles
   By sides:

An **equilateral triangle** has all sides of equal length and angles that are equal. Since sum of angles of a △ is 180°, each angle is 60°.

An **isosceles triangle** has two sides of equal length. Its base angles are equal.

A **scalene triangle** has all sides of different lengths. All its angles are different.

   By angles:

An **acute-angled triangle** has all angles measuring less than 90°.

A **right-angled triangle** has one angle measuring exactly 90°.

An **obtuse-angled triangle** has one angle measuring greater than 90°.

(c) The angle sum of a triangle is 180°,

i.e. $\angle a + \angle b + \angle c = 180°$ ($\angle$ sum of $\triangle$)

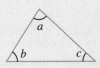

(d) An exterior angle of a triangle is equal to the sum of the interior opposite angles,

i.e. $\angle e = \angle a + \angle b$ (ext. $\angle$ of $\triangle$)

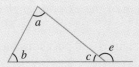

4. Quadrilaterals
   (a) A quadrilateral is a closed plane figure that has four sides.

(b) The sum of the angles of a quadrilateral is 360°,

i.e. $\angle a + \angle b + \angle c + \angle d = 360°$ ($\angle$ sum of quad)

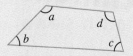

(c) Types of special quadrilaterals

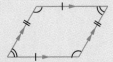   

A **parallelogram** has opposite sides that are equal and parallel. Opposite angles are equal.
Diagonals bisect each other.

A **rectangle** has opposite sides that are equal and parallel, and all angles are 90°.
Diagonals are equal.
Diagonals bisect each other.

A **rhombus** has opposite sides parallel and all sides equal. Opposite angles are equal.
Diagonals bisect all interior angles. Diagonals bisect each other at right angles.

          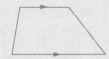

A **square** has opposite sides parallel, all sides equal and all angles are 90°.
Diagonals are equal.
Diagonals bisect each other at right angles.
Diagonals bisect all interior angles.

A **kite** has two pairs of adjacent equal sides. One pair of opposite angles are equal.
One diagonal bisects the other. Diagonals intersect at right angles. One diagonal bisects a pair of opposite angles.

A **trapezium** has one pair of opposite sides that are parallel.

5. Polygons

    (a) A polygon is a closed plane figure formed by three or more line segments.

    (b) A regular polygon has equal sides and equal interior angles. All other polygons are irregular polygons.

    (c) The sum of the interior angles of a polygon is $(n - 2) \times 180°$ where n = number of sides.

    (d) The sum of the exterior angles of any polygon is $360°$.

6. Congruent figures and polygons have the same shape and size. For congruent polygons, their

    • corresponding angles are equal.

    • corresponding sides are equal.

Enrichment
● ● ● **m a t h s** ● ● ●

Fun with Tangrams

The tangram is an interesting Chinese puzzle that consists of seven pieces which fit together to form a square. Among the seven pieces, there are:

    • 5 right isosceles triangles (2 small ones, 1 medium one and 2 large ones),

    • 1 square, and

    • 1 parallelogram

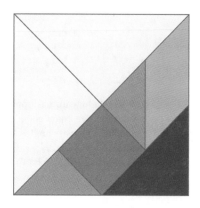

We can form specific shapes or figures using some or all of the seven pieces. For example, the trapezium shown below was formed using two of the isosceles triangles while the rabbit figure was formed using all the seven pieces.

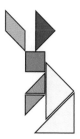

Tangrams can easily be made from cardboard. Try making your own tangram by following the steps given below.

Step 1 Draw a 4 × 4 square on cardboard.

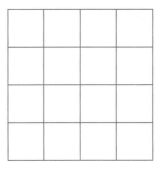

Step 2 Draw diagonals across the squares as shown in the diagram on the right.

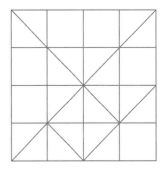

Step 3 Cut out the seven pieces following the outlines shown in the diagram on the right.

1. Using your tangram, check if the following can be done.
   (i) Form a square using two tangram pieces.
   (ii) Form a square using three tangram pieces.
   (iii) Form a square using four tangram pieces.
   (iv) Form a square using five tangram pieces.
   (v) Form a square using six tangram pieces.

2. Which of the following figures can you make using all seven tangram pieces?
   (i) A trapezium
   (ii) A rectangle (that is not a square)
   (iii) A parallelogram (that is not a square)
   (iv) A rhombus (that is not a square)
   (v) A kite
   (vi) A triangle

Have fun using your tangram!

You have 10 minutes to answer the following questions.
Choose the most appropriate answer.

CONCEPT CHECK

6.1 **1.** In the diagram shown on the right,
AP is the angle bisector of $\angle BAC$.
Find the value of $\angle BAC$.

    A   10°   **B**   20°

    C   40°   **D**   70°

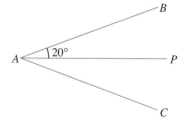

6.1 **2.** In the diagram shown on the right,

    A $AM = BM$.

    B $\angle AMP = \angle BMP$.

    C $\angle AMP = 90°$.

    D   All of the above.

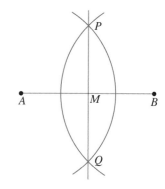

6.2 **3.** Choose the correct statement.

    A   An isosceles triangle is equilateral.

    B   An equilateral triangle is isosceles.

    C   An equilateral triangle is not isosceles.

    D   An isosceles triangle is not equilateral.

6.2 **4.** Which of the mathematical statements given below is correct?

    A $\angle a = 360° - (60° + 70°)$ ($\angle$ sum of $\triangle$)

    B $\angle a = 180° - 60° - 70°$ (adj. $\angle$s on a str. line)

    C $\angle a = 180° - (60° + 70°)$ ($\angle$ sum of $\triangle$)

    D $\angle a = 180° - 60° - 70°$ (int. $\angle$s of $\triangle$)

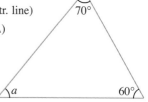

6.2 **5.** Which of the mathematical statements given below is correct?

    A $\angle b = 180° - 55° - 34°$ ($\angle$ sum of $\triangle$)

    B $\angle b = 55° + 34°$ (ext. $\angle$ of $\triangle$)

    C $\angle b = 55° - 34°$ (difference of $\angle$s of $\triangle$)

    D $\angle b + 34° = 55°$ (ext. $\angle$ of $\triangle$)

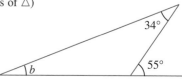

6. The sum of all the interior angles of a quadrilateral

    A is 180°.

    B is 360°.

    C is 400°.

    D depends on the type of quadrilateral.

7. Which quadrilateral has two pairs of equal sides but none of them are parallel to each other?

    A parallelogram   **B** kite

    C trapezium   **D** rhombus

8. The value of each of the interior angles of a regular n-gon is

    A 60°.   **B** $\dfrac{360°}{n}$.

    C $(n-2) \times 180°$.   **D** $\dfrac{(n-2) \times 180°}{n}$.

9. Given that the exterior angles of a pentagon are $x°$, $2x°$, $2x°$, $3x°$ and $4x°$, find the value of x.

    A 75   **B** 60   **C** 45   **D** 30

10. Given that the two quadrilaterals shown below are congruent, write down the values of p, q and r. All sides are in cm.

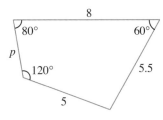 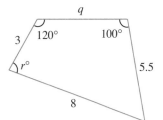

    A $p = 3$, $q = 5$ and $r = 60$.

    B $p = 5$, $q = 3$ and $r = 60$.

    C $p = 3$, $q = 5$ and $r = 80$.

    D $p = 5$, $q = 3$ and $r = 80$.

SECTION A

1. Find the value of ∠x in each of the following figures.

(a)

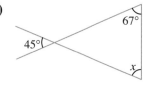

(b)

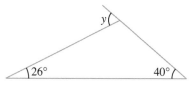

2. Find the value of ∠y in each of the following figures.

(a)

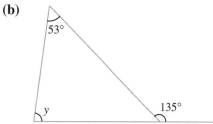

(b)

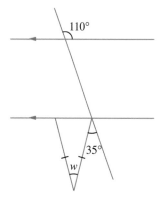

3. Find the value of ∠w in each of the following figures.

(a)

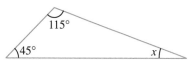

(b)

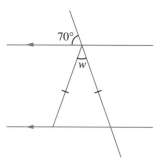

4. The two triangles shown in each of the following figures are congruent. Find the value of the unknown angle u in each case.

(a)

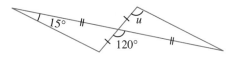

(b)

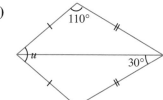

SECTION B

5. Find the value of c in each of the following figures.

(a)

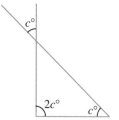

(b)

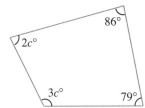

6. For each of the quadrilaterals given below, find the value of ∠z.

(a) Rectangle *ABCD*

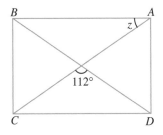

(b) Rhombus *PQRS*

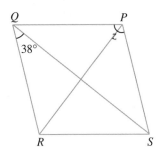

(c) Kite *STUV*

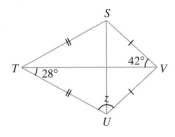

7. (a) How many sides are there in a regular polygon if each exterior angle is 45°?

(b) How many sides does a polygon have if the sum of its interior angles is 1 800°?

8. *PQRST* is a pentagon. Its interior angles, *P*, *Q*, *R*, *S* and *T* are *x*°, 2*x*°, 3*x*°, 4*x*° and 120° respectively.

(a) Calculate the largest exterior angle.

(b) Calculate the largest interior angle.

SECTION C

9. (a) Construct △*ABC* such that *AB* = 3 cm, *BC* = 4 cm and *CA* = 5 cm. Measure and write down ∠*b*.

(b) (i) Construct △*PQR* such that ∠*p* = 50°, *PQ* = 5 cm and *PR* = 5 cm.

   (ii) Construct the perpendicular bisector of *QR* and label the point where it cuts *QR* as *S*.

   (iii) Measure and write down the length of *PS*, in cm.

10. (i) Construct a quadrilateral *WXYZ* such that *WX* = 8 cm, ∠*ZWX* = 90°, *WZ* = 6 cm, ∠*WXY* = 80° and *YZ* = 10 cm.

   (ii) Measure *XZ*, in cm, and state what type of triangle △*XYZ* is.

   (iii) Construct the angle bisector of ∠*XYZ*.

   (iv) Construct a line that passes through the point *Z* and is parallel to *WX*.

Mensuration

Archimedes (287 BC–212 BC) was an ancient Greek mathematician who was considered to be one of the three greatest mathematicians of all time. Although he was best known for having said "Eureka!" ("I have found it!") after discovering a solution to a problem posed to him by a king, Archimedes considered his greatest achievement to be the discovery of the volume and surface area of a sphere.

By comparing a sphere to a cylinder of the same diameter and height, he proved that the volume of the sphere equals two-thirds the volume of the cylinder. He also proved that the surface area of the sphere is two-thirds the total surface area of the same cylinder. He was so excited by this discovery that he requested his tombstone be engraved with a picture of a sphere and its circumscribing cylinder.

In this chapter, you will be learning more about surface areas and volumes of three-dimensional solids such as pyramids, cones and spheres.

Pyramids

7.1.1 Introduction

A **pyramid** is a three-dimensional (3D) figure that has a polygonal base and at least three slanted triangular faces. The slanted triangular faces meet at a common point, called the **vertex**. The vertex is the highest point of the pyramid.

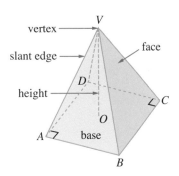

The pyramid shown above has a rectangular base *ABCD* and four slanted triangular faces, *ADV*, *ABV*, *BCV* and *CDV*. The four slanted faces of the pyramid meet at the vertex.

The perpendicular distance from the vertex to the base gives the **height** of the pyramid. A **right pyramid** is one where the perpendicular from the vertex falls onto the centre of the base.

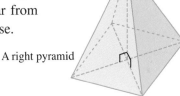

A right pyramid

As mentioned above, a pyramid has a polygonal base. This means that the base of a pyramid can be in the shape of any polygon. Some examples are triangle, square, pentagon and hexagon. Pyramids are named according to the shapes of their bases as shown below.

note

Recall:
A **polygon** is a closed plane figure formed by three or more line segments.

triangular pyramid

square pyramid

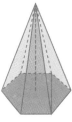

pentagonal pyramid

hexagonal pyramid

7.1.2   Total Surface Area of Pyramids

We can use nets to visualise the surface area of pyramids. In Book 1, you have seen that a **net** is a two-dimensional (2D) figure that can be folded into a three-dimensional (3D) object.

Solids

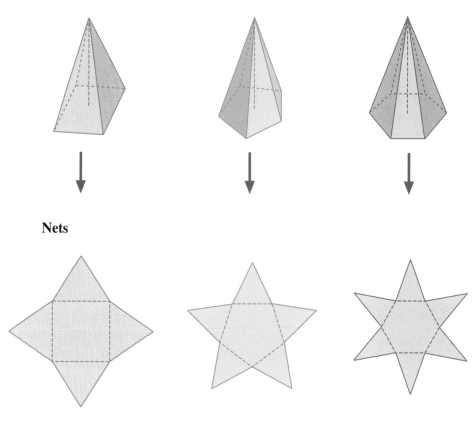

Nets

> The **total surface area** of a pyramid is the sum of the areas of all its faces, i.e., the sum of its base area and all its slanted faces.

Example 1

VABCD is a pyramid with a square base of side 12 cm. Given that the slant height of the triangular faces is 10 cm, find the total surface area of the pyramid.

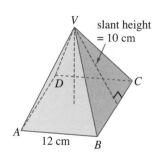

note

The **slant height** of a pyramid is the height of a slanted face.

Solution

The net of a square pyramid is made up of a square and four identical isosceles triangles.

Area of square base = 12 × 12

= 144 cm^2

Area of four triangles

$= 4 \times \left(\dfrac{1}{2} \times 12 \times 10 \right)$

$= 240$ cm^2

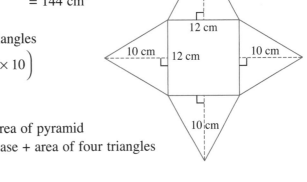

∴   Total surface area of pyramid

= area of the base + area of four triangles

= 144 + 240

= 384 cm^2

7.1.3   Volume of Pyramids

The figure below shows that a cube can be made up of three identical square pyramids. In the figure, the bases of the pyramids are *ABCD*, *CDEH* and *DEFA* with corresponding heights *BG*, *HG* and *FG*.

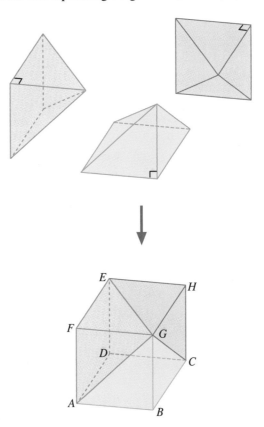

We can see that

Volume of 3 square pyramids = Volume of a cube
∴ 3 × Volume of a square pyramid = $A \times h$
Volume of a square pyramid = $\frac{1}{3}Ah$,

where A = area of cross-section of the cube and h = height.

Through the activity shown below, we can also deduce that the volume of any pyramid is one-third the volume of a **prism** having the same base and height as the pyramid.

Suppose we want to fill the rectangular tank below with water. If we use a container in the shape of a rectangular pyramid, having the same base and height as the rectangular tank, we will find that we will need three such filled containers to fill the tank. Thus, we can say that the container has one-third the volume of the tank.

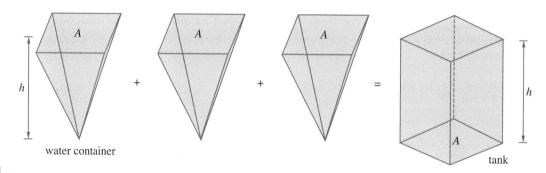

water container

tank

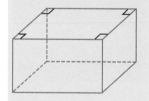
The same result can be observed for a pyramid with another type of polygonal base. Its volume will always be one-third the volume of the prism having the same base and height as the pyramid.

In general,

Volume of pyramid = $\frac{1}{3}Ah$,

where A = area of cross-section of the prism (base area) and h = height.

Example 2

Find the volume of a rectangular pyramid if its base measures 12 cm by 6 cm and its height is 8 cm.

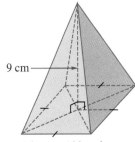

Solution

$$\text{Volume of pyramid} = \frac{1}{3} Ah$$

$$= \frac{1}{3} \times (12 \times 6) \times 8$$

$$= 192 \text{ cm}^3$$

note

h must be the vertical height that is perpendicular to the base, **not** the slant height.

Example 3

Find the height of a tetrahedron (also known as a triangular pyramid) if it has a volume of 80 cm³ and a base area of 24 cm².

Solution

$$\text{Volume of tetrahedron} = 80 \text{ cm}^3$$

$$\frac{1}{3} Ah = 80$$

$$\frac{1}{3} \times 24 \times h = 80$$

$$\therefore \quad \text{Height of tetrahedron, } h = \frac{80 \times 3}{24}$$

$$= 10 \text{ cm}$$

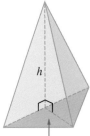

Base area = 24 cm²

note

Notice that the pyramid shown in Example 3 is not a right pyramid. However, we can still use the formula $V = \frac{1}{3} Ah$, as it applies to all pyramids, and not just right pyramids.

Example 4

A square pyramid of height 9 cm has a volume of 108 cm³. Calculate
(a) the area of the base,
(b) the length of each side of the base.

Solution

(a) Volume of pyramid = 108 cm³

$$\frac{1}{3} Ah = 108$$

$$\frac{1}{3} \times A \times 9 = 108$$

$$\therefore \quad \text{Base area, } A = \frac{108 \times 3}{9}$$

$$= 36 \text{ cm}^2$$

9 cm

Volume = 108 cm³

note

$l^2 = 36$
$l = \pm\sqrt{36}$
$\quad = \pm 6$
$l \neq -6$ because $l > 0$.
$\therefore \quad l = 6$

(b) Since the base is a square, base area $= l^2$
$$= 36$$

$$\therefore \quad \text{Length of each side, } l = \sqrt{36}$$

$$= 6 \text{ cm}$$

1. For each of the following pyramids, draw the net and then calculate its total surface area using your net.

   (a)

   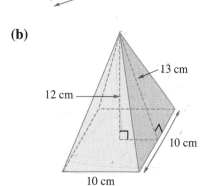

   (b)

   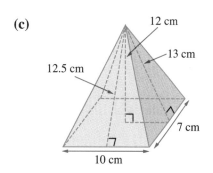

   (c)

   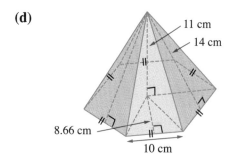

   (d)

   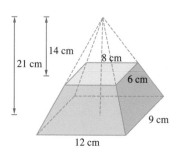

2. Find the volumes of the pyramids shown in Question 1.

3. Find the height of each of the following pyramids with
   (a) volume 72 cm³, base area 36 cm²,
   (b) volume 168 cm³, base area 63 cm²,
   (c) volume 396 cm³, base area 99 cm².

4. For each of the following square pyramids,
   (i) calculate its base area,
   (ii) calculate the length of each side of its base.

   (a) volume = 98 cm³, height = 6 cm
   (b) volume = 216 cm³, height = 8 cm
   (c) volume = 676 cm³, height = 12 cm

5. Calculate the missing values in the table below for the rectangular pyramids in (a) to (h) of length l, breadth b, base area A, height h and volume V.

	l	b	A	h	V
(a)	5 cm	6 cm		7 cm	
(b)	1.2 m	3 m		4 m	
(c)	8 cm	9 cm			144 cm³
(d)	3.4 m	5 m			34 m³
(e)	6 cm			8 cm	112 cm³
(f)	5 m			6 m	67 m³
(g)		8 cm		9 cm	168 cm³
(h)		4 m		5 m	52 m³

6. The diagram below shows part of a pyramid. Calculate its volume.

7.

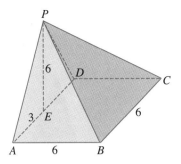

PABCD is a pyramid standing on a horizontal base ABCD. ABCD is a square with sides of length 6 cm.

E is the midpoint of AD. PE is vertical and PE = 6 cm.

Calculate the volume of PABCD.

[The volume of a pyramid = $\frac{1}{3}$ × base area × height]

[O/Jun 94/P1]

★**8.** The diagram shows a model of a building. It consists of a square-based pyramid, VJKLM, attached to a cuboid. The vertical line, VYX, passes through the centres, Y and X, of the horizontal squares JKLM and RSTU. JK = KL = 40 cm and VY = 48 cm.

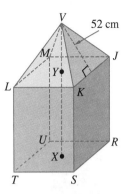

(a) Given also that TL = 70 cm, calculate
   (i) the volume of the model,
   (ii) the total surface area of the sides and top of the model.

(b) Edmund wants to paint the sides and tops of 6 such models. The paint is supplied in tins, each of which contains enough paint to cover a surface area of 5 m². Find the number of tins of paint he would need.

(**7.2**)   **Cones**

7.2.1   Introduction

A **cone** is a three-dimensional figure with a flat circular base and a curved surface. Like the pyramid, a cone also has a vertex.

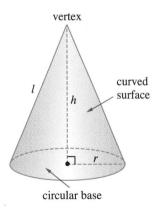

The perpendicular distance from the vertex to the base gives the height of the cone. In the figure above, r is the base of the cone, h is its height and l is the slant height of the cone.

The pictures below show some objects in our daily lives that are conical in shape. Can you recognise these objects?

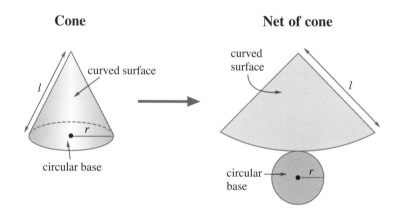

7.2.2 Total Surface Area of Cones

Let us consider the net of the cone shown below.

Cone   **Net of cone**

curved surface

curved surface

l l

r

circular base   circular base r

As with a pyramid, we can find the **total surface area of a cone** by finding the sum of all its faces. Thus,

Total surface area of a cone = curved surface area + area of circular base

Let us now explore how we can find the **curved surface area of a cone**. If we take a piece of paper and cut it in the shape shown on the left below, we can join sides OA and OB to form the curved surface of a cone.

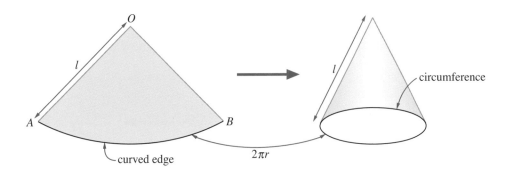

Length of curved edge $AB = 2\pi r$

We can see that the curved surface area of the cone above is equivalent to the area of OAB. As OAB is a part of a circle with centre O, we can use proportion to get the following:

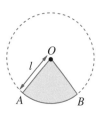

> **note**
>
> The circumference of the circular base of the cone is the length of the curved edge of the sector.

$$\frac{\text{Area of } OAB}{\text{Area of circle of radius } l} = \frac{\text{Length of curved edge } AB}{\text{Circumference of circle of radius } l}$$

$$\frac{\text{Area of } OAB}{\pi l^2} = \frac{2\pi r}{2\pi l}$$

$$\therefore \quad \text{Area of } OAB = \frac{2\pi r}{2\pi l} \times \pi l^2$$

$$= \pi r l$$

We can also make a cone by rotating a right-angled triangle around one of its two short sides. Visit http://www.mathsisfun. com/geometry/cone. html to see the animation.

In general,

> **Curved surface area of cone** $= \pi r l$,
> **Total surface area of cone** $= \pi r l + \pi r^2$,
> where r = radius and l = slant height.

Example 5

Find the total surface area of a solid cone of base radius 7 cm and slant height 25 cm. $\left(\text{Take } \pi = \frac{22}{7} \right)$

Solution

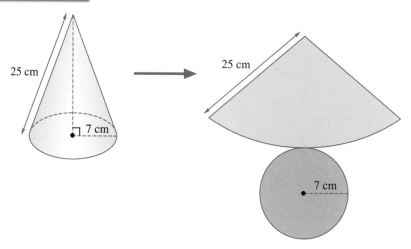

Take out the common factor πr.

Total surface area of a cone = curved surface area + area of circular base

$$= \pi r l + \pi r^2$$
$$= \pi r (l + r)$$
$$= \frac{22}{7} \times 7 \times (25 + 7)$$
$$= \frac{22}{7_1} \times \overset{1}{7} \times 32$$
$$= 704 \text{ cm}^2$$

Example 6

Find the slant height of a cone of curved surface area 19.14 cm² and base radius 2.1 cm. Give your answer correct to 3 significant figures. (Take $\pi = 3.142$)

Solution

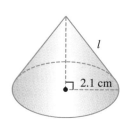

Curved surface area = 19.14 cm²

$$\pi r l = 19.14$$
$$3.142 \times 2.1 \times l = 19.14$$
$$\therefore \quad \text{Slant height, } l = \frac{19.14}{3.142 \times 2.1}$$
$$= 2.90 \text{ cm (correct to 3 sig. fig.)}$$

Example 7

Find the base area of a cone of curved surface area 40.7 cm² and slant height 3.7 cm. Give your answer correct to 3 significant figures.

Solution

note

If value of π is not specified, use your calculator value of π.

$$\text{Curved surface area} = 40.7 \text{ cm}^2$$
$$\pi r l = 40.7$$
$$3.142 \times r \times 3.7 = 40.7$$
$$\therefore \quad r = \frac{40.7}{\pi \times 3.7}$$
$$= 3.50 \text{ cm (correct to 3 sig. fig.)}$$

$$\therefore \quad \text{Base area of cone} = \pi r^2$$
$$= \pi \times (3.50)^2$$
$$= 38.5 \text{ cm}^2 \text{ (correct to 3 sig. fig.)}$$

Example 8

note

Recall:
A circle can be divided into 4 equal quadrants.

The diagram shows a quadrant of radius 28 cm. What is the radius of the base of a cone that can be formed from this quadrant?

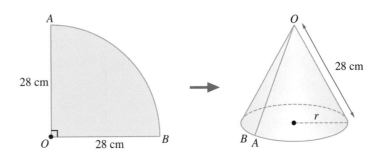

Solution

The strategy is to relate the circumference of the base of the cone to the length of curved edge *AB* since the circumference is formed by the curved edge.

Do not substitute the value of π as it can be cancelled out later.

Circumference of base of cone = $2\pi r$
(*r* is the radius of the cone)

Length of curved edge $AB = \frac{1}{4} \times 2\pi R$
(*R* is the radius of the quadrant)

$$\text{Circumference of base of cone} = \text{Length of curved edge } AB$$
$$2\pi r = \frac{1}{4} \times 2\pi(28)$$
$$\therefore \quad \text{Base radius, } r = \frac{\frac{1}{4} \times 2\overset{1}{\pi}(28)}{2\underset{1}{\pi}}$$
$$= \frac{1}{4} \times 28$$
$$= 7 \text{ cm}$$

1. Taking $\pi = \dfrac{22}{7}$, find the curved surface areas of each of the following cones with
   (a) radius 7 cm, slant height 7.4 cm,
   (b) diameter 8.4 cm, slant height 5.8 cm,
   (c) radius 7 m, slant height 25 m.

2. Taking $\pi = 3.142$, find the total surface areas of the following solid cones, giving your answers correct to 3 significant figures.
   (a) radius = 4 cm, slant height = 5 cm
   (b) diameter = 10 cm, slant height = 13 cm
   (c) radius = 4 m, slant height = 4.1 m

3. Find the slant height of a cone of curved surface area 471.3 cm^2 and base radius 10 cm. (Take $\pi = 3.142$)

4. Find the base area of a cone of curved surface area 157.1 cm^2 and slant length 10 cm. (Take $\pi = 3.142$)

5. A quadrant is cut off from a circle of radius 8 cm. What is the radius of the base of the cone when sides CO and DO of the remaining figure are joined?

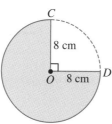

6. Calculate the missing values in the table below for each of the following cones (a) to (h) with slant height l and base radius r.

	l	r	Base area	Curved surface area
(a)	7 cm	4.2 cm		
(b)	11.2 m	10.5 m		
(c)		7 m		550 m^2
(d)		35 cm		4 070 cm^2
(e)	29 cm			1 914 cm^2
(f)	3.5 m			30.8 m^2
(g)	14.8 m		616 m^2	
(h)	12.5 cm		38.5 cm^2	

7. Find the curved surface area of an ice-cream cone with diameter 3.5 cm and slant height 10 cm. Give your answer correct to 3 significant figures.

7.2.3 Volume of Cones

A cone may be considered the result of a sequence of pyramids with an increasing number of faces.

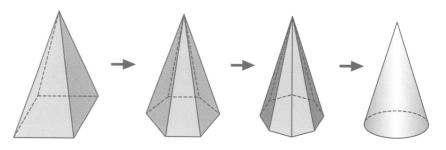

Hence, we can view a cone as a special pyramid with a circular base.

Recall that the volume of a pyramid is one-third the volume of a prism with the same base and height. Since a cone is a special pyramid, this rule should apply to the cone as well.

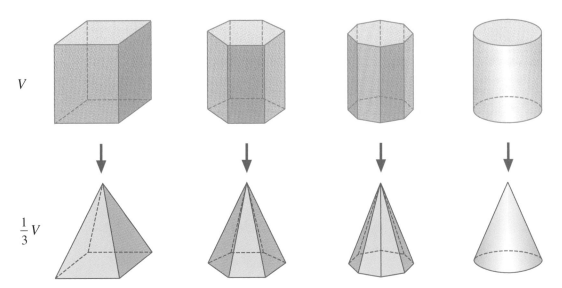

V

$\frac{1}{3}V$

Thus, volume of cone = $\frac{1}{3}$ × volume of cylinder

$= \frac{1}{3}$ × base area × height

$= \frac{1}{3}\pi r^2 h$

In general,

Volume of cone = $\frac{1}{3}\pi r^2 h$,

where r = radius and h = height of the cone.

We can also deduce that the volume of a cone is one-third the volume of a cylinder by doing the following activity. Take a cylindrical tank and a water container in the shape of a cone with the same base and height as the tank. It can be seen that it would take three such filled containers to fill the cylindrical tank with water.

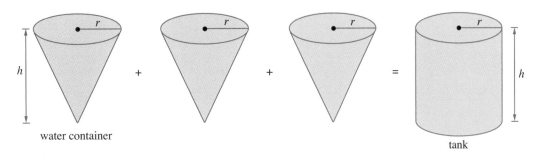

water container

tank

Example 9

Find the volume of the solid cone shown on the right. $\left(\text{Take } \pi = \dfrac{22}{7} \right)$

Solution

note

h must be the vertical height, **not** the slant height.

$$\text{Volume of cone} = \frac{1}{3}\pi r^2 h$$

$$= \frac{1}{3} \times \frac{22}{7} \times (7)^2 \times 24$$

$$= 1\ 232 \text{ cm}^3$$

Example 10

Find the height of a cone of base radius 21 cm and volume $8\ 820\pi$ cm^3.

Solution

$$\text{Volume of cone} = 8\ 820\pi \text{ cm}^3$$

$$\frac{1}{3}\pi r^2 h = 8\ 820\pi$$

Do not substitute the value of π as it can be cancelled out later.

$$\frac{1}{3} \times \pi \times (21)^2 \times h = 8\ 820\pi$$

$$\therefore \quad \text{Height of cone, } h = \frac{8\ 820\overset{1}{\pi}}{\dfrac{1}{3} \times \underset{1}{\pi} \times (21)^2}$$

$$= 60 \text{ cm}$$

Example 11

Find the radius of the base of a cone of height 3 cm and volume 12.56 cm^3. Give your answer correct to 3 significant figures.
(Take $\pi = 3.142$)

Solution

$$\text{Volume of cone} = 12.56 \text{ cm}^3$$

$$\frac{1}{3}\pi r^2 h = 12.56$$

$$\frac{1}{\underset{1}{3}} \times 3.142 \times r^2 \times 3^1 = 12.56$$

$$r^2 = \frac{12.56}{3.142}$$

$$\therefore \quad \text{Base radius, } r = \sqrt{\frac{12.56}{3.142}}$$

$$= 2.00 \text{ cm (correct to 3 sig. fig.)}$$

1. Taking $\pi = \dfrac{22}{7}$, calculate the volumes of each of the following solid cones with
   (a) radius 12 cm, height 35 cm,
   (b) radius 4 cm, height 4.2 cm,
   (c) diameter 7 m, height 1.2 m.

2. Find the height of each of the following cones with
   (a) radius 7 m, volume 392π m^3,
   (b) radius 4.2 cm, volume 23.52π cm^3,
   (c) diameter 4 m, volume 2.8π m^3.

3. Taking $\pi = 3.142$, calculate the height of each of the following cones with
   (a) radius 4 cm, volume 50.24 cm^3,
   (b) radius 2.5 m, volume 78.5 m^3,
   (c) diameter 10 cm, volume 314 cm^3.

4. Find the base area of each of the following cones with
   (a) volume 100 m^3, height 10 m,
   (b) volume 12.3 cm^3, height 3 cm,
   (c) volume 45.6 m^3, height 1.2 m.

5. Taking $\pi = 3.142$, find the radius of each of the following cones. Give your answers correct to 3 significant figures.
   (a) volume = 1 078 cm^3, height = 21 cm
   (b) volume = 528 m^3, height = 14 m
   (c) volume = 6.6 cm^3, height = 0.7 cm

6. A cone has a base radius of 7.7 cm, a vertical height of 26.4 cm and a slant height of 27.5 cm.
   Calculate
   (a) the area of the base,
   (b) the volume of the cone.

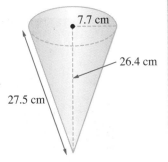

7. [The value of π is 3.142, correct to 3 decimal places.]

   A Large Traffic Marker consists of a solid cone, of height 40 cm and radius 9 cm, with a solid cylindrical base of diameter 30 cm and thickness 2 cm.
   (a) Calculate the volume of the cone.

   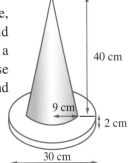

   [Volume of a cone = $\dfrac{1}{3}\pi r^2 h$]

   (b) Calculate the **total** volume of the Marker. [O/Jun 96/P2]

8. A closed container is made by joining together a cylinder and a cone with common radius 6 cm. The length of the cylinder is 12 cm and the height of the cone is 6 cm as shown below.

   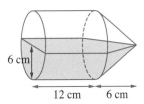

   The container rests on a horizontal surface and is exactly half full of water.
   (a) Show that the volume of water is 252π cm^3.
   (b) The container is now placed with its circular end on a horizontal surface as shown on the right. Calculate the depth of water.
   ★(c) The container is then held with its axis vertical, the cone being at the bottom as shown on the right. Calculate the depth of water.

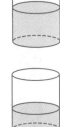

Ratio of Heights

A cone and a cylinder have a common radius and equal volumes. What is the ratio of the height of the cone to the height of the cylinder?

Discuss with your classmates and explain in your Mathematics Journal how you obtained the answer.

7.3 Spheres

7.3.1 Introduction

A **sphere** is a three-dimensional figure that has only one closed curved surface. The distance from any point on its surface to the centre of the sphere is a constant called the **radius**. In the figure below, r is the radius of the sphere. The **diameter** of the sphere, represented by d, is twice the radius of the sphere.

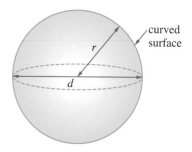

There are many real-life examples of spheres in our world. For example, the balls that are used in games such as soccer and basketball are spherical in shape. There are also buildings and sculptures that are spherical in shape. One such example is the rotating global structure that can be found at the Universal Studios in Hollywood.

7.3.2 Surface Area of Spheres

The figures below show a sphere of radius r and a cylinder of radius r and height $2r$.

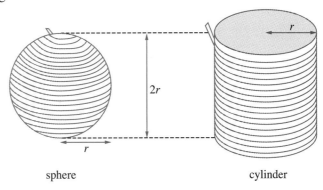

sphere   cylinder

It can be shown that if we use a length of rope to wind around the sphere such that there is no gap between each round of rope, the exact same length of rope can be used to wind around the curved surface area of the cylinder completely. Therefore, in the diagram above,

$$\begin{aligned}
\text{Surface area of sphere} &= \text{Curved surface area of cylinder} \\
&= 2\pi rh \\
&= 2\pi r(2r) \\
&= 4\pi r^2
\end{aligned}$$

note

Finding the surface area of a sphere helps us determine the amount of material needed to cover the sphere. For example, the amount of fabric needed to cover a tennis ball can be determined by finding its total surface area.

In general,

Surface area of sphere = $4\pi r^2$,
where r = radius.

Related Surface Areas

In the chapter opener, it was stated that Archimedes proved that the surface area of a sphere equals two-thirds the total surface area of a cylinder with the same diameter and height as that of the sphere.

Using your knowledge of the formulae for surface area of a sphere and total surface area of a cylinder, can you verify that this is true?

Example 12

Taking $\pi = 3.142$, calculate correct to 3 significant figures, the surface area of a sphere of

(a) radius 3 cm, **(b)** diameter 10 cm.

Solution

(a) Surface area of sphere $= 4\pi r^2$
$$= 4 \times 3.142 \times (3)^2$$
$$= 113.112$$
$$= 113 \text{ cm}^2 \text{ (correct to 3 sig. fig.)}$$

Diameter = 2 × radius

(b) Radius of sphere, $r = \dfrac{10}{2}$
$$= 5 \text{ cm}$$

Surface area of sphere $= 4\pi r^2$
$$= 4 \times 3.142 \times (5)^2$$
$$= 314.2$$
$$= 314 \text{ cm}^2 \text{ (correct to 3 sig. fig.)}$$

7.3.3   Volume of Spheres

Let us do a simple activity to determine the volume of a sphere.

Take two objects – a solid sphere and a cylindrical container with an open end. The radii of both the sphere and cylindrical container must be equal and the height of the cylindrical container must be twice the radius of the sphere.

Place the sphere in the cylinder as shown in the figure on the left below. Then, pour water into the cylinder until the water reaches the brim of the cylinder. Next, take the sphere out of the cylinder carefully without spilling any water.

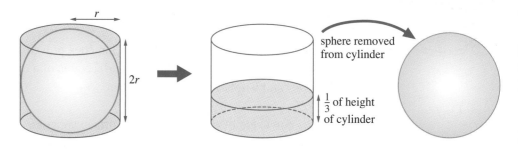

What do you notice about the volume of the water left in the cylinder?

Can you see that the water occupies exactly one-third of the cylinder now? This indicates that the sphere occupied exactly two-thirds of the cylinder. Therefore,

$$\text{Volume of sphere} = \frac{2}{3} \times \text{volume of cylinder}$$

$$= \frac{2}{3} \times \pi r^2 h$$

$$= \frac{2}{3} \times \pi r^2 (2r)$$

$$= \frac{4}{3} \pi r^3$$

note

Finding the volume of a sphere helps us determine the amount of material required to manufacture it. For example, the amount of steel required to manufacture a ball bearing can be determined by finding its volume.

In general,

> **Volume of sphere** $= \dfrac{4}{3} \pi r^3$,
>
> where r = radius.

Example 13

Taking $\pi = 3.142$, calculate correct to 3 significant figures,
(a) the surface area, and
(b) the volume
of a sphere of radius 1.5 cm.

Solution

(a) Surface area of sphere $= 4\pi r^2$
$$= 4 \times 3.142 \times (1.5)^2$$
$$= 28.278$$
$$= 28.3 \text{ cm}^2 \text{ (correct to 3 sig. fig.)}$$

(b) Volume of sphere $= \dfrac{4}{3} \pi r^3$
$$= \frac{4}{3} \times 3.142 \times (1.5)^3$$
$$= 14.139$$
$$= 14.1 \text{ cm}^3 \text{ (correct to 3 sig. fig.)}$$

note

A **hemisphere** is half of a sphere.

Volume of hemisphere

$= \dfrac{1}{2} \times$ volume of sphere

$= \dfrac{1}{2} \times \dfrac{4}{3}\pi r^3$

$= \dfrac{2}{3}\pi r^3$

Do not substitute the value of π as it can be cancelled out later.

A hollow hemisphere is open at the top (like a bowl). Thus, the area of the top circle is not included in the answer to **(b)**.

Example 14

A hollow hemisphere of negligible thickness has a volume of 144π cm^3. Calculate
(a) its radius,
(b) its outer surface area (Leave your answer in terms of π).

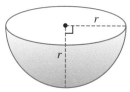

Solution

(a) Volume of hemisphere $= 144\pi$ cm^3

$$\dfrac{1}{2} \times \dfrac{4}{3}\pi r^3 = 144\pi$$

$$r^3 = \dfrac{\overset{1}{\cancel{144}}\,\cancel{\pi}}{\dfrac{1}{2} \times \dfrac{4}{3}\,\underset{1}{\cancel{\pi}}}$$

$$= 216$$

$$\therefore \quad \text{Radius, } r = \sqrt[3]{216}$$

$$= 6 \text{ cm}$$

(b) Outer surface area of hemisphere $= \dfrac{1}{2} \times 4\pi r^2$

$$= \dfrac{1}{2} \times 4\pi \times (6)^2$$

$$= 72\pi \text{ cm}^2$$

Example 15

Calculate, correct to 3 significant figures,
(a) the radius, and **(b)** the volume
of the sphere with a surface area of 1 386 cm^2.

Solution

note

Work to 4 or more significant figures when the answer required is in 3 significant figures.

(a) Surface area of sphere $= 1\ 386$ cm^2

$$4\pi r^2 = 1\ 386$$

$$4 \times \pi \times r^2 = 1\ 386$$

$$r^2 = \dfrac{1\ 386}{4 \times \pi}$$

$$= 110.29$$

$$\therefore \quad \text{Radius, } r = \sqrt{110.29}$$

$$= 10.5 \text{ cm (correct to 3 sig. fig.)}$$

(b) Volume of sphere $= \dfrac{4}{3}\pi r^3$

$$= \dfrac{4}{3} \times \pi \times (10.5)^3$$

$$= 4\ 850 \text{ cm}^3 \text{ (correct to 3 sig. fig.)}$$

1. Taking $\pi = 3.142$, calculate, correct to 3 significant figures,
   (i) the surface area, and
   (ii) the volume
   of each of the following spheres with
   (a) radius 1 cm,
   (b) radius 14 cm,
   (c) diameter 14 cm,
   (d) diameter 2.5 cm.

2. Find
   (i) the radius, and
   (ii) the surface area in terms of π
   of each of the following spheres with
   (a) volume 288π cm³,
   (b) volume 36π cm³.

3. Find
   (i) the radius, and
   (ii) the outer surface area in terms of π
   of each of the following hemispheres with
   (a) volume $83\frac{1}{3}\pi$ cm³,
   (b) volume $5\frac{1}{3}\pi$ cm³.

4. Find, correct to 3 significant figures,
   (i) the radius, and
   (ii) the volume
   of each of the following spheres with
   (a) surface area = 616 cm²,
   (b) surface area = 154 cm².

5. A spherical lead ball of radius 6 cm is remoulded into 216 identical spherical lead shots.
   (a) Calculate the volume of the lead ball in terms of π.
   (b) Find the radius of each lead shot.

6. A dome is in the shape of a hemisphere of diameter 21 m. Calculate the area of coloured glass required to cover the curved surface of the dome.

7. Calculate, correct to 3 significant figures, the total volume of water contained in three bowls, if each bowl is a hemisphere of internal diameter 10 cm and is filled to its rim. (Take $\pi = 3.142$)

8. Taking $\pi = 3.142$, calculate correct to 3 significant figures,
   (i) the total surface area, and
   (ii) the volume
   of each of the following solids.

   (a) 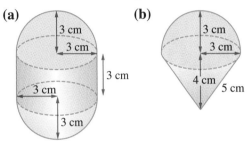 (b)

9. Find the ratio of the surface area of the sphere to that of the total surface area of the circumscribed cylinder shown on the right.

   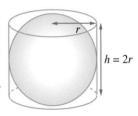

★10. The figure shows a circumscribed 'equilateral' right circular cone. Find the following ratios.
   (a) $\dfrac{\text{Surface area of the sphere}}{\text{Total surface area of the cone}}$

   (b) $\dfrac{\text{Volume of the sphere}}{\text{Volume of the cone}}$

   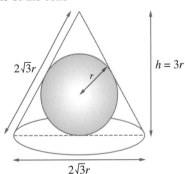

The Eight Little Spheres

Eight little spheres of mercury, each with a radius of 1 mm, are combined to form a single sphere. What is the percentage change in the total surface area?

Discuss with your classmates and show in your Mathematics Journal how you arrive at the answer.

SUMMARY

1. For a pyramid,

    Total surface area = sum of the areas of all its faces

    Volume = $\dfrac{1}{3}Ah$

    where A = base area and h = height.

    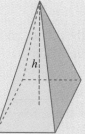

2. For a cone,

    Curved surface area = πrl

    Total surface area = $\pi r^2 + \pi rl$

    Volume = $\dfrac{1}{3}\pi r^2 h$

    where r = radius, h = height and l = slant height.

    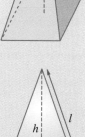

3. For a sphere,

    Surface area = $4\pi r^2$

    Volume = $\dfrac{4}{3}\pi r^3$

    where r = radius.

Tetrahedrons and Octahedrons

Mathematicians use the word **tetrahedron** to describe a triangular pyramid. 'Tetra' means four, and a tetrahedron has four sides.

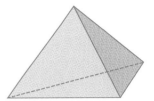

See if you can figure out which of the two nets below will make a tetrahedron. There are two correct nets.

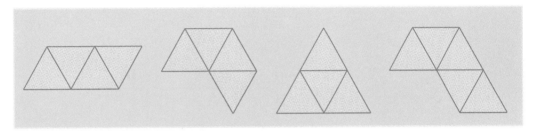

In a tetrahedron, three triangular faces meet at each point. However, when four faces meet at each point, we get an **octahedron**. An octahedron has eight faces.

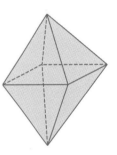

See if you can figure out which of the nets below will fold to give an octahedron. There are only four correct nets in the diagram shown below.

 Surf the Internet or look around you for real-life examples of objects that take the shape of tetrahedrons and octahedrons. Can you find any?

You have 10 minutes to answer the following questions.
Choose the most appropriate answer.

10 MINUTES

CONCEPT CHECK

7.1 **1.** Which of the following is a net of a rectangular pyramid?

A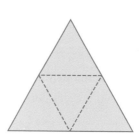

B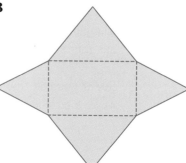

C

D

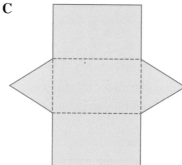

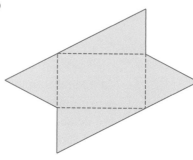

7.1 **2.** Calculate the total surface area of the pyramid shown below.

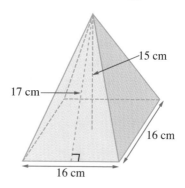

17 cm

15 cm

16 cm

16 cm

    A 544 cm^2 **B** 736 cm^2
    C 800 cm^2 **D** 1 280 cm^2

7.1 **3.** A pyramid with base area 45 cm^2 and height 12 cm has a volume of

    _____.

    A 540 cm^3 **B** 270 cm^3
    C 180 cm^3 **D** 135 cm^3

7.2 **4.** The diagram on the right shows part of a circle with centre O. If we join the sides AO and BO, we will get a _____ .

    A cone
    B cylinder
    C pyramid
    D sphere

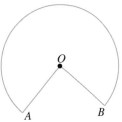

7.2 **5.** Calculate the total surface area of the cone, giving your answer in tems of π.

    A 48π cm^2
    B 84π cm^2
    C 96π cm^2
    D 156π cm^2

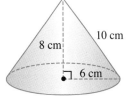

7.2 **6.** Find the volume of a cone if its diameter is x cm and its height is y cm.

    A $\dfrac{1}{12}\pi x^2 y$ cm^3 **B** $\dfrac{1}{6}\pi x^2 y$ cm^3

    C $\dfrac{1}{3}\pi x y^2$ cm^3 **D** $\dfrac{1}{3}\pi x^2 y$ cm^3

7.3 **7.** Find the surface area of a spherical ball given that it has a diameter of 14 cm. Give your answer correct to 3 significant figures.

    A 2 460 cm^2 **B** 616 cm^2
    C 308 cm^2 **D** 154 cm^2

7.3 **8.** A spherical solid has a radius of 1 m. Its volume is _____ .

    A 4π m^3 **B** $\dfrac{4}{3}\pi$ m^3

    C π m^3 **D** $\dfrac{2}{3}\pi$ m^3

7.3 **9.** The total surface area of a solid hemisphere of radius r is

_____ .

    A πr^2 **B** $2\pi r^2$
    C $3\pi r^2$ **D** $4\pi r^2$

7.3 **10.** The volume of a solid hemisphere of radius 10 cm is _____ .
(Take $\pi = 3.142$)

    A 1 050 cm^3 **B** 2 090 cm^3
    C 3 140 cm^3 **D** 4 190 cm^3

SECTION A

1. The dimensions of two pyramids are tabulated as follows. Find the missing values in the table.

	Length	Breadth	Height	Volume
(a)	5 cm	4 cm	3 cm	
(b)	6 m	6 m		72 m³

2. Calculate the missing values in the table for each of the two cones below.

	Base area	Height	Volume
(a)	30 cm²	10 cm	
(b)	40 m²		200 m³

3. **(a)** A cone of height 5 m has a volume of 3 m³. Calculate its base area.
(b) A rectangular pyramid with a height of 21 cm has a volume of 728 cm³. Calculate the length of its base if its breadth is 8 cm.

4. Taking $\pi = \dfrac{22}{7}$, calculate

(a) the surface area of a sphere of radius 7 cm,
(b) the volume of a sphere of radius $10\dfrac{1}{2}$ cm.

SECTION B

5. A solid cone has a curved surface area of 220 cm² and a slant height of 10 cm.

Taking $\pi = \dfrac{22}{7}$, calculate

(a) its radius,
(b) its total surface area.

6. The pyramid shown has a square base of side x cm. Given that its volume is 50 cm³, find

(a) x,
(b) its total surface area.

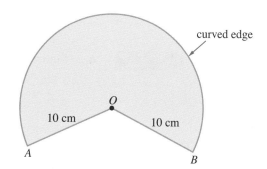

7. The diagram shows part of a circle with centre O and radius 10 cm.

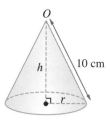

(a) Given that the length of the curved edge of the circle AB is $\dfrac{3}{5}$ of the circumference, express the length of the curved edge AB in terms of π.

(b) AO is joined to BO to make a cone as shown.

(i) Show that the radius, r, of the cone is 6 cm.

(ii) Given that $h = 8$ cm, find the volume of the cone, giving your answer correct to 3 significant figures.

8. (a) A cylindrical container with radius 5 cm contains water to a depth of 8 cm. Find the volume of the water in the container.

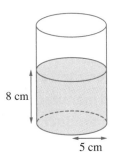

8 cm

5 cm

(b) A solid sphere has a radius of 3 cm. Find the volume of the sphere.

(c) If the sphere is placed into the cylinder of water, find the increase in the depth of the water.

[In this question, use π from your calculator. Give your answer correct to 3 significant figures if it is not exact.]

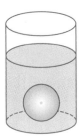

SECTION C

9. In this question, take $\pi = 3.142$ and give your answers correct to 3 significant figures.

A test tube consists of a cylinder of height 9 cm and a hemisphere of diameter 2 cm at the closed end. The test tube contains water to a depth of d cm.

(a) Calculate the volume of water in the hemisphere.

(b) Given that the volume of water in the test tube is 25 cm³, calculate

(i) the height, h cm, of the water in the cylinder,

(ii) the value of d.

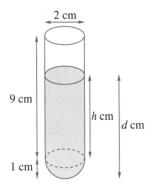

2 cm

9 cm

h cm

d cm

1 cm

10. In this question, take $\pi = 3.142$ and give your answers correct to 3 significant figures.

The diagram shows a metallic silo that a farmer uses for storing winter food for cattle. It is made up of a cylinder and a cone.

The cone has a height of 3.6 m and a slant height of 3.9 m.

The silo has a height of 10 m and a diameter of 3 m. Calculate

(a) the total external surface area of the silo (ignore thickness of the metal),

(b) the capacity (i.e. volume) of the silo.

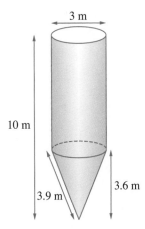

3 m

10 m

3.9 m

3.6 m

8

Statistics and Simple Probability

DISCOVER !

How to:

- interpret and analyse dot diagrams

- interpret and analyse stem-and-leaf diagrams

- find the mean, median and mode of ungrouped data

- find the mean of grouped data

- find the probability of single events

Statistics helps us to understand a large amount of data. For example, when a food manufacturer intends to come up with a more popular product, it has to understand its customers better first. Data has to be collected from surveys before it can be analysed using statistical methods.

In this chapter, you will learn about three statistical averages that can be used to analyse data. These statistical averages are the mean, median and mode. You will also learn about two more statistical representations: dot diagrams and stem-and-leaf diagrams. An introduction to the basic principles of probability is also covered at the end of this chapter.

8.1 Statistical Representations

8.1.1 Dot Diagrams

Consider the spelling scores of a class of 26 pupils as shown in **Table 1** below.

Pupil	Score
A	5
B	6
C	7
D	7
E	4
F	8
G	6
H	7
I	6
J	8
K	5
L	6
M	7
N	7
O	5
P	6
Q	8
R	7
S	9
T	7
U	6
V	7
W	5
X	7
Y	6
Z	5

Table 1 Unsorted scores

Pupil	Score
E	4
A	5
K	5
O	5
W	5
Z	5
B	6
G	6
I	6
L	6
P	6
U	6
Y	6
C	7
D	7
H	7
M	7
N	7
R	7
T	7
V	7
X	7
F	8
J	8
Q	8
S	9

Table 2 Sorted scores

The alphabetical listing of pupils in **Table 1** is useful for looking up the score of a particular pupil. Sometimes however, we may wish to know the highest score and the lowest score at a glance. We can sort (manually or using a computer software) the scores from the lowest to the highest as shown in **Table 2**.

From **Table 2**, we can easily see that the lowest score is 4 (as obtained by Pupil E) while the highest score is 9 (as obtained by Pupil S). We can also look for intermediate scores more easily than in an unsorted list (**Table 1**).

Can we do more than simply listing the scores in ascending order?

If we put the scores in some kind of plot or graph, we may be able to interpret the information more easily. One simple graphical representation is the **dot diagram** (or **dot plot**). A dot diagram uses dots or circles to represent the values in a set of data, arranged along a line or axis showing the scale. Let us draw the dot diagram for the set of data given in **Table 1**.

From the set of data, we can see that the lowest score is 4 and the highest score is 9. Hence, we begin by drawing a number line or axis as shown below.

Since the first score is 5 (for Pupil A), we put a dot above the score 5 on the axis.

The next score is 6. Put a dot above the score 6.

The next two scores are 7. Put two dots above the score 7 as shown.

Continue until all the 26 dots are placed on the diagram. The resulting **dot diagram** is shown below.

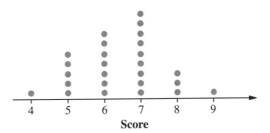

Each dot represents a data value.

A **dot diagram** is a graphical display with dots representing data values positioned along an axis or a number line.

note

Dot diagrams can also be drawn using circles as shown below:

By looking at the dot diagram, we can easily see that the lowest score obtained by this class of pupils is 4 and the highest score obtained is 9. This is similar to our observation made from looking at **Table 2** on page 262. However, notice that it is easier to tell from the dot diagram above than the table that the most common score is 7. This is indicated in the dot diagram by the highest column of dots.

Example 1

A group of students were asked how many times they have travelled on a plane. The result is shown in the dot diagram below.

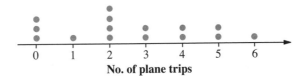

(a) How many students are represented in the dot diagram above?
(b) What was the least number of times a student has travelled on a plane?

Solution

(a) We can get the answer by counting the total number of dots.

(a) There are 15 students represented in the dot diagram.
(b) Least number of times a student has travelled on a plane = 0

Example 2

The dot diagram below shows the results of a survey on the number of children below 12 years old in each household.

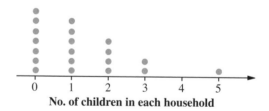

No. of children in each household

(a) How many households were surveyed?

(b) What was the total number of children below 12 years old in the households surveyed?

(c) What percentage of households had no children below 12 years old?

Solution

(a) We can get the answer by counting the total number of dots.

(a) 20 households were surveyed.

(b) Total number of children involved in the survey
$$= (7 \times 0) + (6 \times 1) + (4 \times 2) + (2 \times 3) + (0 \times 4) + (1 \times 5)$$
$$= 0 + 6 + 8 + 6 + 0 + 5$$
$$= 25$$

(c) Percentage of households with no children below 12 years old
$$= \frac{7}{20} \times 100\%$$
$$= 35\%$$

Exercise 8A

1. The dot diagram shows the distance travelled to school by a group of students.

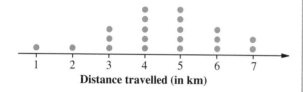

Distance travelled (in km)

Find the total number of students in the group.

2. The dot diagram shows the number of goals scored by a football team per match during a month-long tournament.

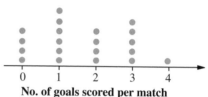

No. of goals scored per match

(a) How many matches did the football team play?

(b) What was the most common number of goals scored per match?

3. The dot diagram shows the number of false alarms received by a security monitoring service on each day in the month of June.

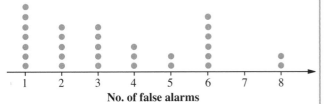

No. of false alarms

(a) What was the greatest number of false alarms received on a single day in that month?

(b) What was the total number of false alarms received in that month?

4. The dot diagram shows the number of teenagers per family in a condominium block.

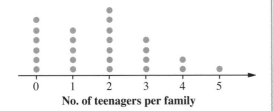

No. of teenagers per family

(a) How many families live in this block altogether?

(b) How many teenagers are there altogether?

(c) What percentage of families in this block have three teenagers in the family?

5. The dot diagram shows the number of people in the cars that passed through a gantry in 1 minute.

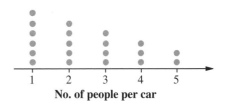

No. of people per car

(a) Explain why the horizontal axis does not start from zero.

(b) How many cars passed through the gantry in 1 minute?

(c) How many people passed through the gantry in their cars during that 1 minute?

ACTIVITY

Comparing Histograms and Dot Diagrams

(a) A group of students was asked how many siblings they have. The results are shown below.

Survey 1:

1	0	1	2	3	2	1	2	0	5
1	0	1	1	2	1	2	1	0	0

(i) Draw a dot diagram to represent the data above.

(ii) Draw a histogram to represent the same data above. You may need to construct a frequency table first.

(iii) Discuss with your classmates and explain in your Mathematics Journal, which of the statistical representations, the histogram or the dot diagram, is easier to construct. Why is this so?

(b) The same survey was done on another group of students. The results are shown below.

Survey 2:

0	1	1	0	2	1	0	2	1	4
0	2	1	3	1	6	1	2	1	0
3	5	1	0	3	1	2	1	1	3
2	0	1	1	1	0	0	0	1	0
2	1	2	2	4	1	0	2	1	2
1	2	0	0	1	3	4	0	1	0
1	0	0	1	1	2	1	0	0	1
1	2	1	2	1	0	0	1	1	0

(i) Discuss in pairs why the histogram is more suitable than the dot diagram to represent the data in Survey 2.

(ii) Hence, list down an advantage and a disadvantage of using dot diagrams to represent statistical data.

8.1.2 Stem-and-Leaf Diagrams

John Tukey, a famous mathematician, developed the **stem-and-leaf diagram** (or **stem-and-leaf plot** or simply just **stemplot**), a technique for summarising data without losing the individual observations.

This technique is particularly useful for detecting patterns and extreme data values. It helps us to explore data to gain initial insights about it. For example, if we have data regarding the masses of a group of Secondary Two students, a stem-and-leaf diagram representing this data can be used to determine whether the masses are uniformly distributed. We can also check if there is any significant difference between the masses of the boys and the girls.

To make a stem-and-leaf diagram, we break the digits of each data into **two** parts. The left group of leading digits is called a **stem** and the remaining group of trailing digits on the right is called a **leaf**. For example, the numerical data value of 36 can be split into 3−6 as shown below.

Stem (Leading digits)	Leaf (Trailing digits)
3	6

The data box below shows the results (in cm) obtained by 20 Secondary Two students at a 'Sit and Reach' event during a physical fitness test. Let us construct a stem-and-leaf diagram of the following data.

41	37	23	48	34	36	30	41	33	28
42	58	29	47	45	47	33	39	46	55

At a quick glance, we see that the data values are in the 20s, 30s, 40s and 50s. Let us use the first digit of each value as the stem and the second digit as the leaf. The stem-and-leaf diagram is usually constructed in a vertical position. Draw a vertical line and place the stems (in order) to the left of this line.

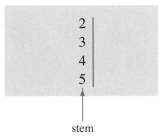

stem

Next, we place the corresponding leaves to the right of the stem. This is done by placing the trailing (remaining) digit on the right side of the vertical line opposite its corresponding leading digit.

Our first data value is 41. For this value, 4 is the stem and 1 is the leaf. Thus, we place 1 next to the stem 4.

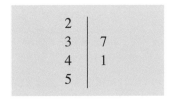

leaf

The next data value is 37, so a leaf of 7 is placed next to the stem 3.

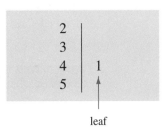

note

The number of leaves in a stem-and-leaf diagram should be equal to the total number of data values.

We continue until each of the 20 leaves is placed on the diagram. The resulting stem-and-leaf diagram is as shown below.

Sit and Reach results (in cm)	
2	3 8 9
3	7 4 6 0 3 3 9
4	1 8 1 2 7 5 7 6
5	8 5

We can rearrange the data to get an **ordered stem-and-leaf diagram**.

note

An **ordered** stem-and-leaf diagram is one where the data is arranged in an ascending order.

Sit and Reach results (in cm)	
2	3 8 9
3	0 3 3 4 6 7 9
4	1 1 2 5 6 7 7 8
5	5 8

Key: 2 | 3 means 23 cm

In the stem-and-leaf diagram above, 2 | 3 can be interpreted as 23 cm or 2.3 cm. Thus, we usually include a **key** with stem-and-leaf diagrams to help us interpret the data correctly. However, in some cases, a key may not be needed as it can be implied in the questions as we shall see later.

From the stem-and-leaf diagram above, we can tell that most of the measurements obtained were between 30 cm and 40 cm. The shortest measurement was 23 cm while the longest measurement was 58 cm.

In the data given on the previous page, the data in the first row are the results from the girls and the data in the second row are the results from the boys. We can draw another ordered stem-and-leaf diagram to study whether there is any difference between the results obtained by the girls and the boys.

note

The diagram on the right is also known as a **comparative stem-and-leaf diagram**. The middle column represents the stems and the left and right sides are the leaves of each of the two data sets.

Sit and Reach results (in cm)		
Girls		**Boys**
8 3	2	9
7 6 4 3 0	3	3 9
8 1 1	4	2 5 6 7 7
	5	5 8

Key (Girls):
3 | 2 cm means 23 cm

↑
common stem

Key (Boys):
2 | 9 cm means 29 cm

This back-to-back stem-and-leaf diagram shows us that there are more boys than girls with measurements more than 40 cm (seven boys compared to three girls). Thus, we can conclude that for this group of students, the boys generally were able to stretch further than the girls and thus performed better at this event.

Example 3

A group of students sat for a common test. Their marks were recorded in the following stem-and-leaf diagram.

Marks	
1	8 9
2	0 2 4 5
3	1 2 6 6 6 7
4	0 3 8 8
5	0

Key: 1 | 8 means 18 marks

(a) How many students are represented above?

(b) What was the lowest mark obtained?

(c) What was the highest mark obtained?

(d) What was the most common mark obtained?

Solution

(a) We can get the answer by counting the number of leaves.

(d) 36 occurs three times.

(a) There are 17 students represented above.

(b) Lowest mark obtained = 18

(c) Highest mark obtained = 50

(d) Most common mark obtained = 36

Example 4

Each scout was asked to estimate the width of a river. Below is a stem-and-leaf diagram showing the widths estimated by a group of scouts.

5	3 5 5 6
6	0 1 1 2 4 4 4 5
7	0 0 1 1 1 2 2 3 4 5 7
8	1 6

(a) How many scouts were there in the group?

(b) If the largest estimated width was 8.6 m, what was the smallest estimated width?

(c) If the actual width of the river is 7.0 m, what percentage of the scouts in the group overestimated the width?

Solution

(a) We can get the answer by counting the number of leaves.

(a) There were 25 scouts in the group.

(b) The smallest estimated width was 5.3 m.

(c) Number of scouts who overestimated = 11

$$\therefore \quad \text{Percentage of scouts who overestimated} = \frac{11}{25} \times 100\%$$

$$= 44\%$$

1. List the data that corresponds to each row of some stem-and-leaf diagrams below.

    (a) 12 | 0 1 3 5 8
         Key: 12 | 0 means 120

    (b) 0 | 1 2 3 5 7
         Key: 0 | 1 means 0.1

    (c) 34 | 01 12 52 55 64 78 89
         Key: 34 | 01 means 3 401

2. The stem-and-leaf diagram shows the time taken by a group of students to complete a particular homework assignment.

Time taken (in minutes)	
1	9
2	1 4 4 4 9
3	1 3 4 6 8 8
4	2 3 4 4 7 8 9
5	4
6	3 5

    Key: 1 | 9 means 19 minutes

    (a) How many students are represented above?
    (b) What was the shortest time taken to complete the assignment?
    (c) What was the longest time taken to complete the assignment?

3. The ordered stem-and-leaf diagram below shows the systolic blood pressure readings of 30 patients.

Blood pressure readings (in mmHg)	
12	3 9 9
13	1 2 5 7
14	4 8
15	0 1 1 3 4 4 8 9
16	0 0 0 1 6
17	0 5 6
18	0 3 5 9
19	
20	6

    Key: 12 | 3 means 123 mmHg

    (a) What was the most common blood pressure reading for this group of patients?
    (b) Find the percentage of patients in this group with blood pressure reading higher than 165 mmHg.

4. A study was done to find out how long a group of listeners would listen to a telephone advertisement before hanging up. The result is shown in the ordered stem-and-leaf diagram below.

Time (in minutes)	
0	1 1 2 2 3 5 8 9
1	1 2 3 3 4 6 6
2	1 1 4 8
3	0 0 0 0 0 0

    Key: 0 | 1 means 0.1 minutes

    (a) How many listeners were surveyed in the study?
    (b) Find the percentage of listeners who hung up before 1.5 minutes was up.
    (c) What do you think was the length of the whole advertisement?

5. The stem-and-leaf diagram shows the total number of hours spent by a housing agent on each of his clients.

Time spent (in hours)	
0	9
1	1 4 0 1 6 0 4
2	6 0 7 1 7 0 7 9
3	2 1 4
4	0

    (a) How many clients did the housing agent have?
    (b) If the least number of hours spent was 9 hours, what was the most number of hours spent?
    (c) What was the most common number of hours spent on a client?

Statistical Averages

8.2.1   Introduction

You have learned about the various ways data can be represented. Some examples of these statistical representations include bar graphs, histograms, pie charts, line graphs, dot diagrams and stem-and-leaf diagrams. We often present data using these representations so that we can interpret and analyse them better to help us make decisions.

Another important tool that helps in statistical analysis is the ability to find the statistical average of a set of data that best describes the data. The three main statistical averages are the **mean**, the **median** and the **mode**. These three statistical averages are also often known as the **measures of central tendency** as they often represent the 'middle value' of the data set.

8.2.2   Mean of Ungrouped Data

> **note**
>
> The mass of canned food is usually given by the label 'net weight'.

A certain brand of canned food is labelled to have a mass of 250 g. However, under careful examination, the masses of some cans from this brand of canned food are found to range from 248 g to 252 g. For example, the masses (in g) of nine randomly selected cans are as shown below:

$$252, 248, 251, 249, 250, 251, 251, 248, 250$$

Let us find the **mean** mass of these nine cans of food.

> **note**
>
> The term 'average' is often synonymously used with the term 'mean'. However, 'average' can actually refer to any of the three main statistical averages — the mean, the median and the mode.

The **mean** is the value that is found by adding all the values and then dividing by the number of values.

$$\text{Mean} = \frac{\text{Sum of values}}{\text{Number of values}}$$

$$\begin{aligned}
\text{Mean mass} &= \frac{252 + 248 + 251 + 249 + 250 + 251 + 251 + 248 + 250}{9} \\
&= \frac{2\,250}{9} \\
&= 250 \text{ g}
\end{aligned}$$

Thus, although the masses of the cans vary a little from 250 g due to the manufacturing process, we say that on the average, the mass is 250 g.

Example 5

Find the mean of the following data.
(a) 47, 52, 41, 49, 51
(b) 1, 1, 1, 1, 2, 2, 3, 3, 3, 4, 4, 4, 5, 5, 6

Solution

note

The mean is not necessarily equal to one of the data values.

(a) Mean $= \dfrac{47 + 52 + 41 + 49 + 51}{5}$

$= \dfrac{240}{5}$

$= 48$

(b) Mean $= \dfrac{1 + 1 + 1 + 1 + 2 + 2 + 3 + 3 + 3 + 4 + 4 + 4 + 5 + 5 + 6}{15}$

$= \dfrac{(4 \times 1) + (2 \times 2) + (3 \times 3) + (3 \times 4) + (2 \times 5) + (1 \times 6)}{15}$

$= \dfrac{45}{15}$

$= 3$

note

Recall that frequency refers to the number of occurrences.

Alternative method:

If we denote the given values by x and the frequencies by f, we can display the data in a frequency table with an additional column 'fx' as shown below.

Number (x)	Frequency (f)	$f \times x = fx$
1	4	$4 \times 1 = 4$
2	2	$2 \times 2 = 4$
3	3	$3 \times 3 = 9$
4	3	$3 \times 4 = 12$
5	2	$2 \times 5 = 10$
6	1	$1 \times 6 = 6$
	Total = 15	*Total* = 45

Mean $= \dfrac{\text{Sum of values}}{\text{Number of values}}$

$= \dfrac{\text{Sum of } fx}{\text{Sum of } f}$

$= \dfrac{45}{15}$

$= 3$

Example 6

The number of goals scored by some football teams in Britain during a particular weekend is shown in the table below.

No. of goals	0	1	2	3	4	5	6
No. of teams	26	27	19	11	3	3	1

Find the mean number of goals scored.

Solution

Let us construct a frequency table to help us calculate the mean.

The number of teams is represented by the frequency, f.

No. of goals (x)	Frequency (f)	fx
0	26	$26 \times 0 = 0$
1	27	$27 \times 1 = 27$
2	19	$19 \times 2 = 38$
3	11	$11 \times 3 = 33$
4	3	$3 \times 4 = 12$
5	3	$3 \times 5 = 15$
6	1	$1 \times 6 = 6$
	Total = 90	*Total* = 131

note

Notice that the mean does not necessarily need to be a whole number.

$$\text{Mean number of goals scored} = \frac{131}{90}$$

$$= 1.46 \quad \text{(correct to 3 sig. fig.)}$$

Example 7

The annual salaries of five people are $15 000, $15 500, $16 000, $16 500 and $52 000.

(a) Find the mean of their salaries.

(b) Is this mean representative of their salaries? Why do you think this is so?

Solution

note

Notice that a disadvantage of the mean is that it is affected by extreme values, i.e., very big or very small values.

(a) Mean salary $= \dfrac{\$15\,000 + \$15\,500 + \$16\,000 + \$16\,500 + \$52\,000}{5}$

$= \dfrac{\$115\,000}{5}$

$= \$23\,000$

(b) The mean $23 000 is certainly not representative of the salaries, as the difference between the mean and each of the values is too great. E.g. $23 000 – $16 000 = $7 000. The extreme value of $52 000 has affected the mean value.

Example 8

The mean mass of 10 students is 55.5 kg.
(a) Find the total mass of the 10 students.
(b) Find the new mean mass, correct to 3 significant figures, if a student whose mass is 62 kg joins the group.

Solution

(a) Mean $= \dfrac{\text{Total mass}}{\text{Number of students}}$

$55.5 = \dfrac{\text{Total mass}}{10}$

Total mass $= 55.5 \times 10$
$= 555$ kg

(b) New mean $= \dfrac{\text{New total mass}}{\text{New number of students}}$

The total number of students is now 11.

$= \dfrac{555 + 62}{11}$

$= \dfrac{617}{11}$

$= 56.1$ kg   (correct to 3 sig. fig.)

Example 9

The mean of a set of eight numbers is 18.5. Given that six of the numbers are 13, 14, 16, 19, 23 and 24, find the mean of the other two numbers.

Solution

Mean $= \dfrac{\text{Sum of values}}{\text{Number of values}}$

Sum of the eight numbers $= 8 \times$ mean
$= 8 \times 18.5$
$= 148$

Sum of the six numbers $= 13 + 14 + 16 + 19 + 23 + 24$
$= 109$

$\therefore$ Sum of the other two numbers $= 148 - 109$
$= 39$

$\therefore$ Mean of these two numbers $= \dfrac{39}{2}$

$= 19.5$

Example 10

The histogram shows the distribution of the number of children per family among a group of married couples. Find the mean of this distribution.

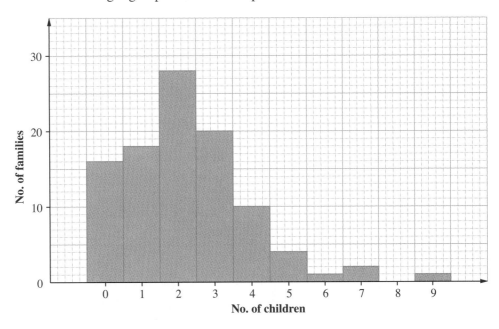

Solution

Let us construct a frequency table to help us calculate the mean.

No. of children (x)	Frequency (f)	fx
0	16	0
1	18	18
2	28	56
3	20	60
4	10	40
5	4	20
6	1	6
7	2	14
8	0	0
9	1	9
	Total = 100	*Total* = 223

$$\text{Mean} = \frac{\text{Sum of } fx}{\text{Sum of } f}$$

$$= \frac{223}{100}$$

$$= 2.23 \text{ children}$$

Example 11

The dot diagram shows the results of a survey of the distances travelled by a group of students to go to school.

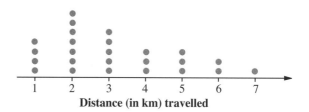

Distance (in km) travelled

(a) How many students were surveyed?

(b) What was the furthest distance travelled by this group of students to go to school?

(c) Calculate the mean distance travelled.

Solution

(a) Number of students surveyed = 25

(b) Furthest distance travelled = 7 km

(c) We can construct a frequency table to help us calculate the mean.

Distance (*x* km)	Frequency (*f*)	*fx*
1	4	4
2	7	14
3	5	15
4	3	12
5	3	15
6	2	12
7	1	7
	Total = 25	*Total* = 79

$$\therefore \quad \text{Mean distance travelled} = \frac{\text{Sum of } fx}{\text{Sum of } f}$$

$$= \frac{79}{25}$$

$$= 3.16 \text{ km}$$

Example 12

The number of hours lost in a particular year due to breakdowns in the machinery of a company is shown in the following stem-and-leaf diagram.

No. of hours lost	
0	1 2 2 5
1	0 1 4 4 8
2	3 6 8
3	1 8
4	0

Key: 0 | 1 means 1 hour

(a) How many breakdowns were there in that year?
(b) What was the least number of hours lost?
(c) What was the most number of hours lost?
(d) Calculate the mean number of hours lost.

Solution

(a) There were 15 breakdowns in that year.
(b) Least number of hours lost = 1 (from 01)
(c) Most number of hours lost = 40

(d)

No. of hours lost
$1 + 2 + 2 + 5 = 10$
$10 + 11 + 14 + 14 + 18 = 67$
$23 + 26 + 28 = 77$
$31 + 38 = 69$
$40 = 40$
Total = 263

$$\therefore \quad \text{Mean number of hours lost} = \frac{263}{15}$$

$$= 17.5 \quad \text{(correct to 3 sig. fig.)}$$

1. Find the mean of each of the following data sets.
   (a) 1, 1, 2, 2, 3, 3, 3, 4, 5
   (b) 4, 4, 4, 6, 6, 7, 7, 7, 9
   (c) 45, 66, 67, 40, 55, 64, 76
   (d) 2.1, 5.1, 2.5, 3.1, 4.3
   (e) 15, 16, 17, 20, 22
   (f) 815, 816, 817, 820, 822

2. (a) Given that 29 is the mean of 22, x, 30, 32 and 35, find x.
   (b) Given that 3.3 is the mean of 4.2, 4.3, x, 3.2, 3.3 and 2.1, find x.

3. The mean of five numbers is 55. Two of the numbers are 144 and 89 and each of the other three is equal to n.
   Find
   (a) the sum of the five numbers,
   (b) the numerical value of n,
   (c) the new mean if another number 40 is included in the group.

4. An examination was taken by four boys and six girls. The mean mark of the 10 pupils was 54.
   (a) Calculate the sum of the marks obtained by all the 10 pupils.
   (b) Given that the mean mark of the four boys were 48, calculate the mean mark obtained by the six girls.

5. The mean of a set of eight numbers is 8 and the mean of a different set of twelve numbers is m. Given that the mean of the combined set of twenty numbers is 5, calculate m.

6. The mean time taken by four runners to complete a race was 11.21 seconds. The time taken by the winner was 10.55 seconds. The winner finished 0.34 seconds ahead of the second runner. Calculate the time taken by each of the other two runners, given that they finished at the same time.

7. The number of workers in a factory reporting sick during a certain period was recorded as shown in the following table.

No. of workers reporting sick	No. of days
0	2
1	3
2	5
3	6
4	7
5	8
6	9
7	7
8	3
9	2
10	2

Calculate the mean number of workers reporting sick per day during that period.

8. Shooting at a target board, a man can score 10, 20, 30, 40, 50 or 60 points. After 100 shots, his scores were as shown in the following table.

Score	No. of times
10	26
20	15
30	14
40	15
50	18
60	12

Calculate his mean score.

9. A survey was carried out to find the number of children in each of 500 families. The results are shown in the following table.

No. of children in each family	No. of families
0	46
1	92
2	198
3	104
4	60

(a) Calculate the mean number of children per family.

(b) A similar survey was carried out on another group of 250 families and in this case, the mean number of children per family was x. Given that the mean number of children per family for all 750 families was 2, calculate the value of x.

10. The table below shows the number of books bought by some people during a book sale.

No. of books	No. of people
0	2
1	7
2	x
3	5
4	6

Given the mean number of books is 2.2, calculate the value of x.

11. The histogram below illustrates the number of broken eggs per crate that arrived at a factory after transportation. Calculate

(a) the total number of broken eggs,

(b) the mean number of broken eggs per crate.

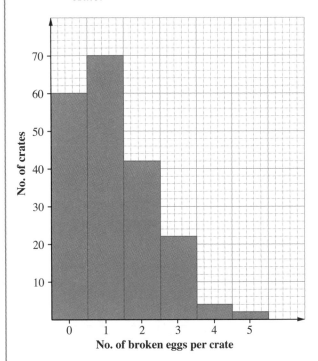

12. The histogram shows the number of occupants per flat in a block of 75 flats in a housing estate. Find the mean number of occupants per flat.

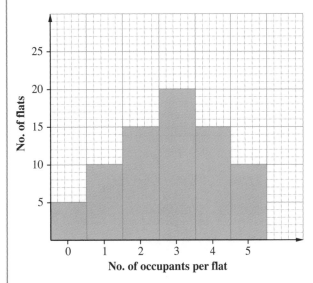

13. The dot diagram shows the results of a survey on the number of children per family.

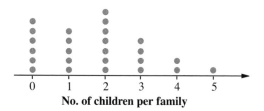

No. of children per family

(a) How many families were surveyed?

(b) How many children were there altogether?

(c) What was the mean number of children per family?

14. The dot diagram shows the number of complaints received by a department store on each day in the month of June.

No. of complaints

(a) What was the total number of complaints received that month?

(b) Calculate the mean number of complaints per day.

15. The stem-and-leaf diagram shows the heights of various trees in a fruit orchard.

Heights (in m)	
1	0 1
2	3 4 4 4 4
3	1 2 2 3 3 4
4	1 2 3 5 7 9
5	
6	5 8

Key: 1 | 0 means 1.0 m

(a) How many trees are represented?

(b) What was the height of the shortest tree in the fruit orchard?

(c) What was the height of the tallest tree in the fruit orchard?

(d) Calculate the mean height of the trees in the fruit orchard.

16. The heights of the Secondary Two students of a class are displayed in the stem-and-leaf diagram.

Heights (in cm)	
13	3 4 4 7 7 8 9
14	0 1 3 4 5 5 6
15	1 1 1 2 3 4 4 5 8
16	1 1 2 2 3 3 3

(a) How many students are there in the class?

(b) If the shortest student has a height of 133 cm, what is the height of the tallest student?

(c) Calculate the mean height of the students.

8.2.3   Median of Ungrouped Data

The monthly salaries of five employees of a company are as shown.

$$\$900, \$1\ 100, \$1\ 050, \$975, \$2\ 300$$

Let us calculate their mean salary.

$$\text{Mean salary} = \frac{\$900 + \$1\ 100 + \$1\ 050 + \$975 + \$2\ 300}{5}$$
$$= \$1\ 265$$

Is the mean shown above representative of the monthly salaries of the employees?

Notice that four out of the five employees earned below $1 265 per month. Thus, the mean is not a good measure of central tendency in this case. The large data value of $2 300 caused the mean to be non-representative of the data.

Similarly, a very small data value can also affect the value of the mean. Thus, extreme values that are either too large or too small can cause the mean of the data to be quite far from most of the data values.

We have seen this disadvantage of mean in Example 7.

If we choose the middle value of the set of data above when it is arranged in ascending order, we see that this value is more representative of the data than the mean.

$$\$900, \$975, \boxed{\$1\ 050}, \$1\ 100, \$2\ 300$$

middle value

Such a 'middle value' is known as the **median**. The median is a statistical average that is not affected by extreme values.

> The **median** of a set of N values is the middle value (if N is odd) or the mean of the two middle values (if N is even) when the values are arranged in ascending or descending order.

Example 13

Find the median of each of the following data sets.

(a) 3, 1, 6, 2, 1, 3, 4, 5, 3

(b) 1, 5, 4, 6, 2, 5, 3, 2, 4, 3

Solution

There are 9 values (odd). Therefore, the middle value, i.e. the 5th value is the median.

(a) Arranging the numbers in ascending order, we have:

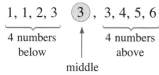

∴   Median = 3

There are 10 values (even). Therefore, the mean of the two middle values, i.e. the mean of the 5th value and 6th value, is the median.

(b) Arranging the numbers in ascending order, we have:

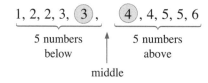

Since there is an even number of values, the median is the mean of the two middle values.

$$\therefore \quad \text{Median} = \frac{3 + 4}{2}$$
$$= 3.5$$

Example 14

The aggregates of the best three subjects, including English Language, for a class of 40 students in the GCE 'N' Level Examinations are as follows:

5	8	6	6	3	12	8	10	7	10
4	6	6	9	4	6	8	5	8	7
4	5	3	6	7	18	9	6	6	4
6	14	8	5	10	6	8	12	8	16

Find the median aggregate.

Solution

Arranging the aggregates in ascending order, we have:

3, 3, 4, 4, 4, 4, ..., ⑥   ⑦, 7, 7, 8, ..., 18

20 students below   20 students above

middle

$$\therefore \quad \text{Median aggregate} = \frac{20^{\text{th}} \text{ value} + 21^{\text{st}} \text{ value}}{2}$$

$$= \frac{6 + 7}{2}$$

$$= 6.5$$

Alternative method:

We can display the data in a frequency table as shown below.

Aggregate	3	4	5	6	7	8	9	10	12	14	16	18
Frequency	2	4	4	10	3	7	2	3	2	1	1	1
Position	1st to 2nd	3rd to 6th	7th to 10th	11th to 20th	21st to 23rd	24th to 30th	31st to 32nd	33rd to 35th	36th to 37th	38th	39th	40th

From the table, the value in the 20th position = 6

and the value in the 21st position = 7.

$$\therefore \quad \text{Median aggregate} = \frac{6 + 7}{2}$$

$$= 6.5$$

Example 15

The number of goals scored by 90 teams that played in a hockey league are shown below.

No. of goals	0	1	2	3	4	5	6
No. of teams	10	42	13	10	9	4	2

(a) Find the median number of goals scored.
(b) Find the mean number of goals scored.

Solution

The total number of teams can also be found by adding up the values in the second row of the table.

(a) Since there is an even number of values (there are 90 teams), we have two middle values at the 45th and the 46th position respectively.

By counting, the value at the 45th position = 1

and the value at the 46th position = 1.

$$\therefore \quad \text{Median number of goals scored} = \frac{1 + 1}{2}$$

$$= 1$$

(b) Mean

$$= \frac{\text{Sum of } fx}{\text{Sum of } f}$$

$$= \frac{(10 \times 0) + (42 \times 1) + (13 \times 2) + (10 \times 3) + (9 \times 4) + (4 \times 5) + (2 \times 6)}{90}$$

$$= \frac{166}{90}$$

$$= 1.84 \text{ goals} \quad \text{(correct to 3 sig. fig.)}$$

Example 16

The students in a particular class are asked to state how many pets they have. The histogram shows the results of the survey. Find
(a) the number of students in this class,
(b) the median number of pets.

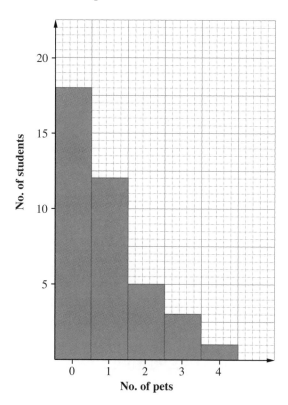

Solution

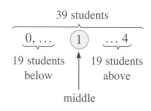

(a) Number of students $= 18 + 12 + 5 + 3 + 1$
$$= 39$$

(b) Since there are 39 students, the median will occur at the 20th position.
$\therefore$ Median number of pets $= 1$

Example 17

The distances (in km) travelled by 20 students to school are shown in the dot diagram below.

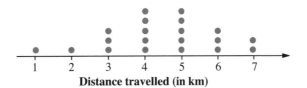

Distance travelled (in km)

Find the median distance travelled by the students.

Solution

Since there are 20 values, the median is the mean of the 10th and 11th values.

Distance travelled by 10th student = 4 km
Distance travelled by 11th student = 5 km

$\therefore$ Median distance travelled $= \dfrac{4 + 5}{2}$

$= 4.5$ km

Example 18

The number of hours spent by a group of teenagers working out at a gym in a particular month is shown in the following stem-and-leaf diagram.

No. of hours	
0	2 2 4 5
1	0 1 4 4 8
2	3 6 8
3	1 8
4	0

Key: 0 | 2 means 2 hours

Find the median number of hours the teenagers spent working out at the gym in that month.

Solution

Since there are 15 values, the median is the 8th value.

There were altogether 15 teenagers in the group.

$\therefore$ Median number of hours spent at the gym
= Hours spent at the gym by the 8th teenager
= 14

1. Find the median of each of the following data sets.
   (a) 1, 2, 3, 4, 5, 3, 2, 1, 3
   (b) 7, 6, 4, 6, 7, 4, 6, 5
   (c) 2, 4, 5, 6, 2, 7, 6, 6
   (d) 89, 95, 76, 71, 88, 78
   (e) $2.50, $3.90, $3.20, $9.20, $3.70
   (f) 6.1, 3.77, 8.9, 2.33, 5.5, 1.48, 3.4, 2.1, 1.3

2. For the numbers 41, 42, 45, 43, 41,
   (a) find the median,
   (b) find the mean.

3. The following shows the numbers of cars sold by 20 salespersons during a trade show.

3	2	2	3	2
2	3	1	3	0
3	1	3	3	1
2	2	3	5	2

   Find the median number of cars sold by each salesperson.

4. The median of a set of six numbers is 2.5. Given that five of the numbers are 8, 1, 2, 5 and 1, find the sixth number.

5. A class of 40 students entered a competition in which the highest possible score was 9. Their scores are given in the following table.

Score	0	1	2	3	4	5	6	> 6
No. of students	1	3	4	8	11	8	3	2

   Find the median score.

6. A survey of the weekly pocket money received by 30 pupils in a class produced the following results.

Amount of pocket money (in $)	10	20	30	40	50	60
No. of pupils receiving this amount	2	6	8	7	6	1

   (a) Find the median amount received.
   (b) Find the mean amount received.

7. The number of absentees in a class for a period of 100 days is shown in the table below.

No. of absentees	0	1	2	3	4
No. of days	20	30	25	20	5

   (a) Find the median number of absentees.
   (b) Find the mean number of absentees.

⋆8. The table below shows the number of pets kept by the students in a class.

No. of pets	No. of students
0	9
1	k
2	2
3	1
4	2

   If the median number of pets is 1, what is the smallest value of k?

9. The histogram shows the results of an observation on the number of passengers per taxi in a shopping district.

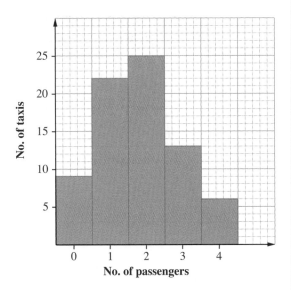

No. of passengers

Calculate

(a) the total number of taxis observed,

(b) the median number of passengers per taxi.

10. The histogram shows the number of the bus trips taken by the employees of a company on a particular day.

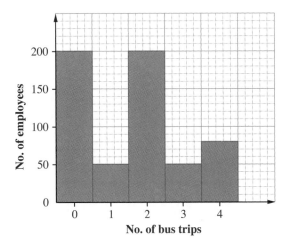

No. of bus trips

Calculate

(a) the median number of bus trips taken per employee,

(b) the mean number of bus trips taken per employee.

11. The dot diagram shows the number of parking fines received by a group of drivers in a one-year period.

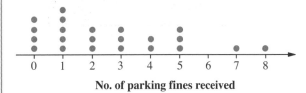

No. of parking fines received

(a) How many drivers are represented in the dot diagram shown?

(b) Find the median number of parking fines received by the group of drivers during this period.

12. The dot diagram shows the results of a survey that was conducted to find the number of children per family.

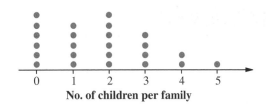

No. of children per family

Find the median number of children per family.

13. The stem-and-leaf diagram below shows the number of sit-ups done by a group of students during a physical fitness test.

No. of sit-ups	
0	1 2 2 2 4 4 5 5 7 9
1	1 3 3 5 5
2	1 1 4 7
3	0 0 1 1 2 4

Key: 0 | 1 means 1 sit-up

Find the median number of sit-ups done.

14. The heights of a class of Secondary Two students are shown in the stem-and-leaf diagram below.

Heights (in m)	
13	3 4 4 7 7 8 9
14	0 1 3 4 5 5 6
15	1 1 1 2 3 4 4 5 8
16	1 1 2 2 3 3 3

Key: 13 | 3 means 1.33 m

Find the median height.

15. The stem-and-leaf diagram shows the time taken by a group of students to complete a particular homework assignment.

Time taken (in minutes)	
1	9
2	4 4 4
3	1 3 4 6 8 8
4	2 3 4 4 7 8 9
5	4
6	3 5

Key: 1 | 9 means 19 minutes

Find the median time taken.

Spot the Mistakes

David, Vincent and Ray were asked to find the median of the following data.

$$1, 1, 2, 3, 5, 8, 1, 3, 2, 1, 3, 4$$

David's solution:

$$\text{Median} = \frac{6^{th} \text{ value} + 7^{th} \text{ value}}{2}$$

$$= \frac{8 + 1}{2} = 4.5$$

Vincent's solution:

Rearrange data: 1, 1, 1, 1, 2, 2, 3, 3, 3, 4, 5, 8

$$\therefore \quad \text{Median} = \frac{6 + 7}{2} = 6.5$$

Ray's solution:

Rearrange data: 1, 1, 1, 1, 2, 2, 3, 3, 3, 4, 5, 8

$$\therefore \quad \text{Median} = \frac{6 + 7}{2}$$

$$= \frac{2 + 3}{2} = 2.5$$

Discuss with your classmates and explain in your Mathematics Journal,
(i) the mistake David made in his solution,
(ii) the mistake Vincent made in his solution,
(iii) the mistake Ray made in the presentation of his solution.

8.2.4 Mode of Ungrouped Data

If a shoe retailer is told that the mean size of men's feet is 7.27 or the median size of men's feet is 7.5, he would not find this information useful. The shoe retailer is more likely to be interested in the most popular size so that he can order more shoes of that size. The most popular size is given by the **mode**.

> The **mode** of a data set is the value that occurs with the highest frequency.

| **Example 19**

Find the mode of the data set: 2, 4, 5, 6, 2, 7, 6, 6

| **Solution**

Looking at the data set, we can see that '6' is the most frequent number. We can see this more clearly if we first rearrange the data in ascending (or descending) order:

6 occurs 3 times (the highest frequency).

$$2, 2, 4, 5, 6, 6, 6, 7$$

$\therefore$ Mode = 6

| **Example 20**

Find the mode of each of the following data sets.
(a) 8, 1, 2, 0, 4, 0, 1, 0
(b) 5, 6, 9, 8, 2, 4
(c) 1, 4, 2, 3, 2, 3, 6

| **Solution**

(a) Rearrange the data: 0, 0, 0, 1, 1, 2, 4, 8
     $\therefore$ Mode = 0

Each value occurs once.

(b) Rearrange the data: 2, 4, 5, 6, 8, 9
     This data set has no mode.

2 and 3 occur twice. Thus, this data set has more than one mode.

(c) Rearrange the data: 1, 2, 2, 3, 3, 4, 6
     $\therefore$ Mode = 2 and 3

Example 21

The sizes of shoes sold in a day are displayed in the dot diagram below.

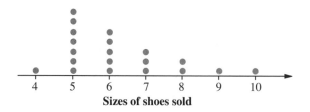

Sizes of shoes sold

(a) How many pairs of shoes were sold altogether?

(b) State the modal size of shoes sold.

Solution

(a) Total number of pairs of shoes sold = 20

(b) Size 5 has the highest frequency (7 pairs).
Therefore, the modal size of shoes sold is 5.

Exercise 8E

1. Find the mode of each of the following data sets.

(a) 5, 3, 7, 3, 3, 9, 0

(b) 3, 6, 8, 1, 8, 3, 3, 6, 1

(c) 53, 5, 23, 58, 6, 20

(d) 110 kg, 100 kg, 120 kg, 110 kg, 100 kg, 110 kg, 100 kg

2. Find the median and the mode of each of the following data sets.

(a) 1, 1, 2, 3, 5, 8, 1, 3, 2, 1

(b) 95, 96, 99, 98, 69, 59, 89

3. The following shows the number of goals scored in 20 football matches.

3	2	2	3	1
3	2	2	3	0
3	1	2	1	3
3	2	3	5	2

Find the modal number of goals scored.

4. The marks scored by 11 children in a spelling test are shown below.

8, 9, 4, 2, 7, 10, 4, 1, 4, 9, 8

Find

(a) the mode,

(b) the median,

(c) the mean.

5. Look at the data set below.

2, 4, 6, 12, 4, 19, 13, 4, 17, 11, 7

(a) State the mode.

(b) Find the median.

(c) Calculate the mean of the numbers in the data set.

(d) When the number x is included in the above group, the new mean is 10. Calculate the value of x.

6. A survey was carried out to find out the number of hours a group of 50 students spend studying each day. The results are shown in the following table.

No. of hours	Frequency
0	2
1	13
2	10
3	14
4	8
5	3

Find

(a) the mode,

(b) the median,

(c) the mean.

7. A group of teenagers were asked how many magazines they had read in a particular week. The results are shown in the table.

No. of magazines	1	2	3	4
No. of teenagers	13	13	20	4

Find

(a) the mode,

(b) the mean.

8. **(a)** By using the tally method or otherwise, copy and complete the frequency distribution of the number of letters in each word in the text below.

The quick brown fox
jumps over the lazy dog.

No. of letters in each word	3	4	5
Frequency			

(b) Find

　(i) the mode,

　(ii) the median.

★**9.** A group of adults were asked about the number of times they had exercised in a specific week. The table below shows the results.

No. of exercises	0	1	2	3
No. of adults	6	8	4	x

(a) Write down the largest possible value of x given that the mode is 1.

(b) Write down the largest possible value of x given that the median is 1.

(c) Calculate the value of x given that the mean is 1.

10. The histogram below shows the number of occupants per apartment for a block consisting of 100 apartments.

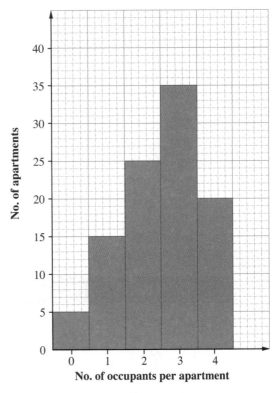

(a) State the modal number of occupants per apartment.

(b) Calculate the mean number of occupants per apartment.

11. The dot diagram shows the grades obtained for a Mathematics examination by students of a Secondary Two class.

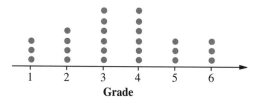

Grade

(a) How many students are there in the class?
(b) Find the median grade.
(c) State the modal grade.

12. The number of people in cars passing a junction during a period of time were noted and displayed in the dot diagram below.

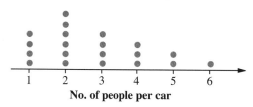

No. of people per car

(a) How many cars were noted passing the junction during that period of time?
(b) State the modal number of people per car.
(c) Find the median number of people per car.
(d) Calculate the mean number of people per car.

13. The stem-and-leaf diagram shows the fortnightly (two-week) wages of workers in a department of a small factory.

Wages (in $)	
5	00 20 40 60
6	00 10 10 20 30 30 30
7	00 30 50 80 80
8	00 10 20 30

(a) If the lowest wage is $500, state the highest wage.
(b) Find
    (i) the mode, (ii) the median,
    (iii) the mean.

14. The stem-and-leaf diagram below shows the marks obtained in a test by students of a class.

Marks		
Girls		Boys
8 5	4	2 3 8
8 5 3 2	5	1 5 5 5 9
7 6 1 1	6	2 3 5
4 1 0	7	1

Key (Girls):   *Key* (Boys):
5 | 4 means 45 marks 4 | 2 means 42 marks

(a) How many students took the test?
(b) Find
    (i) the mode, (ii) the mean.
(c) Find the median mark of
    (i) the girls, (ii) the boys.
(d) Write a brief statement comparing the marks obtained by the girls and the boys.

15. The students of a particular class were asked how many movies they had each watched in the past month. The results are shown in the histogram below.

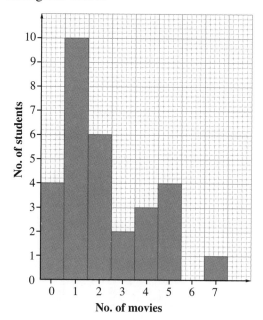

No. of movies

Find
(a) the number of students in the class,
(b) the mode,
(c) the median,
(d) the mean.

8.2.5 Use and Purpose of Mean, Median and Mode

We have learned about the three types of statistical averages or measures of central tendency. How do we know which is the most appropriate type of average to use? Which average (mean, median or mode), for example, should be used to report the results of a survey? Which average should a shopkeeper use to determine the type of goods to top up?

The use of each of these types of averages depends on the type of data and the purpose of interpretation. Using the most suitable average will usually result in a better decision-making process. Consider the scenario below:

General Manager

We should not give overtime allowances to the employees. They are not entitled to it as their average salary of $1 935 is higher than the $1 600 limit.

No, they should be entitled to the overtime allowances. I calculated their average salary to be $1 250.

Level Manager

The table below shows the salaries of the 10 employees under the general manager. The three types of averages have also been calculated.

Employee	Salary
A	$1 100
B	$1 100
C	$1 250
D	$1 250
E	$1 250
F	$1 250
G	$1 250
H	$1 350
I	$1 350
J	$8 200

Mean = $1 935
Median = $1 250
Mode = $1 250

Who was telling the truth? Why are the mean and median in this scenario so different from each other? Which is a better representative of the employees' salaries?

In the scenario on the previous page, both managers were telling the truth. The general manager had taken the mean to be the average while the level manager had taken the median instead. Each of their calculations was correct. However, the general manager's average misrepresents the actual salaries of the employees due to one particular extreme value ($8 200) and thus leads to an inappropriate decision.

The **mean**, which is the most commonly used type of average, is sometimes inappropriate in cases where there are extreme values. In data sets with no extreme values, it is the most suitable representation of the data as it takes into account all the values in the data set.

The **median** however, is a better average to use when extreme values are present. It is less sensitive to such extreme values as it is the middle number in the data set. The median is often used to represent data sets such as salaries, household incomes and so on.

The **mode** is generally preferred by shopkeepers and manufacturers who wish to find out the most typical or popular product they have. This is because it represents the data which occurs the most often. Thus, the mode is especially useful to certain groups of people as it is a measure of popularity and can thus help with business and purchasing decisions.

As can be seen from the observations above, it is often not sufficient in statistics to say, 'The average is …'. It is equally important to know which type of average someone is talking about or which type to use to ensure the correct interpretation of the data values.

Air Quality Index of Singapore

(a) Visit the website of National Environment Agency (NEA) at http://www. nea.gov.sg. Find the data of the Pollutants Standard Index (PSI) readings of Singapore in the past one month. The PSI readings are indications of the air quality in Singapore.

(b) Use the data to find
   (i) the mean,   (ii) the median, and   (iii) the mode
   of the PSI readings of overall Singapore in the past one month.

(c) Assuming that you are a government officer in charge of public education, explain in your Mathematics Journal how you will use any of the statistical averages to help you describe the air quality to the public.

8.2.6 Mean of Grouped Data

Consider the following list of marks obtained by 50 students in a Mathematics examination.

60	51	89	69	66	43	98	60	58	68
80	12	45	64	38	87	59	29	65	56
55	61	77	52	63	22	67	50	49	65
37	40	69	25	52	64	71	44	83	31
41	76	58	62	45	73	56	75	33	63

Recall the formula for the mean of ungrouped data from Section 8.2.2.

If we want to find the mean of the above data, we would first need to add up the 50 values and then divide this sum by 50 as learned in the earlier section.

$$\therefore \quad \text{Mean} = \frac{\text{Sum of values}}{\text{Number of values}}$$

$$= \frac{2\,856}{50} = 57.12 \text{ marks}$$

We have learned in Book 1 that we can also put large sets of data values in groups in a frequency table. These groups can also be known as **classes**. For the data given above, we can choose to group the data values in classes of intervals $0 \leq m < 10$, $10 \leq m < 20$ and so on, where m represents the marks. Thus, the corresponding frequency table is as shown below.

Mark (m)	Tally	Frequency
$0 \leq m < 10$		0
$10 \leq m < 20$	/	1
$20 \leq m < 30$	///	3
$30 \leq m < 40$	////	4
$40 \leq m < 50$	‖‖ //	7
$50 \leq m < 60$	‖‖ ‖‖	10
$60 \leq m < 70$	‖‖ ‖‖ ‖‖	15
$70 \leq m < 80$	‖‖	5
$80 \leq m < 90$	////	4
$90 \leq m < 100$	/	1
		Total = 50

How can we get the mean of such grouped data from a frequency table? Since the frequency table does not show us individual values of the data, it is not possible to calculate the exact value of the mean. However, we can obtain an estimate of the mean using the following steps.

Step 1 Create a new frequency table with columns 'Mark (*m*)', 'Mid-value (*x*)', 'Frequency (*f*)' and '*fx*'. Copy the values of the columns 'Mark (*m*)' and 'Frequency' from the table on the previous page.

note

'**Mid-value**' is also known as '**class mark**' in some books.

Mark (*m*)	Mid-value (*x*)	Frequency (*f*)	*fx*
$0 \leq m < 10$		0	
$10 \leq m < 20$		1	
$20 \leq m < 30$		3	
$30 \leq m < 40$		4	
$40 \leq m < 50$		7	
$50 \leq m < 60$		10	
$60 \leq m < 70$		15	
$70 \leq m < 80$		5	
$80 \leq m < 90$		4	
$90 \leq m < 100$		1	
		Total = 50	

Step 2 Calculate the mid-value of each class by finding the mean of the two ends of the class interval.

note

The **mid-value** of the class $a \leq m < b$ is given by $\dfrac{a + b}{2}$.

E.g.   Mid-value of class $0 \leq m < 10$ is $\dfrac{0 + 10}{2} = 5$.

Step 3 Multiply *f* by *x* for each row and find the sum of *fx* to complete the table.

Mark (*m*)	Mid-value (*x*)	Frequency (*f*)	*fx*
$0 \leq m < 10$	5	0	0
$10 \leq m < 20$	15	1	15
$20 \leq m < 30$	25	3	75
$30 \leq m < 40$	35	4	140
$40 \leq m < 50$	45	7	315
$50 \leq m < 60$	55	10	550
$60 \leq m < 70$	65	15	975
$70 \leq m < 80$	75	5	375
$80 \leq m < 90$	85	4	340
$90 \leq m < 100$	95	1	95
		Total = 50	*Total* = 2 880

Step 4 An estimate of the mean is given by the following formula.

$$\text{Mean} = \frac{\text{Sum of } fx}{\text{Sum of } f}$$

$$= \frac{2\,880}{50}$$

$$= 57.6$$

note

Notice that the mean we have found here is different from the one we calculated on page 296. This is because this method can only give us an estimate of the mean.

For grouped data,

$$\text{Mean} = \frac{\text{Sum of } fx}{\text{Sum of } f}$$

where f is the frequency and x is the mid-value of each class.

Example 22

The heights of a group of students were measured and recorded as shown below.

Height (h cm)	No. of students
$150 < h \leq 155$	3
$155 < h \leq 160$	11
$160 < h \leq 165$	14
$165 < h \leq 170$	10
$170 < h \leq 175$	8
$175 < h \leq 180$	4

(a) How many students are represented in the table above?

(b) Calculate an estimate of the mean height of the students, giving your answer correct to 3 significant figures.

Solution

(a) Total number of students = 3 + 11 + 14 + 10 + 8 + 4
$$= 50$$

The total number of students is the sum of values in the 'No. of students' column.

(b) Let us construct a frequency table to help us calculate an estimate of the mean height.

Height (h cm)	Mid-value (x)	Frequency (f)	fx
$150 < h \leq 155$	152.5	3	457.5
$155 < h \leq 160$	157.5	11	1 732.5
$160 < h \leq 165$	162.5	14	2 275
$165 < h \leq 170$	167.5	10	1 675
$170 < h \leq 175$	172.5	8	1 380
$175 < h \leq 180$	177.5	4	710
		$Total = 50$	$Total = 8\ 230$

$$\text{Mean height} = \frac{\text{Sum of } fx}{\text{Sum of } f}$$

$$= \frac{8\ 230}{50} = 164.6$$

$$= 165 \text{ cm} \quad \text{(correct to 3 sig. fig.)}$$

Example 23

The table below shows the number of apples sold per day by a fruit seller in a month.

No. of apples	No. of days
40 – 44	9
45 – 49	8
50 – 54	4
55 – 59	1
60 – 64	4
65 – 69	4

Calculate an estimate of the mean number of apples sold per day by the fruit seller. Give your answer correct to the nearest whole number.

Solution

Let us construct a frequency table to help us calculate an estimate of the mean.

For class 40 – 44, the mid-value is $\frac{40 + 44}{2} = 42$.

No. of apples	Mid-value (x)	Frequency (f)	fx
40 – 44	42	9	378
45 – 49	47	8	376
50 – 54	52	4	208
55 – 59	57	1	57
60 – 64	62	4	248
65 – 69	67	4	268
		$Total = 30$	$Total = 1\ 535$

$$\text{Mean number of apples} = \frac{\text{Sum of } fx}{\text{Sum of } f}$$
$$= \frac{1\,535}{30}$$
$$\approx 51.17$$
$$= 51 \quad \text{(correct to the nearest whole number)}$$

Exercise 8F

1. The frequency table below shows the masses of some oranges from the same tree.

Mass (m g)	Mid-value (x)	Frequency (f)
$60 < m \leq 70$	65	3
$70 < m \leq 80$	75	5
$80 < m \leq 90$	85	6
$90 < m \leq 100$	95	7
$100 < m \leq 110$	105	10
$110 < m \leq 120$	115	8
$120 < m \leq 130$	125	7
$130 < m \leq 140$	135	4

  (a) How many oranges are represented in the table above?

  (b) Calculate an estimate of the mean mass of the oranges.

2. The frequency table below shows the number of pairs of shoes sold per day at a shop in a particular month.

No. of pairs of shoes sold	Mid-value (x)	Frequency (f)
40 – 44	42	3
45 – 49	47	2
50 – 54	52	3
55 – 59	57	4
60 – 64	62	3
65 – 69	67	5
70 – 74	72	6

  (a) How many days was the shop open for business in that month?

  (b) Calculate an estimate of the mean number of pairs of shoes sold per day. Give your answer correct to the nearest whole number.

3. The frequency table below shows the weekly wages of 200 workers in a company.

Wage ($\$w$)	Mid-value (x)	Frequency (f)
$225 < w \leq 245$	235	26
$245 < w \leq 265$		36
$265 < w \leq 285$		58
$285 < w \leq 305$		42
$305 < w \leq 325$		38
		Total =

  (a) Copy and complete the above table.

  (b) Hence, calculate an estimate of the mean weekly wage.

4. The frequency table below shows the number of spectators per football match held in a stadium in a year.

No. of spectators	Mid-value (x)	Frequency (f)
1 000 – 1 999	1 499.5	4
2 000 – 2 999		5
3 000 – 3 999		2
4 000 – 4 999		5
5 000 – 5 999		12
6 000 – 6 999		14
7 000 – 7 999		5
8 000 – 8 999		1
		Total =

(a) Copy and complete the table.

(b) Hence, calculate an estimate of the mean number of spectators per football match during that year. Give your answer correct to the nearest whole number.

5. The speeds (in km/h) of 50 vehicles passing by a road junction are shown below.

61	53	92	73	71	42	96	57	54	63
85	16	48	66	39	82	55	36	63	55
56	63	80	56	68	31	65	47	45	60
42	44	72	27	53	59	67	41	81	30
42	78	61	66	50	72	54	72	29	58

(a) Copy and complete the following table.

Speed (v km/h)	Mid-value (x)	Tally	Frequency (f)	fx
$9.5 < v \leq 19.5$	14.5			
$19.5 < v \leq 29.5$				
$29.5 < v \leq 39.5$				
$39.5 < v \leq 49.5$				
$49.5 < v \leq 59.5$				
$59.5 < v \leq 69.5$				
$69.5 < v \leq 79.5$				
$79.5 < v \leq 89.5$				
$89.5 < v \leq 99.5$				
			Total =	Total =

(b) Use the table above to calculate an estimate of the mean speed.

6. The number of aeroplanes landing at an airport per day is shown below.

50	50	45	54	62	56	47	58	55	52
44	57	54	56	46	51	51	48	63	52
56	46	50	45	53	58	54	64	49	52
51	57	61	42	53	59	52	48	53	58
51	59	54	52	50	47	53	57	55	40

(a) Copy and complete the following table.

No. of aeroplanes	Mid-value (x)	Tally	Frequency (x)	fx
40 – 44	42			
45 – 49				
50 – 54				
55 – 59				
60 – 64				
			Total =	Total =

(b) Use the table above to calculate an estimate of the mean number of aeroplanes that landed per day.

7. The price of a certain item at 20 shops was investigated. The results are shown in the following table.

Price ($p)	No. of shops
$25.50 < p \leq 26.00$	1
$26.00 < p \leq 26.50$	2
$26.50 < p \leq 27.00$	5
$27.00 < p \leq 27.50$	8
$27.50 < p \leq 28.00$	4

Calculate an estimate of the mean price of the item.

8. The Intelligence Quotient (I.Q.) scores of 80 students are shown in the following table.

I.Q. score (s)	No. of students
$95 < s \leq 100$	5
$100 < s \leq 105$	11
$105 < s \leq 110$	13
$110 < s \leq 115$	16
$115 < s \leq 120$	12
$120 < s \leq 125$	8
$125 < s \leq 130$	8
$130 < s \leq 135$	7

Calculate an estimate of the mean I.Q. score of these students.

9. The weekly expenditure of 35 children is shown in the table below.

Expenditure (m)	No. of children
$5 \leq m < 10$	1
$10 \leq m < 15$	7
$15 \leq m < 20$	8
$20 \leq m < 25$	10
$25 \leq m < 30$	6
$30 \leq m < 35$	3

Calculate an estimate of the mean expenditure of the children.

10. Over a 50-day period, the number of absentees in a private school was recorded as shown in the table below.

No. of absentees	No. of days
0 – 4	5
5 – 9	10
10 – 14	12
15 – 19	15
20 – 24	8

Calculate an estimate of the mean number of absentees per day.

(8.3) Probability

8.3.1 Introduction

Early developments in the theory of probability were inspired by gamblers seeking to predict their chances of winning in a game. Two great French mathematicians, Pierre de Fermat and Blaise Pascal, were the first two mathematicians documented in history to have studied and developed the theory of probability scientifically.

The **probability of any event** is the **measure** of the likelihood or chance that the event will occur. For example, we may wish to know the likelihood of it being a rainy day. Knowing this probability can help us decide if we should carry an umbrella with us when we go out.

The greater the probability of an event, the greater is the likelihood that it will occur.

In modern days, probability has many real-life applications. It is applied in fields such as finance, politics and science to determine risks or predict likely outcomes in future events. For example, probability is used to calculate premiums for insurance coverage schemes (finance), predictions of voting results (politics) and error considerations for scientific experiments (science).

8.3.2   Favourable Outcomes and Sample Space

Consider the event where we obtain an odd number when we roll a die. How many possible outcomes are there for this event?

We can use the letter A (or any other letter) to denote this event, i.e., the event that 'the number rolled on a die is odd'. Since a die has six faces with the numbers 1 to 6, the possible outcomes of A are 1, 3 and 5. We say that the **favourable outcomes** of A are 1, 3 and 5. Therefore, the number of favourable outcomes of A is 3.

The list of all possible outcomes is known as the **sample space**. In the case of the die, the sample space consists of the numbers 1, 2, 3, 4, 5 and 6. Thus, the total number of possible outcomes is 6.

Consider the case when a coin is tossed. What is its sample space?

Example 24

A common die is tossed. P is the event that the number is prime.
(a) State the total number of possible outcomes.
(b) List down the favourable outcomes of P. Hence, write down the number of favourable outcomes of P.

Solution

(a) The list of all possible outcomes (or the sample space) consists of 1, 2, 3, 4, 5 and 6.
∴   the total number of possible outcomes is 6.

1, 4 and 6 are not prime numbers.

(b) The favourable outcomes of P are 2, 3 and 5.
∴   the number of favourable outcomes of P is 3.

Example 25

A box contains 1 red chip, 2 green chips and 3 blue chips. A chip is chosen at random from the box.
(a) List down the sample space and write down the total number of possible outcomes.
(b) B is the event that a blue chip is chosen. List down the outcomes favourable to B and write down the number of favourable outcomes.

Solution

G_1 and G_2 can be used to indicate the 2 green chips. Similarly B_1, B_2 and B_3 are used to indicate the 3 blue chips. Since there is only 1 red chip, the letter R will suffice.

(a) The sample space consists of R, G_1, G_2, B_1, B_2 and B_3.

$\therefore$ the total number of possible outcomes is 6.

(b) The favourable outcomes of B are B_1, B_2 and B_3.

$\therefore$ the number of favourable outcomes of B is 3.

Exercise 8G

1. An octagonal spinner is spun. When it comes to rest, the number it points to is recorded.

(a) List down the sample space and hence state the total number of possible outcomes.

(b) If A is the event that the pointer points to a prime number, list down the favourable outcomes of A.

(c) State the number of favourable outcomes of A.

2. A stationery box contains 2 red pens, 1 green pen and 2 blue pens. A pen is chosen at random from the box.

(a) List down the sample space and hence state the total number of possible outcomes.

(b) B is the event that a blue pen is chosen. List down the favourable outcomes of B.

(c) State the number of favourable outcomes of B.

3. A circular soft board is divided equally into seven sections, each with one of the letters from the word CHANCES. A dart is thrown at the board. Assuming that the dart always lands on the board,

(a) list down the sample space,

(b) write down the total number of possible outcomes,

(c) list down the favourable outcomes of A if A is the event of the dart landing on the letter C.

4. Each of the 11 letters of the word PROBABILITY is written on separate cards. A card is then chosen at random from the 11 cards.

(a) If A is the event that the letter written on the chosen card is a vowel, list down the favourable outcomes of A.

(b) State the number of favourable outcomes of A.

5. If a number is chosen at random from 1 to 30, list down the favourable outcomes of

(a) A, where A is the event that a prime number is chosen,

(b) B, where B is the event that a multiple of 3 is chosen.

8.3.3 Simple Probability

The probability of an event is the likelihood of the event occurring. It is a measure of chance. For example, in one flip of an unbiased (fair, balanced) coin, it is equally likely that the flip will show either a 'head' or a 'tail'. Thus, there is one chance in two of getting a 'head'. We say that the probability of getting a 'head' is $\frac{1}{2}$.

An experiment can be carried out to investigate this probability. We can toss a coin individually many times, say 200 times, and expect the head to appear about 100 times. This practice is rather time-consuming. Let us carry out the experiment in a more efficient way as shown in the activity below.

You can also visit the following website to view an online simulation of the activity on the right:
http://nlvm.usu.edu/en/nav/frames_asid_305_g_3_t_5.html

Activity

To investigate probability through a simple experiment.

1. Assuming that there are 40 pupils in a class, get each pupil to toss a coin at the same time. Record the results on the board (or transparency) in a table as shown below. Repeat the experiment until the total number of tosses reaches a desired figure (say about 200).

Round	Total no. of 'head' (accumulated)	Total no. of tosses (accumulated)	Total no. of 'head' / Total no. of tosses
1		40	
2		80	
3		120	
4		160	
5		200	

Induction

2. If the total number of tosses was increased indefinitely, what do you think the value of $\dfrac{\text{total number of 'head'}}{\text{total number of tosses}}$ would be?

From the previous activity, we can state the definition of **probability** as follows:

$$\text{Probability of any event } A \text{ occurring, P}(A) = \frac{\text{Number of outcomes favourable to } A}{\text{Total number of possible outcomes}}$$

Consider the following example:

Let A be the event that a cat with two tails is chosen. Since there is no such cat in the world, the number of cats with two tails is 0. Hence, A is an impossible event.

$$\therefore \text{P}(A) = \frac{\text{Number of outcomes favourable to } A}{\text{Total number of possible outcomes}}$$

$$= \frac{0}{\text{Total number of possible outcomes}}$$

$$= 0$$

If A is an impossible event, then $\text{P}(A) = 0$.

Consider another example:

Given a class of 40 students in Pine Hill Girls' School, let A be the event that a female student is chosen. Since all the students in a girls' school must be female, the number of female students in the class is 40. Thus, A is also the sample space. Hence, A is a sure event.

$$\therefore \text{P}(A) = \frac{\text{Number of outcomes favourable to } A}{\text{Total number of possible outcomes}}$$

$$= \frac{\text{Total number of possible outcomes}}{\text{Total number of possible outcomes}}$$

$$= \frac{40}{40}$$

$$= 1$$

If A is a sure event, then $\text{P}(A) = 1$.

For some basic examples involving probability, visit: http://www.mathgoodies.com/lessons/vol6/intro_probability.html

For any event A,

If $\text{P}(A) = 0$, then the event will never occur.
If $\text{P}(A) = 1$, then the event will definitely occur.

Thus, the probability of any event occurring is always between 0 and 1. The higher its probability, the greater the chance that the event will occur.

Let us now consider the number obtained when a common die is thrown. If we consider A to be the event of obtaining an odd integer, then

- $P(A)$ is the probability of obtaining an odd integer, and
- $P(\textbf{not } A)$ is the probability of **not** obtaining an odd integer.

Since the number obtained is either an odd or even integer, this means that $P(\textbf{not } A)$ is the probability of obtaining an even integer. The relationship between $P(A)$ and $P(\textbf{not } A)$ can be deduced as follows:

$$\text{Total number of odd integers} + \text{Total number of even integers} = \text{Total number of possible outcomes}$$

Dividing both sides of the above equation by the total number of possible outcomes, we get:

Number of outcomes favourable to A = Total number of odd integers.

LHS
$$= \frac{\text{Total number of odd integers}}{\text{Total number of possible outcomes}} + \frac{\text{Total number of even integers}}{\text{Total number of possible outcomes}}$$
$$= P(A) + P(\textbf{not } A)$$

RHS
$$= \frac{\text{Total number of possible outcomes}}{\text{Total number of possible outcomes}}$$
$$= 1$$

You can check that the relationship deduced on the right is true.

$$P(A) = \frac{3}{6} = \frac{1}{2}$$

$$P(\textbf{not } A) = \frac{3}{6} = \frac{1}{2}$$

$$\therefore \quad P(A) + P(\textbf{not } A) = 1$$

$$\therefore \quad P(A) + P(\textbf{not } A)$$
$$= \frac{1}{2} + \frac{1}{2}$$
$$= 1$$

> For any event A, $P(A) + P(\textbf{not } A) = 1$
> $$\Rightarrow \quad P(\textbf{not } A) = 1 - P(A).$$

Example 26

An unbiased die is thrown. Find the probability that the number obtained is

(a) a prime number,
(b) a number divisible by 3,
(c) a number not divisible by 3,
(d) 7.

Solution

The sample space consists of the numbers 1, 2, 3, 4, 5 and 6.

(a) Let A be the event of obtaining a prime number.
Then the favourable outcomes of A are 2, 3 and 5.
Thus, the number of outcomes favourable to A is 3.

∴ Probability of obtaining a prime number, P(A)

$$= \frac{\text{Number of outcomes favourable to } A}{\text{Total number of possible outcomes}}$$

$$= \frac{3}{6} = \frac{1}{2}$$

(b) Let B be the event of obtaining a number divisible by 3.
Then the favourable outcomes of B are 3 and 6.
Thus, the number of outcomes favourable to B is 2.

∴ Probability of obtaining a number divisible by 3, P(B)

$$= \frac{\text{Number of outcomes favourable to } B}{\text{Total number of possible outcomes}}$$

$$= \frac{2}{6} = \frac{1}{3}$$

(c) Probability of obtaining a number not divisible by 3, P(not B)
$$= 1 - P(B)$$
$$= 1 - \frac{1}{3} = \frac{2}{3}$$

Alternative method:
Let C be the event of obtaining a number not divisible by 3.
Then the favourable outcomes of C are 1, 2, 4 and 5.
Thus, the number of outcomes favourable to C is 4.

∴ Probability of obtaining a number not divisible by 3, P(C)

$$= \frac{\text{Number of outcomes favourable to } C}{\text{Total number of possible outcomes}}$$

$$= \frac{4}{6} = \frac{2}{3}$$

(d) The number 7 is not found on the die. Thus, this is an impossible event.
∴ Probability that the number obtained is 7 = 0

Example 27

A card is randomly drawn from a standard deck of 52 playing cards. Find the probability that the card drawn is
(a) a picture card,   **(b)** a club,
(c) a club or a spade,   **(d)** not a club,
(e) the king of clubs.

Solution

(a) There are 12 picture cards in the deck.

∴ Probability of getting a picture card $= \dfrac{12}{52}$

$$= \frac{3}{13}$$

note

To 'draw' a card means to pick out a card. We can also draw balls from a bag.

(b) There are 13 clubs in the deck.

$$\therefore \quad \text{Probability of getting a club} = \frac{13}{52} = \frac{1}{4}$$

(c) There are 13 clubs and 13 spades in the deck.

$$\therefore \quad \text{Probability of getting a club or a spade} = \frac{13 + 13}{52}$$
$$= \frac{26}{52} = \frac{1}{2}$$

(d) Probability of getting a card which is not a club
= 1 – Probability of getting a club
$$= 1 - \frac{1}{4} = \frac{3}{4}$$

(e) There is only 1 king of clubs.

$$\therefore \quad \text{Probability of getting the king of clubs} = \frac{1}{52}$$

Example 28

There are 36 green chips and some red chips in a bag. One chip is selected at random. Given the probability that it is red is $\frac{4}{13}$, find the number of red chips in the bag.

Solution

Let r be the number of red chips.

$$\text{Probability of selecting a red chip} = \frac{4}{13}$$
$$\frac{\text{Number of red chips}}{\text{Total number of chips}} = \frac{4}{13}$$
$$\frac{r}{36 + r} \diagdown \frac{4}{13}$$
$$13r = 4(36 + r)$$
$$= 144 + 4r$$
$$9r = 144$$
$$r = 16$$

$\therefore$ there are 16 red chips.

Exercise 8H

1. An unbiased die is tossed. Find the probability that the number obtained is
  (a) an odd number, **(b)** greater than 4,
  (c) less than 1, **(d)** less than 10.

2. A card is randomly drawn from a standard deck of 52 playing cards. Find the probability that the card drawn is
  (a) an ace, **(b)** a spade,
  (c) an ace of spades, **(d)** not a spade.

3. A letter is randomly chosen from the word PROBABILITY. What is the probability that it will be
   (a) the letter B,
   (b) a vowel,
   (c) the letter V?

4. A box contains 2 red discs, 3 green discs and 4 blue discs. One disc is randomly drawn from the box. What is the probability that it will be
   (a) a red disc,
   (b) a green disc,
   (c) a red disc or a green disc,
   (d) not a blue disc?

5. An unbiased die is tossed. What is the probability of getting
   (a) a number not divisible by 3,
   (b) a number less than 3,
   (c) a number greater than 6?

6. A card is randomly drawn from a standard deck of 52 playing cards. What is the probability that the card drawn is
   (a) a red card,
   (b) a heart,
   (c) not a heart,
   (d) a queen of hearts?

7. A letter is randomly chosen from the words MATHEMATICS COUNTS. Find the probability that the letter chosen is
   (a) the letter T,
   (b) a vowel,
   (c) a consonant.

8. The pages of a thin book are numbered 1 to 42. A page is chosen at random. Write down, giving your answer as a fraction, the probability that the page number
   (a) contains a single digit,
   (b) contains more than a single digit,
   (c) contains at least one digit that is 2,
   (d) is a perfect square.

9. There are 25 black balls and some white balls in a box. One ball is selected at random. Given the probability that it is white is $\frac{4}{9}$, find the number of white balls in the box.

10. (a) I throw an ordinary six-sided die. Write down, as a fraction, the probability that the number shown on the die is even.
   (b) There are 49 marbles in a bag. Given that the probability of randomly choosing a white marble is exactly $\frac{4}{7}$, calculate the number of marbles in the bag which are not white.

11. The table below shows the number of broken eggs found in each crate.

No. of broken eggs	No. of crates
0	40
1	30
2	20
3	10
4	0

If a crate is selected at random, what is the probability that it has no broken eggs?

12. The stem-and-leaf diagram below shows the number of defective pens found in a few boxes during a quality control check in a factory.

Number of defective pens per box	
0	0 0 0 0 0 0 1 1 1 1 2 5
1	1 1 2 4 6
2	1 2 4

   (a) How many boxes were checked?
   (b) A box is selected at random. What is the probability that the box contains less than 15 defective pens?

1. A dot diagram is a graphical display with dots representing data values positioned along an axis or a number line.
E.g.

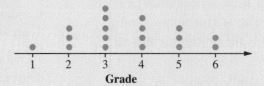

2. A stem-and-leaf diagram offers a quick way to picture the shape of a distribution while displaying the actual numerical values.
E.g.

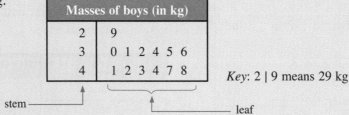

Key: 2 | 9 means 29 kg

3. The three main statistical averages are the mean, median and mode. These are also often known as the measures of central tendency.

4. **(a)** The mean is found by adding all the values and dividing by the number of values added.

$$\text{Mean} = \frac{\text{Sum of values}}{\text{Number of values}}$$

(b) The median of a set of N values is the middle value (if N is odd) or the mean of the two middle values (if N is even) when the values are arranged in ascending or descending order.

(c) The mode is the value that occurs with the highest frequency.

5. For grouped data, $$\text{Mean} = \frac{\text{Sum of } fx}{\text{Sum of } f}$$

where f is the frequency and x is the mid-value of each class.

6. The list of all possible outcomes is called the sample space.

7. Probability of any event A occurring, $P(A) = \dfrac{\text{Number of outcomes favourable to } A}{\text{Total number of possible outcomes}}$

8. If A is an impossible event, then $P(A) = 0$.

9. If A is a sure event, then $P(A) = 1$.

10. For any event A, $P(\textbf{not } A) = 1 - P(A)$.

Spinning Averages

This is a statistical game for two or more players using a roulette. You can buy a toy roulette for a few dollars from a toy shop. Choose one with the possible scores ranging from 0 to 36.

Game 1

Objective:

The target is to get a mean that is the closest to 18 at the end of 10 turns.

Method:

Each player takes his turn to spin the roulette and is allowed to reject the score only once in each turn. Each player is given 10 turns.

Example:

Player 1: Spins a score of 3 – rejects. Spins a second time and obtains a score of 10 – accepts. Records 10 as his first score.

Player 2: Spins a score of 16 – accepts. Records 16 as his first score.

Player 1: Spins a score of 30 (mean of 10 and 30 is 20, which is close to 18) – accepts. Records 30 as his second score.
So his data consists of 10 and 30.

Player 2: Spins a score of 0 (mean of 0 and 16 is 8, which is too far from 18) – rejects. Spins a second time and obtains a score of 22 – accepts. Records 22 as his second score.
So his data consists of 16 and 22, giving a mean of 19.

Player 1: Spins a score of 11 (mean of 10, 30 and 11 is 17) – accepts. Records 11 as his third score.
So his data consists of 10, 30 and 11.

Player 2: . . .

The player who obtains a mean that is the closest to 18 at the end of 10 turns will be the winner.

Game 2

The method is the same as in Game 1, except that the target is to get a median score that is the closest to 18 at the end of 10 turns.

Various rules can be implemented for both games. For a start, allow written calculation. After some practice, allow only mental calculation or set a time for limit calculation. You may also wish to start with Game 2 as it is easier to manage.

You have 10 minutes to answer the following questions.
Choose the most appropriate answer.

CONCEPT CHECK

8.1 1. The dot diagram shows the number of story books read by a group of students in a particular month.

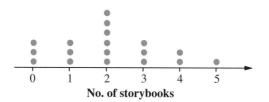

What was the most common number of story books read by the students?

A 2   **B** 3   **C** 5   **D** 18

8.1 2. The stem-and-leaf diagram shows the amounts charged by a taxi for its various trips on a particular day.

Charges (in $)	
4	40 50 70 80 90
5	30 40 50 60 70
6	20 30 50 80
7	00 10 30
8	20 40

Key: 4 | 40 means $4.40

How many trips did the taxi make on that day?
A 5   **B** 19   **C** 24   **D** 30

8.2 3. Find the mean of the following data.

5, 5, 6, 7, 10

A 6.6   **B** 6   **C** 5   **D** 3.3

8.2 4. Find the median of the following data.

9, 5, 6, 5, 7

A 5   **B** 6   **C** 6.4   **D** 9

8.2 5. Find the median of the following data.

4.1, 2.3, 4.1, 2.1, 4.1, 5.5

A 2.1   **B** 3.2   **C** 3.7   **D** 4.1

8.2 **6.** Find the mode of the following data.

1, 2, 8, 2, 1, 3, 1, 8

A 1 **B** 2 **C** 3.25 **D** 8

8.2 **7.** What is the mid-value of class $5 < x \leq 10$?
A 5 **B** 7 **C** 7.5 **D** 15

8.2 **8.** The heights of a group of students are shown below.

Height (h cm)	Mid-value (x)	Frequency (f)	fx
$150 < h \leq 160$	155	4	620
$160 < h \leq 170$	165	10	1 650
$170 < h \leq 180$	175	6	1 050

Calculate an estimate of the mean height.
A 150 cm **B** 164.5 cm
C 166 cm **D** 3 320 cm

8.3 **9.** A number is chosen at random from 1 to 10. If A is the event of obtaining a number which is a multiple of 2, what is the number of favourable outcomes of A?
A 1 **B** 2 **C** 5 **D** 10

8.3 **10.** An unbiased die is tossed and its outcome noted when it lands. What is the probability of obtaining the number 3?

A $\frac{1}{6}$ **B** $\frac{1}{3}$ **C** 1 **D** 3

SECTION A

1. Find the mean of each of the following data sets.
   (a) 1, 1, 2, 3, 5, 8, 1, 3, 2, 1
   (b) 5.2, 7.9, 3.6, 2.1, 7.9, 4.2, 3.6, 7.8, 3.6

2. Find the median of each of the following data sets.
   (a) 5, 3, 7, 3, 3, 9, 0
   (b) 1.1, 1.2, 2.3, 3.5, 5.8, 8.1, 1.3, 3.2, 2.1
   (c) 3, 6, 8, 1, 8, 3, 3, 8, 6, 1

3. Find the mode of each of the following data sets.
   (a) 9, 7, 4, 1, 3, 9, 9, 4, 0
   (b) 2.8, 2.8, 9.3, 7.8, 6.9, 5.6, 2.0, 2.9, 6.9
   (c) 555, 607, 109, 990, 709, 384

4. A letter is randomly chosen from the words RACIAL HARMONY DAY. Find the probability that the chosen letter is
   (a) the letter I,
   (b) the letter R,
   (c) a vowel,
   (d) a consonant.

SECTION B

5. A Mathematics test was taken by 4 boys and 6 girls. The mean mark of the 10 students was 49.
   (a) Calculate the total mark obtained by the 10 students.
   (b) If the mean mark of the 6 girls was 51, calculate the mean mark of the 4 boys.

6. A box contains 4 yellow and 6 black balls. 4 balls are drawn at random from the box and the number of yellow balls among these 4 balls is counted. The 4 balls are then returned to the box before the next draw. The result is displayed in the following dot diagram.

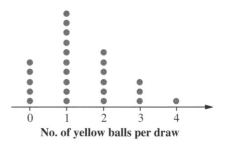

No. of yellow balls per draw

(a) How many times were the balls drawn?
(b) Find
   (i) the mean,
   (ii) the median,
   (iii) the mode.

7. The masses of a group of Secondary Two students are displayed on the stem-and-leaf diagram below.

Masses of Secondary Two students (in kg)	
3	6 9
4	1 3 4 6 7 7 8 8 8 9 9
5	1 1 2 3 4 6
6	1

(a) How many students are represented above?
(b) Find
   (i) the mean,
   (ii) the median,
   (iii) the mode.
(c) A student is selected at random. What is the probability that the student has a mass greater than 50 kg?

★**8.** The table below shows the number of books borrowed from a library by some people.

No. of books	No. of people
0	5
1	9
2	x
3	6
4	2

(a) Given that the mean is 1.64 books, find the value of *x*.

(b) Given that the median is 2 books, find the smallest possible value of *x*.

(c) Given that the mode is 2 books, find the smallest possible value of *x*.

SECTION C

9. The histogram below shows the number of pairs of shoes owned by a group of students.

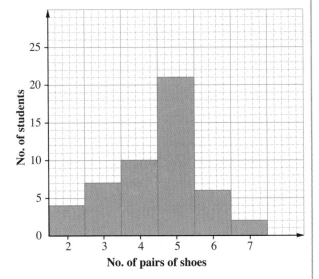

No. of pairs of shoes

(a) How many students are there in the group?

(b) Find
   (i) the mode,
   (ii) the median,
   (iii) the mean.

(c) Find the probability that a randomly chosen student has more than the median number of shoes.

10. The masses, in kg, of 50 soldiers in a training camp are as shown below.

64	76	63	63	52	59	65	68	77	75
71	66	62	51	60	53	58	66	74	56
78	62	49	60	64	67	63	53	58	64
62	47	61	65	79	69	73	54	57	63
43	61	68	68	70	72	80	70	55	56

(a) Using classes $40.5 < m \le 45.5$, $45.5 < m \le 50.5$, and so on, construct a frequency table.

(b) Hence, calculate an estimate of the mean mass.

(c) What is the probability of finding a soldier with a mass
   (i) greater than 70.5 kg,
   (ii) less than or equal to 40.5 kg?

Review Paper 3

SECTION A

1. **(a)** Expand the following.
   (i) $-(2a + 3)$
   (ii) $3(2b - c)$
   (b) Factorise the following.
   (i) $-6z - 9$
   (ii) $4y^2 - 8y$

2. Plot the points $A(1, 2)$, $B(2, -5)$ and $C(7, 0)$ on a piece of graph paper. If these are the three vertices of a rhombus, mark the fourth vertex and write down its coordinates.

3. In the following table, P is directly proportional to I.

P	480	720		1 440
I	2	3	4	

   (a) Find an equation relating P and I.
   (b) Find the missing values in the table.

4. Solve the simultaneous linear equations
$$x + y = 1,$$
$$2x + y = 0.$$

5. Find the value of the unknown angles marked in each of the following figures.
   (a)

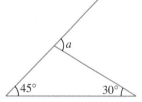

   (b)

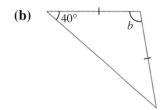

6. In the diagram shown, triangle WQX and triangle ZPY are congruent.

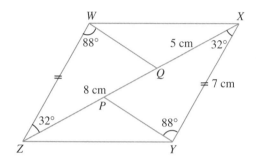

Given that $XQPZ$ is a straight line, find
   (a) the value of $\angle YPZ$ and $\angle WQX$,
   (b) the length of the unknown sides WZ and PQ.

7. The diagram below shows a solid pyramid with a square base. Calculate
   (a) its total surface area,
   (b) its volume.

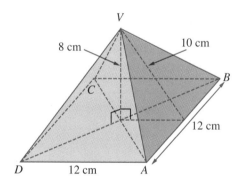

8. Look at the data set below.

$$2, 4, 5, 2, 7, 1, 0$$

Find
   (a) the mean,
   (b) the median,
   (c) the mode.

SECTION B

9. Solve the following equations.

(a) $\dfrac{h}{2} = \dfrac{3}{5}$

(b) $\dfrac{k+1}{2} = \dfrac{3k}{5}$

(c) $\dfrac{x+1}{4} - \dfrac{x}{5} = \dfrac{1}{2}$

10. (a) Write the following scales in the form of $1 : n$, where n is a whole number.

    (i) 1 cm represents 5 km

    (ii) 5 cm represents 60 m

(b) On a map of Malaysia that has a scale of 1 : 2 000 000, the distance between Kuala Lumpur and Johor Bahru is 15 cm. What is the actual distance on the ground in km?

11. Two years ago, the sum of the ages of a boy and his younger sister was 20 years. Three years from now, their ages will differ by 10 years. Form a pair of simultaneous equations and find their present ages.

12. Given that the sum of all the interior and exterior angles of a regular polygon is 1 620°, find

(a) the sum of all the interior angles,

(b) the number of sides the polygon has,

(c) the size of each exterior angle.

13. In this question, take $\pi = 3.142$ and give your answers correct to 3 significant figures.

A cone has a base radius of 7 cm. Calculate

(a) the slant height of the cone if its curved surface area is 124.4 cm²,

(b) the height of the cone if its volume is 462 cm³.

14. A spherical iron ball has a radius of 7 cm. It is melted down and then recast into small spherical balls, each of diameter 2 cm. How many small spherical balls are obtained?

15. The table below shows the number of rotten oranges found in some boxes of oranges.

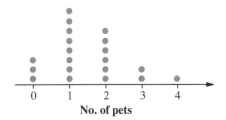

No. of rotten oranges per box	0	1	2	3	4	5
No. of boxes	12	7	15	8	10	1

(a) State the modal number of rotten oranges per box.

(b) Calculate the mean number of rotten oranges per box.

(c) Find the median number of rotten oranges per box.

16. The dot diagram shows the number of pets each child has in Hillview Garden.

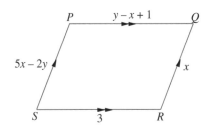

No. of pets

(a) How many children were surveyed?

(b) Find

    (i) the modal number of pets,

    (ii) the median number of pets,

    (iii) the mean number of pets.

SECTION C

17. (a) *PQRS* is a parallelogram.

    (i) Find the values of x and y.

    (ii) Hence, find the perimeter of the parallelogram.

(b) *ABC* is an equilateral triangle.
   (i) Find the values of *x* and *y*.
   (ii) Hence, find the perimeter of the triangle.

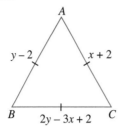

18. Construct a quadrilateral *KLMN* such that *KL* = 4 cm, *LM* = 5 cm, *MN* = 7 cm, *NK* = 6 cm and the diagonal *KM* = 6 cm. Measure and write down
   (a) the length of *LN*,
   (b) ∠*KLM*.

19. The diagram below shows a solid frustum which is formed by cutting off a smaller cone of radius 6 cm from a bigger cone of radius 9 cm.

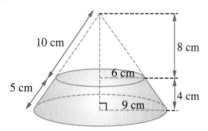

Calculate
   (a) the curved surface area of the frustum,
   (b) the total surface area of the frustum,
   (c) the volume of the frustum.

20. The table below shows the number of people in each car that passed through a gantry in an hour one morning.

No. of people in each car	1	2	3	4	5
No. of cars	10	*x*	18	12	13

   (a) Given that the modal number of people in each car is 3, write down the largest possible value of *x*.
   (b) Given that the median number of people in each car is 3, write down the largest possible value of *x*.
   (c) Given that the mean number of people in each car is 3, calculate the value of *x*.

Review Paper 4

SECTION A

1. **(a)** Expand the following.
    (i) $2(3a - 4)$
    (ii) $3b(5b - 1)$
    (b) Factorise the following.
    (i) $-5xy - 10x^2$
    (ii) $3xy^2 - 6x^2y$

2. Solve the following equations.
    (a) $a + 2 = 1$
    (b) $-\dfrac{b}{3} = 4$
    (c) $\dfrac{1 + 2c}{3} = 4$

3. In the following table, R and r are in inverse proportion.

R	75	25		5
r	3	9	15	

    (a) Find an equation relating R and r.
    (b) Find the missing values in the table.

4. Solve the simultaneous linear equations
    $$3k - 7w = 1,$$
    $$w = k + 5.$$

5. Find the value of the unknown angles marked in each of the following diagrams.
    (a)
    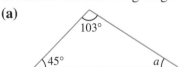
    (b)
    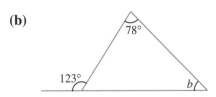

6. Taking $\pi = 3.142$, calculate
    (a) the curved surface area, and
    (b) the volume
    of the cone. Give your answers correct to 3 significant figures.

    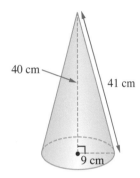

7. The radius of a small sphere is one-quarter of the radius of another bigger sphere. Find the ratio of
    (a) their volumes,
    (b) their surface areas.

8. The scores obtained by 10 students in a spelling test are as shown below.

    $$9, 3, 3, 4, 9, 6, 5, 3, 6, 4$$

    Find
    (a) the mean score,
    (b) the modal score,
    (c) the median score.

SECTION B

9. **(a)** Expand the following.
    (i) $(a + 4)(2a - 7)$
    (ii) $(b + 2c)(3 - 4c)$
    (b) Factorise the following.
    (i) $12 + 5x - 2x^2$
    (ii) $10mp - 2mq + 15np - 3nq$

10. Match the graphs **(a)** – **(d)** sketched below with the equations from the following list **(i)** – **(iv)**:

(i) $y = 3x$

(ii) $y = 3$

(iii) $x = 3$

(iv) $y = -3x$

(a)

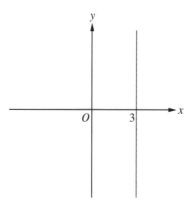

(b)

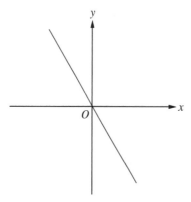

(c)

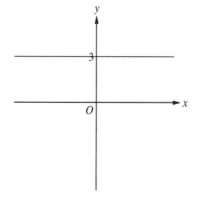

(d)

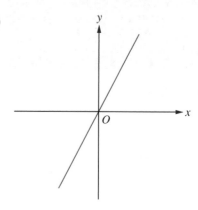

11. The atmospheric pressure, P kPa (unit kPa = kilopascal), is inversely proportional to the height, h km, above sea level.

At 60 km above sea level, the atmospheric pressure is 6 kPa.

(a) Find an equation relating P and h.

(b) Find the atmospheric pressure outside a jetcraft, 20 km above sea level.

(c) Find the height of Mount Everest, given that the atmospheric pressure at the top of the mountain is 40 kPa.

12. Zack has 11 coins in his pocket. Some are 20-cent coins and others are 50-cent coins. Given that the coins have a total value of $3.10,

(a) how many 20-cent coins and 50-cent coins does Zack have?

(b) how many more 20-cent coins does he have than 50-cent coins?

13. Given that the size of each interior angle of a regular polygon is nine times the size of each of its exterior angle, find

(a) the value of each exterior angle,

(b) the number of sides the polygon has,

(c) the sum of all the interior angles.

14. *ABCDEF* is a regular polygon.

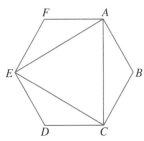

(a) Name the three triangles which are congruent.

(b) Calculate
    (i) $\angle ABC$,
    (ii) $\angle CAB$,
    (iii) $\angle EAC$.

(c) What is the special name given to $\triangle ACE$?

15. A cone and a pyramid have the same height and equal volumes. If the pyramid has a square base of side 10 cm, calculate

(a) the radius of the cone,

(b) the volume of the cone if its height is equal to its radius.

16. The ordered stem-and-leaf diagram below shows the number of hours a group of adults spend on exercising in each month.

Time spent (in hours)	
0	7
1	0 1 2 3 4 5 6
2	0 0 1 2 3 4 8 9
3	1 7 9
4	0

(a) How many adults are there in the group?

(b) If the shortest time spent on exercising is 7 hours, what is the longest time spent?

(c) State the modal time spent on exercising.

(d) Calculate the mean time spent on exercising.

(e) Find the median time spent on exercising.

SECTION C

17. Each diagram in the sequence below consists of a number of matchsticks.

Diagram 1   Diagram 2   Diagram 3

(a) Draw Diagram 4 of the sequence.

(b) Copy and complete the table below.

Diagram	1	2	3	4
No. of matchsticks	12	23		

(c) By considering the number pattern, without drawing further diagrams, write down the number of matchsticks in
    (i) Diagram 10,
    (ii) Diagram 55.

(d) The number of matchsticks in Diagram *n* is denoted by *m*.
Write an equation that expresses *m* in terms of *n*.

(e) Which diagram has 331 matchsticks?

18. (a) Copy and complete the table of values for $y = 2 - 2x$ and $y = 3x - 8$.

    (i) Table of values for $y = 2 - 2x$:

x	0	1	3
y	2		

    (ii) Table of values for $y = 3x - 8$:

x	1	3	5
y		1	

(b) Using a scale of 2 cm to represent 1 unit on the *x*-axis and 1 cm to represent 1 unit on the *y*-axis, draw the graphs of $y = 2 - 2x$ and $y = 3x - 8$. Use the graphs to solve the pair of simultaneous linear equations.

19. A closed container is made by joining together a cylinder and a hemisphere with common radius 6 cm. The length of the cylinder is 15 cm.

The container rests on a horizontal surface and is exactly half full of water as shown in **Figure 1** below.

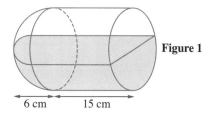

Figure 1

6 cm   15 cm

(a) Show that the volume of water is 342π cm³.

(b) The container is now placed as shown in **Figure 2**. Calculate the depth of water.

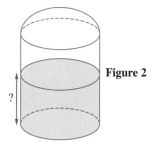

Figure 2

?

(c) The container is then turned around, with the hemisphere being at the bottom as shown in **Figure 3**. Calculate the depth of water.

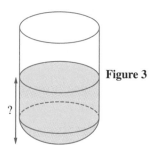

Figure 3

?

20. The table below shows the time taken by the students of a school to complete a certain quiz.

Time (*t* minutes)	No. of students
$40 < t \le 50$	22
$50 < t \le 60$	56
$60 < t \le 70$	70
$70 < t \le 80$	32
$80 < t \le 90$	20

(a) How many students took the quiz?

(b) Calculate an estimate of the mean time taken to complete the quiz.

(c) What is the probability of a student taking

  (i) more than 80 minutes,

  (ii) less than or equal to 1 hour

  to complete the quiz?

Answers

Chapter 1

Exercise 1A

1. (a) $28f + 21$ (b) $42g - 30$
   (c) $25 - 5z$ (d) $-5x - 15$
   (e) $-4n + 28$ (f) $-15w - 40$
   (g) $-35r + 21$ (h) $-16 + 8m$
2. (a) $7x + 34$ (b) $13y - 33$
   (c) $a + 4$ (d) 45
   (e) $5y - 19$ (f) $3a + 42$
3. (a) $3f^2 + 4f$ (b) $12h^2 - 15h$
   (c) $-z^2 - 3z$ (d) $-y^2 + y$
   (e) $-3k^2 - 5k$ (f) $-4x^2 + 6x$
   (g) $4n^2 + 3n$ (h) $2p^2 - 3p$
4. (a) $a^2 + ab$ (b) $c^2 - cd$
   (c) $-gh + g^2$ (d) $-3m^2 - 3mn$
   (e) $8p^2 + 4pq$ (f) $-15r^2 + 10rs$
5. (a) $x^2 + 3x + 4$ (b) $y^2 + 3y - 4$
   (c) $-5a^2 + 3a + 2$ (d) $4n^2 + 11n - 9$
   (e) $2x^2 - 3x - 6$ (f) $2y^2 - 5y - 25$
6. (a) $b^2 + 12b$ (b) $k^2 + 4k$
   (c) $-7m^2 + m$ (d) $45n^2 + 33n$
   (e) $21x^2 - 35x$ (f) $22y^2 - 33y$
7. (a) $11b - 5a$ (b) $23h + 16g$
   (c) $14u^2 + 11uv$ (d) $15w^2 - 10wx + x^2$
   (e) $6m^2 - 5mn - 6n^2$ (f) $-6x^2 + 11xy - 8y^2$

Exercise 1B

1. (a) $a^2 + 5a + 6$ (b) $18 + 11c + c^2$
   (c) $e^2 - 2e - 15$ (d) $6 + n - n^2$
   (e) $k^2 + 6k - 55$ (f) $18 - 3r - r^2$
   (g) $g^2 - 12g + 32$ (h) $15 - 8z + z^2$
   (i) $q^2 + 4q + 4$ (j) $m^2 - 9$
   (k) $w^2 - 25$ (l) $s^2 - 4s + 4$
2. (a) $6c^2 + 19c + 15$ (b) $4t^2 + 15t + 14$
   (c) $18 + 37x + 15x^2$ (d) $12a^2 - 7a - 12$
   (e) $-2d^2 - 3d + 14$ (f) $6 + r - 15r^2$
   (g) $6a^2 - a - 2$ (h) $5h^2 + 13h - 6$
   (i) $15 - t - 2t^2$ (j) $4p^2 - 13p + 10$
   (k) $-12b^2 + 11b - 2$ (l) $10 - 21p + 9p^2$
3. (a) $ac + 2a + bc + 2b$
   (b) $mn + 3m + n^2 + 3n$
   (c) $pr - 4p - qr + 4q$
   (d) $xy + 2x + 2y^2 + 4y$

(e) $lm - ln + m^2 - mn$
(f) $ac + ad - bc - bd$
(g) $xy - yz - 2x^2 + 2xz$
(h) $3p^2 + pq - 2q^2$
(i) $2yz + 2xy + z^2 + xz$
(j) $3x^2 + 3xz - 2xy - 2yz$

Exercise 1C

1. (a) $x^2 + 16x + 64$ (b) $x^2 + 20x + 100$
   (c) $x^2 - 14x + 49$ (d) $x^2 - 8x + 16$
   (e) $p^2 + 2pq + q^2$ (f) $s^2 + 2st + t^2$
   (g) $p^2 - 2pq + q^2$ (h) $s^2 - 2st + t^2$
2. (a) $4x^2 + 4x + 1$ (b) $9a^2 + 6a + 1$
   (c) $9m^2 + 12m + 4$ (d) $4a^2 + 12a + 9$
   (e) $25a^2 - 20a + 4$ (f) $16a^2 - 24a + 9$
   (g) $49y^2 - 56y + 16$ (h) $64n^2 - 80n + 25$
3. (a) $4a^2 + 4ab + b^2$ (b) $9h^2 + 6hk + k^2$
   (c) $16m^2 + 24mn + 9n^2$ (d) $25p^2 + 20pq + 4q^2$
   (e) $4r^2 - 4rs + s^2$ (f) $9u^2 - 6uv + v^2$
   (g) $16v^2 - 24vw + 9w^2$ (h) $25x^2 - 20xy + 4y^2$

Exercise 1D

1. (a) $x^2 - 1$ (b) $m^2 - 100$
   (c) $64 - u^2$ (d) $81 - n^2$
   (e) $h^2 - k^2$ (f) $r^2 - s^2$
2. (a) $4p^2 - 1$ (b) $16q^2 - 1$
   (c) $1 - 9x^2$ (d) $1 - 25y^2$
   (e) $9a^2 - 16$ (f) $25b^2 - 9$
   (g) $9 - 4k^2$ (h) $4 - 25h^2$
3. (a) $4x^2 - y^2$ (b) $x^2 - 9y^2$
   (c) $16a^2 - 9b^2$ (d) $4a^2 - 25b^2$

Time-Out Activity:
(a) For Ali's expansion, when $a = 1$,
   LHS $= [2(1) + 3]^2 = 25$
   RHS $= 4(1)^2 + 9 = 13$
   $\therefore$ LHS $\neq$ RHS
   Therefore, Ali's expansion is wrong.

   For Benny's expansion, when $a = 1$,
   LHS $= [3(1) - 2]^2 = 1$
   RHS $= 9(1)^2 - 4 = 5$
   $\therefore$ LHS $\neq$ RHS
   Therefore, Benny's expansion is wrong.

For Chandra's expansion, when $a = 1$,
LHS $= [4(1) + 1][4(1) - 1] = 15$
RHS $= 16(1)^2 - 8(1) - 1 = 7$
$\therefore$ LHS $\neq$ RHS
Therefore, Chandra's expansion is wrong.

(c) $(2a + 3)^2 = (2a)^2 + 2(2a)(3) + (3)^2$
$= 4a^2 + 12a + 9$

$(3a - 2)^2 = (3a)^2 + 2(3a)(-2) + (-2)^2$
$= 9a^2 - 12a + 4$

$(4a + 1)(4a - 1) = (4a)^2 - (1)^2$
$= 16a^2 - 1$

Exercise 1E

1. **(a)** $3(x + 4)$ **(b)** $7(x + 7)$
     (c) $7(8 + x)$ **(d)** $49(2 + x)$
     (e) $4(x - 4)$ **(f)** $8(x - 6)$
     (g) $8(2 - x)$ **(h)** $12(1 - 4x)$

2. **(a)** $3(2x + 7y)$ **(b)** $2(2m + 3n)$
     (c) $4(2m + 3n)$ **(d)** $5(2y + 5z)$
     (e) $9(2p - 3q)$ **(f)** $3(5a - 4b)$
     (g) $7(2c - 7d)$ **(h)** $8(2b - 5c)$

3. **(a)** $x(x + 4)$ **(b)** $y(y - 4)$
     (c) $p(3 + 4p)$ **(d)** $5y(y - 3)$
     (e) $4a(1 - 3a)$ **(f)** $2s(8 - 5s)$
     (g) $5y(3 + 2y)$ **(h)** $4a(2 + 3a)$

4. **(a)** $-8(6 + p)$ **(b)** $-12(2 + m)$
     (c) $-5(3p + 2q)$ **(d)** $-4(2y + 5z)$
     (e) $-y(4 + y)$ **(f)** $-p(3p + 1)$

5. **(a)** $a(1 + b)$ **(b)** $c(c - d)$
     (c) $3e(e + 2f)$ **(d)** $2g(2g - 3h)$
     (e) $mn(1 + n)$ **(f)** $pq(p - q)$

6. **(a)** $(x + 1)(x + 2)$ **(b)** $(m + 1)(m + 4)$
     (c) $(t - 2)(t + 2)$ **(d)** $(y - 5)(y + 5)$
     (e) $(4b - 3)(b - 3)$ **(f)** $(1 - 3x)(x + 2)$
     (g) $(y + 1)(y + 1)$ **(h)** $(q - 4)(q - 4)$

Exercise 1F

1. **(a)** $(z + 1)(a + 2)$ **(b)** $(x - 3)(c + 3)$
     (c) $(v + 5)(e - 6)$ **(d)** $(t - 6)(g - 7)$
     (e) $(2r + 1)(m + 1)$ **(f)** $(z - 1)(2a + 3)$
     (g) $(x + y)(b - c)$ **(h)** $(t - 3u)(2f - g)$

2. **(a)** $(p + q)(m + n)$ **(b)** $(y + z)(2a + b)$
     (c) $(u - t)(f + g)$ **(d)** $(2s - r)(2h + k)$
     (e) $(p + q)(m - 1)$ **(f)** $(y + z)(2n - 1)$
     (g) $(b + 1)(a - 1)$ **(h)** $(3d + 1)(c - 1)$
     (i) $(k - 3)(h + 2)$ **(j)** $(2s - 1)(2r + 3)$
     (k) $(2p - q)(3a + 2b)$ **(l)** $(5m - 2n)(3y - 4z)$

3. **(a)** $(v + 4)(3u + 1)$ **(b)** $(x - 3y)(2m + n)$
     (c) $(a + 2)(p + 3q)$ **(d)** $(2p + q)(5a + b)$
     (e) $(2 + x)(3a - b)$ **(f)** $(a + 3b)(c - 2d)$

Exercise 1G

1. **(a)** $(z + 1)(z + 2)$ **(b)** $(y + 1)(y + 3)$
     (c) $(x + 1)(x + 6)$ **(d)** $(w + 1)(w + 5)$
     (e) $(v + 6)^2$ **(f)** $(u + 9)^2$
     (g) $(s + 3)(s + 7)$ **(h)** $(r + 2)(r + 9)$
     (i) $(p - 6)^2$ **(j)** $(n - 4)^2$
     (k) $(m - 3)(m - 4)$ **(l)** $(k - 5)(k - 6)$
     (m) $(h - 3)(h + 4)$ **(n)** $(g - 1)(g + 6)$
     (o) $(f - 2)(f + 6)$ **(p)** $(e - 2)(e + 3)$
     (q) $(d + 3)(d - 8)$ **(r)** $(c + 2)(c - 6)$
     (s) $(b + 2)(b - 12)$ **(t)** $(a + 3)(a - 4)$

2. **(a)** $(2a + 1)(a + 2)$ **(b)** $(3b + 1)(b + 3)$
     (c) $(3c + 2)(4c + 3)$ **(d)** $(2d + 3)(3d + 2)$
     (e) $(4e + 3)(3e - 2)$ **(f)** $(2f + 3)(3f - 2)$
     (g) $(3g - 1)(g - 1)$ **(h)** $(h - 4)(4h - 1)$
     (i) $(z - 2)(5z + 2)$ **(j)** $(2y + 1)(3y - 2)$
     (k) $2(k + 4)(k + 5)$ **(l)** $2(x + 2)(x + 5)$
     (m) $3(m - 2)(m + 5)$ **(n)** $3(n - 1)(n + 3)$
     (o) $2(w - 3)(w - 4)$ **(p)** $2(p - 2)(p - 6)$
     (q) $3(v - 2)(v + 1)$ **(r)** $5(r + 1)(r - 3)$

3. **(a)** $(w - 4)(w - 9)$ **(b)** $(y + 5)^2$
     (c) $(y + 2)(y + 3)$ **(d)** $(x + 2)(x - 5)$
     (e) $(y - 5)^2$ **(f)** $(x + 1)(x - 5)$

4. **(a)** $(u + 4s)(u + 5s)$ **(b)** $(6d + y)(8d - y)$
     (c) $5(m - 2n)(m - 4n)$ **(d)** $5(s + t)(s - t)$

Exercise 1H

1. **(a)** $(a + 2)^2$ **(b)** $(m + 5)^2$
     (c) $(b - 1)^2$ **(d)** $(w - 4)^2$

2. **(a)** $(2c + 3)^2$ **(b)** $(5x + 4)^2$
     (c) $(2d - 1)^2$ **(d)** $(8x - 7)^2$

3. **(a)** $2(h + 1)^2$ **(b)** $3(5x + 3)^2$
     (c) $3(b - 5)^2$ **(d)** $8(3x - 2)^2$

4. **(a)** $(m + n)^2$ **(b)** $(3x + 5y)^2$
     (c) $(p - 2q)^2$ **(d)** $(5h - 3k)^2$

Exercise 1I

1. **(a)** $(a + 7)(a - 7)$ **(b)** $(b + 5)(b - 5)$
     (c) $(12 + d)(12 - d)$ **(d)** $(10 + g)(10 - g)$
     (e) $(5m + 1)(5m - 1)$ **(f)** $(2z + 9)(2z - 9)$
     (g) $(1 + 8n)(1 - 8n)$ **(h)** $(11 + 5x)(11 - 5x)$
     (i) $5(w + 10)(w - 10)$ **(j)** $2(p + 4)(p - 4)$
     (k) $3(6 + v)(6 - v)$ **(l)** $4(4 + r)(4 - r)$

2. **(a)** $(a + z)(a - z)$ **(b)** $(c + 2x)(c - 2x)$
 (c) $(4e + v)(4e - v)$ **(d)** $(5f + u)(5f - u)$
 (e) $(4g + 5t)(4g - 5t)$ **(f)** $(7h + 8s)(7h - 8s)$
 (g) $(r + 3)(r - 1)$ **(h)** $(p + 5)(p - 3)$
 (i) $(k + 8)(k - 12)$ **(j)** $(a + 1)(a - 9)$
 (k) $(15 + m)(9 - m)$ **(l)** $(9 + n)(17 - n)$

3. **(a)** 7 600 **(b)** 5 400
 (c) 30.8 **(d)** 8.6
 (e) $\dfrac{1}{2}$ **(f)** $\dfrac{1}{4}$
 (g) 113 **(h)** 56
 (i) 8 **(j)** 1.1

4. **(a)** $(v + 5)(v - 5)$ **(b)** $(3m + 1)(3m - 1)$
 (c) $(x + 3)(x - 3)$ **(d)** $3(c + 2d)(c - 2d)$

Time-Out Activity:

(i) LHS $= a^2 - 1$
 RHS $= (a - 1)^2$
 $= a^2 - 2a + 1$
 $\therefore$ LHS $\neq$ RHS

(ii) $(2a + 6)^2 = (2a + 6)(2a + 6)$
 $= (2)(a + 3)(2)(a + 3)$
 $= (2)^2(a + 3)^2$
 $= 4(a + 3)^2$

(iii) $4a^2 + 24a + 36$
 $= 4(a^2 + 6a + 9)$
 $= 4[(a)^2 + (2)(a)(3) + (3)^2]$
 $= 4(a + 3)^2$

10 Minutes Concept Check

1. B **2.** A **3.** D **4.** D **5.** D
6. B **7.** A **8.** B **9.** A **10.** C

Revision Paper 1

1. **(a)** $6 + 3a$ **(b)** $-30y + 24$
 (c) $6a - 3b$ **(d)** $-5x^2 - 5xy$
2. **(a)** $5(4c + 3)$ **(b)** $6(1 - 2d)$
 (c) $-4(2x + 3)$ **(d)** $-3(2y - 7)$
3. **(a)** $4a^2 + 14a + 10$ **(b)** $13b^2 + 10b$
 (c) $2c^2 - 5cd$ **(d)** $8e^2 + 3ef - 10f^2$
4. **(a)** $3(2x - 3y)$ **(b)** $ab(a + b)$
 (c) $3x(x - 2)$ **(d)** $-2ky(5y + 2)$
5. **(a)** $3m^2 + 10m + 8$ **(b)** $6n^2 + 5n - 25$
 (c) $5p^2 - 22p + 21$
6. **(a)** $(h + 1)(h + 2)$ **(b)** $(k - 1)(k + 6)$
 (c) $(r + 2)(r - 3)$

7. **(a)** $36a^2 + 60a + 25$ **(b)** $16 - x^2$
 (c) $16x^2 - 24xy + 9y^2$
8. **(a)** $4(e + 3f)(e - 3f)$ **(b)** $(2x - y)^2$
 (c) $2(y + x)^2$
9. **(a)** $(a + b)(a - b)$
 (b) **(i)** 23.88 **(ii)** 10
10. **(a)** **(i)** $(5 - b)(a + 2)$
 (ii) $(5y + 1)(x - 1)$
 (iii) $(5c - 3d)(7a + 2b)$
 (b) **(i)** 49 **(ii)** 1
 (iii) -7 or 7

Chapter 2

Exercise 2A

1. **(a)** $\dfrac{2y}{3}$ **(b)** $\dfrac{3x}{4}$ **(c)** $\dfrac{9p}{8}$
 (d) w^2 **(e)** $3e$ **(f)** $\dfrac{4x^2}{3}$
 (g) $\dfrac{1}{z}$ **(h)** $\dfrac{2}{d}$ **(i)** $\dfrac{2}{3f^2}$

2. **(a)** $\dfrac{1}{2a}$ **(b)** $2b$ **(c)** $\dfrac{2c}{3}$
 (d) $\dfrac{3d^2}{8}$ **(e)** $\dfrac{2}{9e^2}$ **(f)** $\dfrac{v}{2g}$
 (g) $\dfrac{3h^2}{4}$ **(h)** $\dfrac{x}{2k^2}$ **(i)** $\dfrac{3x}{2y}$

3. **(a)** $\dfrac{a}{b}$ **(b)** $\dfrac{a - b}{a + b}$ **(c)** $\dfrac{x}{x + y}$
 (d) $\dfrac{3}{5(x + y)}$ **(e)** $\dfrac{qr}{q + r}$ **(f)** $\dfrac{a - t}{f^2}$
 (g) $t(a + f)$ **(h)** $\dfrac{k + 1}{k - 1}$

Exercise 2B

1. **(a)** 6 **(b)** $\dfrac{5t}{16s}$ **(c)** $\dfrac{3s}{2}$
 (d) $\dfrac{5g}{4k^2}$ **(e)** $\dfrac{6}{x^2 y}$ **(f)** $\dfrac{f^2}{2}$
 (g) $\dfrac{5m}{26n}$ **(h)** $\dfrac{3u}{16v^2}$

2. **(a)** $\dfrac{4b}{c}$ **(b)** $5m^2$ **(c)** $\dfrac{12}{n}$
 (d) $\dfrac{16z}{21}$ **(e)** $\dfrac{10e}{21}$ **(f)** $\dfrac{3u^2}{10v}$
 (g) $\dfrac{4a}{3}$ **(h)** $\dfrac{10x}{9y}$

3. (a) $\dfrac{2}{3a}$ (b) $\dfrac{h}{2}$ (c) $\dfrac{3(3k-2)}{2k}$

(d) $\dfrac{2a^2}{b}$ (e) $\dfrac{m(m+5)}{m-5}$ (f) $\dfrac{3}{4}$

(g) $\dfrac{x}{y}$ (h) $w(w+1)$

Exercise 2C

1. (a) $b=6$ (b) $d=-3$
(c) $f=-6$ (d) $h=3$

(e) $y=\dfrac{1}{2}$ (f) $w=-1$

(g) $n=4$ (h) $v=-6$

2. (a) $a=5$ (b) $c=3$
(c) $e=-1$ (d) $g=0.9$
(e) $x=0.4$ (f) $k=-0.4$

(g) $m=\dfrac{1}{2}$ (h) $u=\dfrac{1}{7}$

3. (a) $a=3$ (b) $c=-5$
(c) $b=-4$ (d) $g=6$

(e) $x=\dfrac{1}{3}$ (f) $c=-\dfrac{1}{5}$

(g) $m=-\dfrac{1}{4}$ (h) $u=\dfrac{1}{6}$

4. (a) $b=35$ (b) $d=-18$

(c) $y=\dfrac{5}{8}$ (d) $w=5$

(e) $f=-28$ (f) $h=72$

5. (a) $d=1$ (b) $f=15$

(c) $b=1\dfrac{1}{3}$ (d) $h=90$

(e) $w=-27$ (f) $y=-1$

(g) $n=-\dfrac{1}{4}$ (h) $v=-6$

Exercise 2D

1. (a) $b=3$ (b) $d=-1$
(c) $f=2$ (d) $h=-2$

(e) $y=-\dfrac{1}{2}$ (f) $n=\dfrac{2}{3}$

(g) $r=-\dfrac{3}{2}$ (h) $v=2$

2. (a) $b=\dfrac{1}{8}$ (b) $d=-\dfrac{1}{5}$

(c) $h=\dfrac{5}{24}$ (d) $k=-\dfrac{1}{5}$

(e) $y=0.4$ (f) $w=-0.3$

(g) $v=2.5$ (h) $x=0.8$

3. (a) $a=4$ (b) $c=-3\dfrac{2}{3}$

(c) $y=-1$ (d) $e=5$

(e) $k=-\dfrac{1}{4}$ (f) $z=3$

(g) $m=1\dfrac{1}{2}$ (h) $u=\dfrac{4}{9}$

Exercise 2E

1. (a) $a=2$ (b) $c=2$
(c) $d=1$ (d) $e=-4$
(e) $g=1$ (f) $h=1$
(g) $x=1$ (h) $y=-2$

2. (a) $a=1$ (b) $c=6$
(c) $g=1$ (d) $k=2$
(e) $u=3$ (f) $q=2$
(g) $w=-2$ (h) $y=-1$

3. (a) $a=10$ (b) $c=2\dfrac{3}{4}$

(c) $d=-\dfrac{2}{13}$ (d) $f=10$

(e) $g=1\dfrac{1}{3}$ (f) $h=1\dfrac{10}{13}$

4. (a) $x=1$ (b) $x=-1$

(c) $x=2\dfrac{2}{3}$ (d) $x=-2$

5. (a) $x=4\dfrac{1}{2}$ (b) $p=10$

(c) $x=14$ (d) $y=3\dfrac{1}{4}$

Exercise 2F

1. (a) $a=25$ (b) $b=-28$
(c) $c=-54$ (d) $d=28$
(e) $e=21$ (f) $f=2$

2. (a) $b=10$ (b) $d=-1\dfrac{1}{5}$

(c) $q=1\dfrac{1}{2}$ (d) $g=-\dfrac{1}{6}$

(e) $p=\dfrac{5}{8}$ (f) $r=-\dfrac{9}{16}$

3. (a) $a=6$ (b) $b=10$
(c) $c=4$ (d) $d=-7$

(e) $l=-1\dfrac{3}{5}$ (f) $m=0$

4. (a) $e=3$ (b) $h=-8$
(c) $k=1$ (d) $n=6$

(e) $p=2\dfrac{1}{10}$ (f) $r=-2\dfrac{1}{2}$

Exercise 2G

1. (a) $a = 2\frac{2}{5}$ (b) $v = 2\frac{1}{4}$

  (c) $c = 4\frac{1}{2}$ (d) $u = \frac{2}{3}$

  (e) $e = \frac{3}{5}$ (f) $x = -8$

  (g) $w = 3$ (h) $z = 12$

2. (a) $h = -3$ (b) $y = -5$
  (c) $k = 7$ (d) $z = 39$

  (e) $m = \frac{5}{7}$ (f) $n = -\frac{11}{13}$

  (g) $r = -\frac{4}{5}$ (h) $s = 13$

3. (a) $x = 9$ (b) $x = 0$
  (c) $x = 3$ (d) $x = 29$

  (e) $y = 1\frac{16}{19}$ (f) $y = 7\frac{9}{19}$

  (g) $y = \frac{31}{39}$ (h) $x = 5$

4. $x = 5$

5. (a) $x = \frac{3}{4}$ (b) $x = 7$

Exercise 2H

1. (a) $n + 4 = 7$, $n = 3$ (b) $n - 23 = 12$, $n = 35$
  (c) $3n = 15$, $n = 5$ (d) $8n = 32$, $n = 4$

  (e) $\frac{n}{3} = -12$, $n = -36$ (f) $\frac{n}{4} = 3$, $n = 12$

2. (a) $a + 3 = 5$, $a = 2$
  (b) $c + 11 = 6$, $c = -5$
  (c) $e - 2 = 8$, $e = 10$
  (d) $f - 7 = 1$, $f = 8$

3. (a) $n + 5 = 12$ (b) $n = 7$
4. 3
5. -6
6. 5
7. 9
8. (a) $5x - x = 32$ (b) 8 yrs
9. 10 kg, 60 kg
10. 12 yrs, 48 yrs
11. $48 + x = 3(12 + x)$, $x = 6$
12. (a) $n + 2$ (b) $n + (n + 2) = 42$
  (c) 20, 22
13. 31, 33, 35
14. (a) $\$(m + 2)$ (b) $3m + 4(m + 2) = 29$
  (c) \$5

15. 80¢
16. (a) $x = 2$ (b) 12 cm

Exercise 2I

1. $x = 60$
2. $x = 12$
3. $x = 480$
4. $x = 4$

5. (a) $\frac{5 + x}{19 - x}$ (b) $x = 4$

6. $x = 8$

7. (a) $\frac{x}{x + 6}$ (b) $x = 11$

8. $x = 3\,280$
9. 90 km

10. (a) (i) $(240 - x)m$ (ii) $\frac{x}{30}$ min

      (iii) $\frac{240 - x}{150}$ min

  (b) $x = 165$
11. 200 km
12. 144 minutes

Time-Out Activity:
84 years

Exercise 2J

1. (a) $>$ (b) $<$ (c) $>$ (d) $<$
  (e) $<$ (f) $<$ (g) $>$ (h) $>$

2. (a) 3, 3, 5   (b) 3, 3, -6 (c) $\frac{3}{2}$, $\frac{3}{2}$, -6

3. (a) $a \le 3$ (b) $b > -4$
  (c) $c < -5$ (d) $d \ge 16$
  (e) $m > 6$ (f) $n < -20$

4. (a) 10   (b) 16   (c) 11
5. (a) 8   (b) 4   (c) 7

6. (a) 4   (b) 11   (c) $12\frac{1}{4}$

7. (a) $4x \ge 300$ (b) $x \ge 75$ (c) 75 marks
8. (a) $4x \le 60$ (c) $x \le 15$ (c) 225 cm²
9. 13 bookshelves
10. 208 students

10 Minutes Concept Check

1. B   2. C   3. D   4. B   5. A
6. C   7. D   8. B   9. C   10. C

Revision Paper 2

1. **(a)** $\dfrac{3}{2b}$ **(b)** $\dfrac{7n}{8m}$

2. **(a)** $a = 10\dfrac{1}{2}$ **(b)** $b = 4\dfrac{2}{3}$

3. **(a)** $x = \dfrac{9}{10}$ **(b)** $y = 1\dfrac{16}{19}$

4. **(a)** $u = 3$ **(b)** $w = 14$

5. **(a)** $k = \dfrac{1}{4}$ **(b)** $s = 15$

   (c) $m = 4$

6. **(a)** $n = -1$ **(b)** $u = -27$

   (c) $x = -1$

7. **(a)** $u > -4$ **(b)** $v < -14$

   (c) $w \geq 5$

8. **(a)** $4y + y = 50$, 40, 10

   (b) $4m - m = 51$, 17 kg

9. **(a)** 3 334 tickets

   (b) $x + (x + 2) = 96$, 47, 49

10. **(a)** $3(n + 6) = 7(n - 2)$, $n = 8$

    (b) $x = 25$

Chapter 3

Exercise 3A

1. $A(4, 1)$; $B(2, 3)$; $C(-2, 3)$; $D(-5, 2)$; $E(-6, -2)$; $F(-3, -3)$; $G(1, -2)$; $H(4, -3)$; $I(6, 0)$; $J(-4, 0)$; $K(0, 1)$; $L(0, -3)$

2. $A(1.5, 1)$; $B(3, 2.5)$; $C(0, 1.5)$; $D(-1.5, 3)$; $E(-3.5, 2)$; $F(-4.5, 0)$; $G(-3.5, -1.5)$; $H(-2.5, -2.5)$; $I(0, -2.5)$; $J(2, -3.5)$; $K(5, -2.5)$; $L(4.5, 0)$

5. **(b) (i)** They lie on the x-axis. They have '0' as the y-coordinate.

   (ii) They lie on the y-axis. They have '0' as the x-coordinate.

6. **(b)** a star

7. **(b)** a straight line

   (c) The value of the y-coordinate is always twice the value of the x-coordinate.

Time-Out Activity:

The gold was hidden at the Bear Pit since that was the only location marked on the map which the pirates had not searched.

Exercise 3B

1. **(a)** $y = x$ **(b)** $y = -x$ **(c)** $y = 4x$

   (d) $y = x + 2$ **(e)** $y = x - 1$ **(f)** $y = -x + 1$

2. **(a)** $y = 5x$

x	−2	−1	0	1	2
y	−10	−5	0	5	10
(x, y)	(−2, −10)	(−1, −5)	(0, 0)	(1, 5)	(2, 10)

(b) $y = -x$

x	−2	−1	0	1	2
y	2	1	0	−1	−2
(x, y)	(−2, 2)	(−1, 1)	(0, 0)	(1, −1)	(2, −2)

(c) $y = -3x$

x	−2	−1	0	1	2
y	6	3	0	−3	−6
(x, y)	(−2, 6)	(−1, 3)	(0, 0)	(1, −3)	(2, −6)

(d) $y = x + 5$

x	−3	−2	−1	0	1
y	2	3	4	5	6
(x, y)	(−3, 2)	(−2, 3)	(−1, 4)	(0, 5)	(1, 6)

(e) $y = x - 3$

x	−1	0	1	2	3
y	−4	−3	−2	−1	0
(x, y)	(−1, −4)	(0, −3)	(1, −2)	(2, −1)	(3, 0)

4.

x	−2	0	2
y	−14	0	14

5.

x	−1	0	1	2	3	4
y	−7	−6	−5	−4	−3	−2

Exercise 3C

1.

x	–2	–1	0	1	2
y	–3	1	5	9	13

4. $a = 7, b = 1$
    (a) $y = -1.4$; $y = 6.4$
    (b) $x = 0.5$; $x = -1.5$
5. **(b)** 5 kg
6. **(b)** The \$280 could be the start-up cost.
    (c) 55

Time-Out Activity:

(a) Substituting $x = 0$ into $y = 3 - \dfrac{1}{2}x$ would give us $y = 3$. Thus, the correct graph of $y = 3 - \dfrac{1}{2}x$ should pass through (0, 3). As such, Bala's graph is wrong.

(b) Use at least 3 points for drawing a straight line graph with the third point to serve as a check.

Exercise 3D

1. **(a)** **(i)** (–1, –2); (3, –2); (0, –2)
        (ii) (3, 3); (3, –2); (3, –1); (3, 0)
2. **(a)** **(i)** (0, 1); (2, 1); (–1, 1); (–3, 1)
        (ii) (–1, 0); (–1, 1); (–1, –3)
5. **(a)** $y = 2$ **(b)** $x = 3$ **(c)** $x = -3$
    (d) $y = -4$ **(e)** $x = 1$ **(f)** $y = -2$
    (g) $y = 1$ **(h)** $x = -2$
6. **(a)** $y = 0$ **(b)** $x = 0$

Time-Out Activity:
(a) Lines sloping up to the right have positive gradients.
(b) Lines sloping down to the right have negative gradients.

Exercise 3E

1. **(a)** $\dfrac{1}{2}$ **(b)** $-\dfrac{1}{2}$

2. **(a)** –1   **(b)** $\dfrac{2}{3}$

3. Gradient of $AB = -1$
    Gradient of $BC = 2$
    Gradient of $AC = \dfrac{1}{2}$

4. **(a)** 2   **(b)** $\dfrac{1}{2}$ **(c)** $-1\dfrac{1}{2}$ **(d)** $-\dfrac{3}{4}$

5. **(a)** positive   **(b)** negative
    (c) positive   **(d)** positive
    (e) negative   **(f)** positive
    (g) negative   **(h)** positive

6. **(a)** 3   **(b)** $\dfrac{1}{2}$ **(c)** $3\dfrac{1}{2}$
    (d) $-\dfrac{3}{4}$ **(e)** $-3\dfrac{1}{2}$ **(f)** $1\dfrac{1}{2}$

7. **(a)** 1   **(b)** $-\dfrac{2}{3}$ **(c)** $\dfrac{1}{2}$
    (d) –2   **(e)** 1   **(f)** –1

8. **(a)** 2   **(b)** 3
    (c) $-\dfrac{1}{2}$ **(d)** –1

9. **(a)** horizontal line, gradient = 0
    (b) vertical line, gradient is undefined.
10. **(a)** 0   **(b)** undefined
    (c) 0   **(d)** 0
    (e) undefined   **(f)** undefined
11. **(a)** 30 cents
    (b) **(i)** 60 cents   **(ii)** 140 cents
    (c) 5
    (d) This gradient represents the rate of charge, i.e., the amount charged (in cents) per minute by the telecommunications company.
12. **(a)** \$3 000
    (b) **(i)** \$2 400   **(ii)** \$1 600
    (c) 200
    (d) This gradient represents the rate at which the value of the article is decreasing every year.

10 Minutes Concept Check

1. B   **2.** C   **3.** B   **4.** A   **5.** A
6. C   **7.** A   **8.** D   **9.** B   **10.** D

Revision Paper 3

1. $A(3, 2)$; $B(2, -1)$; $C(-2, 0)$; $D(0, 3)$
2. isosceles triangle
3. (2, –3)
4. (2, 2)

5.

x	–2	0	2
$y = 2x - 4$	–8	–4	0

(0, –4)
6. **(a)** $y = x$ **(b)** $y = 2$ **(c)** $x = 2$
    (d) $y = -x$ **(e)** $y = x + 2$

7. (a) (i) undefined (ii) $\frac{1}{2}$
  (b) -2
8. (a) (i) 0 (ii) $-1\frac{1}{2}$
  (b) 4
9. parallelogram
10. (b) (i) \$20 (ii) 0.1
  (c) This gradient represents the rate of charge, i.e., the amount charged (in \$) per minute of talk time.

Chapter 4

Exercise 4A

1. 9 litres **2.** 360 g
3. \$6.72 **4.** 0.25 km
5. (a) \$18 (b) 10 kg
6. (a) \$63 (b) 24 hours
7. (a) \$650 (b) 3 days
8. (a) 100 km (b) 18.4 seconds
9. (a) \$1.26 (b) 350 g
10. (a) 2.5 km (b) 500 m

Exercise 4B

1. (a) y is directly proportional to x. The equation is $y = 3x$.
  (b) y is directly proportional to x. The equation is $y = \frac{1}{2}x$.
  (c) y is not directly proportional to x.
  (d) y is not directly proportional to x.
2. (a) (a), (b) and (c)
  (b) (a) and (b)
  (c) (a) and (b)
  (d) The graph of two variables that are in direct proportion is a straight line passing through the origin.
3. (a) a and b are in direct proportion.
  (b) y and x are not in direct proportion.
  (c) T and P are not in direct proportion.
  (d) C and N are in direct proportion.
  (e) y and x are not in direct proportion.
  (f) d and t are not in direct proportion.
4. (b) $y = kx$, where k is a constant.
  (c) $c = kd$, where k is a constant.
  (d) $v = kt$, where k is a constant.
5. (a) $y = \frac{1}{2}x$ (b) $y = 3$ (c) $x = 8$

6. (a) $P = 3T$ (b) $P = 30$ (c) $T = 3\frac{1}{3}$
7. (a) $V = 52$ (b) $h = 10$
8.

T	10	40	**50**
V	**50**	200	250

9. (a) $y = \frac{9}{2}x$
  (b)

x	2	4	**18**
y	9	**18**	81

10. (a) $P = \frac{3}{2}T$
  (b)

P	**3**	51	81
T	2	**34**	54

11. 4.5 hours
12. (a) 180 km (b) 13 litres
  (c) $12x$ km (d) $\frac{m}{12}$ litres

Time-Out Activity:
Bala is correct. The equation is $y = 3(x + 2)$.

Exercise 4C

1. 10 soldiers
2. 14.4 km/h
3. 18 pieces
4. 7 carpenters
5. (a) 40 days (b) 60 men
6. (a) 10 days (b) 20 farmers
7. 30 sheep
8. $2\frac{2}{3}$ hours
9. 12 days
10. (a) 12 days (b) 18 men

Exercise 4D

1. (a) y is inversely proportional to x. The equation is $y = \frac{20}{x}$.
  (b) y is not inversely proportional to x.
  (c) y is inversely proportional to x. The equation is $y = \frac{60}{x}$.

(d) y is inversely proportional to x. The equation is $y = \dfrac{96}{x}$.

2. (b) $p = \dfrac{k}{q}$, where k is a constant.

(c) $m = \dfrac{k}{n}$, where k is a constant.

(d) $a = \dfrac{k}{b}$, where k is a constant.

3. (a) $y = \dfrac{60}{x}$ **(b)** $y = 15$

(c) $x = 120$

4. (a) $a = 2$ **(b)** $b = \dfrac{20}{7}$

5.

x	2	3	**3.6**
y	9	6	5

6. (a) $y = \dfrac{36}{x}$

(b)

x	2	3	**6**	9
y	18	12	6	**4**

7. (a) $Q = \dfrac{1}{2P}$

(b)

P	0.25	0.5	1	**1.25**
Q	2	1	0.5	0.4

8. 112.5 cm of mercury

9. 4 h

10. (a) $320   **(b)** $20

(c) 40 people   **(d)** $\$\dfrac{320}{x}$

(e) $\dfrac{320}{M}$ people

11. 25°C

Time-Out Activity:

Both Gerald and Melanie are wrong.

The correct working should be:
Given that 4 cats can catch 4 mice in 4 days, each cat thus takes 4 days to catch 1 mouse. The number of cats and the number of mice caught in 4 days are in direct proportion. Thus, 2 cats can catch 2 mice in 4 days. In fact, 3 cats can catch 3 mice in 4 days, 100 cats can catch 100 mice in 4 days and so on.

Exercise 4E

1. (a) $1 : 125$ **(b)** $1 : 80$
(c) $1 : 80\,000$ **(d)** $1 : 125\,000$

2. 4.5 cm   **3.** 8 cm

4. (a) Actual length = 600 m, Actual breadth = 128 m.
(b) 7.68 ha

5. (a) 12.5 cm   **(b)** $0.5\ \text{km}^2$

6. (a) 200 km   **(b)** $1\,600\ \text{cm}^2$

7. (a) (i) 4.4 cm   **(ii)** 4.5 cm
(iii) 3.7 cm
(b) (i) 4.40 km   **(ii)** 4.50 km
(iii) 3.70 km

8. (a) 7 m   **(b)** 22 cm

9. (a) 200 m   **(b)** $1 : 20\,000$
(c) 720 m

10. (a) 16 cm   **(b)** $48\ \text{cm}^2$

11. (a) 3.2 m   **(b)** 10.6 m

10 Minutes Concept Check

1. C   **2.** A   **3.** A   **4.** B   **5.** D
6. D   **7.** B   **8.** A   **9.** C   **10.** C

Revision Paper 4

1. (a) $U = kv$, where k is a constant.
(b) $S = \dfrac{k}{T}$, where k is a constant.
(c) $Y = \dfrac{k}{x}$, where k is a constant.

2. (a) $9.45   **(b)** 4 kg

3. (a) p and q are not in direct proportion.
(b) q and r are in direct proportion.
(c) r and s are not in direct proportion.
(d) s and t are not in direct proportion.

4. (a) 20 days   **(b)** 45 men

5. (a) $m = 15n$ **(b)** $m = 45$ **(c)** $n = 6$

6. (a) $V = \dfrac{1\,000}{I}$ **(b)** $V = 200$ **(c)** $I = 8$

7. (a) 10 km   **(b)** 2 cm

8. (a) 19 km   **(b)** 36 cm

9. (a) y is not directly or inversely proportional to x.
(b) y is directly proportional to x. The equation is $y = 9x$.
(c) y is inversely proportional to x. The equation is $y = \dfrac{300}{x}$.

10. (a) (i) 1 : 25 000   (ii) 1 : 2 000 000
    (b) 110 km   (c) 5.184 km²

Review Paper 1

1. (a) (i) $35a + 21$ (ii) $-18b - 12$
    (b) (i) $2(1 - 2m)$ (ii) $3(7 - 3n)$
2. (a) (i) $6c + 2d$ (ii) $-3e^2 - 3ef$
    (b) (i) $2p(p - 3)$ (ii) $-3r(qr + 2)$
3. (a) (i) $6uv - 48u^2$ (ii) $-5t^2 - 5st$
    (b) (i) $2c(c + 5e)$ (ii) $-fg(f + g)$
4. (a) (i) $\dfrac{5}{2w}$ (ii) $\dfrac{5x}{12y}$

    (b) (i) $g = 5\dfrac{1}{2}$ (ii) $h = -\dfrac{1}{3}$
5. (a) (i) $x = \dfrac{3}{5}$ (ii) $y = \dfrac{13}{17}$

    (b) (i) $\dfrac{27}{35}$ (ii) $2\dfrac{5}{8}$
6. (a) $A(2, 1), B(0, 2), C(-1, 0)$
    (b) $D(1, -1)$
7. (a) $7.20   (b) 5.5 kg
8. (a) $c = kd$ (b) $a = \dfrac{k}{b}$
9. (a) $3a^2 + 10a + 8$ (b) $8b^2 + 2b - 15$
    (c) $15c^2 - 38c + 24$ (d) $ac - 3a + 2bc - 6b$
10. (a) $(u + 2v)(3w - 4)$ (b) $(x - 2y)(3h - 4k)$
11. (a) $(y + 6)(y - 1)$ (b) $(3b - 4)(b - 7)$
12. (a) 35 yrs, 7 yrs   (b) 13 yrs
13. (a) $\left(1\dfrac{1}{2}, 0\right)$ (b) $(0, -3)$
14. (a) (i) undefined   (ii) $\dfrac{2}{3}$

    (b) $1\dfrac{1}{2}$
15. (a) $y = 5x$ (b) $y = 45$ (c) $x = 2$
16. (a) 1 : 2 000   (b) 8 cm
17. (a) 62   (b) 5   (c) 10
18. (a) $120
    (b) (i) $8d \le 500$ (ii) 62 days
19. (b) (i) $40   (ii) $58
    (iii) 6.7 hours
20. (a) y is not directly or inversely proportional to x.
    (b) y is inversely proportional to x. The equation is $y = \dfrac{60}{x}$.
    (c) y is directly proportional to x. The equation is $y = 7x$.

Review Paper 2

1. (a) (i) $15b - 5$ (ii) $-20y + 15$
    (b) (i) $5(3c + 4)$ (ii) $4(2 - 3x)$
2. (a) (i) $12b + 8c$ (ii) $-6x + 3xy$
    (b) (i) $3(3x - 2y)$ (ii) $-3x(1 + 4y)$
3. (a) (i) $6c + 8c^2$ (ii) $-6y^2 + 3y$
    (b) (i) $3x(2x - 1)$ (ii) $3(2 - 3x)(2 + 3x)$
4. (a) $p < -5$ (b) $q > -36$
    (c) $r \ge 5\dfrac{1}{3}$
5. $(1, 1)$
6. $(-2, -1)$ and $(3, 2)$
7. (a) 196 km   (b) 30 litres
8. (a) 15 soldiers   (b) 5 hours
9. (a) $x^2 + 5x - 50$ (b) $4x^2 - 9$
    (c) $25x^2 + 10x + 1$ (d) $9x^2 - 12xy + 4y^2$
10. (a) $(y + 3)^2$ (b) $(3y - 1)^2$
    (c) $(2y - 7)(2y + 7)$ (d) $(4m - 3n)(2m - n)$
11. (a) $\dfrac{5p - 2q}{6q}$ (b) $\dfrac{w + 1}{2}$
12. (a) 21   (b) $1\dfrac{5}{29}$
13. (a) $3x \le 50$
    (b) $x \le 16\dfrac{2}{3}$, 16 hairclips
14. (a) (i) 0   (ii) $\dfrac{1}{2}$

    (b) -1
15. (a) 12.5 km   (b) 1.2 cm
16. (a) $l = \dfrac{300}{f}$
    (b) (i) 3.20 m   (ii) 88.90 MHz
17. (a) (i) $2(3x - 5y)(3x + 5y)$
      (ii) $(a + 2)(3 - 5b)$
    (b) (i) 64   (ii) 16   (iii) -32 or 32
18. (a) $x + (x + 2) + (x + 4) = 87$, 27, 29, 31
    (b) $y = 0.3$
19. (b) (i) $F = 32$ (ii) $F = 212$
    (c) $\dfrac{5}{9}$
    (d) 1 unit of F is equivalent to $\dfrac{5}{9}$ unit of C.
20. (a) (i) 1 : 12 500   (ii) 1 : 250 000
    (b) 100 km   (c) 16 km²

Chapter 5

Exercise 5A

1. (a) $x = -2, y = -3$ (b) $x = 5, y = 2$

   (c) $x = 5, y = -1$ (d) $x = \frac{1}{2}, y = 1$

   (e) $x = -1, y = -2$ (f) $x = -3, y = -\frac{5}{3}$

   (g) $x = 2, y = 1$ (h) $x = 1, y = 1$

2. (a) $x = -1, y = 2$ (b) $x = -1, y = 1$
   (c) $x = -1, y = 1$ (d) $x = 0, y = 4$
   (e) $x = 1, y = 2$ (f) $x = 2, y = 3$

3. (a) $x = 0, y = -1$ (b) $x = 5, y = -5$

   (c) $x = \frac{1}{2}, y = 1$ (d) $x = -1, y = -\frac{3}{2}$

   (e) $x = -4, y = 1$ (f) $x = 3, y = -5$
   (g) $x = 5, y = 1$ (h) $x = 7, y = 4$

Time-Out Activity:

Mistake 1:

When he substituted *(1)* into *(2)*, the expression on the LHS should be $2x - 3x + 3$ and not $2x - 3x - 3$.

Mistake 2:

Since he substituted $x = -7$ into *(1)* to get y, he should check his solution by substituting the values into *(2)* instead.

Check: Substitute $x = -7$ and $y = -8$ into *(2)*,

      LHS $= 2x - 3y$
           $= 2(-7) - 3(-8)$
           $= 10$
      RHS $= 4$
      $\therefore$ LHS $\neq$ RHS

Therefore, Anthony's solution is wrong.

Exercise 5B

1. (a) $x = 2, y = 1$ (b) $a = 5, b = -2$
   (c) $p = 5, q = 2$ (d) $x = 1, y = -2$
   (e) $f = -1, g = -3$ (f) $c = -2, d = -5$

2. (a) $x = 3, y = 2$ (b) $p = -1, q = -2$
   (c) $e = 3, f = -1$ (d) $r = -1, s = 4$
   (e) $j = -6, k = -5$ (f) $v = 1, w = -4$

3. (a) $a = -3, b = 4$ (b) $c = 3, d = -3$
   (c) $x = 4, y = -3$ (d) $x = -1, y = -1$
   (e) $x = 7, y = 2$ (f) $x = -1, y = 5$

4. (a) $c = \frac{2}{3}, d = \frac{3}{2}$ (b) $m = -\frac{1}{2}, n = -\frac{1}{3}$

   (c) $x = 3, y = 2$ (d) $x = 4, y = 3$

5. (a) $a = 0, b = -2$ (b) $c = \frac{3}{8}, d = \frac{1}{8}$

   (c) $e = \frac{1}{2}, f = -2$ (d) $x = 1, y = 2$

   (e) $x = 2, y = -5$ (f) $x = 3, y = \frac{1}{2}$

   (g) $x = 3, y = -2$ (h) $x = 2, y = 3$

   (i) $x = -4, y = 9$ (j) $x = 4, y = \frac{5}{2}$

Exercise 5C

1. (a) $x = 2, y = 0$ (b) $x = 2, y = 5$
   (c) $x = -3, y = -9$ (d) $x = -5, y = 10$

   (e) $x = -2, y = -5$ (f) $x = 1, y = 2\frac{1}{2}$

2. (a) $x = 5, y = 1$ (b) $x = 2, y = 0$
   (c) $x = -1, y = 3$ (d) $x = 1, y = 3$
   (e) $x = 3, y = -2$ (f) $x = -3, y = 5$
   (g) $x = 1, y = -1$ (h) $x = -3, y = -1$

Time-Out Activity:

(b) From the graph, $x = 0.3$ and $y = 3.4$.

(c) No, solution obtained: $x = \frac{2}{7}, y = 3\frac{2}{7}$.

(d) The graphical method does not always give accurate answers especially when the actual answers are in the form of fractions.

Exercise 5D

1. 8, 7
2. 4, 3
3. Science: 65, Maths: 80
4. length: 18 cm, width: 16 cm
5. English book: $10, Maths book: $12
6. cows: 13, chickens: 22
7. Ahmad: 28, Weihui: 12
8. Ganesh: 85, Ajit: 25

9. (a) $x = 1\frac{1}{2}, y = 1$ (b) 18

10. (a) $3s + 2t = 200$ (b) $s = 30, t = 55$

Time-Out Activity:

Each carries 3 bundles.

10 Minutes Concept Check

1. C   2. C   3. B   4. A   5. A
6. A   7. C   8. D   9. C   10. B

1. $x = 7$, $y = 5$
2. $x = 3$, $y = -1$
3. $x = 1$, $y = 3$
4. $x = 5$, $y = 7$
5. $x = 2$, $y = 3$
6. 13, 17
7. mutton: \$8, chicken: \$12
8. (a) (i) Table for $y = 4x - 3$:

x	0	2	4
y	-3	5	13

(ii) Table for $y = -2x + 3$:

x	0	2	4
y	3	-1	-5

(c) $x = 1$, $y = 1$
9. Liza: 17, Petrina: 7
10. (a) $x = 0$, $y = 3$　　(b) 12 units^2

Chapter 6

Exercise 6B

1. (a) (i) scalene triangle
      (ii) right-angled triangle
   (b) (i) scalene triangle
      (ii) obtuse-angled triangle
   (c) (i) equilateral triangle
      (ii) acute-angled triangle
   (d) (i) isosceles triangle
      (ii) obtuse-angled triangle
   (e) (i) isosceles triangle
      (ii) acute-angled triangle
   (f) (i) isosceles triangle
      (ii) right-angled triangle

Time-Out Activity:
(a) (i) acute-angled isosceles triangle
    (ii) right-angled isosceles triangle or right isosceles triangle
    (iii) obtuse-angled isosceles triangle
    The three triangles are all isosceles triangles.
(b) No. All the angles in an equilateral triangle are 60°. Thus, it is only possible to have an acute-angled equilateral triangle.

Exercise 6C

1. (a) 47°　　(b) 90°　　(c) 50°
   (d) 60°　　(e) 45°　　(f) 46°
2. (a) 30　　(b) 20　　(c) 20
   (d) 30　　(e) 20
3. (a) 66°　　(b) 114°

Exercise 6D

1. (a) 66°　(b) 80°　(c) 158°　(d) 135°
   (e) 140°　(f) 120°　(g) 105°　(h) 38°
2. 160°
3. (a) 65°　(b) 30°　(c) 95°
4. (a) 115°　(b) 65°　(c) 135°

Exercise 6E

5. (a) 9.2 cm or 92 mm
   (b) 116°

Time-Out Activity:
The set of measurements in (a) and (d) can be used to construct a triangle. The sets of measurements in (b), (c), (e) and (f) cannot be used to construct a triangle. The sum of the lengths of the shorter sides of a triangle is always greater than the length of the longest side.

Exercise 6F

1. (a) 50°　(b) 90°　(c) 85°　(d) 80°
   (e) 75°　(f) 113°　(g) 70°　(h) 130°
2. 40
3. (a) $x = 36$　　(b) $y = 105$

Exercise 6G

1. (a) $x = 36°$, $y = 54°$　(b) $x = 20°$, $y = 10°$
2. (a) 70°　　(b) 40°
3. (a) $x = 29°$, $y = 119°$　(b) $x = 120°$, $y = 75°$
4. (a) 67.5°　　(b) 22.5°
5. (a) $x = 60$, $y = 120$　(b) $x = 37$, $y = 32$
6. (a) 70°　　(b) 100°
7. (a) $x = 80°$, $y = 50°$　(b) $x = 50°$, $y = 100°$
8. (a) 70°　　(b) 110°
9. (a) $x = 50°$, $y = 100°$　(b) $x = 60°$, $y = 100°$
10. (a) 50°　　(b) 110°
11. (a) $x = 80°$, $y = 120°$　(b) $x = 110°$, $y = 50°$
12. (a) (i) 40°　　(ii) 55°
    (b) trapezium

Exercise 6H

6. kite
7. 107°
8. 3.0 cm
9. (a) 7.5 cm (c) 4.6 cm
10. (b) (i) 38° (ii) 5.5 cm

Exercise 6I

1. triangle, quadrilateral, pentagon and octagon.
2. (a) (i) 60° (ii) 60°
   (b) equilateral triangle
   (c) trapezium
3. (a) (i) isosceles triangle
      (ii) right-angled triangle
   (b) (i) kite (ii) square
4. (a) (i) AC, BD (ii) 2
   (b) (i) AC, AD, BD, BE, CE
      (ii) 5
   (c) 1 175 diagonals

Exercise 6J

1. (a) 720° (b) 1 260°
2. (a) 108° (b) 135°
3. (a) 7 (b) 4
4. (a) 12 (b) 10
5. 100°
6. 108°
7. 8
8. 50
9. $\angle a = 108°$, $\angle b = 36°$
10. $\angle x = 120°$, $\angle y = 60°$, $\angle z = 30°$
11. (a) 30° (b) 120°
12. 24
13. (a) 20° (b) 18 sides
14. (a) (i) 144 (ii) 108
    (b) 10

Exercise 6K

1. (a) No (b) Yes
2. (a) 1 & 3 (b) 1 & 2 (c) 2 & 3
3. (a) PQ ; $\angle P$. (b) RP; $\angle R$. (c) PQ: $\angle P$.
4. (a) $a = 2.7$ (b) $\angle b = 48°$
   (c) $\angle c = 100°$; $d = 5$
   (d) $\angle e = 110°$; $\angle f = 125°$; $h = 3$
5. (a) $\angle x = 50°$; $\angle y = 30°$.
   (b) $\angle p = 30°$; $\angle q = 30°$.

(c) $\angle x = 106°$; $y = 2.2$.
(d) $\angle a = 60°$; $\angle b = 30°$; $\angle c = 30°$; $x = 6.5$

10 Minutes Concept Check

1. C 2. D 3. B 4. C 5. D
6. B 7. B 8. D 9. D 10. C

Revision Paper 6

1. (a) 20° (b) 68°
2. (a) 66° (b) 82°
3. (a) 30° (b) 40°
4. (a) 105° (b) 80°
5. (a) 45 (b) 39
6. (a) 34° (b) 104° (c) 110°
7. (a) 8 (b) 12
8. (a) 138° (b) 168°
9. (a) 90°
   (b) (iii) 4.6 cm
10. (ii) $XZ = 10$ cm; $\triangle XYZ$ is an isosceles triangle.

Chapter 7

Exercise 7A

1. (a) 138 cm² (b) 360 cm²
   (c) 286 cm² (d) 679.8 cm²
2. (a) 72 cm³ (b) 400 cm³
   (c) 280 cm³ (d) 952.6 cm³
3. (a) 6 cm (b) 8 cm
   (c) 12 cm
4. (a) 49 cm², 7 cm (b) 81 cm², 9 cm
   (c) 169 cm², 13 cm
5. (a) 30 cm², 70 cm³ (b) 3.6 m², 4.8 m³
   (c) 72 cm², 6 cm (d) 17 m², 6 m
   (e) 7 cm, 42 cm² (f) 6.7 m, 33.5 m²
   (g) 7 cm, 56 cm² (h) 7.8 m, 31.2 m²
6. 532 cm³
7. 72 cm³
8. (a) (i) 137 600 cm³ (ii) 15 360 cm²
   (b) 2

Exercise 7B

1. (a) 162.8 cm² (b) 76.56 cm² (c) 550 m²
2. (a) 113 cm² (b) 283 cm² (c) 102 m²
3. 15 cm
4. 78.55 cm²
5. 6 cm

6. **(a)** 55.4 cm², 92.4 cm²
   (b) 346 m², 369 m²
   (c) 25.0 m, 154 m²
   (d) 37.0 cm, 3 850 cm²
   (e) 21.0 cm, 1 390 cm²
   (f) 2.80 m, 24.6 m²
   (g) 14.0 m, 651 m²
   (h) 3.50 cm, 137 cm²
7. 55.0 cm²

Exercise 7C

1. **(a)** 5 280 cm³ **(b)** 70.4 cm³ **(c)** 15.4 m³
2. **(a)** 24 m   **(b)** 4 cm   **(c)** 2.1 m
3. **(a)** 3.00 cm **(b)** 12.0 m   **(c)** 12.0 cm
4. **(a)** 30 m²   **(b)** 12.3 cm² **(c)** 114 m²
5. **(a)** 7.00 cm **(b)** 6.00 m   **(c)** 3.00 cm
6. **(a)** 186 cm²   **(b)** 1 640 cm³
7. **(a)** 3 390 cm³   **(b)** 4 810 cm³
8. **(b)** 7 cm   **(c)** 11 cm

Time-Out Activity:
The ratio is 3 : 1.
Let the radius of the cone and the cylinder be r,
   the height of the cone be h,
   and the height of the cylinder be H.
Since their volumes are equal, therefore

$$\frac{\text{Volume of cone}}{\text{Volume of cylinder}} = 1 = \frac{\frac{1}{3}\pi r^2 h}{\pi r^2 H}$$

$$= \frac{h}{3H}$$

$$\frac{h}{H} = \frac{3}{1}$$

$$\therefore \quad h : H = 3 : 1$$

Time-Out Activity:
Surface area of sphere

$$= \frac{2}{3} \times \text{total surface area of cylinder}$$

$$= \frac{2}{3} \times (2\pi rh + 2\pi r^2)$$

$$= \frac{2}{3} \times [2\pi r(2r) + 2\pi r^2]$$

$$= \frac{2}{3} \times (4\pi r^2 + 2\pi r^2)$$

$$= \frac{2}{3} \times 6\pi r^2$$

$$= 4\pi r^2$$

Exercise 7D

1. **(a)** **(i)** 12.6 cm² **(ii)** 4.19 cm³
   (b) **(i)** 2 460 cm² **(ii)** 11 500 cm³
   (c) **(i)** 616 cm²   **(ii)** 1 440 cm³
   (d) **(i)** 19.6 cm² **(ii)** 8.18 cm³
2. **(a)** **(i)** 6 cm   **(ii)** 144π cm²
   (b) **(i)** 3 cm   **(ii)** 36π cm²
3. **(a)** **(i)** 5 cm   **(ii)** 50π cm²
   (b) **(i)** 2 cm   **(ii)** 8π cm²
4. **(a)** **(i)** 7.00 cm   **(ii)** 1 440 cm³
   (b) **(i)** 3.50 cm   **(ii)** 180 cm³
5. **(a)** 288π cm³   **(b)** 1 cm
6. 693 m²
7. 786 cm³
8. **(a)** **(i)** 170 cm²   **(ii)** 198 cm³
   (b) **(i)** 104 cm²   **(ii)** 94.3 cm³
9. $\dfrac{2}{3}$

10. **(a)** $\dfrac{4}{9}$ **(b)** $\dfrac{4}{9}$

Time-Out Activity:
The percentage change is –50%.

Volume of 1 small sphere $= \dfrac{4}{3}\pi \, \text{mm}^3$

Volume of 1 big sphere = Volume of 8 small spheres

$$= 10\frac{2}{3}\pi \, \text{mm}^3$$

Volume of big sphere $= \dfrac{4}{3}\pi r^3$

$$10\frac{2}{3}\pi = \frac{4}{3}\pi r^3$$

$$\frac{4}{3}r^3 = 10\frac{2}{3}$$

$$r^3 = 8$$

$$r = 2$$

$\therefore$ Radius of big sphere = 2 mm
Total surface area of big sphere $= 4\pi(2)^2$
$$= 16\pi \, \text{mm}^2$$
Total surface area of small spheres $= 4\pi(1)^2 \times 8$
$$= 32\pi \, \text{mm}^2$$

$\therefore$ Percentage change $= \dfrac{16\pi - 32\pi}{32\pi} \times 100\%$

$$= -50\%$$

10 Minutes Concept Check

1. B **2.** C **3.** C **4.** A **5.** C
6. A **7.** B **8.** B **9.** C **10.** B

1. (a) 20 cm^3 (b) 6 m
2. (a) 100 cm^3 (b) 15 m
3. (a) 1.8 m^2 (b) 13 cm
4. (a) 616 cm^2 (b) 4 851 cm^3
5. (a) 7 cm   (b) 374 cm^2
6. (a) 5 cm   (b) 90 cm^2
7. (a) 12π cm   (b) (ii) 302 cm^3
8. (a) 628 cm^3 (b) 113 cm^3 (c) 1.44 cm
9. (a) 2.09 cm^3 (b) 7.29 cm   (c) 8.29
10. (a) 78.7 m^2 (b) 53.7 m^3

Chapter 8

Exercise 8A _____

1. 20
2. (a) 20   (b) 1
3. (a) 8   (b) 106
4. (a) 25   (b) 44   (c) 16%
5. (a) There must be at least one person (driver) in the moving car.
   (b) 20   (c) 50

Time-Out Activity:

(a) (iii) The dot diagram is easier to construct as the construction of a frequency table is not necessary.

(b) (i) In this case, as the number of data is large, it will be easier to read off the values from the histogram rather than counting the number of dots from the dot diagram.

     (iii) Advantage – Easy to construct for a small number of data.
        Disadvantage – Hard to interpret for a large number of data.

Exercise 8B _____

1. (a) 120, 121, 123, 125, 128
   (b) 0.1, 0.2, 0.3, 0.5, 0.7
   (c) 3 401, 3 412, 3 452, 3 455, 3 464, 3 478, 3 489
2. (a) 22   (b) 19 minutes (c) 65 minutes
3. (a) 160   (b) 30%
4. (a) 25   (b) 52%   (c) 3.0 minutes
5. (a) 20   (b) 40 hours   (c) 27

Exercise 8C _____

1. (a) 2.67   (b) 5.78   (c) 59
   (d) 3.42   (e) 18   (f) 818
2. (a) 26   (b) 2.7
3. (a) 275   (b) 14   (c) 52.5
4. (a) 540   (b) 58
5. 3   6. 11.7 seconds
7. 4.89   8. 32
9. (a) 2.08   (b) 1.84
10. 10
11. (a) 246   (b) 1.23
12. 2.8
13. (a) 25   (b) 44   (c) 1.76
14. (a) 99   (b) 3.3
15. (a) 21   (b) 1.0 m
    (c) 6.8 m   (d) 3.5 m
16. (a) 30   (b) 163 cm   (c) 149 cm

Exercise 8D _____

1. (a) 3   (b) 6   (c) 5.5
   (d) 83   (e) $3.70   (f) 3.4
2. (a) 42   (b) 42.4
3. 2   4. 3   5. 4
6. (a) $30   (b) $34
7. (a) 1.5   (b) 1.6
8. 5
9. (a) 75   (b) 2
10. (a) 2   (b) 1.59
11. (a) 22   (b) 2
12. 2   13. 13
14. 1.51 m   15. 40 minutes

Time-Out Activity:

(i) David should have rearranged the data first before taking the average of the 6th and 7th values.

(ii) Vincent should have taken the average of the 6th and 7th values instead of the numbers 6 and 7.

(iii) Ray should have written $\dfrac{6^{th} + 7^{th}}{2}$ instead of $\dfrac{6 + 7}{2}$.

Exercise 8E _____

1. (a) 3   (b) 3
   (c) None   (d) 100 kg and 110 kg
2. (a) 2, 1   (b) 95, None

3. 3

4. (a) 4 marks   (b) 7 marks
    (c) 6 marks

5. (a) 4   (b) 7
    (c) 9   (d) 21

6. (a) 3 hours   (b) 2.5 hours
    (c) 2.44 hours

7. (a) 3 pens   (b) 2.3 pens

8. (a)

No. of letters	3	4	5
Frequency	4	2	3

    (b) (i) 3 letters   (ii) 4 letters

9. (a) 7   (b) 9   (c) 1

10. (a) 3   (b) 2.5

11. (a) 25   (b) 3   (c) 3 and 4

12. (a) 20   (b) 2
    (c) 2.5   (d) 2.8

13. (a) $830
    (b) (i) $630   (ii) $630
       (iii) $672.50

14. (a) 25
    (b) (i) 55 marks   (ii) 58 marks
    (c) (i) 61 marks   (ii) 55 marks
    (d) Generally, the girls scored better in the test than the boys.

15. (a) 30   (b) 1 movie
    (c) 2 movies   (d) 2.23 movies

Time-Out Activity:

(b) The answers will vary as PSI readings change constantly. Please visit the website for the latest PSI readings.

Exercise 8F

1. (a) 50   (b) 102.6 g

2. (a) 26   (b) 60

3. (a)

Wage ($w)	Mid-value (x)	Frequency (f)
$225 < w \leq 245$	235	26
$245 < w \leq 265$	255	36
$265 < w \leq 285$	275	58
$285 < w \leq 305$	295	42
$305 < w \leq 325$	315	38
		Total = 200

    (b) $278

4. (a)

No. of spectators	Mid-value (x)	Frequency (f)
1 000 – 1 999	1 499.5	4
2 000 – 2 999	2 499.5	5
3 000 – 3 999	3 499.5	2
4 000 – 4 999	4 499.5	5
5 000 – 5 999	5 499.5	12
6 000 – 6 999	6 499.5	14
7 000 – 7 999	7 499.5	5
8 000 – 8 999	8 499.5	1
		Total = 48

    (b) 5 229

5. (a)

Speed (v km/h)	Mid-value (x)	Tally	Frequency (f)	fx
$9.5 < v \leq 19.5$	14.5	/	1	14.5
$19.5 < v \leq 29.5$	24.5	//	2	49
$29.5 < v \leq 39.5$	34.5	////	4	138
$39.5 < v \leq 49.5$	44.5	### ///	8	356
$49.5 < v \leq 59.5$	54.5	### ### //	12	666
$59.5 < v \leq 69.5$	64.5	### ### /	11	720.5
$69.5 < v \leq 79.5$	74.5	### /	6	453
$79.5 < v \leq 89.5$	84.5	////	4	342
$89.5 < v \leq 99.5$	94.5	//	2	191
			Total = 50	Total = 2 930

    (b) 58.6 km/h

6. (a)

No. of aeroplanes	Mid-value (x)	Tally	Frequency (f)	fx
40 – 44	42	///	3	126
45 – 49	47	### ////	9	423
50 – 54	52	### ### ### ###-/	21	1 092
55 – 59	57	### ###-///	13	741
60 – 64	62	////	4	248
			Total = 50	Total = 2 630

    (b) 52.6

7. $27.05

8. 114 (correct to 3 sig. fig.)

9. $20.64 (correct to 2 dec. pl.)

10. 13.1

Exercise 8G

1. (a) 1, 2, 3, 4, 5, 6, 7 and 8; 8
   (b) 2, 3, 5 and 7
   (c) 4

2. (a) R_1, R_2, G, B_1 and B_2; 5
   (b) B_1 and B_2
   (c) 2

3. (a) C_1, H, A, N, C_2, E and S
   (b) 7
   (c) C_1 and C_2

4. (a) O, A, I_1 and I_2
   (b) 4

5. (a) 10   (b) 10

Exercise 8H

1. (a) $\dfrac{1}{2}$ (b) $\dfrac{1}{3}$
   (c) 0   (d) 1

2. (a) $\dfrac{1}{13}$ (b) $\dfrac{1}{4}$
   (c) $\dfrac{1}{52}$ (d) $\dfrac{3}{4}$

3. (a) $\dfrac{2}{11}$ (b) $\dfrac{4}{11}$ (c) 0

4. (a) $\dfrac{2}{9}$ (b) $\dfrac{1}{3}$
   (c) $\dfrac{5}{9}$ (d) $\dfrac{5}{9}$

5. (a) $\dfrac{2}{3}$ (b) $\dfrac{1}{3}$ (c) 0

6. (a) $\dfrac{1}{2}$ (b) $\dfrac{1}{4}$
   (c) $\dfrac{3}{4}$ (d) $\dfrac{1}{52}$

7. (a) $\dfrac{3}{17}$ (b) $\dfrac{6}{17}$ (c) $\dfrac{11}{17}$

8. (a) $\dfrac{3}{14}$ (b) $\dfrac{11}{14}$
   (c) $\dfrac{1}{3}$ (d) $\dfrac{1}{7}$

9. 20

10. (a) $\dfrac{1}{2}$ (b) 21

11. 0.4

12. (a) 20   (b) 0.8

10 Minutes Concept Check

1. A   **2.** B   **3.** A   **4.** B   **5.** D
6. A   **7.** C   **8.** B   **9.** C   **10.** A

Revision Paper 8

1. (a) 2.7   (b) 5.1
2. (a) 3   (b) 2.3   (c) 4.5
3. (a) 9   (b) 2.8 and 6.9
   (c) None
4. (a) $\dfrac{1}{16}$ (b) $\dfrac{1}{8}$
   (c) $\dfrac{3}{8}$ (d) $\dfrac{5}{8}$
5. (a) 490   (b) 46
6. (a) 25
   (b) (i) 1.4 balls   (ii) 1 ball
   (iii) 1 ball
7. (a) 20
   (b) (i) 48.15   (ii) 48   (iii) 48
   (c) 0.35
8. (a) 3   (b) 7   (c) 10
9. (a) 50
   (b) (i) 5 pairs (ii) 5 pairs   (iii) 4.48 pairs
   (c) 0.16
10. (a)

Mass (m kg)	Frequency
$40.5 < m \leq 45.5$	1
$45.5 < m \leq 50.5$	2
$50.5 < m \leq 55.5$	6
$55.5 < m \leq 60.5$	8
$60.5 < m \leq 65.5$	14
$65.5 < m \leq 70.5$	9
$70.5 < m \leq 75.5$	5
$75.5 < m \leq 80.5$	5

   (b) 63.4 kg
   (c) (i) 0.2   (ii) 0

Review Paper 3

1. (a) (i) $-2a - 3$ (ii) $6b - 3c$
   (b) (i) $-3(2z + 3)$ (ii) $4y(y - 2)$
2. $(6, 7)$
3. (a) $P = 240I$

(b)

P	480	720	**960**	1 440
I	2	3	4	**6**

4. $x = -1, y = 2$
5. (a) $a = 75°$ (b) $b = 100°$
6. (a) $\angle YPZ = 120°, \angle WQX = 120°$
   (b) $WZ = 7$ cm, $PQ = 3$ cm
7. (a) 384 cm²   (b) 384 cm³
8. (a) 3   (b) 2   (c) 2
9. (a) $h = 1\frac{1}{5}$ (b) $k = 5$ (c) $x = 5$
10. (a) (i) 1 : 500 000   (ii) 1 : 1 200
   (b) 300 km
11. boy's age = 17 years, sister's age = 7 years
12. (a) 1 260°   (b) 9   (c) 40°
13. (a) 5.66 cm   (b) 9.00 cm
14. 343
15. (a) 2   (b) 2   (c) 2
16. (a) 20
   (b) (i) 1   (ii) 1   (iii) 1.5
17. (a) (i) $x = 2, y = 4$ (ii) 10 units
   (b) (i) $x = 4, y = 8$ (ii) 18 units
18. (a) $LN = 9.0$ cm   (b) $\angle KLM = 83°$
19. (a) 236 cm²   (b) 603 cm²   (c) 716 cm³
20. (a) 17   (b) 32   (c) 18

Review Paper 4

1. (a) (i) $6a - 8$ (ii) $15b^2 - 3b$
   (b) (i) $-5x(y + 2x)$ (ii) $3xy(y - 2x)$
2. (a) $a = -1$ (b) $b = -12$
   (c) $c = 5\frac{1}{2}$
3. (a) $R = \dfrac{225}{r}$

(b)

R	75	25	**15**	5
r	3	9	15	**45**

4. $k = -9, w = -4$

5. (a) $a = 32°$ (b) $b = 45°$
6. (a) 1 160 cm²   (b) 3 390 cm³
7. (a) 1 : 64   (b) 1 : 16
8. (a) 5.2   (b) 3   (c) 4.5
9. (a) (i) $2a^2 + a - 28$
     (ii) $3b - 4bc + 6c - 8c^2$
   (b) (i) $(2x + 3)(4 - x)$
     (ii) $(2m + 3n)(5p - q)$
10. (a) $x = 3$ (b) $y = -3x$
   (c) $y = 3$ (d) $y = 3x$
11. (a) $P = \dfrac{360}{h}$ (b) 18 kPa   (c) 9 km
12. (a) eight 20-cent coins and three 50-cent coins
   (b) five more 20-cent coins
13. (a) 18°   (b) 20   (c) 3 240°
14. (a) $\triangle ABC \equiv \triangle CDE \equiv \triangle EFA$
   (b) (i) 120°   (ii) 30°   (iii) 60°
   (c) equilateral triangle
15. (a) 5.64 cm   (b) 188 cm³
16. (a) 20   (b) 40 hours
   (c) 20 hours   (d) 21.6 hours
   (e) 20.5 hours
17. (a)

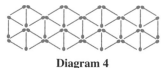

Diagram 4

(b)

Diagram	1	2	3	4
No of matchsticks	12	23	**34**	**45**

   (c) (i) 111   (ii) 606
   (d) $m = 11n + 1$
   (e) Diagram 30

18. (a) (i)

x	0	1	3
y	2	**0**	**-4**

     (ii)

x	1	3	5
y	**-5**	1	7

   (b) $x = 2, y = -2$
19. (a) 9.5 cm   (b) 11.5 cm
20. (a) 200 students   (b) 63.6 minutes
   (c) (i) 0.1   (ii) 0.39